Exam Ref 70-687:

Configuring Windows 8

Mike Halsey
Andrew Bettany

Published with the authorization of Microsoft Corporation by:

O'Reilly Media, Inc.
1005 Gravenstein Highway North
Sebastopol, California 95472

ISBN: 978-0-7356-7392-2

2 3 4 5 6 7 8 9 10 QG 8 7 6 5 4 3

Printed and bound in the United States of America.

Microsoft Press books are available through booksellers and distributors worldwide. If you need support related to this book, email Microsoft Press Book Support at mspinput@microsoft.com. Please tell us what you think of this book at *http://www.microsoft.com/learning/booksurvey*.

Acquisitions and Developmental Editor: Russell Jones

Production Editor: Kara Ebrahim

Editorial Production: Box Twelve Communications

Technical Reviewer: Todd Meister

Copyeditor: Box Twelve Communications

Indexer: Box Twelve Communications

Cover Design: Twist Creative • Seattle

Cover Composition: Zyg Group, LLC

Illustrator: Rebecca Demarest

For Zeshan Sattar, I couldn't have done it without you.

—MIKE HALSEY

I would like to dedicate this book to Tommy and Netty. You continue to be awesome.

—ANDREW BETTANY

Contents at a glance

Contents

What do you think of this book? We want to hear from you!

Microsoft is interested in hearing your feedback so we can continually improve our books and learning resources for you. To participate in a brief online survey, please visit:

www.microsoft.com/learning/booksurvey/

Chapter 2   Configure hardware and applications   55

Chapter 4   Configure access to resources   171

Chapter 6 Monitor and maintain Windows clients   321

What do you think of this book? We want to hear from you!

Microsoft is interested in hearing your feedback so we can continually improve our books and learning resources for you. To participate in a brief online survey, please visit:

www.microsoft.com/learning/booksurvey/

Introduction

Microsoft's flagship operating system, Windows 8, includes significant changes to the user interface compared to previous versions and is intended to unify the user experience across desktops, laptops, and mobile devices such as tablets. Windows 8 replaces the familiar Start menu with an all-new Start screen—but that's just one of dozens of exciting new features that offer challenges for users moving from earlier versions of Windows but also showcases how Microsoft Windows continues to evolve.

This book focuses on describing and explaining the new material in Windows 8. Throughout the book, we have broken down each of the key examination domains, following the specific exam objectives that Microsoft has provided. Although readers of the this Exam Ref guide might have already earned a Microsoft certification in a previous version of Windows, this guide should be useful for both those experienced with certification exams and people who are new to certification.

By using this book as your companion guide to learning the skills and knowledge required, our belief is that you will significantly increase the likelihood of succeeding at the exam 70-687: Configuring Windows 8. Although we don't want to heap additional expectations on you, success at passing the 70-687 examination could open the opportunity for you to continue your skills development and to set your targets on the Microsoft Certified Solutions Associate (MCSA): Windows 8.

In addition to your study of this book, you should also seek and obtain real-world experience. As you read the book, if you encounter an area that you are unfamiliar with, consider seeking additional knowledge from other sources such as Microsoft TechNet, forums, and hands-on experience. After you believe that you've thoroughly studied, researched, and practiced the topics covered in this book, you should be sufficiently prepared to attempt the 70-687 exam.

Over the last couple of years, Microsoft has quietly made substantial changes to its certification program to improve the rigor of the certifications, preserve exam integrity, and build the relevance and value that Microsoft certifications bring to candidates who earn the certifications.

To you, these changes might make the exams "feel" a lot harder to pass than in previous years. This increase in subjective difficulty could be solely in the authors' perceptions—but it could also be because of the changes Microsoft has made. The bottom line is that you need to be fully prepared. The revised certification program ensures that holders of Microsoft certifications have the knowledge, skills, abilities, and experience required—and that being Microsoft Certified sets you apart from the rest.

This book covers every exam objective, but it does not cover every exam question. Only the Microsoft exam team has access to the exam questions themselves and Microsoft regularly adds new questions to the exam, making it impossible to cover specific questions. You should consider this book a supplement to your relevant real-world experience and other study materials. If you encounter a topic in this book that you do not feel completely comfortable with, use the links you'll find in text to find more information and take the time to research and study the topic. Great information is available on MSDN, TechNet, and in blogs and forums.

Microsoft certifications

Microsoft certifications distinguish you by proving your command of a broad set of skills and experience with current Microsoft products and technologies. The exams and corresponding certifications are developed to validate your mastery of critical competencies as you design and develop, or implement and support, solutions with Microsoft products and technologies both on-premise and in the cloud. Certification brings a variety of benefits to the individual and to employers and organizations.

> **MORE INFO ALL MICROSOFT CERTIFICATIONS**
>
> For information about Microsoft certifications, including a full list of available certifications, go to *http://www.microsoft.com/learning/en/us/certification/cert-default.aspx.*

Who should read this book

This book is intended for IT professionals who want to achieve certification on the Windows 8 operating system. Specifically, this book prepares readers to take and pass exam 70-687: Configuring Windows 8. Successfully passing the 70-687 also counts as credit toward the Microsoft Certified Solutions Associate (MCSA): Windows 8 certification.

IT professionals reading this book should have hands-on experience installing, configuring, and supporting Windows 8 computers, devices, users, and the networking environment in which they can be found. As an IT professional, you might be a consultant, a full-time desktop support technician, or an IT generalist who has experience administering Windows 8 in addition to other duties.

Assumptions

You should have at least a working understanding of administering Microsoft Windows 8 and configuring common Internet technologies. As you progress with your learning through this book and other study resources, you will become proficient at configuring, supporting, and troubleshooting Windows 8. This book is focused on helping those of you whose goal is to become certified on Windows 8 configuration.

You can find information about the audience for the 70-687: Configuring Windows 8 exam in the exam preparation guide, available at *http://www.microsoft.com/learning/en/us/exam.aspx?id=70-687*.

Who should not read this book

Readers who need a fundamental understanding of the Windows 8 operating system should instead consider reading the book *Training Guide: Configuring Windows 8* published by Microsoft Press.

Organization of this book

This book is divided into seven chapters. Each chapter focuses on a different exam domain related to the exam 70-687: Configuring Windows 8. Each chapter is further broken down into specific exam objectives that have been published by Microsoft and can be found in the "Skills Being Measured" section of the *Exam 70-687: Configuring Windows 8* website available at *http://aka.ms/ER70-687/details*.

The material covered by the exam domain and the objectives has been incorporated into this book so that you have concise, objective-by-objective content together with strategic real-world scenarios, thought experiments, and end-of-chapter review questions to provide readers with professional-level preparation for the exam.

Conventions and features in this book

This book presents information using conventions designed to make the information readable and easy to follow:

- Each exercise consists of a series of tasks, presented as numbered steps listing each action you must take to complete the exercise.
- Boxed elements with labels such as "Note" provide additional information or alternative methods for completing a step successfully.

- Boxed elements with "Exam Tip" labels provide additional information which might offer helpful hints or additional information on what to expect on the exam.

- Text that you type (apart from code blocks) appears in bold.

- A plus sign (+) between two key names means that you must press those keys at the same time. For example, "Press Alt+Tab" means that you hold down the Alt key while you press the Tab key.

- A vertical bar between two or more menu items (for example, File | Close), means that you should select the first menu or menu item, then the next, and so on.

System requirements

Where you are unfamiliar with a topic cover in this book, you should practice the concept on your study PC. You will need the following hardware and software to complete the practice exercises in this book:

- One study PC that can be installed with Windows 8 (see hardware specification below) or a PC that can allow the installation of Windows 8 within a virtualized environment.

- Windows 8 requires the following minimum hardware requirements: 1 GHz processor, 512 MB RAM, network card, video card, DVD-ROM drive, and at least 25 GB of available disk space available on each computer.

- If you plan to install Windows 8 in a virtualized environment, you should consider using Hyper-V and ensure that the minimum hardware requirements are as follows: x64-based processor, which includes both hardware-assisted virtualization (AMD-V or Inter VT) and hardware data execution protection; 4 GB RAM (more is recommended); network card; video card; DVD-ROM drive; and at least 100 GB of available disk space available to allow for the storage of multiple virtual machines.

- If you don't own Windows 8, you can download a 90-day evaluation of Windows 8 Enterprise from the Microsoft Springboard Series website available at *http://technet. microsoft.com/en-us/springboard.aspx*.

Errata & book support

We've made every effort to ensure the accuracy of this book and its companion content. Any errors that have been reported since this book was published are listed on our Microsoft Press site at oreilly.com:

http://aka.ms/ER70-687/errata

If you find an error that is not already listed, you can report it to us through the same page.

If you need additional support, email Microsoft Press Book Support at:

mspinput@microsoft.com.

Please note that product support for Microsoft software is not offered through the addresses above.

We want to hear from you

At Microsoft Press, your satisfaction is our top priority, and your feedback our most valuable asset. Please tell us what you think of this book at:

http://www.microsoft.com/learning/booksurvey

The survey is short, and we read every one of your comments and ideas. Thanks in advance for your input!

Stay in touch

Let's keep the conversation going! We're on Twitter: *http://twitter.com/MicrosoftPress*

Preparing for the exam

Microsoft certification exams are a great way to build your resume and let the world know about your level of expertise. Certification exams validate your on-the-job experience and product knowledge. While there is no substitution for on-the-job experience, preparation through study and hands-on practice can help you prepare for the exam. We recommend that you round out your exam preparation plan by using a combination of available study materials and courses. For example, you might use the Exam Ref and another study guide for your "at home" preparation, and take a Microsoft Official Curriculum course for the classroom experience. Choose the combination that you think works best for you.

Note that this Exam Ref is based on publically available information about the exam and the author's experience. To safeguard the integrity of the exam, authors do not have access to the live exam.

CHAPTER 1

Install and upgrade Windows 8

You might have heard the phrase "if a job is worth doing, it's worth doing well." Personally, I prefer to say "if a job's worth doing, it's worth doing only *once*." This is especially true when installing or migrating to a new operating system, which can be time-consuming, especially if you have many machines onto which you need to install the Windows operating system, software, and updates—a process that can be tricky in places and is rarely as simple as it might first appear. With Windows 8, for example, the basic hardware requirements of the operating system are effectively *lower* than they were with Windows 7; however, this doesn't mean that Windows 8 will work properly on every computer that Windows 7 ran on.

> **important**
>
> ## Have you read page xxiii?
>
> It contains valuable information regarding the skills you need to pass the exam.

If you want to upgrade their existing copy of the operating system to the new version, you face a different set of issues with Windows 8. Windows 8, Windows 7, and Windows Vista are all very similar "under the hood," but some upgrade paths that were previously blocked are now open, whereas others that were simple and straightforward are now much more complex.

Finally, you have the issue of software compatibility. In theory, all software that works in Windows 7 and Windows Vista will work in Windows 8. In reality, the sheer number of software packages available for the platform and the complexity of the operating system mean that complete software compatibility can't be guaranteed. In addition, there are many scenarios in which you or a computer user might prefer—or when a situation might demand—a new-style app instead.

This chapter shows how to plan effectively for installing or migrating to Windows 8, how to install the operating system in a trouble-free manner, and how to migrate user files, settings, and programs to the new operating system.

Objectives in this chapter:

- Objective 1.1: Evaluate hardware readiness and compatibility
- Objective 1.2: Install Windows 8
- Objective 1.3: Migrate and configure user data

Objective 1.1: Evaluate hardware readiness and compatibility

The following are primary considerations when installing or upgrading a computer to Windows 8:

- Windows 8 edition required
- 64-bit hardware support
- 64-bit software support
- 64-bit device driver availability

In addition, you need to be aware of common application compatibility problems and how to manage them.

> **This objective covers how to:**
> - Identify the correct version of Windows 8 for your needs
> - Manage hardware and software compatibility in Windows 8
> - Understand common application compatibility problems
> - Manage application compatibility

Identifying the correct version of Windows 8

When you set out to install Windows 8 in any environment, you need to consider whether the hardware onto which you will be installing the operating system is suitable for running both Windows 8 and the version of Windows 8 you want to install. This means breaking the various Windows 8 editions down so that you can see, at a glance, what hardware and edition you require to use the features you want and need on a particular computer. The base hardware requirements of Windows 8 are shown in Table 1-1.

TABLE 1-1 Windows 8 hardware requirements

	32-bit (x86)	64-bit (x64)
Processor	1 GHz	1 GHz
Memory	1 GB	2 GB

	32-bit (x86)	64-bit (x64)
Graphics	DirectX 9 with WDDM 1.0	DirectX 9 with WDDM 1.0
HDD	16 GB	20 GB
Secure boot	UEFI-based BIOS	UEFI-based BIOS

In addition to these requirements, each edition of Windows 8 has its own limitations, such as the maximum amount of memory that it can access and the location from which it is available. These are shown in Table 1-2.

TABLE 1-2 Memory and availability limits

	32-bit memory limit	64-bit memory limit	availability
Windows 8	4 GB*	16 GB	Retail/OEMs
Windows 8 Pro	4 GB*	192 GB	Retail/OEMs
Windows 8 Enterprise	4 GB*	192 GB	Volume licensing

*including graphics card memory

> **NOTE SCREEN RESOLUTION ISSUES**
>
> If users want to use side-by-side apps, they need a minimum screen resolution of 1,366 × 768 pixels. If the screen has a vertical resolution of less than 768 pixels, which is common on some netbooks, the Start screen won't display at all.

The editions also have feature differences, as shown in Table 1-3.

TABLE 1-3 Feature differences among versions

	Windows 8	Windows 8 Pro	Windows 8 Enterprise
Bitlocker and bitlocker to go	No	Yes	Yes
Boot from virtual hard disk (VHD)	No	Yes	Yes
Client hyper-V	No	Yes	Yes
Domain join	No	Yes	Yes
Encrypting file system	No	Yes	Yes
Group policy	No	Yes	Yes
Applocker	No	No	Yes
Branchcache	No	No	Yes

	Windows 8	Windows 8 Pro	Windows 8 Enterprise
Directaccess	No	No	Yes
Side-load apps	No	No	Yes
Virtualization through remotefx	No	No	Yes
Windows to go	No	No	Yes

If you know that you will need to use BranchCache or Group Policy on a system, the base edition of Windows 8 won't be suitable. Indeed, the standard edition of Windows 8 is aimed primarily at consumers and will unlikely support any features a business will usually require.

EXAM TIP

Ensure that you have learned the Windows 8 system requirements for both x86 and x64, key feature differences between the versions.

Hardware support: differences between 32-bit and 64-bit Windows 8

What about the 32-bit/64-bit question? Determining which to use isn't simply a case of installing the best available edition of Windows 8 because you might find that the hardware and even software you require won't work with that edition.

The 32-bit and 64-bit operating systems have the following differences:

- A 64-bit processor can process more data in each clock cycle, enabling applications to run more quickly.

- A 64-bit operating system can access significantly more memory than its 32-bit counterpart. For a 32-bit operating system, the maximum memory ceiling is 4 GB, which includes the memory on the graphics card. Also, memory can be seen by the Windows operating system only in discrete memory card units, meaning that if a computer has 4×1 GB memory cards and a graphics card with 1.5 GB of its own memory, only two of the motherboard memory cards will be seen (2×1 GB + 1.5 GB graphics = 3.5 GB seen). Each 64-bit processor has a memory ceiling so high that if you work on a computer that has reached that ceiling, you should consider yourself very lucky indeed.

- A 64-bit processor supports additional security features, such as Kernel Patch Protection (KPP), kernel-mode driver signing, and Data Execution Prevention (DEP).

- As shown in Table 1-3, the Hyper-V virtualization client is supported only in the 64-bit editions of Windows 8 Pro and Enterprise. But Hyper-V also requires a processor that supports Second Level Address Translation (SLAT), which reduces the overhead incurred with virtual-to-physical address mapping.

- A 64-bit operating system can be installed only on hardware with 64-bit architecture support, whereas a 32-bit operating system can be installed on 32-bit and 64-bit architecture.

- A 64-bit version of Windows 8 doesn't support older 16-bit Windows software. That software will need to be installed on a 32-bit version of Windows 8 or within a Hyper-V virtualized environment.

> **_NOTE_ MIGRATING BETWEEN 32-BIT AND 64-BIT WINDOWS**
>
> If you want to perform an in-place upgrade of any 32-bit Windows version, you can't upgrade to a 64-bit version of Windows 8. Upgrading from Windows XP or Windows Vista doesn't migrate any software, and upgrading from Windows XP doesn't allow you to migrate any operating system settings. The Windows 8 installer doesn't support any move between 32-bit and 64-bit operating systems. As a result, you need to perform a clean installation of Windows 8.

Software compatibility and Windows 8

Assume that you will install Windows 8 in an accounting or financial business where the staff needs to work on extremely large Excel spreadsheets that have in excess of 256 columns or 65,536 rows. The 64-bit edition of Excel allows for up to 16,384 columns and 1 million rows.

Suppose also that the company needs to use specific 64-bit software, which could include such programs as AutoCAD or Adobe Photoshop, where the 64-bit version is required either due to nature of the work the staff does, or because the company doesn't have a 32-bit license for the software.

No 64-bit software will run on a 32-bit Windows version. Therefore, if your company is moving from the 32-bit version of software such as Microsoft Office or Adobe Photoshop to the 64-bit version as part of a planned upgrade, you should first ensure that 64-bit versions of the plug-ins for the software exist. Many plug-ins have yet to be rewritten for the 64-bit architecture.

Also consider support for Hyper-V. If the business requires client virtualization, remember that only the 64-bit editions of Windows 8 Pro and Windows 8 Enterprise include this feature.

Hardware compatibility in Windows 8

After identifying any software compatibility issues, you need to identify any hardware compatibility issues such as problems with drivers. You should check the manufacturer's website for the latest compatible versions of hardware drivers before migrating to Windows 8. Indeed, you should download and store all of these. Check that a 64-bit version of the driver is available for any hardware the client uses, including any external peripherals such as printers, scanners, and biometric devices.

> **MORE INFO WINDOWS 8 DEVICE COMPATIBILITY**
>
> You can read more about Windows 8 device compatibility at *http://www.microsoft.com/ en-us/windows/compatibility/en-us/compatcenter/home*.

Common application compatibility problems

As mentioned previously in this objective, not all existing software will run (or run happily) on Windows 8. The two most common reasons for this problem are:

- **Changes to the underlying architecture that Microsoft implemented with Windows Vista** This new architecture removed some components that earlier Windows versions required to operate fully and changed other components in significant ways, also resulting in incompatibilities with older software.

- **Workarounds that software authors occasionally employed before User Account Control was introduced** These workarounds would often use the blanket administrator privileges of Windows users to provide quick workarounds for programming issues that otherwise would have required more complex coding.

Some older software won't run or will produce errors in the operating system for other reasons as well.

User Account Control

Considering the problems just discussed, some legacy and older software was written by programmers who designed software that included tasks that require administrator rights. This was done primarily to simplify the programmer's life because writing code to perform the same tasks using standard user rights is more complex. The User Account Control (UAC) program will prompt you for your credentials when it encounters a program that requires administrator rights. If the user does not have the required administrator rights, UAC will block the program and the program will not run.

Other software types might be blocked by UAC for a variety of reasons. These include the following:

- Poorly written installers, updaters, and uninstallers might not be automatically elevated to have administrator rights by Windows 8.

- Standard application events, as detailed previously, that require elevated privileges might not be able to obtain them.

- Applications to be run specifically by administrators can fail when used by people on standard user accounts.

- Dynamic Link Library (DLL) applications using the RunDLL32.exe program might not function properly if they try to perform global operations that affect other user accounts or core Windows 8 settings.

- Everyday applications that attempt to make file-level changes to Windows operating system areas or those of other user accounts will be blocked.

Windows Resource Protection

Windows Resource Protection (WRP) is a system that maintains critical Windows resources, files, folders, and registry entries in a read-only state. Access to these resources is permitted only to trusted software and hardware installers. These kinds of problems can occur:

- Any installers that attempt to overwrite, modify, or delete registry keys, files, or folders protected by WRP can fail with a message informing users that the resource can't be updated.

- Installers that attempt to create new registry keys or values in protected registry keys can fail with a message saying that access is denied.

- Any application that attempts to write to protected resources can fail if it relies on the use of protected registry keys.

Incompatibilities of 64-bit

The 64-bit version of Windows 8 can run all 32-bit Windows 8 software, thanks to the Windows 32-bit on Windows 64-bit (WOW64) emulator. However, software can fail on a 64-bit installation of Windows 8 under some circumstances:

- Older 16-bit software won't run on the 64-bit version of Windows 8. To use such legacy software, you need a 32-bit version of Windows installed on a Hyper-V virtualization client.

- All 32-bit hardware and kernel drivers will fail to work or will malfunction in the 64-bit version of Windows 8. You need 64-bit versions of all your drivers.

- Attempting to install unsigned 64-bit drivers will fail on Windows 8, including drivers added manually by editing the Windows registry.

Windows Filtering Platform

The Windows Filtering Platform (WFP) includes application program interfaces (APIs) that allow developers to write code that interacts with the data packet processing and filtering that occurs in the Windows 8 networking stack and elsewhere in the operating system. Problems can occur if software uses an earlier version of the API, resulting in errors when applications such as firewalls, anti-malware programs, and other security software are running.

Kernel-mode drivers

Any kernel-mode hardware drivers in Windows 8 need to be written or recoded to follow the Microsoft Windows User Mode Driver Framework (UMDF), a device-driver platform first introduced with Windows Vista. Incompatible drivers will fail to install or will cause errors in operation.

Operating system version number changes

Occasionally when older software looks for a Windows version number, it might not recognize Windows 8 as a new version of the operating system. This can happen if the software is poorly coded. Should this happen, the software will return an Incompatible Version of Windows error.

Managing application compatibility in Windows 8

If you are performing a stand-alone installation of Windows 8, the installer will inform you of any local hardware and software incompatibilities. However, this last-minute approach to determining application and hardware compatibility isn't ideal because if you encounter a significant problem, you have to decide whether to continue with an installation that's already partly underway or to abandon it and try again later. The best way to determine application compatibility in Windows has always been and continues to be to download the free Application Compatibility Toolkit (ACT) from *http://technet.microsoft.com/en-US/windows//aa905066.aspx*.

Using ACT is advantageous for multiple reasons. The ACT allows you to verify compatibility with Windows 8 for any software. (Note that this will apply only to desktop programs, because Windows Store apps will already be written to be compatible.) Another benefit of the ACT is that it allows you to test web applications with the latest version of the Internet Explorer web browser. Many compatibility problems in business are caused by older web applications originally written for the non-standards–compliant IE6 browser.

> **MORE INFO** **WINDOWS 8 APPLICATION COMPATIBILITY**
>
> You can read more about Windows 8 application compatibility at *http://technet.microsoft. com/en-us/windows/aa905066.aspx*.

If you encounter an application that has compatibility problems with Windows 8, you can rectify the situation by following several possible courses of action—although some will require some software recoding:

- Update the software so that stored file locations, registry entries, or file and folder permissions can be changed.
- Change the security configuration for the software. Remember that the UAC displays an alert if software tries to perform an action that changes a setting or perform a

modification in folder locations that affects other computer users, even if no other user accounts currently exist.

- Find fixes, updates, and service packs for the software that will rectify the problems and issues that cause incompatibilities. If you are using off-the-shelf software, finding these items is reasonably likely unless all development on the product has ceased.

- Upgrade the software to a newer and compatible version. If a newer version of the software exists, investigate whether the company can migrate to that version while also moving to Windows 8.

- Use Hyper-V in Windows 8 to run the application in a virtualized environment. This will require installing an earlier Windows version into the Hyper-V client software. You will see more about this topic shortly.

- Migrate to a different software package that is compatible with Windows 8. Sometimes moving to a different software package can be a good thing, because it can introduce new features and other enhancements while maintaining file compatibility.

- Use the application compatibility features in Windows 8 to run the software in compatibility mode (more information about this shortly).

Running earlier Windows versions in Hyper-V: What to look for

You see how to set up and configure an operating system in Hyper-V in Chapter 2, "Configure hardware and applications," but here you need to look at the issue of security and stability when using earlier versions of the operating system. Consider some of the potential problems and pitfalls involved with using an earlier Windows version:

- **When will support for security and stability updates end?** Extended product support for Windows 7 won't end until 2020. However, with Windows 7 and Windows 8 sharing much of the same core architecture, any software that works properly in Windows 7 will likely also run in Windows 8, so using Windows 7 in Hyper-V really isn't necessary. With Windows XP, however, you more than likely need to run a copy in the virtual machine. All support for Windows XP with Service Pack 3 installed (the final service pack for the operating system) ends in April 2014. After that date, Microsoft will no longer support that operating system.

- **Does the application need access to the Internet?** If you can completely isolate the operating system by denying it access to the Internet and to files held on local computers (which have a risk of malware infection), it is highly unlikely that the copy of Windows XP will ever be exposed to malware itself. Indeed, Hyper-V can be set up so that a virtual machine can get network access only to other virtual machines, so that data can be shared between them.

- **Will the virtualized operating system also require maintenance by the systems team?** If the virtualized operating system requires access to the local file system on your Windows 8 computers, you will need to maintain the security on those virtualized copies of Windows XP, which adds an extra layer of complexity to your overall systems support role. Most importantly, if network access is granted, Internet access is automatically granted with it. One way around this is on computers that connect to the Internet via Wi-Fi. On such systems, the virtual machine's networking can be set to use the physical Ethernet system. If no cable is plugged into this on the host computer, the virtual machine will have local file access but no Internet access.

Regarding the final support date of April 2014, any remaining security problems left unrepaired on this date will likely be exploited by malware writers extensively because Windows XP is still widely used in some emerging economies.

Setting application compatibility in Windows 8

You can manually set compatibility for desktop programs that are installed in Windows 8 but were written either for an earlier version of the operating system or aren't included with the operating system as it ships from Microsoft. These compatibility settings run the program with parameters that tell the operating system how to modify its interaction with the program to ensure it runs smoothly and properly.

To access the program compatibility settings, follow these steps:

1. From the Start screen or the All Apps view, right-click the program you want to set compatibility for and click Open File Location.

2. File Explorer opens on the desktop, displaying the link to the program. Right-click the program and click Properties from the options that appear.

3. In the dialog box that appears for the program, click the Compatibility tab (see Figure 1-1).

Here, you can choose from several options. If you aren't sure which compatibility options to set for the program, you can run the compatibility troubleshooter program. This troubleshooter will ask you a series of questions about the circumstances under which the program ran previously, and will then automatically set compatibility options based on the answers you provide.

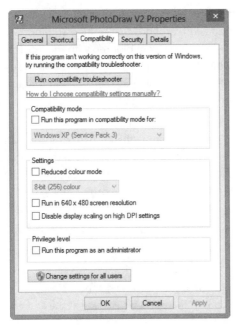

FIGURE 1-1 Setting program compatibility in Windows 8

If you choose to set compatibility manually, you can choose from the following main options:

- **Compatibility mode** This option sets general, overall compatibility for the program for a previous Windows version (including service pack builds) going all the way back to Windows 95. Service pack builds are included for Windows XP and Windows Vista because some service packs included significant changes that can alter how software works in the operating system.

- **Reduced Ccolor mode** If an older program isn't displaying correctly onscreen, you can set it to work in either 8-bit (256 color) or 16-bit (65,536 color) mode.

- **Run in 640 x 480 screen sesolution** If an older program isn't displaying correctly, this setting locks the program into 640×480 pixel resolution.

- **Run this program as an administrator** Some older software might not work correctly if it was coded using what shortcuts and workarounds that require administrator-level access to system files and folders—and these were blocked with the introduction of User Account Control (UAC) in Windows Vista. If a program requires administrator rights to function correctly, you can enable this setting, but keep in mind that the program will *always* open a UAC dialog box when it is run, and some users might not have password access to authorize this action.

- **Change settings for all users** Setting program compatibility changes the registry settings for that program, but each user has her own registry file, so setting compatibility will make the changes only for the user who is logged in at that time. Clicking this button will set program compatibility for all users on the computer.

Thought experiment
Upgrading a branch office

In the following thought experiment, apply what you've learned about this objective. You can find answers to these questions in the "Answers" section at the end of this chapter.

You are upgrading a small branch office of computers from the 32-bit version of Windows XP to Windows 8. Staff members don't need to use any 64-bit software and their computers all have less than 3 TB of installed RAM. You also have to set up a connection to the servers of their parent company using BranchCache.

1. Describe what you will need before upgrading these computers.

2. Make a recommendation for which edition of Windows 8 should be deployed in the office.

Objective summary

- Not all editions of Windows 8 support the features required in the workplace, such as Group Policy or BitLocker.

- No migration path exists between 32-bit and 64-bit Windows editions.

- Windows 8 allows you to upgrade from Windows XP while keeping your files and folders intact.

- The Application Compatibility Toolkit (ACT) can help you to determine the readiness of your software and hardware for Windows 8.

- You can manually set compatibility for older software.

Objective review

Answer the following questions to test your knowledge of the information in this objective. You can find the answers to these questions and explanations of why each answer choice is correct or incorrect in the "Answers" section at the end of this chapter.

1. A business is upgrading its copy of Microsoft Office alongside its Windows 8 installations, and the accounting department has said it needs to work with Excel files in excess of 256 columns. That department also has several third-party Excel plug-in apps that it needs to continue using. What does this mean for your deployment plans?

   A. The accounting department needs the 64-bit version of Windows 8 installed.

   B. The accounting department needs 64-bit Windows 8 and 64-bit Microsoft Office.

   C. The accounting department can install 64-bit Excel in compatibility mode in 32-bit Windows 8.

   D. The accounting department needs 64-bit Windows 8, 64-bit Office, and also compatible 64-bit third-party plug-ins.

2. A business is upgrading several computers from the 64-bit version of Windows Vista to Windows 8. Which one of these statements is true?

   A. You can perform a straight upgrade, keeping the existing software.

   B. You have to perform a clean installation on each workstation.

   C. The company's existing software won't work with Windows 8.

   D. You can upgrade the company computers, keeping files and settings, but will need to reinstall all software afterward.

3. You are planning to upgrade several computers running Windows XP to Windows 8. Which of the following factors do you need to consider? Select all that apply.

   A. You need updated drivers for all the hardware, including external devices.

   B. You need new drivers for the internal hardware, but USB devices will be fine.

   C. You can check your hardware on the Microsoft website to determine Windows 8 compatibility.

   D. You might need to install some software in a Hyper-V environment running Windows XP.

4. Some older software a company has been using doesn't work properly in Windows 8 and keeps reporting a Cannot Write To File error. What is the cause of this?

   A. The file the software is attempting to write to is protected by User Account Control (UAC).

   B. The software isn't being run in compatibility mode.

C. The software is attempting to write to a system file or folder location that is protected by Windows Resource Protection (WRP).

D. The software is being run inside Hyper-V.

Objective 1.2: Install Windows 8

Installing Windows 8 isn't a simple matter of running Setup.exe from a DVD or USB flash drive and entering a product key. Objective 1.1 detailed some of the obstacles facing users who are migrating to Windows 8—for example, moving from a 32-bit version of Windows XP to the 64-bit version of Windows 8 on the same hardware.

This objective covers how to:

- Choose the best method for you to install Windows 8
- Create a custom Windows 8 installation
- Install Windows 8 into a Virtual Hard Disk
- Deploy Windows 8 using Windows To Go
- Understand common installation errors

What are the installation methods?

So how should you install Windows 8, and what media can you use to do so? How can you migrate user files and software on the computers in such a way to provide as seamless and trouble-free an experience for users as possible?

First, look at the different ways you can move computers to Windows 8:

- **Clean Installation** is how many IT professionals recommend migrating from one operating system to another. A clean install completely wipes away any traces of the old operating system, and with that wipes away any problems that could be brought into the new installation. Performing a clean installation has definite advantages, one being that since Windows Vista, the operating system has created a 100 MB System Reserved partition at the beginning of drive 0 in the computer that contains startup and rescue files. With Windows 8, the size of this partition has grown to 350 MB, so an upgrade might not bring all the startup benefits Windows 8 offers because it won't change the size of this partition. You can perform a clean installation from a DVD, a USB flash drive, and a network share.

- **In-Place Upgrade** is an excellent solution, especially if you need to keep user files, settings, and programs. Although all versions of the operating system from Windows XP onward support upgrading, not all files, settings, and software can be migrated. You can run an in-place upgrade from a DVD, a USB flash drive, or a download.

- **Automated Installation** is the method of choice in enterprise environments, using tools such as the Microsoft Deployment Toolkit (MDT) and Windows Deployment Services. You can create answer files that will lead the Windows 8 installer to configure the operating system as you require.
- **Migration** is the process of moving files, settings, and software from an older computer running Windows 7 to a new machine running Windows 8, known as a *side-by-side* migration, or where you perform a clean installation of Windows 8 on a Windows 7 computer but put back all user files, settings, and programs as they were previously, a process known as a *wipe-and-load* migration.

Following a pre-installation checklist

Before you upgrade to or clean install a copy of Windows 8, ensure that all the items on this list have been completed:

- All user files and settings have been backed up.
- You are installing the correct edition of Windows 8 for the features that will be required in the business.
- You have compatible hardware drivers for the edition of Windows 8 you are going to install.
- You have versions of your software that are Windows 8 compatible (as much as possible, anyway).
- You have Windows 8 compatible plug-ins required for software, such as Microsoft Office, additions.

These are all important, because they will help ensure that the installation will go smoothly and that you will have access to the assets you need.

Choosing between an upgrade or a clean installation

It can be argued that it's always a good idea to perform a clean installation of any operating system. The primary reason is that you won't carry over any problems with the existing operating system, software, or drivers to the new operating system. You can also be much more certain that any hardware drivers you install in the new operating system are the correct ones.

In the past, a clean install typically resulted in a faster operating system than an upgrade did. However, this does not apply. With Windows 8, things aren't quite that simple because the upgrade process for this operating system is very different. Table 1-4 shows the differences between the last few Windows versions with respect to what can be migrated from an existing Windows installation to Windows 8.

TABLE 1-4 Migration differences

	Windows XP	Windows Vista	Windows 7	Windows 8
Windows 98, Windows Me	Files, Settings, Software	None	None	None
Windows XP		None	None	Files
Windows Vista			Files, Settings, Software	Files, Settings
Windows 7				Files, Settings, Software

By looking at Table 1-4, you might think that people have preferred a clean installation in recent years because upgrade paths have been blocked. For example, in no way could you upgrade Windows XP to either Windows Vista or Windows 7.

For Windows 8, the only full upgrade path available is from Windows 7. If you are upgrading from Windows Vista, you can migrate only your files and settings; if you are upgrading from Windows XP, you can migrate only your files.

What is the difference, then, between an upgrade from Windows XP or Windows Vista and a clean install? If Windows 8 is wiping the earlier operating system and hardware drivers, it's still a clean installation, right? You have two considerations here: Carry forward any problems with the partition formatting or use the System Reserved partition.

EXAM TIP

Questions may focus on your understanding of the upgrade process and migration differences to ensure that you are able to accurately recommend the most appropriate course of action.

The System Reserved partition

The System Reserved partition was first introduced with Windows Vista as a 100 MB hidden drive but is now expanded to 350 MB in Windows 8. It contains the boot files for the operating system and the system re-imaging and rescue tools. The installer places this small partition just ahead of your Windows installation on drive 0 (zero).

The benefit to having this partition is that the Windows system rescue tools can operate from startup without requiring a Windows installation DVD or restore drive. If this partition is missing or too small, you could experience one or more of the following scenarios:

- Windows Startup Repair won't run from the hard disk.
- Windows System Image Backup won't function.

These are important considerations because any PC that malfunctions can commonly be fixed simply and automatically using Windows Startup Repair, and also because you might require the Windows 8 in-built System Imaging Tool to create backup copies of your installations.

When to perform a clean install

You will always want to perform a clean installation of Windows 8 under certain circumstances:

- The computer currently has no operating system.
- You are migrating a user from one computer to a different computer.
- The existing operating system is Windows 2000, Windows ME, Windows 98, or earlier.
- The computer is currently running a non-Windows operating system.

Methods for performing a clean installation

You can perform a clean installation of Windows 8 in three ways:

- By running Setup.exe from an installation DVD or USB flash drive
- By running Setup.exe from a network share
- By installing using an image

First look at creating an installable DVD or USB flash drive, because these are very common. Installable USB flash drives will likely be a tool you will want to create.

To create an installation DVD or USB flash drive, you need a copy of the correct Windows 8 ISO disc image file. You might have downloaded this as part of your volume licensing program or through a program such as Software Assurance. In both Windows 7 and Windows 8, you can easily burn a disc image of this file to a blank DVD, because you need just to double-click the file to open the Disc Image Burner tool.

To create a bootable USB flash drive (you need a drive of 4 GB or more in size), you need to download the Microsoft Windows USB/DVD download tool. By using this tool, you can select the ISO file and USB flash drive to use, and the tool then creates the media for you. You can also use this tool in Windows XP and Windows Vista to create a bootable installation DVD of Windows 8.

> **MORE INFO DOWNLOAD THE WINDOWS USB/DVD TOOL**
> You can find the Microsoft Windows USB/DVD tool at *http://www.microsoftstore.com/ store/msstore/html/pbpage.help_win7_usbdvd_dwntool.*

To install Windows 8 from a network share, how you begin the installation will vary depending on whether you already have an operating system installed on the destination computer. You can, for example, create a Windows Preinstallation Environment (Windows PE) drive and start the computer from that, or you can use a network Pre-boot Execution Environment (PXE) boot.

Creating a custom Windows 8 installation

You will often find that you want to create a custom Windows 8 installation to include specific hard drivers, software, or updates. You might want something as simple as the company desktop wallpaper on all machines by default. The following steps show how to create a custom install image of Windows 8.

Step 1: Create a Windows PE drive

To start the Windows installer from a network share, you can create Windows PE bootable media, but you will also need the following:

- A *technician computer* on which to install the Windows Assessment and Deployment Kit (Windows ADK). Having the 32-bit Windows version running on the technician computer is best because you can use that version to create media that supports both the 32-bit and 64-bit versions of the operating system.

> **MORE INFO** **WINDOWS ADK**
>
> You can download the Windows Assessment and Deployment Kit from *http://technet. microsoft.com/library/hh824947.aspx.*

- A *reference computer* that represents a typical computer in the organization. This computer shouldn't require any special hardware drivers, but it must have at least one free USB port.
- A *test computer* on which you can make sure everything works afterward.
- A Windows 8 installation DVD and valid product key.
- An empty USB Flash drive with at least 4 GB of free space, if you want to run Windows PE from a USB flash drive.
- An external storage device with at least 8 GB of free space. This can be a network location that you create using the **net use e: \\server\share** command.

When you have these items available, as well as the Windows ADK, you can begin the process of creating your Windows PE bootable media. Follow these steps:

1. On the technician computer, run the Deployment and Imaging Tools environment as an administrator.

2. At the command prompt, type **copype amd64 C:\winpe_amd64** (you can also use **copype amd64 C:\winpe_x86** to create a 32-bit Windows PE disc only). You don't need to create the destination folder in advance.

3. Mount the Windows PE base-image file by typing **dism /mount-image /imagefile:c:\ winpe_amd64\media\sources\boot.wim /index:1 /mountdir:C:\winpe_amd64\ mount**. This command unpacks its contents to a folder so that you can make changes, such as adding boot-specific drivers.

4. Add required drivers by typing the command **dism /image:C:\winpe_amd64\mount /Add-Driver /Driver:C:\Drivers\network.inf**.

5. Add any required packages to the base image file, such as service packs, by using the /Add-Package command in this format:

```
Dism /Image:C:\winpe_amd64\mount /Add-Package /PackagePath:"C:\Program Files
(x86)\Windows Kits\8.0\Assessment and Deployment Kit\Windows Preinstallation
Environment\amd64\WinPE_OCs\WinPE-WinReCfg.cab"
```

Also use the following, because when you add a package, you must also add its corresponding language packs:

```
Dism /Image:C:\winpe_amd64\mount /Add-Package /PackagePath:"C:\Program Files
(x86)\Windows Kits\8.0\Assessment and Deployment Kit\Windows Preinstallation
Environment\amd64\WinPE_OCs\en-us\WinPE-WinReCfg_en-us.cab"
```

6. Commit your changes and unmount the image by typing **Dism /unmount-image /mountdir:C:\winpe_amd64\mount /commit**.

7. To copy your Windows PE image to a USB flash drive, type **MakeWinPEMedia /UFD C:\winpe_amd64 F:**, where *F* represents the drive letter of the destination USB flash drive. You can also use the command **MakeWinPEMedia /ISO C:\winpe_amd64 c:\ winpe_amd64\winpe.iso** to create a Windows PE DVD.

MORE INFO **DISM TECHNICAL REFERENCE**

The Deployment Image Servicing and Management (DISM) tool is used to service offline images. The Technical Reference can be found here: *http://technet.microsoft.com/en-us/library/hh824821.aspx*.

Step 2: Create an unattended answer file

You can optionally create an unattended answer file for your Windows 8 installation. This can include information such as a product key and configuration information for software and/or Windows 8 system components. Follow these steps:

1. On the technician computer, copy the file \Sources\Install.wim to the desktop.

2. Start the Windows System Image Manager from the Windows ADK.

3. From the File menu, click Select Windows Image.

4. Select the correct Install.wim file.

5. From the File menu, click Open Answer File, and then select a sample file from the folder C:\Program Files (x86)\Windows Kits\8.0\Assessment and Deployment Kit\Deployment Tools\Samples\Unattend on the technician computer. Notice in Figure 1-2 that different files are available depending on the computer's BIOS and processor type.

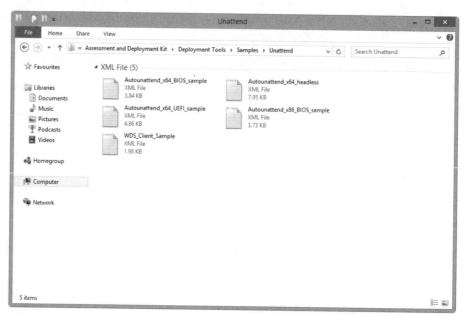

FIGURE 1-2 The different default unattend.txt files available in the Windows ADK

The different components of the Answer File now appear in the Answer File pane and can be easily modified (see Figure 1-3).

MORE INFO **CREATING UNATTENDED INSTALLATION FILES**

You can read more about creating unattended installation files at *http://technet.microsoft. com/en-us/library/ff699038.aspx.*

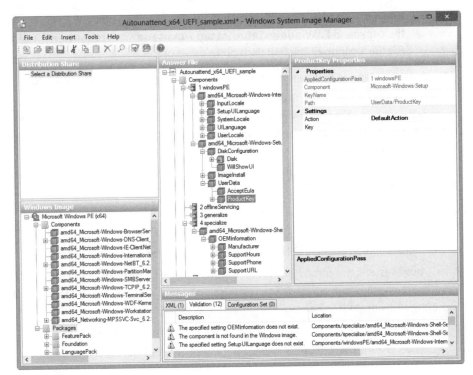

FIGURE 1-3 Modifying an unattended installation file

6. When you have finished making changes to your answer file, choose Save Answer File As from the File menu and save the file as CopyProfileunattend.xml on the USB flash drive.

> **NOTE ADDING DRIVERS AND PACKAGES**
>
> You can add a driver to the unattended installation file by choosing Driver Path from the Insert menu, and then Pass 1 Windows PE. To add packages such as updates of service packs to the unattended installation file, from the Insert menu select Package.

Step 3: Install Windows 8

You now need to install Windows 8 so that you can perform tests and check that the installation file you have created works as required. Follow these steps:

1. Start the reference computer from the Windows 8 installation DVD (the simplest option) or from your newly created Windows PE drive, as follows:

   A. If you are installing from a Windows 8 installation DVD, follow the installation instructions as they are presented.

B. If you are installing from a Windows PE drive, after the computer is started, type the command **F:\WindowsSetup\setup /unattend:F:\autounattend.xml,** where *F* is the location of the USB flash drive.

2. Enter audit mode by pressing Ctrl+Shift+F3 when the installation is complete.

You can now change certain aspects of the default user profile, such as the desktop wall-paper and specific environment variables. You can also install additional software, but keep in mind that if you want to run the installation image from a DVD, the final image must not be too large to fit on the disc.

At this point, it's worth discussing the SysPrep command-line options. The main format of the command is

```
sysprep.exe [/oobe | /audit] [/generalize] [/reboot | /shutdown | /quit] [/quiet] [/
unattend:answerfile]
```

The more common command-line switches for the SysPrep tool are as follows:

- *ated/audit* restarts the computer in audit mode, which is a special mode that allows you to make changes to the default user account and to the operating system, such as install-ing software, before locking down the image.
- */generalize* prepares the installation for locking down and use by a user.
- */oobe* restarts the computer in welcome mode, the first startup mode for a new user of the computer.
- */reboot* restarts the computer.
- */shutdown* shuts down the computer.
- */quiet* runs the SysPrep tool while hiding messages.
- */quit* closes the SysPrep tool after running specified commands.
- */unattend:answerfile* uses the specified unattended answer file with SysPrep.

Step 4: Capture the image

In the final phase of the image-creation process, you need to capture the modified Windows installation. Follow these steps:

1. Boot the reference computer from the Windows PE drive.

2. At the Windows PE command prompt, type **diskpart**.

3. Type **list volume** and write down the drive letters and names that are reported.

4. Type **exit** to leave Diskpart.

5. To capture the Windows partition as an image, type the **dism /Capture-Image / CaptureDir:D:\ /ImageFile: E:\ThinImage.wim /Name:"Contoso"** command, where *D* is the drive letter for the Windows drive and *E* is the drive letter your external hard disk will use later, usually the first unused drive letter after *C* that is available.

6. Connect your external USB hard disk to the computer and create an Images folder by typing the command **md E:\Images**.

7. Type **copy D:\ThinImage.wim E:\Images** to copy the newly created image to the drive.

8. Turn off the reference computer.

You can also use the command-line tool ImageX to capture a Windows image. It is used in the following format:

```
ImageX [/flags "EditionID"] [{/dir | /info | /capture | /apply |
/append | /delete | /export | /mount | /mountrw | /unmount | /split} [Parameters]
```

The switches you can use with the ImageX command are as follows:

- */flags "EditionID"* specifies the Windows version you want to capture. This switch is required (including the quotation marks) if you want to deploy a custom image.

- */dir* displays a list of files and folders inside the image.

- */info* displays information about the .wim image file, including its size and image index number.

- */capture* captures a volume image from a drive into a new .wim file. This includes all subfolders and files.

- */apply* applies a volume image to a specified drive. All hard disk partitions must be created before starting this process, and then you can run this option from Windows PE.

- *append* adds a volume image to an existing .wim file.

- *delete* removes a specified volume from a .wim file.

- *export* exports the contents of a .wim file to another .wim file.

- *mount* mounts a .wim file.

- *mountrw* mounts a .wim file with read/write permission.

- *unmount* unmounts a .wim file.

- *split* breaks large .wim files into smaller, multiple files.

Step 5: Deploy the image to the test computer

You still have some steps to go through to complete your installation image:

1. Start your technician computer and attach your USB hard disk to it.

2. Create an E:\CreatePartitions.txt file in Notepad, where *E* is the location of the USB hard disk.

    A. For Unified Extensible Firmware Interface (UEFI) computers, create a script based on the following, which creates five partitions: Windows RE Tools, System, Windows, Microsoft Reserved (MSR), and Recovery Image.

```
rem These commands are used with DiskPart to
rem erase the drive and create five partitions
rem for a UEFI/GPT-based computer.
rem Adjust the partition sizes to fill the drive as necessary.
select disk 0
clean
convert gpt
rem === 1. Windows RE tools partition ===========
create partition primary size=300
format quick fs=ntfs label="Windows RE tools"
set id="de94bba4-06d1-4d40-a16a-bfd50179d6ac"
assign letter="T"
rem === 2. System partition ====================
create partition efi size=100
format quick fs=fat32 label="System"
assign letter="S"
rem === 3. Microsoft Reserved (MSR) partition ===
create partition msr size=128
rem === 4. Windows partition ===================
rem ==     a. Create Windows partition ==========
create partition primary
rem ==     b. Create space for recovery image ====
shrink minimum=15000
rem ==     c. Prepare the Windows partition ======
format quick fs=ntfs label="Windows"
assign letter="W"
rem === 5. Recovery image partition ============
create partition primary
format quick fs=ntfs label="Recovery image"
gpt attributes=0x8000000000000001
assign letter="R"
```

A. **For older BIOS computers that don't run the UEFI system, create a script that creates three partitions:** System, Windows, and Recovery Image.

```
rem These commands are used with DiskPart to
rem erase the drive and create three partitions
rem for a BIOS/MBR-based computer.
rem Adjust the partition sizes to fill the drive as necessary.
select disk 0
clean
rem === 1. System partition ====================
create partition primary size=350
format quick fs=ntfs label="System"
assign letter="S"
active
rem === 2. Windows partition ===================
rem ==    a. Create Windows partition ==========
create partition primary
rem ==    b. Create space for recovery image ====
shrink minimum=15000
rem ==    c. Prepare the Windows partition ======
format quick fs=ntfs label="Windows"
assign letter="W"
rem === 3. Recovery image partition =============
create partition primary
format quick fs=ntfs label="Recovery"
assign letter="R"
attributes volume set nodefaultdriveletter
exit
```

3. Create a deployment script called *E:\ApplyImage.bat*. This script creates the partitions, applies the Windows 8 image, copies the Windows Recovery Environment (Windows RE) tools, along with the System Partition, and then configures the partitions.

A. For UEFI computers, use this script as your baseline:

```
rem These commands use the specified Windows image file
rem to deploy Windows, system, and recovery tools
rem to a UEFI-based computer.
rem Usage: ApplyImage WimFileName
rem Example: ApplyImage E:\Images\ThinImage.wim
rem === Apply the image to the Windows partition ========
dism /Apply-Image /ImageFile:%1 /Index:1 /ApplyDir:W:\
rem === Copy tools to the Windows RE Tools partition ====
md T:\Recovery\WindowsRE
copy W:\windows\system32\recovery\winre.wim T:\Recovery\WindowsRE\winre.wim
rem === Copy boot files to the System partition =========
W:\Windows\System32\bcdboot W:\Windows /s S:
rem === Set the location of the WinRE tools =============
W:\Windows\System32\reagentc /setreimage /path T:\Recovery\WindowsRE /target
W:\Windows
rem === Create the recovery image =======================
Mkdir R:\RecoveryImage
Copy %1 R:\RecoveryImage
W:\Windows\System32\reagentc /setosimage /path T:\RecoveryImage /target W:\Windows
/index 1
```

B. For BIOS computers, use this script as your baseline:

```
rem These commands use the specified Windows image file
rem to deploy Windows, system, and recovery tools
rem to a BIOS-based computer.
rem Usage: ApplyImage WimFileName
rem Example: ApplyImage E:\Images\ThinImage.wim
rem === Apply the image to the Windows partition ====================
dism /Apply-Image /ImageFile:%1 /Index:1 /ApplyDir:W:\
rem === Copy the Windows RE Tools to the system partition ===================
md S:\Recovery\WindowsRE
copy W:\windows\system32\recovery\winre.wim S:\Recovery\WindowsRE\winre.wim
rem === Copy boot files from the Windows partition to the System partition ===
W:\Windows\System32\bcdboot W:\Windows /s S:
rem === In the System partition, set the location of the Windows RE tools
=========
W:\Windows\System32\reagentc /setreimage /path S:\Recovery\WindowsRE /target
W:\Windows
rem === Create the recovery image ===========================
Mkdir R:\RecoveryImage
copy %1 R:\RecoveryImage
W:\Windows\System32\reagentc /setosimage /path R:\RecoveryImage /target W:\Windows
/index 1
```

MORE INFO DOWNLOAD THESE SCRIPTS

You can get copies of the scripts detailed here at *http://technet.microsoft.com/en-gb/library/hh825212.aspx*.

4. Boot the Test Computer into Windows PE from your USB flash drive.

5. At the command line, type **diskpart /s E:\CreatePartitions.txt**.

6. To verify that the script worked successfully, type **diskpart**.

7. At the Diskpart prompt, type **list volume**. This displays the list of partitions that have been created by Windows PE, such as *E* for External USB Hard Disk, *F* for USB Flash Drive, *R* for Recovery Image, *S* for System, *T* for Windows RE Tools, and *W* for Windows.

8. Type **exit** to return to the command prompt.

9. To test your deployment script, type **E:\ApplyImage E:\Images\ThinImage.wim**, where *E* is the drive letter for your USB hard disk.

10. After the image is applied, restart the computer. You should have a working Windows 8 installation.

EXAM TIP

Ensure that you have a good understanding of what the key Windows 8 automation tools for installation are, including sysprep, DISM, WinPE, unattended answer files and the Windows SIM.

Installing Windows 8 into a Virtual Hard Disk (VHD)

Quite possibly one of the most useful features that's ever been built into Windows from the perspective of an IT support and deployment professional is the ability to boot natively into a VHD. Although this might on the face of things sound like a rather odd idea, let's look at some scenarios to see what this actually means and just how useful this actually is in practice.

On a typical computer where you boot from a VHD you will have a standard installation of Windows 8, installed onto the hard disk in the usual way (and presumably backed up as an image as well) and then you will have a separate VHD file, which does not need to be on its own partition and can reside on the C: drive with Windows 8.

When you boot your computer from a VHD you'd never know that you're not using an operating system that's installed on the hard disk in the usual way. You still have full access to the computer's hardware resources and everything seems normal, except crucially that you're isolated from the main installation of Windows 8 on the hard drive that now can't be interfered with. Additionally you can use 64-bit editions of Windows 8 with this feature, there is no limitation to 32-bit only.

This is useful in many ways. If you run an internet café, library, or training provider for example the VHD is very simple to restore as and when it is needed. All that is required is that you boot into the standard copy of Windows 8 and copy your master VHD (because you obviously made a copy of it!) back, overwriting the current VHD.

In business the applications for booting from a VHD are even more useful because it means you can very quickly and simply repurpose any computer, laptop, or tablet. Let's say, for example, that you have different Windows 8 installations for management, accounts, sales, design, administration, and development departments, each containing different software packages and settings, and privileges unique to the role for which they will be used.

In this scenario you might need to repurpose a laptop from the accounts department for the sales team, because one on-the-go laptop has failed and needs replacing. In the usual scenario you'd re-image the entire computer, but this would wipe out the full installation on the machine.

With a VHD you simply boot into that installation and either copy an already configured and purposed VHD over to the computer or, rename a couple files if you already have multiple VHDs on the computer just in case.

> **NOTE MAKE SURE YOU HAVE APPROPRIATE WINDOWS LICENSES**
>
> Each copy of Windows 8 you install onto a computer, whether in a VHD or not, will require its own valid product key and activation. You should ensure that you have an adequate number of product keys to cover the VHDs that you use in your organization.

So let's look at how you can install Windows 8 into a VHD.

1. Boot your computer from your Windows 8 installation media. Note that you cannot install to a VHD from Within an already running copy of Windows 8.

2. Select your installation language.

3. At the install screen, press Shift+F10 to open the DOS command window.

4. Type **diskpart** and press Enter.

Using an Existing VHD

1. Type **select vdisk file=C:\path1\path2\disk.vhd**, substituting the drive letter, path, and file name of the VHD you wish to use.

2. Type a**ttach vdisk.**

Creating a new VHD

1. Type **create vdisk file=C:\path1\path2\disk.vhd maximum=40000 type=fixed** and press Enter, substituting the drive letter, path, and file name of the VHD you wish to create and changing the VHD size (20480, for example, would create a drive 20GB in size) and swapping fixed for expandable if you want a dynamically expanding disk size.

2. Type **select vdisk file=C:\path1\path2\disk.vhd** to select the disk you have just created and press Enter.

3. Type **attach vdisk** and press Enter.

4. Type **exit** and press Enter.

5. Type **exit** again and press Enter.

6. Click Install and then select Custom: Install Windows 8 Only (Advanced).

7. Click the VHD you have created and select Drive Options (Advanced).

8. Create a new partition inside the VHD using all the space available.

9. Format this new drive.

10. Ensure that the VHD drive is highlighted as the drive on which you wish to install Windows 8 and click Next to begin the installation.

11. Windows 8 will now install the OS and automatically configure the boot loader; however, you will now have two copies of Windows 8 in that boot loader, both of which will be called "Windows 8." Thus you might want to edit the boot menu and change the name of one of these to something else. To do this follow these instructions after Windows 8 starts.

12. Open the Win+X menu and run Command Prompt (Admin).

13. Type **bcdedit /v** and press Enter.

14. Locate the VHD copy of Windows in the list of operating systems that appears and copy its GUID code. This is a long string of numbers and letters that appears as its identifier parameter.

15. Type **bcdedit /set {GUID} description "OS Name"** and press Enter, substituting GUID for the string you copied in step 3 and with the name you wish for the VHD to have (see Figure 1-4).

FIGURE 1-4 A command prompt window showing the GUIDs for several Windows installations

16. Optionally you might want to set your VHD to boot by default when the computer starts. You can do this with the command **bcdedit /default {GUID}**.

Deploying via Windows To Go

You might want to give some users a Windows To Go USB flash drive that they can use to run an Windows 8 Enterprise edition installation on computers when they are away from the office. You can create this flash drive complete with a user's profile, software, and even files intact. The Windows To Go USB flash drive is usable on any computer that can boot from USB.

> **NOTE TO GIVE OR NOT TO GIVE?**
>
> You really don't want to give users their own Windows To Go devices solely, unless you have a very good reason why they shouldn't get a laptop or desktop computer. However, a Windows To Go device can help people who work out of the office or even at home.

Keep in mind some considerations for Windows To Go:

- Windows To Go drives can be created only from Windows 8 Enterprise edition.

- Hibernate and sleep are disabled by default.

- Windows To Go blocks access to the local drives on the host computer to help maintain the security of that computer.

- If you use BitLocker to encrypt a Windows To Go drive, you will need a password to unlock the drive, because USB flash drives don't have TPM chips as of this writing.

- The Windows RE isn't available, so if the Windows To Go drive becomes corrupt, it will be need to be re-created.

- You need a compatible USB flash drive with a 32 GB capacity or larger. Note, however, that not all flash drives are compatible. In Figure 1-5, notice the 64 GB USB3 flash drive that won't run Windows To Go.

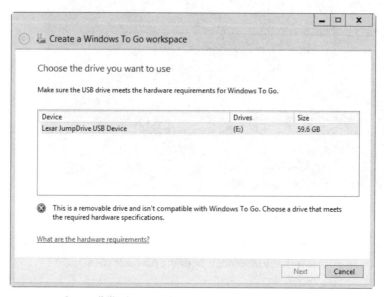

FIGURE 1-5 Compatibility issues with some USB flash drives

When you use Windows To Go on a computer for the first time, it will detect and install the hardware drivers for that computer. As a result, the first run can take some time to start up, although it will be much faster for subsequent uses on that same computer. You should make users aware of this first-time delay if they plan to use the drive on many different computers.

> **MORE INFO COMPATIBLE USB FLASH DRIVES**
>
> You can find out more details about compatible USB flash drives at
> *http://technet.microsoft.com/en-us/library/hh831833.aspx#wtg_hardware.*

Understanding common Windows 8 installation errors

So far, the methods for installing Windows 8 detailed in this chapter assume that nothing will go wrong during the installation. However, you sometimes might encounter a problem, such as the following:

- Not being able to read from the installation DVD doesn't necessarily mean that it is faulty. Try reading the disc on another computer to see whether you need to use a lens cleaner on the optical drive. Alternatively, you can try cleaning the disc itself with a small amount of glass cleaner and a soft cloth.

- On some older computers, the BIOS firmware might need updating. You might find, for example, that the firmware won't allow you to boot the computer from a USB device.

- When starting from a USB device, you might find at computer startup that you need to press the key that displays the boot options menu. If your computer doesn't boot from a USB drive, you can select a one-time boot option here.

- If hardware isn't properly installed, you can have trouble installing drivers. Some hardware, such as RAID cards, requires a driver to be loaded at startup. You need to make sure such drivers are included in your Windows 8 image.

- If you're upgrading older computers, you might find that their hardware doesn't meet the minimum hardware requirements for Windows 8. Performing a hardware audit of your computers is a good idea before rolling out any new operating system.

- Any error messages that you see during the process can be checked at the Microsoft knowledge base online at *http://support.microsoft.com*. Carefully write down, in full, any error messages that you receive.

If you need to troubleshoot a problem, first determine what it is that might have changed. Problems are commonly caused by recent changes to software, drivers, or updates. You might find that reversing any recent changes might rectify the problem.

Activating Windows 8

You can use the Volume Activation Management Tool (VAMT), included within the Windows 8 WDK, to manage the activation of a group of computers in an enterprise environment based on their Active Directory Domain Services (AD DS), workgroup names, IP addresses, or computer names.

Each computer requires only a single activation connection with Microsoft, after which no further connection to Microsoft is made. This system uses a product key that is permitted to activate a certain number of computers.

In larger enterprise environments, activation can be managed by the Key Management Services (KMS) without connecting to Microsoft at all. To use this, you need a KMS server within the enterprise that manages your licensing. You can then activate the Windows installation from the command line by typing **cscript C:\windows\system32\slmgr.vbs -ipk \<KmsKey\>**.

However, computers activated through a KMS server must reactivate via that server once every 180 days. This consideration must be made if remote work is required, where the computer can be mobile or out of touch with the server for long periods of time.

To check the activation status of a Windows 8 client at any time, use the System item in Control Panel or type the **slmgr.vbs -dli** command. If a copy of Windows 8 isn't activated, an activation option will also appear in PC Settings.

Upgrading to Windows 8

If you now use Windows Vista or Windows 7 and are moving to Windows 8, an in-place upgrade of the operating system might be a good option. You can perform an in-place upgrade from the Windows 8 installation media. If you are upgrading from Windows 7, you can keep all your settings, accounts, and files. If you are upgrading from Windows Vista, you can keep your user account and settings, but you will have to reinstall your software.

You can still use an answer file to automate an upgrade, although the overall interaction required from the user is minimal.

> **IMPORTANT** **A CRUCIAL CONSIDERATION FOR ANY UPGRADE**
>
> The most important consideration when upgrading a computer to Windows 8, or any operating system, is to ensure that you have a full and up-to-date backup of all your data.

You will find that some software will need to be removed (such as your anti-virus software, if you want to use the in-built anti-virus protection of Windows 8 or a server-based solution such as InTune). Other software might need updating, and hardware drivers might also need updating.

The final consideration is that if you are upgrading to the Standard edition of Windows 8, rather than Windows 8 Pro, you can't upgrade from the Professional or Ultimate editions of Windows 7.

If you want to upgrade from Windows XP, the computer's user accounts and files will be retained but all the computer's settings and installed software will need to be redone.

EXAM TIP

Because Microsoft certification exams often focus on the command-line aspect of tools and utilities, you should consider this when preparing for your final exam.

Thought experiment
Upgrading a small business

In the following thought experiment, apply what you've learned about this objective. You can find answers to these questions in the "Answers" section at the end of this chapter.

The business has ten computers to upgrade, all of which are running Windows Vista, and the user files and data are stored on a separate file server that doesn't need upgrading. With this in mind, complete the following exercises:

1. How do you propose it is best to keep a bespoke software package required for all the computers but unlikely to need upgrading in the future?

2. You need to create a custom installation image for the computers. Describe the tools and utilities you will need to create this.

3. Describe how you would activate each copy of Windows 8 used in the business.

Objective summary

- You can perform a clean installation of Windows 8, upgrade an existing installation, or migrate user data to a new Windows 8 computer.

- Only an upgrade from Windows 7 will permit migration of installed desktop software.

- You can create a custom or automated Windows 8 installation by downloading and installing the Windows 8 Assessment and Deployment Kit (ADK) onto a technician computer.

- You can create an unattended answer file to automate much of the Windows 8 installation process.

- You can use SysPrep, the System Preparation tool, to customize a Windows 8 default installation before an installation image is captured.

- You can use Windows To Go to provide users with mobile, USB-based Windows 8 installations.

- The Windows 8 ADK includes tools to aid the automation of Windows 8 product activation.

Objective review

Answer the following questions to test your knowledge of the information in this objective. You can find the answers to these questions and explanations of why each answer choice is correct or incorrect in the "Answers" section at the end of this chapter.

1. You need to upgrade a few computers in an office running Windows 7 and a few slightly older Windows XP computers to Windows 8. What is the best method to deploying the new operating system?

   A. Performing clean installations

   B. Upgrading each machine in place

   C. Upgrading the Windows 7 computers and performing a clean installation on the Windows XP computers

   D. Migrating user data on each machine to a new computer

2. You need to install both 32-bit and 64-bit versions of Windows 8. Which sections of the Deployment and Imaging Tools do you need?

   A. Just the x86 tools

   B. The x86 tools and the x64 tools

   C. The x86 tools and the amd64 tools

   D. Just the amd64 tools

3. You are using the SysPrep command to configure a custom installation before you capture the image and need to restart the computer after installing an update before you can continue configuring it. Which SysPrep command-line switch do you use?

   A. /audit

   B. /restart

   C. /generalize

   D. /oobe

4. Which command-line tool can you use to capture a custom Windows 8 image?

   A. Dism /capture

   B. SysPrep /capture

   C. ImageX /capture

   D. DiskPart /capture

5. Which method can you use to check the activation status of any computer?

   A. Type **slmgr.vbs -dli** at the command prompt.

   B. Type **vlmgr.vbs /license** at the command prompt.

   C. Open the System panel from the Control panel and type **vlmgr.vbs /license** at a command prompt.

   D. Open the System panel from the Control Panel and type **slmgr.vbs -dli** at a command prompt.

Objective 1.3: Migrate and configure user data

An installation solution that commonly best suits businesses is called *migration*. This involves saving portions of the current installation, such as the user account and data and files, by backing them up to a temporary store while you reimage the computer. This saved state data can later be returned to the computer.

This objective covers how to:

- Choose how best to migrate user data to Windows 8
- Migrate files and settings using Windows Easy Transfer
- Migrate user files and settings using the User State Migration Tool
- Set up folder redirection

Choosing to migrate

Migration to Windows 8 is recommended for many reasons, especially for Windows XP installations. For example, you can ensure that no problems associated with the previous Windows installation, including malware and viruses, carry over to the new Windows 8 installation. You can also easily restore user accounts with not just the main enterprise-set account permissions but also a user's individual preferences.

***IMPORTANT* BACKUP, BACKUP, BACKUP!**

You probably don't need to be reminded of two things: that you can try turning the computer off and on again if a problem occurs, and that you should keep current backups. Because backups are absolutely essential, they are mentioned here because, although the tools available to migrate a user's settings and files from one computer to another are excellent, Murphy's law dictates that whatever can go wrong, will go wrong. It's therefore during this essential transition that you can reasonably guarantee that it will.

Before migrating user data, you should create a complete backup of the computer's entire hard disk. You might need this in case the Windows 8 installation fails or encounters a problem, and you find that you need to restore the older operating system until you can rectify the error. Alternatively, you could experience something catastrophic such as a power outage during the installation or migration.

You can perform a data migration from one computer to another in two ways: by using Windows Easy Transfer, a feature built into Windows 8, and by using the User State Migration Tool (USMT), which is provided as part of the Microsoft Deployment Toolkit (MDT).

Migration using Windows Easy Transfer

Don't think of Windows Easy Transfer as a basic tool to help consumers switch to another computer at home because it's much more useful and full featured than you might imagine. For example, you can use it to migrate files, settings, and accounts from one computer to another over a network and in a secure manner. Follow these steps to perform a migration with Windows Easy Transfer:

1. Start Windows Easy Transfer on the host and target PCs. On the target (Windows 8) PC, search for Windows Easy Transfer from the Start screen. On the host PC, run Windows Easy Transfer from a Windows 8 installation DVD or flash drive; you can find it in the E:\ support\migwiz folder (assuming *E* is the letter associated with the installation media). You need to run the program Migwiz.exe (see Figure 1-6).

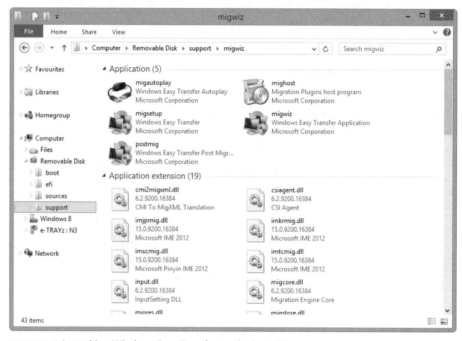

FIGURE 1-6 Launching Windows Easy Transfer on the host PC

On startup, Windows Easy Transfer tells you what it can transfer (see Figure 1-7). This, frankly, is anything and everything from the host PC except the operating system. This makes Windows Easy Transfer a very powerful tool.

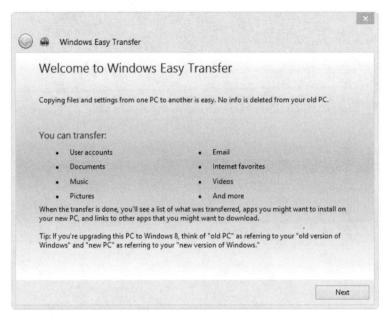

FIGURE 1-7 Starting Windows Easy Transfer

2. Decide how you want to transfer the user accounts and data (see Figure 1-8). You can perform this transfer using an external USB hard disk or, if you have one large enough, a USB flash drive. You can also perform the transfer over a wired or wireless network, although using a wireless network isn't recommended in case the signal is lost during the transfer.

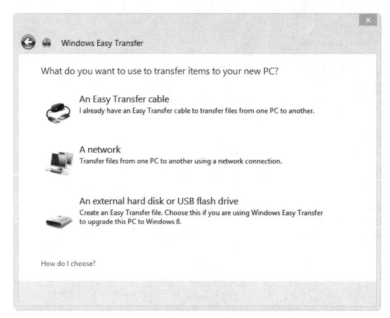

FIGURE 1-8 Choosing how to transfer the user data

Until now, you have been selecting the same options on both host and target PCs.

3. Specify which is the host (old) PC and which is the target (new) PC (see Figure 1-9).

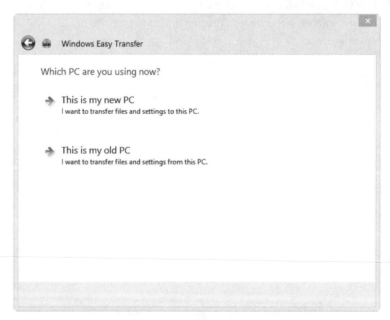

FIGURE 1-9 Choosing which is the target PC

If you are transferring files over a network, Windows Easy Transfer will give you a security code on the host PC that needs to be typed into the target PC to make the connection (see Figure 1-10).

FIGURE 1-10 Security code from Windows Easy Transfer

4. Select what to transfer from the host PC while the target PC waits for the transfer to begin. The choices screen is simply laid out and easy to use, with Customize and Advanced links available to help you choose which aspects of a user's account and what else on the computer's hard drive to transfer (see Figure 1-11).

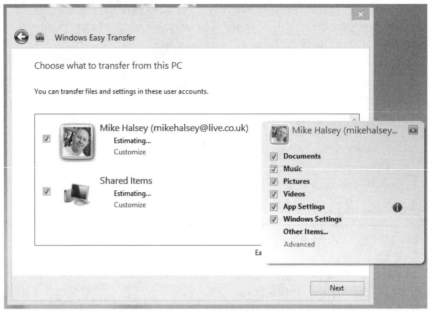

FIGURE 1-11 Choosing what to migrate in Windows Easy Transfer

Migration using the User State Migration Tool (USMT)

You can find the command-line User State Migration Tool in the C:\Program Files (x86)\ Windows Kits\8.0\Assessment and Deployment Kit\User State Migration Tool folder of your hard disk after you install the ADK. Here, you will see different x86 and amd64 versions of the tool; you should use the one that matches the operating system you are using. (On 32-bit Windows versions, this path will read C:\Program Files\Windows Kit... and so on, because the x86 part of the folder address isn't used.)

The main tools in this folder, for which you will need to open a command prompt, are as follows:

- **ScanState.exe** The migration tool for files, settings, and accounts from the host computer.
- **LoadState.exe** The migration import tool for the target computer.
- **MigApp.xml** This tool contains details of software that migrates from a Windows 7 computer to a Windows 8 computer.
- **MigUser.xml** This tool contains details of the user accounts to migrate.
- **MigDocs.xml** This tool contains details of the documents and files to migrate.
- **Custom.xml** This tool enables you to create custom XML files that can migrate additional files and data, such as a line-of-business (LOB) application, or to modify the default migration behavior.
- **Config.xml** This tool can be used to exclude certain items from migration. You can create this file using the /genconfig option in the scanstate tool.

You run the ScanState command-line tool on the host computer with the following format:

```
scanstate [StorePath] [/i:[path\]FileName] [Options]
```

The /i[*path*\]FileName option specifies an XML file that contains rules determining what's to be migrated. You can specify this option multiple times to include all your necessary .xml files.

With those options is a great menu to choose from, and you can find descriptions of them by using the /? switch with the ScanState.exe command. Another switch that you certainly want to know about is /hardlink, which you can use to create hard links to the migration store location. If you use this switch, you must also use the /nocompress switch.

On the target PC, you would use the LoadState command with this format:

```
Loadstate [StorePath] [/i:[path\]FileName] [Options]
```

Again, you can read about many command-line switches with the /? switch, but the most important is /lac:[*password*] (local account create), which specifies that a local user account is to be created on the target computer. By default, the account will be disabled if it doesn't already exist on the target computer, and you should use the /lae (local account enable) switch to enable it.

EXAM TIP

Because LoadState.exe and ScanState.exe offer the administrator the ability to migrate to Windows 8 securely, efficiently and importantly at scale, you should ensure that your exam preparation includes these two commands.

Using folder redirection

You might want to consider redirecting a user's files, or all users' files, to a central server when you migrate the user files to a new Windows 8 computer. This isn't the same as users having a roaming profile where their files and documents are always kept on the server as well as on their own computer and synched whenever they log in. This method uses either a server in the office or one of the computers as a file server.

All files and documents for all users will always be stored solely on this central server and nowhere else. Doing so has certain advantages, not the least of which is file security if anybody uses a laptop, because files stored on this computer won't be available outside the immediate network.

REAL WORLD CREATING A BACKUP FOR A LOCAL AREA NETWORK OR VPN

When I was working in a small training center with five staff members who were part of a national education charity, we had huge amounts of resources (teaching and paperwork) that everybody wanted access to. We each had our own PC but no server.

I moved all files to one computer—the one the administrator used that was most commonly going to be switched on all the time—and updated the documents folders (this was Windows XP, pre-libraries) to point to the shared folder that contained all the resources. Then, on another computer I created a hidden backup folder and used a free backup tool to ensure that a second copy of all the files was kept up-to-date.

Nobody outside the office could access these files because they were available only on the local network. This suited us for security, however, because the files contained personal data about learners in the center.

If we had a small server in the office, however, I could have set up a virtual private network (VPN) to allow access to these files for staff when they were out and about on their laptops or when they were working at home. Today you can also set this up on Windows To Go drives.

You can add the central storage, which can be per user or shared between users, to the main libraries in Windows 8 as follows:

1. Create a folder on the target computer for the network share—for example, C:\Shared.

2. Create another folder within that folder—for example, C:\Shared\Documents.

3. Select the subfolder that you just created. On the Home tab on the ribbon, click Easy Access, and then click Include In Library.

4. Delete the folder.

5. Press Win+X to open the Administration menu and then click Command Prompt (Admin).

6. Type **mklink /d** followed by the path of the folder you just deleted and the path of the network folder—for example, mklink /d C:\Share\Documents\\Server\SharedDocs—to create a symbolic link between the two folders.

   Doing so adds the network files to your library, something that can't be done from within File Explorer itself.

You can also use the Sync Center in Windows 8 to maintain a synchronized copy of the server files on the local computer—useful if the user is working on a laptop—by right-clicking the folder you want to make available and clicking Always Available Offline from the options that appear (see Figure 1-12).

FIGURE 1-12 Syncing a network folder

The first synchronization will then take place, which can take some time if you have many files, and a copy of the network files will then be kept on the local computer.

To manage this sync partnership, open the Sync Center by searching for it at the Start screen. You will want to use two main options most of all:

- To manage the schedule when the files are synched with the server, double-click the sync relationship in the main Sync Center view and then click the Schedule link that appears on the toolbar. Figure 1-13 shows how you can set the frequency or specific times when synchronization takes place.

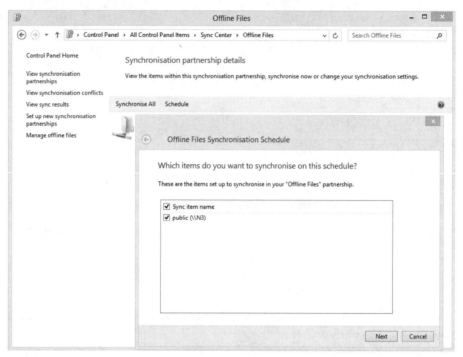

FIGURE 1-13 Changing the synch schedule for offline files

■ The other aspect of synchronization over which you might want finer control is the offline copy of the server files. To access these controls, click the Manage Offline Files link. Here you can enable and disable synchronization, but on the Disk Usage tab you can change the amount of local disk space allocated for synchronized files, which is useful for laptops with small hard disks. You can also remove any temporary files that might not have been cleaned up (see Figure 1-14). On the Encryption tab you can also force encryption of the offline files, which can be useful if those files include anything that would be covered by data protection legislation, such as personal details of individuals.

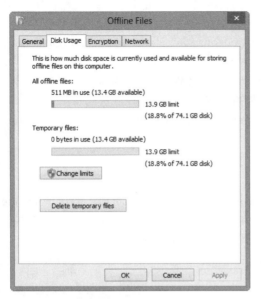

FIGURE 1-14 Managing offline files

Thought experiment

Upgrading for mobile workers

In the following thought experiment, apply what you've learned about this objective. You can find answers to these questions in the "Answers" section at the end of this chapter.

A small office doesn't have a server but requires mobile workers to have access to files at all times when out on the road. Which of the following statements is true and why?

1. You can set the encryption status of files in the office by using Encrypting File System (EFS) and then open them on local PCs using the correct EFS decryption key.

2. You can use the Windows 8 Sync Center to encrypt files that are synched from the office.

3. Secure encrypted access to files from a remote location can be gained only by logging on to the server via a VPN.

Objective summary

- To migrate user accounts and files from one computer to another, use either the Windows Easy Transfer tool or the User State Migration Tool.
- The ScanState command offers many more configurability options than Windows Easy Transfer but requires some knowledge of XML.
- You can relocate user files to a server or central file store and still maintain access to them in Windows 8 libraries.

Objective review

Answer the following questions to test your knowledge in this objective. You can find the correct answers to these questions and explanations of why each answer choice is correct or incorrect in the "Answers" section at the end of this chapter.

1. In which folder on the Windows 8 installation media will you find the Windows Easy Transfer tool?

   A. \support\wet

   B. \support\migwiz

   C. \support\migration

   D. \sources\migwiz

2. Which .xml file should you use to specify items to exclude from a migration?

   A. Custom.xml

   B. Exclude.xml

   C. Config.xml

   D. MigDocs.xml

3. Which LoadState command-line switch or switches are required to create a user account on a new computer?

   A. /createuser

   B. /lua and /lae

   C. /lac and /lae

   D. /lac

4. How can you make server files available on a local computer?

   A. By applying them to a local library

   B. By setting their offline availability status

   C. By setting up a new sync partnership

   D. Server files are available only when connected to the local network

5. Setting a sync partnership between server files and a local PC stores how many of the server files locally?

   A. All shared server files

   B. All server files up to a maximum specified local storage amount

   C. The most recently accessed server files

   D. Server files that don't have their archive switch activated

Chapter summary

- Not all editions of Windows 8 support the features required in the workplace, such as Group Policy or BitLocker.
- No migration path exists between 32-bit a 64-bit Windows editions.
- Windows 8 allows you to upgrade from Windows XP while keeping your files and folders intact.
- The Application Compatibility Toolkit (ACT) can help you to determine the readiness of your software and hardware for Windows 8.
- You can manually set compatibility for older software.
- You can perform a clean installation of Windows 8, upgrade an existing installation, or migrate user data to a new Windows 8 computer.
- Only an upgrade from Windows 7 will permit migration of installed desktop software.
- You can create a custom or automated Windows 8 installation by downloading and installing the Windows 8 Assessment and Deployment Kit (ADK) onto a technician computer.
- To automate much of the Windows 8 installation process, you can create an unattended answer file.
- You can use SysPrep, the System Preparation tool, to customize a Windows 8 default installation before an installation image is captured.
- You can use Windows To Go to provide users with mobile, USB-based Windows 8 installations.
- The Windows 8 ADK includes tools to aid the automation of Windows 8 product activation.

- You can migrate user accounts and files from one computer to another using either the Windows Easy Transfer tool or the User State Migration Tool (USMT).

- The ScanState command offers many more configurability options than Windows Easy Transfer (but requires some knowledge of XML).

- You can relocate user files to a server or central file store and still maintain access to them in Windows 8 libraries.

Answers

This section contains the solutions to the thought experiments and answers to the objective review questions in this chapter.

Objective 1.1: Thought experiment

1. Because you don't need the 64-bit Windows version, you need only the 32-bit (x86) Windows 8 installation media—unless, of course, you will want to upgrade the computers to 4 GB or more of memory in the future. You also need Windows 8 compatible drivers for all your hardware and software installers that are compatible with Windows 8.

2. You need to install Windows 8 Enterprise because only this edition of the operating system supports BranchCache.

Objective 1.1: Review

1. **Correct answer:** D

   A. **Incorrect:** Although the 64-bit version of Windows 8 can handle numbers larger than 65,536 on its own and memory addressing above 4 GB, you also need to have 64-bit software installed to take advantage of this extra functionality. Using 32-bit software still can address only the same memory and perform the same calculations as a 32-bit version of the Windows operating system.

   B. **Incorrect:** Although the 64-bit version of Excel, when paired with the 64-bit version of Windows 8, can handle more than 256 columns required, the plug-ins won't work if they're not coded specifically to work with the 64-bit version of Microsoft Office.

   C. **Incorrect:** You can't install any 64-bit application in the 32-bit Windows version, not even in compatibility mode. Attempting to install 64-bit software in a 32-bit operating system will report an error that the software is incompatible.

   D. **Correct:** The workers in the accounting department will have the facilities they need only if the operating system, version of Microsoft Office, and all required Office plug-ins are all coded for 64-bit processors.

2. **Correct answer:** D

   A. **Incorrect:** Although many software packages that run on Windows Vista will run on Windows 8 without incident, the Windows 8 installer doesn't support migration of any software from Windows Vista. It will allow you to migrate only user settings, accounts, and files.

   B. **Incorrect:** Although you *can* perform a clean installation on each workstation, doing so isn't absolutely necessary because upgrading to Windows 8 from Windows Vista supports all user accounts, settings, and documents and only your software will need reinstalling.

   C. **Incorrect:** Although a few changes that have been made to the Windows operating system since Windows Vista means some software won't work with Windows 8, this situation will arise very rarely. Almost every piece of software that runs on Windows Vista will run on Windows 8.

   D. **Correct:** The Windows 8 installer allows you to migrate your user accounts, settings, and files from Windows Vista. It is only your software that needs reinstalling afterward when performing an in-place upgrade.

3. **Correct answers:** A, C, and D

   A. **Correct:** No hardware drivers that worked with Windows XP will work with Windows 8 because the hardware driver model was changed completely with Windows Vista. Thus, you will need new drivers for all your hardware.

   B. **Incorrect:** When the hardware driver model changed with Windows Vista, this change included all drivers, including those attached to a computer via USB. The USB attachment doesn't guarantee that all external devices operate the same way. While this might be generally true for some devices such as external hard disks, so many different device types can be attached via USB that the USB driver system itself can't provide hardware compatibility with all devices.

   C. **Correct:** Microsoft provides an online device compatibility database that you can access at http://www.microsoft.com/en-us/windows/compatibility/win8/CompatCenter/Home?Language=en-US. This database details every device that is certified for use on a Windows computer. If your device doesn't appear in this list, it doesn't necessarily mean that it won't work; it simply might not have been submitted for compatibility testing.

D. Correct: Although many software packages that worked in Windows XP will also work in Windows 8, much of the core operating system architecture has changed between the two operating systems and many functions called by software in Windows XP no longer exist or have changed radically since. This means that some software will need to be run in a virtualized Windows XP environment because Windows 8 compatibility mode can't maintain full compatibility where Windows features are missing or have changed.

4. Correct answer: C

A. Incorrect: The User Account Control is activated when software is installed, at which time its UAC permissions are set. If a user permits software to install, the UAC will give it the appropriate permissions in Windows 8.

B. Incorrect: A Cannot Write to File error means that the software is trying to access a protected part of the Windows file system. Running the program in compatibility mode won't rectify this problem because allowing older software to access protected Windows files in this way would compromise the operating system's security.

C. Correct: Windows Resource Protection (WRP) is a security feature designed specifically to protect write access to critical operating system files and folders. This error is the only one ever generated by WRP.

D. Incorrect: Technically, you can get this error inside Hyper-V if you install a copy of Windows 8 into a virtual machine and then install legacy software into that. This is unlikely, however, and not the answer sought for this question.

Objective 1.2: Thought experiment

1. If the software is bespoke and doesn't get upgraded, when computers come to be reinstalled or when new computers are bought, the software won't have changed. The best way to deploy this software, then—assuming it's not too large—is by using SysPrep so that it is already installed on any new Windows 8 systems installed from a custom image.

1. To create a custom image, you need three computers: a technician computer; a target computer, which is a typical computer broadly representing the computers in the office; and a test computer. You also need a USB flash drive for your Windows PE boot loader and an external USB hard disk or network storage location for the image storage.

2. You need to use the Volume Activation Management Tool (VAMT) provided in the Windows 8 ADK. If you use the Key Management Services (KMS), each computer will need to be activated (and reactivated every 180 days) through a server. The only available server is only a file server, which might not have the installed software you need to run the KMS service.

Objective 1.2: Review

1. **Correct answer:** B

   A. **Incorrect:** You can perform clean installations, but you also can upgrade each computer so that the ones running Windows 7 will keep all their current software. On the Windows XP computers, the software, operating system, and hardware drivers are all replaced during an upgrade, effectively making this a clean install anyway, but performing the same installation method on every machine simplifies the overall process.

   B. **Correct:** This is the best option because it will keep any Windows 7 software in place and effectively perform a clean installation on the XP computers. Performing the same installation method on all computers simplifies the overall process.

   C. **Incorrect:** Like with answer A, you can perform clean installations but you also can upgrade each computer so that the ones running Windows 7 will keep all their current software. On the Windows XP computers, the software, operating system, and hardware drivers are all replaced during an upgrade, effectively making this a clean install anyway, but performing the same installation method on every machine simplifies the overall process.

   D. **Incorrect:** This can't be done. Because you need to upgrade existing computers, you can't migrate the user data to any new computers.

2. **Correct answer:** D

A. Incorrect: The 32-bit (x86) tools support creation of only a 32-bit Windows PE disc.

B. Incorrect: You can use the 64-bit tools to create a Windows PE disc compatible with both 64-bit and 32-bit operating systems. Creating a second Windows PE disc isn't necessary.

C. Incorrect: No x64 tools are supplied; the tools for 64-bit operating systems are all labeled amd64.

D. Correct: The x64 tools support installations of both the 32-bit and 64-bit Windows 8 editions.

3. **Correct answer:** A

A. Correct: /audit is the correct command-line switch to restart the computer in a mode in which you can continue modifying the installation before sealing it for capture.

B. Incorrect: No /restart switch is available for use with the SysPrep tool.

C. Incorrect: The /generalize switch seals the current configuration and prepares it for capture. You would need to open SysPrep again after the reboot if this switch is used accidentally.

D. Incorrect: The /oobe switch restarts the computer in Out of Box Experience mode, which is what users see when they first turn on a new computer. You can't capture the image if you use this switch.

4. **Correct answer:** C

A. Incorrect: The Deployment Image Servicing and Management (DISM) tool is used to service offline images that already exist. It can't be used to create new images.

B. Incorrect: You can use the SysPrep tool to make changes to the default Windows installation before capture. It can't be used to capture the image itself.

C. Correct: ImageX is the command-line tool used to capture disc images.

D. Incorrect: The DiskPart tool configures the hard disks and other storage on a computer before deployment of the operating system.

5. **Correct answer:** D

A. Incorrect: While this is the correct command-line tool to use to check the activation status of the Windows operating system, you can also see the activation status from the System panel in the main control panel.

B. Incorrect: This is an incorrect format for the command; the /license switch doesn't exist. You can also check the activation status from the System panel in the main control panel.

C. Incorrect: This format is incorrect for the command; the /license switch doesn't exist.

D. **Correct:** This is the correct use of the command-line tool. You can also check activation status in the Control Panel.

Objective 1.3: Thought experiment

1. This statement is true because you can use the Encrypting File System (EFS) to encrypt files on the server and then read them on a remote computer if the user has a copy of the correct EFS key to decrypt them. Unlike BitLocker, EFS encryption is an encryption method tied to the file rather than the drive.

2. This statement is also true. You can have the Sync Center automatically encrypt offline files synced with the target computer using EFS by clicking the Manage Offline Files option in the Sync Center.

Objective 1.3: Review

1. **Correctanswer:** B

   A. **Incorrect:** The \support\wet folder doesn't exist on the Windows 8 installation media.

   B. **Correct:** The \support\migwiz folder on the Windows 8 installation media includes the Windows Easy Transfer tool.

   C. **Incorrect:** The \support\migration folder doesn't exist on the Windows 8 installation media.

   D. **Incorrect:** The \sources\migwiz folder doesn't exist on the Windows 8 installation media.

2. **Correct answer:** C

   A. **Incorrect:** The custom.xml file allows you to create custom XML files that can migrate additional files and data, such as a line-of-business (LOB) application, or to modify the default migration behavior.

   B. **Incorrect:** No exclude.xml file exists.

   C. **Correct:** The config.xml file specifies items to exclude from a migration.

   D. **Incorrect:** The migdocs.xml specifies which documents are migrated. Although not all document locations need to be included, it can't be used specifically to exclude items from a migration.

3. **Correct answer:** C

   A. **Incorrect:** The LoadState command doesn't have a */createuser* switch.

   B. **Incorrect:** The LoadState command doesn't have a */lua* switch.

   C. **Correct:** You need to use */lac* (local account create) and */lae* (local account enable) to successfully create a new user account using the LoadState command-line tool.

D. Incorrect: Although the */lac* switch will create a user account, you also need to enable the account by using the */lae* switch.

4. **Correct answer:** B

    A. Incorrect: In a way, this was a trick answer. To best see the files you have synched with a server, it's best to add them to a library. If you said this answer was necessary, you have identified an important part of the process.

    B. Correct: You need to make the networked files available offline by right-clicking the network folder and selecting Make Available Offine from the options that appear.

    C. Incorrect: Performing the action described in answer B automatically creates a new Sync Partnership. Although it is possible to create the sync partnership, you first need to make the folder available offline.

    D. Incorrect: You have several options available to make server files available offline on computers taken away from the office.

5. **Correct answer:** B

    A. Incorrect: Again, this is a trick answer. By default, all files in the synced folder will be copied to the target computer, so this part is correct. You can manage the amount of space available on the target computer, however, making B the most technically accurate answer.

    B. Correct: You can manage the amount of space available on the target computer for offline files in the Sync Center.

    C. Incorrect: The sync relationship doesn't distinguish between the most recently accessed and least commonly accessed files; it assumed that you will need them all.

    D. Incorrect: The archive switch on a file or folder has no bearing on what files or folders are synched with offline files.

CHAPTER 2

Configure hardware and applications

An operating system is like an island; it has enough resources of its own to keep ticking but cannot be expanded or improved unless it gets connections to the outside world's residents and infrastructure. Thus it is with Windows 8. Using the operating system would be very difficult without adding hardware, such as printers, and extra software to enable you to perform tasks. For businesses, just having a web browser isn't good enough.

This chapter shows the various methods available to install, maintain, and manage hardware device drivers, and how to install and manage the software and new Windows 8 apps that you will use on your computer. You also learn how to manage usage of the Internet Explorer web browser and use Hyper-V to maintain application compatibility with your older software.

Objectives in this chapter:

- Objective 2.1: Configure devices and device drivers
- Objective 2.2: Install and configure desktop applications
- Objective 2.3: Install and configure Windows Store applications
- Objective 2.4: Control access to local hardware and applications
- Objective 2.5: Configure Internet Explorer
- Objective 2.6: Configure Hyper-V

Objective 2.1: Configure devices and device drivers

In Windows, users are mostly accustomed to being able to plug a device into their computers and for the driver to be installed automatically, after which they expect it to just work and be updated invisibly in perpetuity. Alas, although this is true for some hardware, other—and often more critical—hardware such as display drivers can often cause problems.

This objective doesn't reiterate the basics of how to install, remove, and maintain hardware drivers; instead, it guides you through some of the more advanced tools available and some of the tricks you might want to use to make management more simple and efficient.

This objective covers how to:

- Understand the differences between different types of device driver
- Maintain hardware device drivers
- Manage device drivers using different views in Device Manager
- Install hardware in Device Manager
- Install legacy hardware in Windows 8
- Configure faulty device drivers
- Troubleshoot and repair device drivers
- Use devices that include a Device Stage window

32-bit versus 64-bit and unsigned drivers

Considering that hardware used today comes with both 32-bit and 64-bit drivers, the driver type you use has to match the version of Windows 8 that you've installed. When you are using Windows 8 in a business environment, however, you might come across older hardware that the business still wants to use, perhaps because it "still works" or it's critical to a certain aspect of the business and a replacement would be expensive. In such cases, you might find that you are forced to install the 32-bit version of Windows on computers where this older hardware is required. This can potentially cause problems when that computer is now or might later be required for performing work that needs a 64-bit operating system and 64-bit software to do such work as editing large spreadsheets. Assigning a separate older machine to be used exclusively with the older hardware, or finding a suitable piece of alternative hardware with a 64-bit driver, might be the best option in such a scenario.

Unsigned hardware drivers are another concern. Hardware manufacturers can submit their hardware for certification from Microsoft through its Windows Certification Program. Hardware that passes certification can display a Windows 8 Compatible logo like the one shown in Figure 2-1. In practice, getting this certification can be expensive, and some manufacturers choose not to go through the certification process, confident that their hardware and drivers are of a high enough quality and stability not to cause problems. Indeed, some unsigned hardware drivers work perfectly fine with Windows products.

FIGURE 2-1 The Windows 8 hardware certification logo

NOTE WINDOWS 8 COMPATIBLE LOGO BENEFITS

Hardware certified and carrying the Windows 8 Compatible logo benefits from drivers being distributed on Windows Update

By default, Windows 8 doesn't install any unsigned driver, but you can still install one. Windows 8 displays a Windows Security dialog box for unsigned drivers (see Figure 2-2), warning you that the publisher of the driver can't be verified and that the driver doesn't contain a valid digital signature.

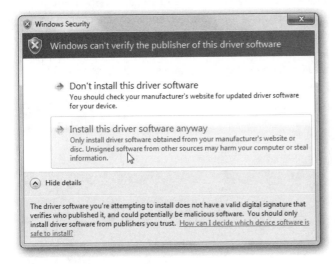

FIGURE 2-2 A security warning about unsigned drivers

You will probably find that one of the following is true:

- You won't have a choice but will need to install the driver because the hardware is critical to the business.

- The hardware will work perfectly well with this hardware anyway.

- Both of the above.

If you have an external support contract for your computers or your copy of Windows 8, however, it might be advisable to check whether installing unsigned drivers affects the support you receive.

NOTE USING THE DRIVER SIGNATURE VERIFICATION TOOL

You can check the status of signed drivers on your computer by running the signature verification tool sigverif from the command prompt. Running this tool displays a small desktop utility that provides a report detailing whether any unsigned drivers have been installed on the computer.

EXAM TIP

By default Windows 8 will enforce the digital signing of all x64 drivers. A digitally signed driver is a quality control measure which ensures that the driver has not been modified after it has been published. Signing does not guarantee functionality.

Maintaining hardware device drivers

Device drivers are kept in the \Windows\System32\DriverStore folder, as shown in Figure 2-3. Each driver consists of an .inf file, any related files for the driver, and a .cat file containing details of the digital signature. When you add new hardware to your computer—for example, you plug in a USB device—the operating system searches the DriverStore folder for a compatible driver and then searches online on Windows Update if you have an Internet connection.

FIGURE 2-3 Contents of the DriverStore folder

If you want to install a driver manually, however, you need to install it before plugging the device into the computer. To install a driver manually, use the Pnputil.exe tool, which is accessible from the Windows 8 command prompt. You need to run the command prompt as an administrator to give the tool the permissions it requires to write to a Windows 8 system folder.

The format you need to use for the tool is as follows when you want to add a driver to Windows 8:

```
pnputil.exe -a <PathtoDriver>/<Driver>.inf
```

This command renames all driver files to oem*.inf to guarantee unique naming. At any time, you can use the –e switch to display the full details of all the installed drivers (see Figure 2-4).

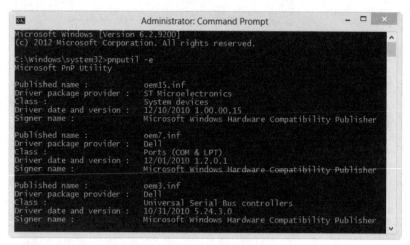

FIGURE 2-4 Running the pnputil command with the *–e* switch

If you want to add all drivers in a folder to Windows 8, use the following command

```
pnputil -a <PathToDriver>/*.inf
```

The wildcard then automatically adds all drivers in the specified folder to the DriverStore folder.

You can also have Windows 8 automatically install the drivers after they are added by using the *–i* switch. Doing so can often save you from having to restart the computer to install the drivers.

If you want to delete a specific driver from the DriverStore folder—perhaps because it is an incorrect version or causes instability—use the command **pnputil –d OEM<#>.inf**, specifying the driver you want to uninstall. If the driver is currently in use and you need to force its removal, add the *–f* switch to the command.

Managing device drivers with Device Manager

Windows 8 provides three main tools for controlling hardware devices: the Devices and Printers, Device Stage, and Device Manager. When you open the venerable Device Manager, the default view is a list of installed devices organized by category. Because Device Manager also hides many devices, it can display considerably more information. It also offers ways to manage devices that aren't immediately obvious.

The main power of the Control Panel comes from its View menu (see Figure 2-5).

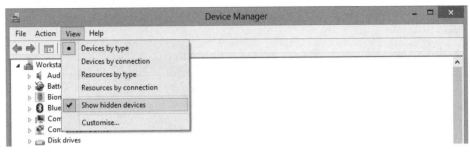

FIGURE 2-5 The View menu in Control Panel

As mentioned previously, the Control Panel hides many hardware drivers that you don't commonly need to access or modify. However, as a system administrator, you might need access to these drivers. Select Show Hidden Devices on the View menu. In Figure 2-6, you can see on the left the standard Control Panel and on the right all the additional devices that you can reveal.

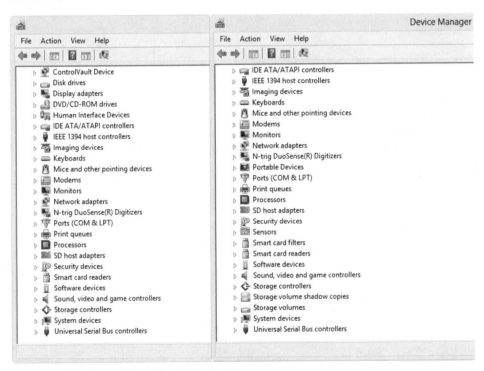

FIGURE 2-6 Showing hidden devices in Device Manager

You can also display hardware devices in different ways. For example, you can view devices based on their base hardware connection by selecting Devices By Connection on the View menu. This view can be useful for viewing everything connected to a virtual machine (see Figure 2-7).

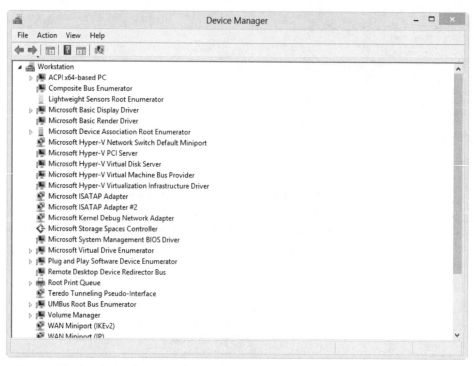

FIGURE 2-7 Viewing devices by connection

Select Resources By Connection on the View menu if you want to view the device hardware resources, such as interrupt requests (IRQs) or memory addresses. This view, shown in Figure 2-8, is most useful for troubleshooting and repairing problems.

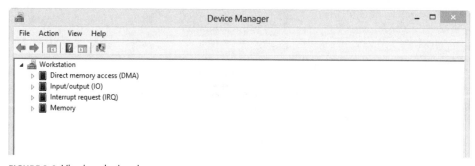

FIGURE 2-8 Viewing devices by resource

When you want to manage a device, you can do so by right-clicking it and selecting its properties. The most useful controls are on the Driver tab of the Properties sheet (see Figure 2-9). By using the controls on this tab, you can view Driver Details, which lists all files in the DriverStore folder associated with that driver. If a driver is misbehaving after an update, you can roll it back to a previous version by selecting Roll Back Driver.

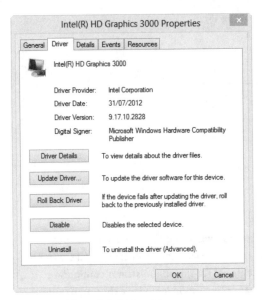

FIGURE 2-9 Managing device drivers

You can also disable a hardware device from this tab (also available by right-clicking the device in Device Manager). This feature enables you to switch a device off while leaving it attached to the computer.

> **NOTE MANAGING MISBEHAVING DRIVERS IN WINDOWS UPDATE**
>
> You might on occasion find that a driver update that was installed through Windows Update causes a computer to become unstable or unreliable. Simply rolling back the driver in this circumstance won't be enough to rectify the problem, because the update service simply reinstalls the offending driver the next time Windows Update runs.
>
> If you manage Windows Update locally on each computer, you can right-click the driver update as it appears in Windows Update and select Hide from the options that appear. The update then won't be installed on the computer.

If you want to completely uninstall and reinstall a driver—perhaps because it is faulty or misbehaving—you might still find that the moment the driver for that device is reinstalled, the unwanted version of the driver is reinstalled with it.

You can delete the driver files from the DriverStore folder in Windows 8 for some—but not all—devices in Device Manager by selecting the Delete The Driver Software For This Device check box when uninstalling the device (see Figure 2-10). If this check box isn't available, you can force deletion of the driver files by using the Pnputil.exe command-line tool with the –*f* and –*d* switches.

FIGURE 2-10 Deleting the files associated with a device driver

EXAM TIP

Windows 8 offers support for new and improved and emerging hardware such as Location Sensors, Trusted Platform Module (TPM) and Near Field Communications (NFC). The Device Manager continues to remain an essential tool for the administrator configuring devices and device drivers. Ensure that your exam preparation includes a thorough understanding of Device Manager.

Installing hardware in Windows 8 using Device Manager

Microsoft has gone to great lengths in recent years to simplify the installation of hardware device drivers into Windows products. This simplicity doesn't mean you can't get a high level of fine control when you need it. For example, you might have to force the installation of a driver that Windows 8 insists is incompatible when you know it is compatible, such as one for an older device.

You can do this when installing a driver by telling Windows 8 not to search for the correct driver automatically, but to let you choose the driver to install. In the next window (see Figure 2-11), you can either click the Have Disk button to choose the correct driver for the device Windows 8 lists (the one it believes the hardware to be), or you can clear the Show Compatible Hardware check box to show all the drivers installed located in the DriverStore folder for that particular hardware type.

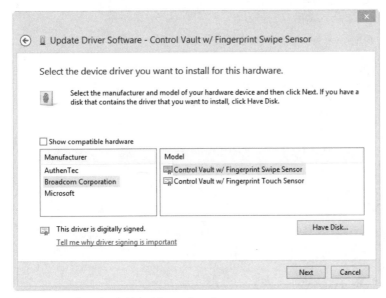

FIGURE 2-11 Choosing which driver to install

You might need to follow this installation process for a device when you know of a compatible driver from another product that can work or when the device is being incorrectly identified. Such substitution was common in the days of dial-up modems, where they were all based on just a few chipsets.

Installing legacy hardware in Windows 8

Do you work in an office that still requires the use of a dot-matrix printer connected to a computer via a serial or parallel cable? If so, you aren't alone, because all sorts of dot-matrix printers and other legacy hardware are still in use in the world of business.

Windows 8 still allows you to install and configure these devices and it knows that they're not going to be Plug-and-Play, so it enables you to specify what communications port they are attached to.

The default driver settings for legacy devices are also well programmed so that Windows 8 understands by default how to communicate with a wide variety of older hardware.

You can install a legacy hardware device from the Action menu, which lets you choose from a wide selection of hardware types (see Figure 2-12).

FIGURE 2-12 Installing legacy hardware in Windows 8

Configuring device drivers

Sometimes you will need to manually configure settings for a hardware or software device, perhaps to resolve a conflict with another driver. You will normally be alerted to this by a small red stop sign on the device's icon in Device Manager.

You can configure drivers from within the Device Manager itself by right-clicking on the driver and selecting its Properties. If there are any configurable options, you will see a tab labelled as Advanced, Power Management, or Resources. The advanced tab will include options specific to that driver, such as a Wi-Fi channel setting and the power management tab will commonly include the option to turn on and off an "allow this device to wake the computer" setting. This is commonly switched off and might be useful to activate if you use remote deployment and management in your organization.

Additionally some devices will include other tabs with options you can set for a driver. These can include Modem and Diagnostics for network and modem adapters and Volume and Policies for hard disk drives.

If there is a conflict with another device, open its properties and on the Resources tab you should find yourself able to uncheck the Use automatic settings option (see Figure 2-13). This is normally greyed out for working drivers, but it does allow you to manually change memory and some other settings to resolve a conflict with another driver.

FIGURE 2-13 Manually setting the resources for a driver

Troubleshooting and repairing device drivers

Device drivers can cause problems, conflict,s and instabilities with Windows. This is just something we've become accustomed to over the years. The driver creation model used for Windows 8, however, is by far the most robust in the life of the OS and, as such, it is only poorly written drivers that cause problems and issues. Despite this reliability and robustness, however, many IT departments like to soak test drivers on an isolated machine before deploying them.

One of the reasons why this is a good idea, assuming you even have a spare machine available, is that even drivers that come through Microsoft's Windows Update service aren't immune and can cause blue screens or instabilities, and this is something I've seen several times on my own computers.

I'm a great fan of the motto "if it ain't broke, don't fix it" and when a driver works, there's no need to update it, certainly not manually. Let's spend a little time though looking at how we can repair drivers if something does go wrong.

Rolling back a device driver

Probably the simplest way to deal with a faulty driver upgrade is to use Windows' automatic roll-back feature. When you open the properties for a driver, click on the Driver tab to see the options for managing the driver.

EXAM TIP

Windows 8 offers support for new and improved and emerging hardware such as Location Sensors, Trusted Platform Module (TPM) and Near Field Communications (NFC). The Device Manager continues to remain an essential tool for the administrator configuring devices and device drivers. Ensure that your exam preparation includes a thorough understanding of Device Manager.

Here you will see a Driver Details button, which provides detailed information on precisely what files on your hard disk are related to this driver. There is also a Roll Back Driver button and this is what you click to restore the last installed version of the hardware driver (see Figure 2-14).

FIGURE 2-14 If you have upgraded a driver you can roll it back to the previous version

Hiding drivers in Windows Update

Let's say, for example, that the driver you have just rolled back came through Windows Update. Obviously you will want to make sure that the service doesn't automatically reinstall the driver again, causing a recurrence of the problem.

You can hide updates in Windows Update by opening the main Windows Update panel and manually checking to see whether the offending driver appears in the list (note that you might need to click the Check for Updates link on the left of the panel.

With the list of available updates displayed, you can right-click on the offending driver (or on any update you don't want installed automatically) and from the context menu that appear,s click Hide Update (see Figure 2-15).

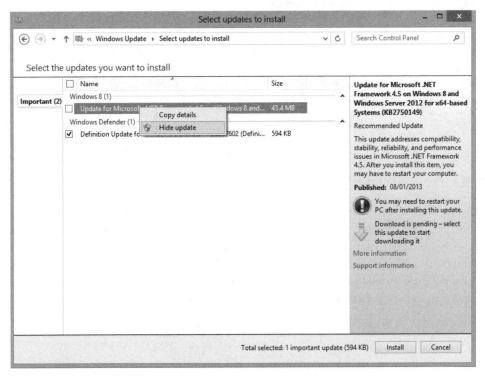

FIGURE 2-15 Hiding updates in Windows Update

Once this is done, the update will no longer appear in the updates list and won't be installed on your computer. One thing, however, that it is important to note, is that should you hide any updates before creating a Windows System Image Backup, they will not still be hidden when time comes to restore Windows from that image. The reason for this is that this configuration data is not stored within the backup image itself.

Removing and reinstalling a driver

I mentioned previously that when you remove a driver, you can optionally remove all the files associated with it from your computer. The reason for this is that Windows installs device drivers automatically and keeps them in the DriverStore folder. If you have a faulty or misbehaving driver on your computer and remove it, when you next come to reinstall it the OS might automatically reinstall the faulty driver before you have a chance to specify a new one to install.

Not all devices support this, however, and you'll see when you uninstall a driver if you can permanently delete the driver files from your computer by way of a check box (see Figure 2-16). If this check box does not appear it could be that Windows believes that some of the driver files are being shared by other devices.

FIGURE 2-16 Some drivers allow you to delete their files when you uninstall them

One possible way around this, but I would always advise using extreme caution with this method, is by opening the Properties for the driver before uninstalling it and from the Driver tab clicking the Driver Details button. This will reveal a complete list of all the files on your computer that make up the device driver (see Figure 2-17). After you have uninstalled the driver, you can verify whether these files have been deleted and, if they have not, manually delete them. This will prevent reinstallation of the driver later.

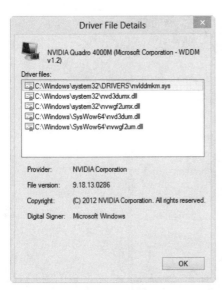

FIGURE 2-17 You can view the files associated with a device driver

The reason I say you should do this with extreme caution is that there's no real way to know whether one or more of those files isn't also being used by another driver or by a Windows process or service. Thus deleting the wrong file from your computer could cause a malfunction or possibly even a failure of Windows itself.

Once the driver files have been completely removed from your computer, you can reinstall the correct driver version for your hardware.

Using Devices and Printers and Device Stage

You can access Devices and Printers from Control Panel. Devices and Printers is often thought of as an easy-to-use Device Manager for consumers. However, it does have some uses for system administrators, not only because it can provide direct access to help and support specific to a particular hardware device, but also when you are using wireless devices on your network such as Wi-Fi printers.

The Add Device and Add Printer options on the toolbar searches automatically for wireless network devices (something Device Manager won't do) and displays them with their IP or Mac address as appropriate when it finds them (see Figure 2-18).

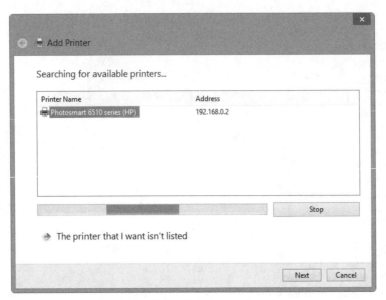

FIGURE 2-18 Installing wireless devices in Windows 8

You can access the Device Stage view for most devices (see Figure 2-19). A photorealistic icon replacing the default icon for the actual device in Devices and Printers indicates that a device has a Device Stage view installed.

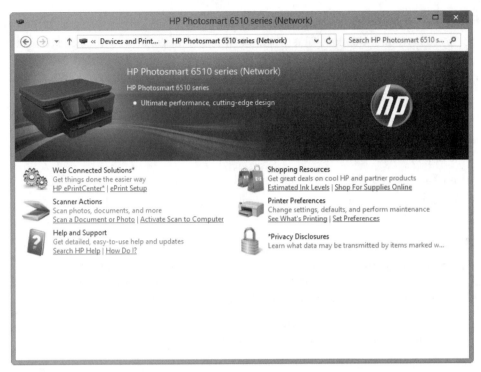

FIGURE 2-19 The Device Stage view

From the Device Stage view, you can typically get quick access to help, support, and other links associated with the device. This information can significantly speed up troubleshooting and the process of obtaining updated drivers.

Thought experiment
Installing hardware drivers

In the following thought experiment, apply what you've learned about this objective. You can find answers to these questions in the "Answers" section at the end of this chapter.

You discover that when the Windows 8 installation completes, not all required hardware device drivers are installed, even though the computer was connected to the Internet during installation and the Windows Update service was active afterward.

Describe how you would install all the remaining device drivers with a single command, ensuring that the hardware is installed in a way that shouldn't require the computer to be restarted.

Objective summary

- To use hardware with the 64-bit (x64/amd64) version of Windows 8, you need compatible 64-bit drivers for the hardware.
- Windows 8 keeps hardware drivers in the \Windows\System32\DriverStore folder.
- You can install, audit, and delete drivers from the command line with the pnputil.exe command.
- Device Manager lets you view installed devices in several ways, and includes the ability to display hidden devices.
- You can force Windows 8 to install a specific driver, should that be required.
- You can use the Devices and Printers panel to install wireless network devices.

Objective review

Answer the following questions to test your knowledge of the information in this objective. You can find the answers to these questions and explanations of why each answer choice is correct or incorrect in the "Answers" section at the end of this chapter.

1. You need to forcibly remove a driver from Windows 8 using the pnputil command-line tool. Which is the correct syntax for the command?

   A. pnputil –a <PathToDriver>/<Driver>.inf

   B. pnputil –d OEM<#>.inf

   C. pnputil –e –d <PathToDriver>/<Driver>.inf

   D. pnputil –f –d OEM<#>.inf

2. What is the best way to install a wireless device in Windows 8?

   A. By using the pnputil command-line tool

   B. By using Device Manager

   C. By using the Devices and Printers panel

   D. By using Windows Update

3. You need to install a parallel-interfaced dot-matrix printer into Windows 8. How can you do this?

   A. By using the Devices and Printers panel through the Add Printer option

   B. By using Device Manager

   C. By using the pnputil command

   D. You cannot install a parallel interface device into Windows 8.

4. The Device Stage view can give you quick access to which of the following? Select all that apply.

    A. Drivers and software updates

    B. Manufacturer help

    C. Related hardware devices from the same manufacturer

    D. Supplies and resources

5. You need to check which files are associated with a device driver. How can you do this?

    A. By running the pnputil tool with the *–e* switch

    B. By opening the Device Stage for the hardware

    C. By opening a device's Properties in Device Manager

    D. By opening the DriverStore folder and finding a subfolder for the device

Objective 2.2: Install and configure desktop applications

This objective won't talk you through how to install desktop programs on a PC. However, if you have software on a server, you can use a useful command-line tool to automate the process.

The inevitable move away from Windows XP has created a greater need to maintain compatibility with older software, especially bespoke company software. Here you might face problems, because with Windows Vista the underlying Windows architecture was almost completely rewritten and then further refined in Windows 7.

The fundamental changes to the operating system make up the primary reason programs can be upgraded only from Windows 7, and presents challenges for many people wanting to use older software with Windows 8. Objective 2.6, "Configure Hyper-V," shows how to set up Hyper-V to run another operating system, possibly a legacy one, and to maintain software compatibility, but in the meantime this objective focuses on the desktop.

This objective covers how to:

- Automate software installation from a Windows Server
- Set the default program options in Windows 8
- Manage program compatibility

Automating software installs from a server

Many businesses have a central store for their apps. If the installer for these programs comes with an .msi file, you can use a command-line version of the Windows installer package to automate the process. You can also write a batch file that wraps up the installers and can be run on each computer. The command you need is as follows:

```
Msiexec.exe /i \\server\apps\app1.msi
```

You need to specify the correct folder and .msi file.

You also need to ensure that you are running the command prompt window or the batch file as an administrator; otherwise, it won't have the required permissions to install the software and the installations will fail.

Setting default program options in Windows 8

You can find the main default program options (see Figure 2-20) by searching for "default" at the Start screen. These default program options include four items that are explained individually. You must change these options to select what file type opens with what program; what external hard disks, USB flash drives, and media do when inserted into your computer; and whether certain Microsoft software is blocked completely.

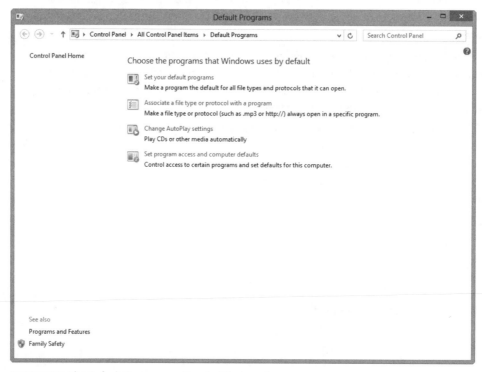

FIGURE 2-20 The Default Programs options in Windows 8

Set Your Default Programs option

Clicking Set Your Default Programs displays the window shown in Figure 2-21. On the left is a list of every installed program and app in Windows 8. When you select a program or an app in this list, the details about the selected item are shown in the right pane. Below this pane is a statement of how many defaults this program has.

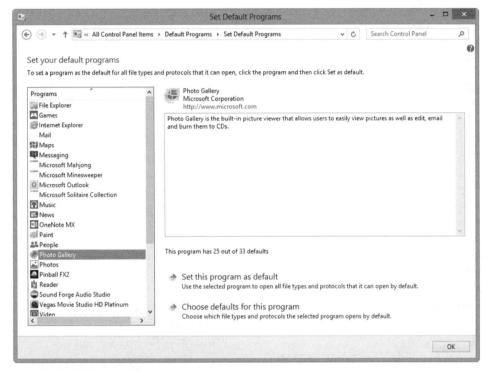

FIGURE 2-21 Setting the default programs

Each default is an individual file type with which this program is associated. If you want this program—for example an image editor or an accountaning package—to open every file type it is associated with by default, you can click Set This Program As Default. Choosing this option sets every default for the program. For finer control, click Choose Defaults For This Program to display a list of every file type that the program can open, allowing you to choose which ones to associate.

Associate A File Type Or Protocol With A Program option

In Default Programs (see Figure 2-20), click Associate A File Type Or Protocol With A program to open the Set Associations window shown in Figure 2-22. This option can be useful when you have a bespoke file type associated with a custom business application, and the application files aren't being recognized.

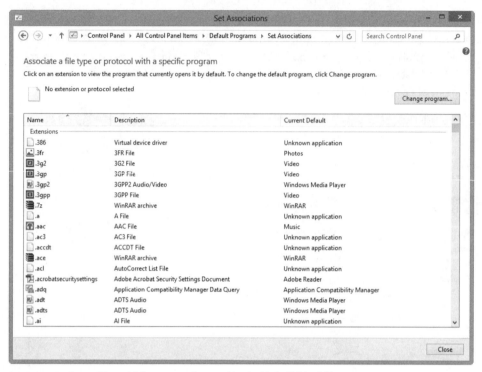

FIGURE 2-22 Controlling which program is associated with individual file types

In this window you can choose the file associations based on file type. Doing so can be very awkward, but for some less common file types this tool can be very valuable.

Change AutoPlay Settings option

In Default Programs (see Figure 2-30), click Change AutoPlay Settings to open the AutoPlay window shown in Figure 2-23. With AutoPlay, you can choose what happens when someone plugs an external hard disk, USB flash drive, memory card, DVD, CD, or other device into the computer. You can control what happens based not only on the device type, but also the type of content on that device.

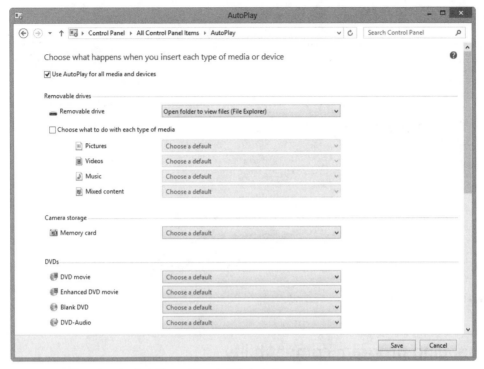

FIGURE 2-23 Changing the AutoPlay settings in Windows 8

Most helpful for businesses, you also can turn off the AutoPlay settings completely. Objective 2.4, "Control access to local hardware and applications," explains how to block external storage devices completely with Group Policy so that you can enhance security on your computers.

Set Program Access And Computer Defaults option

In Default Programs (see Figure 2-20), click Set Program Access And Computer Defaults to open the window shown in Figure 2-24. In some ways this option is similar to the Set Your Default Programs option, except that its window isn't as well featured. Here you can select Microsoft applications for email, web browsing, and other software to be the default on the computer.

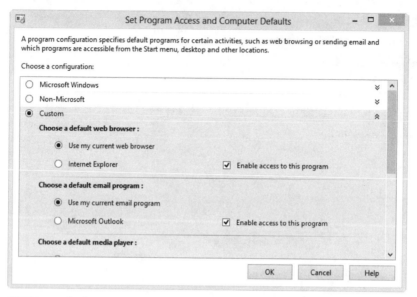

FIGURE 2-24 Setting program access in Windows 8

Managing program compatibility

You can maintain compatibility with older software in Windows 8 in several ways, one of which is to right-click the program and run the program compatibility troubleshooter. This tool won't give you the finer control that you need to maintain compatibility, however. The compatibility tools in Windows 8 exist for older desktop software and won't appear by default every time for some programs, such as some written by Microsoft or those included with Windows 8.

In Windows 8, even opening the properties for a program can be difficult because they're quite well hidden. You can open the properties in two ways:

- Open the All Apps view from the Start screen, right-click the program, click Open File Location from the app bar, right-click the actual program, and click Properties.

- Open the jump list for a program on the desktop Taskbar by right-clicking its icon. In the jump list that appears, right-click the program's title again; an option to open its properties appears.

You want to use the Compatibility tab in the Properties sheet (see Figure 2-25). The main option, Run This Program In Compatibility Mode For, enables you to select which version of Windows—even including service pack installations—the program worked with stably and reliably before. You can choose versions going back to Windows 95.

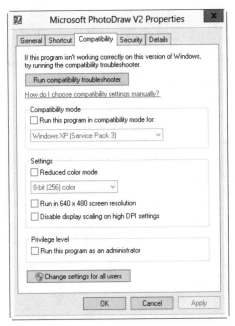

FIGURE 2-25 Setting program compatibility in Windows 8

If you need to, you can also force the program to run in a low-color mode, run in a low-resolution mode, and—if you find text and other items in the program difficult to read—turn off display scaling that can sometimes make old software look fuzzy.

You also have an option to always run this program as an administrator. In the days before Windows Vista, it wasn't uncommon for business programs to be written using what can only be described as "sloppy" workarounds that saved development time by forcing the program to access system files and features it really should have had access to. Running a program as an administrator can get around this problem, but please consider not only that it displays a UAC prompt every time the software is run that usually requires an administrator password that the user might not have, but also that this opens up possible security problems.

Even with these settings in place, the program might not work because it could require access to Windows components that have changed significantly or that have been removed altogether. This is where you need to consider running the program in a virtual machine.

Thought experiment

Installing software that requires administrator rights

In the following thought experiment, apply what you've learned about this objective. You can find answers to these questions in the "Answers" section at the end of this chapter.

Your problem with a particular piece of software is that it requires administrator rights to run because it accesses protected areas of the Windows file system when processing data and needs to be used by only a small number of people in the company.

Make a recommendation for how the software should be installed, taking into account the Windows 8 program compatibility settings, user permissions, and use of the Hyper-V virtual machine.

Objective summary

- You can use the msiexec.exe command to automate software installations from a server or file share.
- You can set a program to open different types of compatible files and have control over which ones it can open.
- You can choose what happens when removable media is plugged into the PC.

Objective review

Answer the following questions to test your knowledge of the information in this objective. You can find the answers to these questions and explanations of why each answer choice is correct or incorrect in the "Answers" section at the end of this chapter.

1. What command format do you need to use to install software using the Windows installer from a server or file share?

   A. msiexec.exe \\server\apps\app1.msi

   B. msiexec.exe /install \\server\apps\app1.msi

   C. msiexec.exe -install \\server\apps\app1.msi

   D. msiexec.exe /i \\server\apps\app1.msi

2. You need to specify that a bespoke program open a file type Windows doesn't recognize. How do you do this?

   A. Choose the Set Your Default Programs option.

   B. Choose the Associate a File Type or Protocol with a Program option.

   C. Choose the Set Program Access and Computer Defaults option.

   D. Open the program's Properties sheet.

3. The compatibility settings for programs in Windows 8 allow you to specify that a program worked in which versions of Windows?

   A. Windows XP, Windows Vista, and Windows 7

   B. Windows 2000 onward

   C. Windows 98 to Windows Vista

   D. Windows 95 onward

4. You can force a program to work at a lower maximum resolution, but what is this?

   A. 640 by 480 pixels

   B. 800 by 600 pixels

   C. 1024 by 768 pixels

   D. EGA Compatibility Mode for DOS

Objective 2.3: Install and configure Windows Store applications

The new Windows Store is the central location—and, indeed the only location unless you include AppLocker in Windows Server—for finding and installing apps in Windows 8. Already, high-quality business apps—some even costing up to $499—are appearing in the Windows Store, and this trend is set to continue.

This objective covers how to:

- Disable user access to the Windows Store
- Sideload apps into Windows 8
- Sync your App licences between different Windows 8 computers

Disabling access to the Windows Store

You might want to disable employees' access to the Windows Store to prevent them from finding, downloading, and playing games. You can disable access to the Windows Store on both a computer and a user level through the Group Policy Editor. Follow these steps:

1. Search for gpedit.msc at the Start screen to find and open the Group Policy Editor.

2. Navigate to Computer/User Configuration | Administrative Templates | Windows Components | Store.

3. Use the Turn Off The Store Application setting to prevent users from accessing the store on that computer, or to prevent a specific user from accessing it (see Figure 2-26).

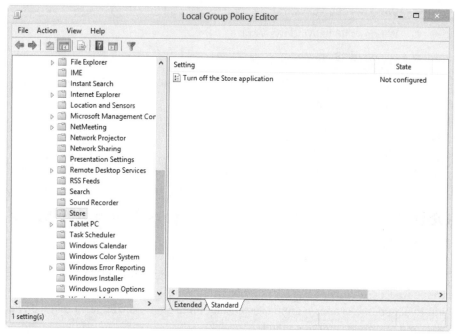

FIGURE 2-26 Disabling the Windows Store in Group Policy

Sideloading apps in Windows 8

Although the Windows Store is the main location for installing apps, in a Windows 8 Enterprise environment you can also use a method known as *sideloading* to install your own apps onto computers. You need to activate this feature before you can use it, and you do so in the Group Policy Editor. Follow these steps:

1. Search for and open gpedit.msc at the Start screen.

2. Navigate to Computer Configuration | Administrative Templates | Windows Components | App Package Deployment.

3. Enable the Allow All Trusted Apps To Install setting (see Figure 2-27).

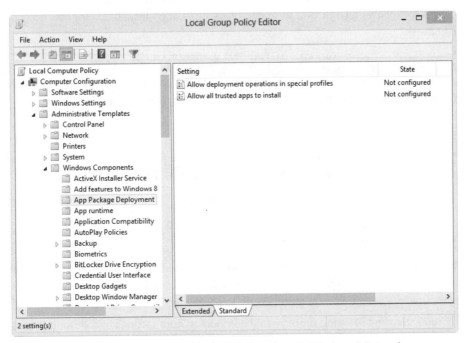

FIGURE 2-27 Using Group Policy to disable the Windows Store in Windows 8 Enterprise

After you enable the sideloading of apps in Group Policy, you can install your own business app onto computers, bypassing the Windows Store. Follow these instructions.

1. Open PowerShell from the All Apps view.

2. Type **import-module.appx** and press Enter..

3. Install your app by typing **add-appxpackage C:\apps1.appx**, where *C:\apps1.appx* is the name and location of your app. Then press Enter.

4. If you are adding an app to a Windows 8 image, use the following PowerShell command:

```
Add-AppxProvisionedPackage -Online -FolderPath C:\Appx
```

You can also add an app to a Windows 8 image by using the DISM command in the following format (you need elevated privileges to run this PowerShell command):

```
DISM /Online /Add-ProvisionedAppxPackage /PackagePath:C:\App1.appx /SkipLicence
```

If you need to remove an app for a specific user, use the following PowerShell command, where Package1 is the name of the app:

```
Remove-AppxPackage Package1
```

Use the following command format to prevent the app's installation for new users on the computer:

```
Remove-AppxProvisionedPackage -Online -PackageName MyAppxPkg.
```

To remove an app from a Windows image using the DISM command, type **DISM.exe / Online /Remove-ProvisionedAppxPackage /PackageName:App1.`**

EXAM TIP

With the triple combination of the new Windows Store Apps, new Appx PowerShell commands and new SideLoading capabilities, you could reasonably expect some exam questions on these topics.

Synching app licenses

When you buy an app, you typically find that it is licensed for installation for only a maximum number of computers. You might discover that after uninstalling a copy of the app from one computer, the license doesn't then transfer to another computer.

You can fix the licensing problem in the Windows Store settings by following these steps:

1. Open the Charms from within the Windows Store and click the Settings charm. You should see not just access to the standard Windows 8 settings, but also on the top left of your screen settings for the Windows Store itself (see Figure 2-28).

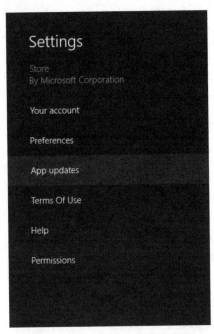

FIGURE 2-28 Opening the Windows Store settings

2. Click the App Updates option.

3. In the next screen that appears should be a Sync Licences button (see Figure 2-29). Click this button to bring your licenses for the app up-to-date and activate the app on this computer.

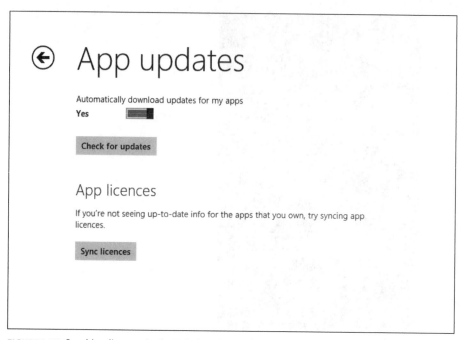

FIGURE 2-29 Synching licenses in the Windows Store

Sometimes you need to deactivate one of the computers for your Windows Store account before you can add another computer and activate an app. You do this by opening the Settings charm from within the Windows Store and clicking the Your Account option (refer to Figure 2-28). In the screen that appears is a complete list of all computers attached to your account (see Figure 2-30). Each one of these computers can be removed by clicking the Remove button.

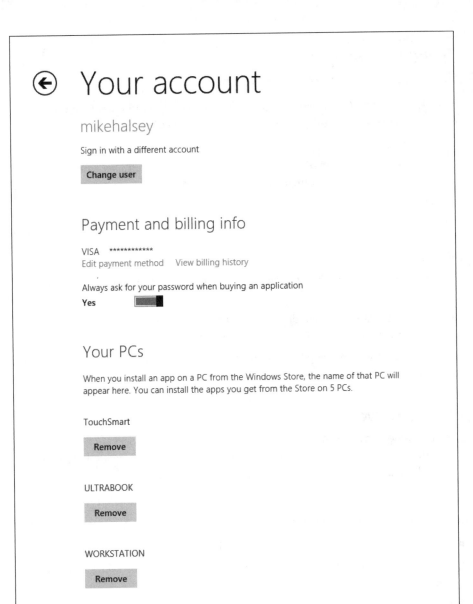

Your account

mikehalsey

Sign in with a different account

Change user

Payment and billing info

VISA ************
Edit payment method   View billing history

Always ask for your password when buying an application
Yes

Your PCs

When you install an app on a PC from the Windows Store, the name of that PC will
appear here. You can install the apps you get from the Store on 5 PCs.

TouchSmart

Remove

ULTRABOOK

Remove

WORKSTATION

Remove

FIGURE 2-30 Removing computers from Your Account in the Windows Store

Objective summary

- You can disable access to the Windows Store on a user or computer level through Group Policy.
- You can sideload apps into Windows 8 by using a PowerShell command, or by using the DISM command when building a Windows 8 installation image.
- You can synchronize your app licenses to bring them up-to-date in the Windows Store if you find that an app won't activate.

Objective review

Answer the following questions to test your knowledge of the information in this objective. You can find the answers to these questions and explanations of why each answer choice is correct or incorrect in the "Answers" section at the end of this chapter.

1. What is the correct PowerShell command to sideload an app into Windows 8?

    A. add-appxpackage C:\apps1.appx

    B. add-AppxProvisionedPackage –Online –FolderPath C:\Appx

    C. DISM /Online /Add-ProvisionedAppxPackage /PackagePath:C:\App1.appx /SkipLicence

    D. import-module.appx

2. If an app won't activate on a computer, what should you do first to rectify the problem?

    A. Remove a computer from your Windows Store account

    B. Uninstall and reinstall the app

    C. Install the app the Administrative permissions

    D. Synchronize the app licenses

3. Which Group Policy settings must you change to allow the sideloading of apps?

   A. Administrative Templates | Windows Components | App Package Deployment

   B. Administrative Templates | Windows Components | Store

   C. Software Settings

   D. Windows Settings | Security Settings

Objective 2.4: Control access to local hardware and applications

Objective 2.2 said that you can use Group Policy settings to block access to local hardware on the computer in the context of permitting software installers. Objective 2.4 examines this concept in detail and talks about the specific types of hardware you can block and why you might want to do block them.

This objective covers how to:

- Block external media and storage access
- Block specific program and app access

Blocking external media access using Group Policy

As mentioned previously, you can completely block access to removable media devices by using Group Policy. Doing so by user or by computer is a great way to prevent the spread of malware and viruses as well as prevent unauthorized copying of files and data. On this second point, however, note that on some occasions staff members need to be able to copy data onto USB flash drives and other media, so you should carefully audit which computers need this feature disabled.

You access the Group Policy Editor by searching for gpedit.msc at the Start screen. When the Editor opens, you need to navigate to Computer Configuration | Administrative Templates | System | Removable Storage Access (see Figure 2-31). You can also find this screen for individual users under User Configuration.

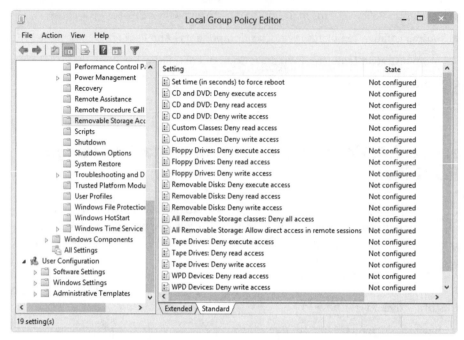

FIGURE 2-31 Setting external device access in Windows 8

On this screen you should find options to block access to many types of removable storage. You could, for example, allow read access to USB flash drives and CDs/DVDs (remember malware again, though) while denying them write access. You achieve this control based on device type by enabling the block for each device you don't want people to be able to use with the computer.

Blocking program and app access using AppLocker

In a similar way to how you can block hardware devices in Windows 8, you can also control access to programs and apps by using a feature called *AppLocker* (see Figure 2-32).

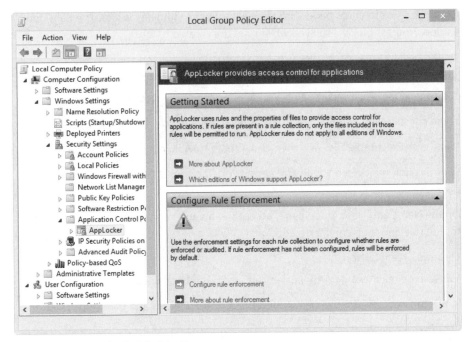

FIGURE 2-32 AppLocker in Windows 8

You can create and control AppLocker rules in several ways. You start by creating the default rules for AppLocker through the Local Security Policy Editor:

1. Open the Local Security Policies panel by searching for secpol.msc at the Start screen.

2. In the console tree, double-click Application Control Policies and then double-click AppLocker.

3. To create default rules for Applocker, right-click Executable Rules and then click Create Default Rules.

After you create the default rules, you can set AppLocker to create new rules automatically for all the programs or apps in a specific folder, such as all Office applications in the C:\Programs Files\Office15 folder. Follow these steps:

1. Open the Local Security Policy Editor.

2. In the console tree, double-click Application Control Policies and then AppLocker.

3. Right-click Executable Rules and then click Automatically Generate Rules.

4. On the Folder and Permissions page, click Browse.

5. In the Browse For Folder dialog box, select the folder containing .exe files for which you want rules generated automatically. Click OK and then click Next.

6. On the Rule Preferences page, click Next without changing any values. The Rule Generation Progress box is displayed while rules are created.

7. On the Review Rules page, click Create to close the wizard and add the rules.

You might also want to set rules allowing only signed applications to run on the computer. This too is done in the Local Security Policies panel. Follow these steps:

1. In the console tree, double-click Application Control Policies and then AppLocker.

2. Right-click Executable Files and then click Create New Rule.

3. Click through the Before You Begin, Permissions, Conditions, Publisher, and Exceptions pages.

4. On the Name and Description page, accept the default name or enter a custom name for the rule and then enter a description.

5. Click the Create button.

You can also delete unwanted AppLocker rules from the Local Security Policies panel:

1. In the console tree, double-click Application Control Policies and then AppLocker.

2. Click Executable Rules.

3. In the Details pane, right-click the rule you want to delete and then click Delete from the options that appear. You will be asked to confirm your deletion.

When you want to add specific AppLocker rules, follow these steps from within the Group Policy Editor:

1. Navigate to Computer Configuration | Windows Settings | Security Settings | Application Control Policies | AppLocker.

2. In the left panel of the Group Policy Editor, right-click Executable Rules and select Create New Rule.

3. Set the conditions for your rule, which includes excluding specific users (or groups of users) from using the program.

Thought experiment
Managing Removable Hardware

In the following thought experiment, apply what you've learned about this objective. You can find answers to these questions in the "Answers" section at the end of this chapter.

Describe the two primary reasons for blocking removable hardware on a computer.

Objective summary

- You can block specific hardware types from being used on the computer.
- You can use AppLocker to specify rules for individual or groups of applications and programs on the computer.

Objective review

Answer the following questions to test your knowledge of the information in this objective. You can find the answers to these questions and explanations of why each answer choice is correct or incorrect in the "Answers" section at the end of this chapter.

1. How do you access the Group Policy Editor in Windows 8?
   A. By running it from the Control Panel
   B. By opening Administrative Tools from the Control Panel and running it there
   C. By searching for gpedit.msc
   D. By running it from the All Apps view

2. Where do you create AppLocker rules types?
   A. The Local Security Policy panel
   B. The Group Policy panel
   C. Both the Local Security Policy panel and the Group Policy panel
   D. Windows System Center Configuration Manager

3. Before you create AppLocker rules, what do you first need to create?
   A. Individual rules for apps and programs
   B. AppLocker default rules
   C. A signed applications rule
   D. Remove all previous rules

Objective 2.5: Configure Internet Explorer

Not installing any software that duplicates features or functionality that already exists in an operating system is highly recommended. All you're doing is adding bloat and complexity to the operating system, which can serve only to cause problems earlier than they otherwise might happen.

This objective shows you how to configure Internet Explorer so that it causes the least amount of problems in the business space. You also look at some of its security features, some of which you might not be aware of.

This objective covers how to:

- Configure website compatibility views
- Set IE10 browser security options
- Allow specific websites through SmartScreen security

Configuring compatibility view in IE10

One common problem with using Internet Explorer (IE) in business is that the browser has moved in recent years to being 100 percent compatible with web standards. Many company and Intranet sites were designed and built in the days of Windows XP and IE6 , however, meaning they won't render properly. It's one thing for Microsoft to provide a Compatibility View icon in the IE10 address bar that users can click to render the current website in a mode that displays these pages properly, but another thing entirely to expect users to know that this button even exists, let alone what it's there for.

This is why you can configure and manage Compatibility View through Group Policy in Windows 8. You find it in the Group Policy Editor (again, search for gpedit.msc at the Start screen) under the Administrative Templates | Windows Components | Internet Explorer | Compatibility View options (see Figure 2-33).

FIGURE 2-33 The IE10 Compatibility View options in Group Policy Editor

First, look at the two main options that you will want to use:

- **Turn on Internet Explorer Standards Mode for Local Intranet** ensures that your company intranet will always display properly on every computer and for every user on which this setting is in place.

- **Use Policy List of Internet Explorer 7 Sites** allows you to specify within the Group Policy Editor which company websites require the use of compatibility mode so that you can have IE10 turn it on automatically (see Figure 2-34).

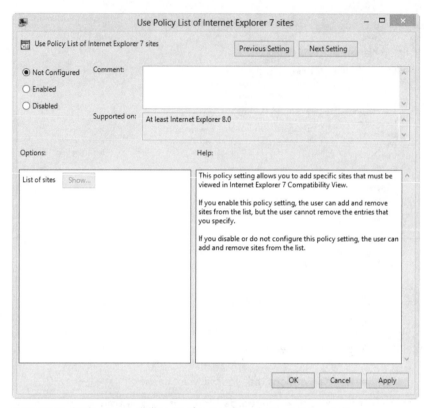

FIGURE 2-34 Setting compatibility view for specific websites in Group Policy

Setting browser security options in IE10

Now look at some of the most important security options within IE10, many of which can be controlled by Group Policy. The first is InPrivate browsing. Turning this feature on prevents the browser from collecting any data about that session, including tracking or other cookies, search or browsing history, usernames, and passwords. Thus, when you're shopping online, other users can't see what you've been viewing.

Although this feature might not be necessary for office computers or even for laptops used outside the office, informing users of the mode can be wise if they will access work websites from computers outside the company's control.

Tracking Protection is a security feature that for the first time is switched on by default in Windows 8. This feature can prevent tracking cookies from building up a profile of the user(s) on a particular computer. Such information is used to sell targeted advertising to users but it is increasingly being seen as an unwelcome intrusion.

Deleting the browsing history in IE10 is also a good option for businesses in which multiple people are using a computer. You can delete browsing history in IE10 on the desktop by choosing Tools | Internet Options (this also deletes the browsing history for the IE10 app that runs from the Start screen). A user is handing a computer over to another employee—especially if that user is in a different grade or department—might want to delete the history of his or her previously visited websites and searches.

The Group Policy features extend this functionality considerably (see Figure 2-35). At Administrative Templates | Windows Components | Internet Explorer | Security Features you can block all web browser add-ons, for example. Browser add-ons can include not just toolbars that redirect searches and spyware/malware extensions, but also common browser add-ins, such as the Adobe Acrobat Reader, which are regularly vulnerable to attack.

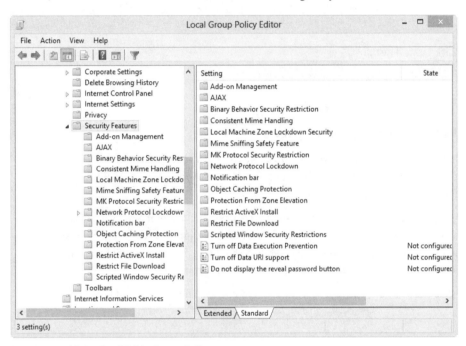

FIGURE 2-35 Managing IE10 in Group Policy

Also notice the settings that can block all file downloads from the Internet. You should test these settings with your company intranet, but they can help protect your computers from malware and virus infection considerably.

You also can block ActiveX controls, which can be used to launch malware attacks via infected websites and restrict website scripting. The latter setting needs to be tested with the websites your business requires to ensure that it doesn't block any necessary functionality on the sites.

Allowing websites through SmartScreen security

Another previous IE feature that IE10 has beefed up is SmartScreen. This cloud-backed service checks websites and downloads against whitelists and blacklists maintained by Microsoft into which many security companies contribute. You might find, however, that websites required for your business are considered suspicious by SmartScreen, perhaps because of the way they've been coded.

You can add specific websites to SmartScreen within the desktop version of IE10:

1. Open the IE10 Tools menu and click Internet Options.

2. On the Security tab, click the Trusted Sites icon and then click Sites.

3. In the Add This Website To The Zone text box, type the name of the websites you want to add.

4. Click OK to finish.

 Thought experiment

Setting up browser security

In the following thought experiment, apply what you've learned about this objective. You can find answers to these questions in the "Answers" section at the end of this chapter.

You need to design a strategy for employees using the Internet and local intranet at your company. You want to set the maximum browser security for the company, but employees regularly need to be able to share files over the Intranet and use websites that process large amount of user-entered data.

Which Group Policy security settings should you use and which should you omit?

Objective summary

- You can use Group Policy to specify websites that automatically display in Compatibility View in IE10.

- Group Policy can be used to block malware and virus infection routes through scripting, ActiveX controls, downloads, and browser add-ins.

- You can manually permit websites that could be blocked automatically by IE10's Smart-Screen filter.

Objective review

Answer the following questions to test your knowledge of the information in this objective. You can find the answers to these questions and explanations of why each answer choice is correct or incorrect in the "Answers" section at the end of this chapter.

1. Your company has employees who sometimes access sensitive company websites and data through your clients' computers. Which IE10 features should you teach them to use? (Select all that apply.)

   A. SmartScreen

   B. InPrivate mode

   C. Delete browser history

   D. Compatibility mode

2. Which Group Policy settings do you use to list websites that should always be displayed in compatibility mode?

   A. Turn on Internet Explorer 7 Standards Mode.

   B. Turn off Compatibility View.

   C. Turn on Internet Explorer Standards Mode for Local Intranet.

   D. Use Policy List of Internet Explorer 7 Sites.

3. Which of the following cannot be blocked using Group Policy in Windows 8?

   A. ActiveX controls

   B. Specific websites

   C. Downloads

   D. Browser toolbars

Objective 2.6: Configure Hyper-V

Microsoft first shipped the Hyper-V virtualization client with Windows Server 2008. Now it's included in the Windows client for the first time, but only in the 64-bit editions of Windows 8 Pro and Windows 8 Enterprise. (In other words, if you are using a 32-bit edition of Windows 8, you won't have Hyper-V available to you.) Your computer must also have at least 4 GB of RAM and a compatible processor.

The client version isn't as fully featured as the server version of Hyper-V because it doesn't support Hyper-V replica, Remote FX Graphics virtualization, and Virtual Machine Live Migration, all of which are available in the server edition. Otherwise, it is fully featured and even includes a couple of features not available in the server version: Sleep and Hibernate support for the host as well as the virtual machines (VMs) and virtual wireless network adapters.

> **This objective covers how to:**
>
> - Use Hyper-V in Windows 8 Pro and Enterprise
> - Set up network and other connection types in Hyper-V
> - Connect Virtual Machines together in Hyper-V
> - Import and Export Virtual Machines on the same PC and between computers
> - Understand the limitations of Hyper-V

Using Hyper-V in Windows 8 Pro

Hyper-V is commonly hidden in Windows 8 Pro, making it inaccessible. To activate the feature, select the Turn Windows Features On Or Off setting from the Programs and Features panel. You should see Hyper-V listed in the features list. Activating Hyper-P requires restarting your computer.

You can find Hyper-V in the All Apps view from the Start screen. The main administration interface for Hyper-V is very similar to the administrative tools in Windows 8, featuring a console tree on the left and context-sensitive actions on the right (see Figure 2-36).

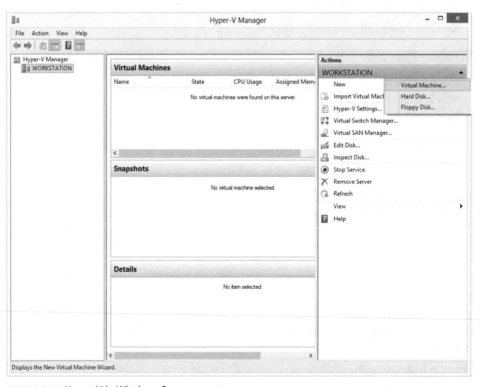

FIGURE 2-36 Hyper-V in Windows 8

You begin on the Actions panel on the right. Here (with your computer name selected in the left panel) you should see a New option that displays a wizard to help you create a virtual machine. The options you will have when creating a new VM are as follows:

- **Virtual Machine Name** helps you to identify the VM in the Hyper-V manager.

- **Virtual Machine Location** is the physical location on the computer's hard drive or on a network where the files for the virtual machine are stored.

- **Memory** is the amount of the computer's physical memory allocated to the VM.

- **Network Connection** enables you to specify multiple network adaptors for a VM (the different types are explained shortly).

- **Virtual Hard-Disk Location** is the location of the actual VHD file and can be separate from the main virtual machine location, if you want.

- **Operating System Installation Media** enables you to choose from several options, including a DVD or an ISO image file, if you want to install an operating system into the VM immediately.

After you create your virtual machine, you can start it by highlighting it in the Virtual Machines panel of Hyper-V Manager (top center in the window) and clicking the Connect link in the bottom right panel (see Figure 2-37). Clicking the link displays the VM, but it still won't be running. To activate the virtual machine, open the Action menu in the VM windows and click Start; the virtual machine now activates.

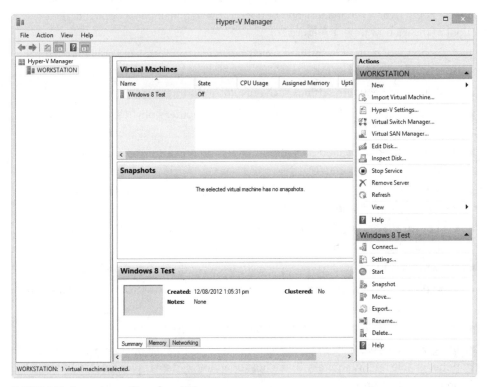

FIGURE 2-37 Accessing settings for a VM

Using the Virtual Machine Connection utility in Windows 8

You can run and access virtual machines in Windows 8 without having to access the Hyper-V Manager, and doing so is the best option for employees who need to access a VM. You can find Virtual Machine Connection in the All Apps view but need to know the server name (if appropriate) and the virtual machine name to gain access (see Figure 2-38).

FIGURE 2-38 The Virtual Machine Connection utility in Windows 8

Configuring virtual machines in Hyper-V

When a virtual machine is created, you can highlight it in the main Virtual Machines panel (top center in the Hyper-V Manager), and options to use and maintain it appear in the bottom right of the window (refer to Figure 2-32).

Chief among these options is Settings, which allows you to control and configure a great many aspects of the VM and its use:

- **BIOS** Used to configure settings such as NumLock on startup
- **Memory** Used to configure the amount of the computer's physical memory allocated for the VM
- **Processor** Used to configure what processors and processor resources in your computer are allocated to the VM
- **IDE Controllers** Used to connect to the VM virtual IDE disks, which can be created at Virtual Hard Disks in the Hyper-V Manager
- **SCSI Controllers** Used to connect to the VM virtual SCSI disks, which can also be created in the Hyper-V Manager as virtual hard disks
- **Network Adapter** Used to specify the virtual network adapter(s) used by the VM
- **COM Ports** Used to specify the virtual COM port the VM uses to communicate with the physical computer
- **Diskette Drive** Used to connect a virtual floppy disk to the VM
- **Integration Services** Used to add valuable tools to a virtual operating system that better enable it to integrate with the host operating system, which can include mouse and network control

- **Automatic Start Action** Used to specify whether the VM starts when the host computer does

Creating virtual switches and sandboxing VMs

You can create several different types of virtual network adapters (known as *switches*) in Hyper-V, and each has its own distinct purpose:

- **External switches** allow the VM to access physical computers on the network and provide access to the Internet.
- **Internal switches** allow the VM network access only to other VMs running on the same physical computer. This allows both outbound and inbound communications between VMs on the same computer.
- **Private switches** allow only outbound communications to other VMs running on the same computer.

Security is obviously a major factor when it comes to running an operating system in Hyper-V. Each operating system must be required to maintain updates and security in the same way as your main copy of Windows 8 does.

Some operating systems, especially older ones such as Windows XP (you might even have software that requires the use of Windows 2000), have significant problems when products go out of extended support from Microsoft. This means that they no longer get any updates for security or other vulnerabilities that either already exist or can be created.

One solution is to sandbox a VM, but if the VM also requires access to files or other resources stored on the physical host computer or of the physical network, you can set up only an external switch. This also gives the VM Internet access, inbound as well as outbound.

One solution is to use a Wi-Fi connection to connect the physical computer to the Internet while having no Ethernet cable plugged in. You can then use that Ethernet adapter to create an external connection, which gives the VM access to files stored physically on the host computer but won't give it access to the Internet. You can also block the VM at the router level, however, because the VM receives its own unique IP address on the network.

This limited solution won't work in many environments, but for some applications it works fine for sandboxing a VM to help enhance security.

Managing snapshots in Hyper-V

A snapshot is a means to capture the state of a virtual machine at a specific point in time so that you can roll the VM back to this point as needed. When Hyper-V creates a snapshot, it pauses the virtual machine and creates differencing disks associated with all the VHDs in the VM. It also makes a copy of the virtual machine's configuration file and then saves this information to disk.

The snapshot data consists of several files: an .xml configuration file, a .vsv virtual machine saved state file, a .bin virtual machine memory contents file, and .avhd snapshops of the different disks.

You manage snapshots from the Settings menu when the virtual machine is running. You can open the Virtual Machine Settings dialog box and perform snapshot operations such as apply, restore, export, rename, delete, and revert.

Importing and exporting virtual machines

You can import virtual machines into Hyper-V on Windows 8 that have been created on another Windows 8 computer or on Windows Server. If you import by simply copying the virtual machine files from one computer to another, you need to create a new VM using the VHD because all the virtual machine changes will be lost.

Instead, you should use the Import and Export options on the Action menu of the Hyper-V Manager. These correctly maintain the four parts of the virtual machine:

- An .exp file containing the globally unique identifier (GUID) of the VM file
- The virtual hard disks folder containing copies of each VHD associated with the virtual machine
- The snapshots folder containing an .exp file for each snapshot taken of the virtual machine
- A config.xml file used during the import process

Note that when you are importing a VM using Hyper-V, the import process doesn't copy the files provided; instead, it uses them as is. This means that if you have a master copy of the VM, you should create a copy of the exported files in the location on the host PC from which you want the VM run and maintained.

Understanding Hyper-V limitations

When you are using Hyper-V in Windows 8, you need to be aware of a few limitations:

- Hyper-V is available only in Windows 8 Pro and Windows 8 Enterprise, and even then only in the 64-bit versions of those editions.
- Hyper-V requires a minimum of 4 GB physical memory on the host computer.
- The virtual IDE controller allows for VHDs up to 2,048 GB in size and can manage up to four VHDs simultaneously.
- The virtual SCSI controller supports up to 256 VHDs with no disk size limitation.
- The new .VHDX file format adds support for storage up to 64 TB and resiliency against data corruption during power failures, but it is incompatible with Hyper-V in Windows Server 2008 and its family of products.

EXAM TIP

Windows 8 is Microsoft's first client operating system to include virtualization software as a core feature. Because of this inclusion don't assume that Hyper-V will only be tested on server focussed exams!

Thought experiment
Creating a VM environment

In the following thought experiment, apply what you've learned about this objective. You can find answers to these questions in the "Answers" section at the end of this chapter.

You need to run a copy of Windows XP inside a virtual machine to maintain compatibility with older software. The VM will run on laptops used away from the office but will need access to files stored on the laptop itself. You want the VM and laptops to be as secure as possible, because the employees using them will be away from the office for sometimes weeks at a time.

Describe the network switch type you would set up and explain why you would use it.

Objective summary

- Hyper-V is available within Windows 8 Pro and Windows 8 Enterprise 64-bit editions.
- You can export and import virtual machines between computers running Windows 8, Windows Server 2008, and Windows Server 2012.
- You can create snapshots of VMs so that you can roll them back if required for testing or other purposes.
- Employees can use the Virtual Machine Connection utility to connect to VMs.

Objective review

Answer the following questions to test your knowledge of the information in this objective. You can find the answers to these questions and explanations of why each answer choice is correct or incorrect in the "Answers" section at the end of this chapter.

1. In which editions of Windows 8 can Hyper-V be found?

   A. All editions of Windows 8

   B. Windows 8 Pro and Windows 8 Enterprise

   C. Windows 8 Enterprise x64

   D. Windows 8 Pro (where it is hidden) and Windows 8 Enterprise x64

2. Which virtual switch type would you use to allow a virtual machine full inbound and outbound communications with just other VMs on the host computer?

   A. External

   B. Internal

   C. Private

   D. Restricted

3. What is the best way for employees to access a virtual machine in Hyper-V?

   A. Through the Hyper-V Manager

   B. Through a virtual private network (VPN)

   C. Through the Virtual Machine Connection utility

   D. Through a Windows Server system

4. What are the limits for IDE-attached virtual disks?

   A. 2,048 GB and 4 disks

   B. 4,096 GB and 4 disks

   C. 8,192 GB and 6 disks

   D. 12,228 GB and 2 disks

5. What do you need to do to import a .VHDX file into Windows 8?

   A. Copy the virtual machine files from the host computer.

   B. Export the VHD from Windows Server 2008 or Windows Server 2012.

   C. Access the files from a currently running Windows Server–hosted VHD.

   D. Export the VHD from another Windows 8 PC or from Windows Server 2012.

Chapter summary

- To use hardware with the 64-bit (x64/amd64) version of Windows 8, you need compatible 64-bit drivers for the hardware.

- Windows 8 stores hardware drivers in the \Windows\System32\DriverStore folder.

- You can install, audit, and delete drivers from the command line with the pnputil.exe command.

- Device Manager allows you to view installed devices in several ways, including displaying hidden devices.

- You can force Windows 8 to install a specific driver if it's required.

- You can use the Devices and Printers panel to install wireless network devices.

- You can use the msiexec.exe command to automate software installs from a server or file share.

- You can set a program to open different types of compatible files and have control over which ones it can open.

- You can choose what happens when removable media is plugged into the PC.

- You can disable access to the Windows Store on a user or computer level through Group Policy.

- You can sideload apps into Windows 8 by using a PowerShell command or by using the DISM command when building a Windows 8 installation image.

- You can synchronize your app licenses to bring them up-to-date in the Windows Store if you find that an app won't activate.

- You can block specific hardware types from being used on the computer.

- You can use AppLocker to specify rules for individual or groups of applications and programs on the computer.

- You can specify websites to automatically display in Compatibility View in IE10 using Group Policy.

- You can use Group Policy to block malware and virus infection routes through scripting, ActiveX controls, downloads, and browser add-ins.

- You can manually permit websites that could be automatically blocked by IE10's Smart-Screen filter.

- Hyper-V is available within Windows 8 Pro and Windows 8 Enterprise 64-bit editions.

- You can export and import virtual machines between computers running Windows 8, Windows Server 2008, and Windows Server 2012.

- You can create snapshots of VMs so that you can roll them back if required for testing or other purposes.

- Employees can use the Virtual Machine Connection utility to connect to VMs.

Answers

This section contains the solutions to the thought experiments and answers to the objective review questions in this chapter.

Objective 2.1: Thought experiment

Installing all the drivers a computer needs requires a two-stage process using a single command. The first stage is to put all the drivers that need to be installed into a single folder.

When this is done, type the command **pnputil –i –a <PathToDriver>/*.inf** from a command prompt to install all the .inf files in that folder through the use of the * wildcard symbol. The *–i* switch tells Windows 8 to then automatically install all the new hardware devices.

Objective 2.1: Review

1. **Correct answer:** D

   A. **Incorrect:** This is the syntax you would use to install a single device driver.

   B. **Incorrect:** Although this command deletes a device driver, it cannot forcibly remove it because it is missing the forcibly remove switch.

   C. **Incorrect:** This is an incorrect syntax for the command and won't work. You cannot use the audit (*–e*) switch with the delete (*–d*) switch.

   D. **Correct:** You need to use the *–d* (delete) switch with the *–f* (forcibly delete) switch; they must be used together.

2. **Correct answer:** C

   A. **Incorrect:** Although you can install the driver for a wireless device in Windows 8, you cannot get the operating system to search for it.

   B. **Incorrect:** Device Manager can install hardware, but it's not designed to search for remote devices. The Add New Hardware option here can scan only for devices physically connected to the computer.

   C. **Correct:** The Devices and Printers panel is the only location in Windows 8 from which you can scan for and install wireless network hardware.

   D. **Incorrect:** Windows Update can provide driver updates for existing hardware and drivers for newly located hardware, including wireless hardware, but it cannot scan for hardware.

3. **Correct answer:** B

    A. **Incorrect:** A parallel device is legacy hardware and can be installed in Windows 8 only through the Install Legacy Device option in the Control Panel.

    B. **Correct:** Only Device Manager has an Install Legacy Device option.

    C. **Incorrect:** You can use the pnputil command to install the hardware driver for a legacy device, but Windows can't scan for it. You still need to set the device up with the Install Legacy Device option to specify which communications port it's attached to.

    D. **Incorrect:** Windows 8 supports a wide range of legacy devices, including parallel and serial devices.

4. **Correct answers:** A, B, and D

    A. **Correct:** Although the actual links and help provided will vary from one device to the next, this information can be gained from Device Stage.

    B. **Correct:** Again, it can vary, but very often direct links to online help can be found in the Device Stage.

    C. **Incorrect:** The Device Stage view is intended to provide help and support for that specific device. Hardware manufacturers aren't permitted to promote additional devices through this panel.

    D. **Correct:** Links to supplies and resources that you can buy online are commonly included in the Device Stage.

5. **Correct answer:** C

    A. **Incorrect:** The pnputil command can provide general information about the driver, but it doesn't give specific information about which files are installed on the computer for that driver.

    B. **Incorrect:** The Device Stage view doesn't give in-depth technical information about a product; it's intended as a way for the manufacturer to provide quick help, support, and supplies links.

    C. **Correct:** To find out which files are installed for a driver, you need to open its Properties in Device Manager. On the Driver tab, you then click on the Driver Details button to display a complete list of all files associated with that driver that are installed on your computer.

    D. **Incorrect:** You can't find the files for a specific driver in the DriverStore folder as Windows 8 doesn't organize that folder alphabetically.

Objective 2.2: Thought experiment

The critical point with this thought experiment was that only a very small number of people within the company need to use the program. This then presents you with two options, both of which can be considered correct:

- You can install the program in a virtual machine running Windows XP, although you have to take into account the complete ending of support for Windows XP in April 2014 and, as a result, such a VM would need to be completely isolated from any sources of infection, including the Internet, which can be tricky.

- Because not many users need the program, you can give them administrator permission on one or two computers that can be used exclusively for older software and hardware that pose compatibility problems.

Objective 2.2: Review

1. **Correct answer:** D

   A. **Incorrect:** The syntax in this example is missing the */i* switch, which is necessary to tell Windows to install the program.

   B. **Incorrect:** No */install* switch is associated with this command.

   C. **Incorrect:** No *-install* switch is associated with this command. Also, its switches use the / (slash) character to activate them instead of the - (hyphen) character.

   D. **Correct:** The msiexec.exe /i \\server\apps\app1.msi syntax is correct to install an msi-packaged program on the computer.

2. **Correct answer:** B

   A. **Incorrect:** The Set Program Defaults options can be used only when Windows recognizes the file type and can identify broadly what type of program it should be opened with.

   B. **Correct:** If Windows cannot recognize the file type at all, you need to find that file type in the Associate a File Type panel and set it manually.

   C. **Incorrect:** You can't set file type associations in the Program Access or Computer Defaults panel; this is for allowing and disabling Microsoft and third-party software on the computer.

   D. **Incorrect:** You can't set what files a program will open in its Properties sheet; you need the Default Programs panel to set these.

3. **Correct answer:** D

   A. Incorrect: The compatibility options allow you to specify that a program worked as far back as Windows 95.

   B. Incorrect: The compatibility options allow you to specify that a program worked as far back as Windows 95.

   C. Incorrect: The compatibility options allow you to specify that a program worked as far back as Windows 95.

   D. Correct: Windows 95 is the oldest Windows version you can specify in the compatibility options.

4. **Correct answer:** A

   A. Correct: Setting a program to run in low-resolution mode locks it to 640 by 480 pixels onscreen.

   B. Incorrect: The only setting available for low resolution programs in the compatibility settings is 640 by 480 pixels.

   C. Incorrect: The only setting available for low resolution programs in the compatibility settings is 640 by 480 pixels.

   D. Incorrect: DOS programs don't have a resolution compatibility mode. These would appear in a command prompt and could be individually scaled within that environment.

Objective 2.3: Thought experiment

You can add an app to a Windows image through either the command line or by using PowerShell, whichever is most convenient and accessible. You would use these two commands:

- PowerShell:

```
Add-AppxProvisionedPackage –Online –FolderPath C:\Appx
```

- Command line:

```
DISM /Online /Add-ProvisionedAppxPackage /PackagePath:C:\App1.appx /SkipLicence
```

Objective 2.3: Review

1. **Correct answer:** A

   A. **Correct:** add-appxpackage is the correct PowerShell command to sideload an app in Windows 8.

   B. **Incorrect:** Add-AppxProvisionedPackage isn't used for adding apps in Windows 8; instead, it's the PowerShell command you would use to inject an app into a Windows image.

   C. **Incorrect:** You use DISM commands when working with Windows images, and you use this particular command to inject an app into an image file.

   D. **Incorrect:** You need to run the import-module command in PowerShell before you can install an app, but this isn't the command you use to install the app itself.

2. **Correct answer:** D

   A. **Incorrect:** Although you might need to remove a computer from your Windows Store account if you have an old computer on which an app was activated that's no longer in use, you should first try to synchronize your licenses.

   B. **Incorrect:** Uninstalling and reinstalling an app won't circumvent problems with license activation.

   C. **Incorrect:** You cannot install an app in Windows 8 with administrator rights, because all apps in the operating system are installed in the same way. This is different from the way desktop programs are installed and doesn't require clicking through a UAC prompt.

   D. **Correct:** You should first try to synchronize the app licenses on your computers.

3. **Correct answer:** A

   A. **Correct:** Administrative Templates | Windows Components | App Package Deployment is the correct location in the Group Policy Editor for authorizing the sideloading of apps.

   B. **Incorrect:** Administrative Templates | Windows Components | Store is where you can disable access to the Windows Store for users in the Group Policy Editor.

   C. **Incorrect:** By default, Software Settings has no options unless they are added specifically by a systems administrator.

   D. **Incorrect:** The Windows Settings | Security Settings option doesn't deal with app installation.

Objective 2.4: Thought experiment

The two primary reasons for blocking removable hardware devices in Windows 8 are as follows:

- To help prevent malware and viruses from being transferred on those devices from outside of company premises and onto your computers

- To help ensure that sensitive company information cannot be easily copied onto the devices and removed from the premises without permission

Objective 2.4: Review

1. **Correct Aanswer:** C

   A. **Incorrect:** You cannot access the Group Policy Editor from the Control Panel in Windows 8.

   B. **Incorrect:** Although you can access the Local Security Policy Editor from the Administrative Tools in Windows 8, you cannot access the Group Policy Editor there.

   C. **Correct:** You must remember to search for gpedit.msc, not just gpedit, for it to appear in the search results.

   D. **Incorrect:** The Group Policy Editor doesn't appear in the All Apps view in Windows 8.

2. **Correct answer:** A

   A. **Correct:** You can create specific rules for programs in the Group Policy Editor, but you use the Local Security Policies Editor to define rule types.

   B. **Incorrect:** You use the Group Policy Editor to create individual rules for specific programs or users. General rule types are defined in the Local Security Policy Editor.

   C. **Incorrect:** You use the Group Policy Editor to create individual rules for specific programs or users. General rule types are defined in the Local Security Policy Editor.

   D. **Incorrect:** You don't need to use System Center Configuration Manager to create and manage AppLocker rules in Windows 8.

3.   Correct answer: B

   A.   Incorrect: Creating individual rules for apps and programs is what you're doing when you're creating AppLocker rules.

   B.   Correct: You need to create the AppLocker default rules before creating any specific rules.

   C.   Incorrect: You need to create a signed applications rule only if you want to prevent unsigned applications from being installed and used on the computer.

   D.   Incorrect: You don't need to remove any rules before creating a new rule.

Objective 2.5: Thought experiment

The Group Policy settings you should activate are those to block ActiveX controls and browser add-ons. You need to allow downloads, because they are required on your intranet so that users can work with files stored on SharePoint or another intranet service. You also most likely need to allow scripting because if websites used by employees use scripts to process entered data, those websites might stop functioning if scripting is blocked.

Objective 2.5: Review

1.   Correct answer: B and D

   A.   Incorrect: The SmartScreen feature blocks unsafe websites and downloads based in whitelists and blacklists maintained by Microsoft.

   B.   Correct: InPrivate mode prevents the local computer from storing any information about the current browsing session. Use of this mode prevents clients' computers from keeping a record of any web browsing activity by employees.

   C.   Incorrect: Although you can delete the browser history, this also deletes it for your client, who might want to keep it.

   D.   Correct: Compatibility mode might be required if the user is accessing a website or intranet that doesn't display correctly in IE10 with the default settings.

2. **Correct answer:** D

   A. Incorrect: This mode enables compatibility mode for every website and you might find that some websites don't display properly when forced into compatibility mode.

   B. Incorrect: Turning off compatibility mode completely prevents older websites that require it from displaying correctly.

   C. Incorrect: This setting forces your local company intranet to use only compatibility mode. The settings aren't automatically applied to other websites.

   D. Correct: You can manually specify a list of which websites used by the company require compatibility mode. This ensures that any websites detailed here will always display correctly.

3. **Correct answer:** B

   A. Incorrect: You can use Group Policy to block ActiveX controls from running on web pages in IE10.

   B. Correct: You cannot block access to specific websites in Group Policy. Instead, you will commonly use a third-party hardware appliance on your network to block unwanted websites.

   C. Incorrect: You can use Group Policy to block users from activating file downloads from web pages in IE10.

   D. Incorrect: You can use Group Policy to block browser toolbars from installing in IE10.

Objective 2.6: Thought experiment

In this scenario, the two critical points are that the VMs are to be used only on laptops, which have both wireless and Ethernet connections, and that security is paramount. Because each virtual machine requires access to files on the host computer, you need to set up an external virtual switch; it's the only switch type that supports accessing files on the host PC.

However, the external switch type also grants the VM both inbound and outbound Internet access, which is a security risk for Windows XP for which no support is available after April 2014. Using the laptop's Ethernet connection to set up the virtual switch is best but isn't commonly used for Internet access (assuming the laptop connects via Wi-Fi). Ethernet gives the VM access to files on the host computer while denying it Internet access.

Objective 2.6: Review

1. **Correct answer:** D

   A. **Incorrect:** Hyper-V is used in only the 64-bit versions of Windows 8 Pro and Windows 8 Enterprise.

   B. **Incorrect:** Although Hyper-V is indeed in the Pro and Enterprise editions of Windows 8, it is available only in the 64-bit versions of those editions.

   C. **Incorrect:** Hyper-V can also be found in Windows 8 Pro.

   D. **Correct:** Hyper-V is found only in the 64-bit editions of Windows 8 Pro and Windows 8 Enterprise. In Windows 8 Pro, however, it is hidden by default and first needs to be activated in the Programs and Features panel by clicking the Add and Remove Windows Features link.

2. **Correct answer:** B

   A. **Incorrect:** An external virtual switch would give a VM access to the files on the host computer and would also give it access to the physical network and Internet. This includes traffic going inbound as well as outbound.

   B. **Correct:** The internal switch allows the VM access to other virtual machines on the host computer and allows for full inbound and outbound connections between those hosted VMs.

   C. **Incorrect:** Although a private switch allows for communications between VMs hosted in the same computer, it allows for only outbound connections, not inbound ones.

   D. **Incorrect:** Hyper-V has no restricted switch option.

3. **Correct answer:** C

   A. **Incorrect:** The Hyper-V manager allows for full control of all virtual machines on the computer, including deletion. This isn't a good way for employees to access Hyper-V.

   B. **Incorrect:** Although you can use a VPN to access VMs on a Windows Server, this isn't the best way for employees to access local virtual machines.

   C. **Correct:** The Virtual Machine Connection utility in Windows 8 allows employees to access VMs in Hyper-V without being able to modify or damage them.

   D. **Incorrect:** You don't need a Windows Server to access VMs because the Hyper-V client is available in Windows 8 Pro and Windows 8 Enterprise 64-bit editions.

4. **Correct answer:** A

   A. **Correct:** The maximum available disk size for virtual IDE VHDs in Hyper-V is 2,048 GB, and the system can access up to four of these disks.

   B. **Incorrect:** The maximum available disk size for virtual IDE VHDs in Hyper-V is 2,048 GB, and the system can access up to four of these disks. To access disks larger than this, you need virtual SCSI disks.

   C. **Incorrect:** The maximum available disk size for virtual IDE VHDs in Hyper-V is 2,048 GB, and the system can access up to four of these disks. To access disks larger than this, you need virtual SCSI disks that also have no limit on the number of VHDs that can be attached to a VM.

   D. **Incorrect:** The maximum available disk size for virtual IDE VHDs in Hyper-V is 2,048 GB, and the system can access up to four of these disks. To access disks larger than this, you need virtual SCSI disks that also have no limit on the number of VHDs that can be attached to a VM.

5. **Correct answer:** D

   A. **Incorrect:** If you copy a VHD directly from one computer to another, you need to re-create the VHD file at the destination. The best way to use a VHD on a different computer is through the export/import mechanism.

   B. **Incorrect:** .VHDX files are incompatible with Windows Server 2008.

   C. **Incorrect:** You cannot import files from a virtual machine now in use on another computer or a server. You must first export the files so that they can be copied locally to the destination computer.

   D. **Correct:** .VHDX files can be used in Windows 8 and Windows Server 2012 and swapped between the two operating systems.

CHAPTER 3

Configure network connectivity

Of all the aspects of an operating system that need setting up and configuring, networking can sometimes be complicated. This isn't helped by the adoption of IPv6 technologies and a need for heightened security that's further complicated by the growth of bring-your-own-device (BYOD) schemes in the workplace (sometimes also known in IT circles as "bring your own disaster").

The networking settings and configuration options in Windows have also had a long-held reputation for being quite widely scattered and often hidden from view completely. Also, the growth in remote working and remote management needs to be cared for.

This chapter shows you the quick and easy ways to configure networking in Windows using various tools including the command line, explains what the different aspects of networking actually are and what the terminology means, and shows you how to implement best practice in configuring your network.

Objectives in this chapter:

- Objective 3.1: Configure IP settings
- Objective 3.2: Configure networking settings
- Objective 3.3: Configure and maintain network security
- Objective 3.4: Configure remote management

Objective 3.1: Configure IP settings

Networking is much more than just connecting your computer to other computers and to the Internet, although it's simpler than it used to be. Whatever operating system you use, it will conform to the same basic standards, but even those standards are evolving.

This objective covers how to:

- Configure IPv4 settings
- Configure IPv6 settings
- Use IPConfig

Comparing IPv4 to IPv6

The Internet Protocol (IP) standard ensures that every device connected to a network and to the Internet has its own unique address. This way, when you ask a website or a remote computer for information, the website or server knows where to send the reply.

Most commonly used is IPv4, a numeric 32-bit binary address system. With this system, a standard IP address, as processed by your computer, can read 11000000 10101000 00000001 00000011, even though that's difficult to read and complex for a human to work with. However, it can be translated into decimal as 192.168.1.3. A 32-bit system has a finite number of numbers that can be generated, and many more numbers are in use now worldwide than was ever expected when the system was conceived and before just about every device and appliance in our homes and workplaces, from fridges to photocopiers, became IP connected.

Newer IPv6 addresses can provide up to 128-bit addressing, allowing considerably more addresses than with the IPv4 system, but still not unlimited. IPv6 also brings additional benefits such as the ability to autoconfigure without requiring a separate Dynamic Host Configuration Protocol (DCHP) server and built-in support for Internet Protocol Security (IPsec), Authentication Header (AH), and Encapsulating Security Payload (ESP).

The IPv6 protocol also carries much of the configuration detail for which IPv4 must use additional tools, such as restored end-to-end communication, a global addressing model done by network address translation (NAT) in IPv4. This simplifies communication because you don't need separate NAT devices for such communications as peer-to-peer or videoconferencing.

IPv6 traffic also contains a data packet that can inform the receiving computer how important the data is and how quickly it should be processed. Overall, IPv6 was designed to do more configuration itself, taking the strain off other services and, ultimately, the systems administrator.

In short, IPv6 was designed to be extendable and to require less setup and configuration than IPv4 addresses.

Configuring the IPv4 subnet mask

IPv4 is still the most common network address system and the most widely used. In fact, it's so widely adopted that it won't be going away for many years yet.

IPv4 addresses, as already explained, require more configuring than IPv6 addresses, and one of these configuration requirements is a *subnet mask*. A subnet mask specifies what parts of an IPv4 address are for the network ID and which parts are for the host ID. It's formatted similar to an IPv4 address, with four blocks of numbers. Whereas the numbers in an IPv4 address range from 0 to 255, the subnet mask numbers are usually either only 0 (representing a host ID) or 255 (representing a network ID).

So what is a subnet and how is it important in network configuration? A subnet is a network segment, a subnetwork of the main network. Subdividing a network allows you to isolate internal and external traffic. Your main subnet mask will vary depending on the network class (A, B, or C) that you are using. Table 3-1 shows what the subnet mask is for computers with different IP addresses on networks of different classes.

TABLE 3-1 Subnet mask addresses by IP address type

Class	IP address range	Default subnet mask	Number of supported networks	Number of supported hosts per network
A	1.x.x.x to 127.x.x.x	255.0.0.0	126	16,777,214
B	128.x.x.x to 191.x.x.x	255.255.0.0	16,384	65,534
C	192.x.x.x to 223.x.x.x	255.255.255.0	2,097,152	254

You can see in Table 3-1 how the use of subnets can divide a main network into smaller network groups. This can help reduce congestion across the network and can overcome limitations with the IPv4 addressing system, effectively permitting considerably more computers to be attached to a network than would otherwise be allowed if the IPv4 address was used on its own. Remember, this would limit you to fewer than 256 total devices.

To calculate a subnet mask for your network and create a custom subnet, follow this process, using 255.0.0.224 as the example subnet mask:

1. Determine what type of network you have according to its IP address in Table 3-1. This network type will be either A, B, or C.

2. Determine how many subnets you require. This is worked out via the formula 2^n-2, where n is the number of bits. Because you don't know the number of bits, you need to work the formula backward using $Log2(s+2)$, where s is the number of subnets required. For example, if you require six subnets, the formula would be $Log2(6+2)$, which equals 3; three bits in the IP address are used as a subnet portion.

3. Compose the subnet mask in binary. This is where the class type comes in: Class A, 8-bits = 11111111.00000000.00000000.00000000; Class B, 16-bits = 11111111.11111111.00000000.00000000; and Class C, 24 bits = 11111111.11111111.11111111.00000000. Add your three-bit extension, making the final part of the binary address 11100000.

4. Convert this binary address to decimal form so that you can use it. You know that 11111111 = 255 and 00000000 = 0, but if a segment includes both 1s and 0s, you use the formula $(128*n)+(64*n)+(32*n)+(16*n)+(8*n)+(4*n)+(2*n)+(n)$. This would translate a binary address of 11111111.00000000.00000000.11100000 as 255.0.0.224, which is your final subnet mask.

Configuring the IPv4 default gateway

The default gateway on a network is a device, usually a router, that forwards Transmission Control Protocol/Internet Protocol (TCP/IP) packets to other computers and devices on or outside the network. A company intranet might have several routers connecting local, remote, and Internet traffic, but one of these routers must be configured as the default gateway for the local hosts—a "master router," as it were.

When a host sends an IPv4-addressed packet, the subnet mask is used to determine whether the destination is on the same or a different network. If the destination is on the same network, the packet is delivered directly; if it's on a different network, the packet is sent to the default gateway to be passed on.

The default gateway consults its internal routing table to determine the best route to send the packet, whether it's directly or through an additional router. The host computer assumes that the default gateway contains the required route information.

The default gateway address is usually assigned automatically using the DHCP server, which automatically assigns and allocates addresses for all devices on a network. This also gets around the problem of having to manually assign the default gateway IP address on each device. It's much simpler using DHCP to have the host receive the default gateway information automatically when it attempts to join the network.

Configuring IPv6 addresses

IPv6 addresses contain much more information than IPv4 addresses; as a result, they can include information such as the subnet and DHCP information. IPv6 is enabled by default in Windows 8 and is used by the DirectAccess and Remote Desktop features.

IPv6 addresses are written in number base 16 (Hexadecimal) and derived from 128-bit binary numbers in much the same way IPv4 addresses are. The binary number is split into 16-

bit boundaries in much the same way that IPv4 addresses are split into 8-bit (*octal*) segments. IPv4 addresses separate these octals with a period (.), but IPv6 addresses separate them with a colon (:).

The best way to convert an IP4v address to an IPv6 address is to use a conversion tool; many of these can be found online. Simplified, however, the IPv4 address 192.168.0.1 and subnet mask 255.255.255.0 would convert to an IPv6 address of fe80:0:0:0:0:0:c0a8:1.

You can remove unwanted zeros in an IPv6 address, which would condense the address down to fe80::c0a8:1. You can see the beginning and end of the IPv6 address and can easily tell how many 0s would be found in the middle of the address.

Understanding different types of IP addresses

IP addresses change depending on what type of network the device is attached to, whether public or private, and this is the same of both IPv4 and IPv6 addresses. This section lists the main address types and shows how to identify them.

IPv4 address types

IPv4 address comes in two main types: public and private. A private IP address is one that is unique to your network, such as 192.x.x.x (class C), 172.x.x.x (Class B), and 10.x.x.x (Class A). A public address is one assigned by the Internet Corporation for Assigned Names and Numbers (ICANN) and appears differently from private IPv4 addresses.

IPv6 address types

IPv6 has more address types than IPv4:

- Unicast addresses are used for communication between single hosts only. They use the FE80: address header.

- Multicast addresses can deliver packets to multiple addresses simultaneously. They use the FF02: address header.

- Anycast addresses use the nearest router for locating computers and services.

EXAM TIP

For the exam ensure that you have a good understanding of IPv6 addressing. You should be able to recognise link local (FE80), global (2001), special addresses and the various transition mechanisms (6to4, Teredo, ISATAP).

Configuring IPv4 and IPv6 in Windows 8

Windows 8 is extremely good at automatically managing your computer's IP address. However, you can change that IP address in the Network and Sharing Center, which you can access by searching for it from the Start screen or finding it in the Control Panel. An easier way to access it is by right-clicking the taskbar Network icon on the desktop and opening it directly.

In the Network and Sharing Center, click the name of the network to bring up its status panel, and then click the Properties button to display advanced configuration options (see Figure 3-1).

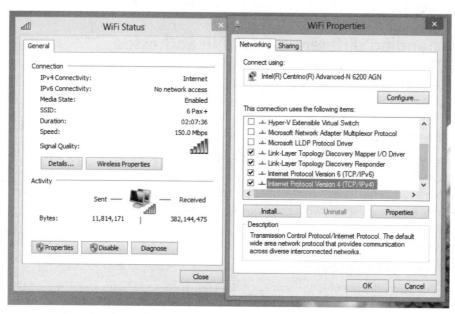

FIGURE 3-1 Accessing the IP address settings in Windows 8

On the Properties sheet, notice the options to configure the IPv4 and IPv6 connectivity separately from one another. By default, they are set to obtain IP addresses and Domain Name System (DNS) server addresses automatically. If you want, you can set specific and locked addresses here. When you are changing the IPv4 settings, you can also set an alternate configuration (this doesn't apply to IPv6). An alternate configuration might be required if the computer is used on more than one network, in which either both require set IP addresses, subnet masks, or DHCP servers that manage IP addresses automatically on a network, or in which one network is configured automatically by a DCHP server and the other network needs to be configured manually.

NOTE IF IN DOUBT, PING IT!

If you are concerned that network connectivity isn't working on a particular computer, you can use the ping command at a command prompt to test the connection. Start by testing the loopback address of the computer:

```
ping 127.0.0.1
```

followed by the default gateway and perhaps also external addresses.

Using IPConfig

If you are experiencing problems with a network connection on a Windows 8 PC, you can use the IPConfig command-line tool. You can use IPConfig with several switches, and the ones you will most commonly use are as follows:

- **/all** You can verify all the IP and MAC addresses for your network connections with this switch.
- **/release** Use this switch to release a DHCP client lease, forcing the computer to release an IP address. (You can use the switch */release6* to force the release of an IPv6 address.)
- **/renew** Use this switch to renew your DHCP client lease and IP address. (You can use the switch */renew6* for IPv6 addresses.)
- **/displaydns** Use this switch to display the contents of the DNS cache.
- **/flushdn**s Use this switch to clear the DNS cache.

Additional network troubleshooting tools in Windows 8

In addition to the ping and IPConfig tools, you can use additional command-line tools to diagnose and troubleshoot network problems in Windows 8. These tools are in addition to the standard Windows 8 diagnostic tools that you can find in the "Troubleshooting" section of the Action Center. You can use these troubleshooting tools to reset Windows components to their default state, rectifying common problems:

- **Tracert** determines the route data takes from the host to the destination computer by sending Internet Control Message Protocol (ICMP) echo requests. This path is displayed to you as a list of router interfaces that detail the speed at which the data traveled.

- **Pathping** is similar to tracert but provides more detailed information on the individual steps taken through the network.

- NSlookup displays information that can help diagnose DNS problems on your network and to confirm connection to a DNS server.

Thought experiment

Configuring a custom subnet mask

In the following thought experiment, apply what you've learned about this objective. You can find answers to these questions in the "Answers" section at the end of this chapter.

You need to configure a subnet mask for an office that usually contains between 300 and 400 individual computers, and all of them need to be connected together in such a way that you won't use a subnet.

Explain what IP address range and what network class you would configure and why.

Objective summary

- Whereas IPv4 is a 32-bit addressing system, IPv6 uses 128-bits, allowing for more information to be carried in the IP address itself.

- You can configure subnet masks on IPv4 networks to create subnetworks, allowing for more computers to be attached overall.

- You can use various command-prompt tools to troubleshoot and diagnose problems with network connectivity.

- The default gateway for a network is automatically configured by Windows 8, although you can set it manually.

Objective review

Answer the following questions to test your knowledge of the information in this objective. You can find the answers to these questions and explanations of why each answer choice is correct or incorrect in the "Answers" section at the end of this chapter.

1. Which of the following is a private IPv4 address?

A. 235.0.0.1

B. 255.255.255.0

C. 172.0.8.0

D. 191.0.1.4

2. Which IPv6 address type would you use to deliver a data packet to a single computer on the same subnet?

   A. Anycast

   B. Unicast

   C. Singlecast

   D. Multicast

3. What boundary segment sizes are used to separate the different sections of IPv4 and IPv6 addresses?

   A. 8-bit and 16-bit

   B. Binary and hexadecimal

   C. 32-bit and 128-bit

   D. 3 character and 4 character

4. How many different IP address configurations can you set in Windows 8 for IPv4 and IPv6 networks on an individual computer?

   A. 2 and 2

   B. 2 and 1

   C. 1 and 4

   D. 4 and unlimited

5. Which command would you use to provide the maximum information when trying to diagnose a network connection problem?

   A. Tracert

   B. IPConfig

   C. Pathping

   D. Ping

Objective 3.2: Configure networking settings

IP addresses are just a very small proportion of the overall network settings in Windows 8, although they're essential to get you initially connected to the network. This objective explains how to manually connect to a network, how to change network settings, and what the different network settings do.

You can connect to a network in several ways. Perhaps the easiest way in Windows 8 is from the Settings charm for connecting to Wi-Fi or mobile broadband. When you connect to a network in this way, it displays only a list of visible networks and, when you connect, it sensibly asks whether you want to permit file and printer sharing. However, you can get much more control over network connections elsewhere.

This objective covers how to:

- Configure network connections
- Reset network connections
- Set up VPN connections
- Resolve network conflicts
- Use the network troubleshooter

NOTE RESETTING FAULTY WI-FI CONNECTIONS

If you find that a Wi-Fi connection becomes faulty and either won't connect or remember the password, you can reset it from the network connections panel, available from the Settings charm. By right-clicking a network, you can tell Windows 8 to Forget This Network (see Figure 3-2). This removes all the settings for the network. The next time you connect to it will be like the first time.

FIGURE 3-2 Telling Windows 8 to forget a wireless network

The Network and Sharing Center in Figure 3-3 is where you get full control over network connections in Windows 8. If the computer is already connected to a network, this displays the View Your Active Networks panel at the top of the window. The name of the current network is clickable so that you can display further information and configuration options for it. (Later, this objective covers configuring a network.)

You set up a new network connection by clicking the Set Up A New Connection Or Network link in the center panel. This displays a dialog box, allowing you to create new Internet or other network connections or to turn your computer into a network or Internet access point, perhaps to share your existing ad hoc network connection with wireless devices such as tablets or smartphones (see Figure 3-4).

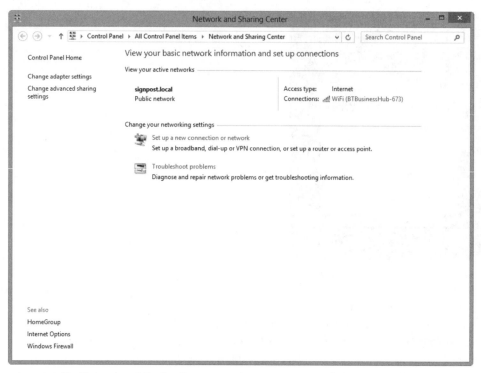

FIGURE 3-3 The Network and Sharing Center

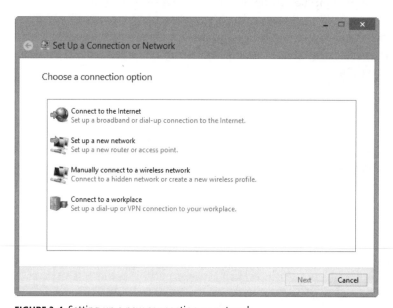

FIGURE 3-4 Setting up a new connection or network

Look at the different connection types and how they are configured:

- **Connect To The Internet** is used if you already have a router that you can connect to with a physical Ethernet cable or if you are using a dial-up Internet connection via a modem. Here you might be in a situation where you have to have a username and password to gain Internet access, such as with an ISDN phone line. The Connect to the Internet wizard asks you for the username and password and, if you are using dial-up Internet, the phone number to connect to. Note that if you are using dial-up Internet, your computer needs a modem, which are no longer installed in computers. You can add a modem via USB or an ExpressCard if you are using a laptop with a compatible slot.

- **Set Up A New Network** allows you to access a new router or access point on your network to configure it for the first time. This is most useful if you don't know the IP address of the device to access it through a web browser.

- **Manually Connect To A Wireless Network** enables you to connect to a hidden network. With wireless network security scares becoming increasingly common, it's also becoming more common for individuals and businesses to hide their network from plain sight. This means that the network is still active but its service set identifier (SSID, the name you assign to a wireless network) won't be visible. You can use this option to connect to a hidden network, but you need some information about the network first, including what type of password encryption it uses. You should ask the network administrator for both the security type and the encryption type.

- **Connect To A Workplace** is perhaps the most commonly used option in business, because it allows users to connect to virtual private networks (VPNs) set up by the business. This option can allow them to access the corporate network while at home or on the road. When you connect to a VNP, you are asked for the server address; this can be a web address (such as Contoso.com), an IPv4 address, or an IPv6 address.

Setting up VPN connections in Windows 8

You can set up a VPN connection in Windows 8 in the Network and Sharing Center by using the Connect To A Workplace option just mentioned. After you set up a VPN connection on your computer, you might need to modify or add some configuration options, which the network administrator should provide. To access these in the Network and Sharing Center, click the Change Adapter Settings link in the top left of the window; you should see the VPN listed as a network connection in the new window that appears.

You can right-click the VPN here and select its Properties (see Figure 3-5). On the Properties sheet, you can change various settings and options for the VPN, including all-important security settings that probably need additional configuring to match those set by the network administrator.

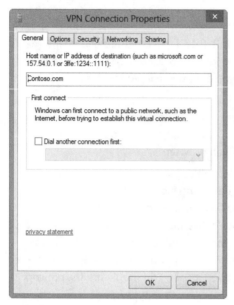

FIGURE 3-5 Changing the properties for a VPN

When a VPN is configured, it can be accessed in the same way as any other network in Windows 8—through the Settings charm and then the Network icon. VPNs are listed in the main panel on the left side of the screen above any wireless networks that are in range (see Figure 3-6).

To connect to a VPN, you also need a current Internet connection, either wired through an Ethernet cable or via Wi-Fi.

FIGURE 3-6 Accessing a VPN in Windows 8

When you are connected to a network, it's listed in the View Your Active Networks section of the Network and Sharing Center. The network name is highlighted as a link, which you can click for current information about the network, including the status and connection speed. You can click the Wireless Properties button to reveal more information and configuration options for the network (see Figure 3-7). Here you can change settings for the network, such as automatic connection to wireless networks. You can also change the password and security settings for a network without having to delete the network profile and rebuild it.

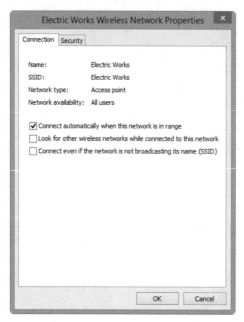

FIGURE 3-7 Settings and changing network properties

Also, on the network status panel you can click the Properties button to display additional network options that you might want to enable, disable, or modify (see Figure 3-8). This panel can be handy if you want to ensure that a feature such as file and printer sharing is enabled or disabled. You can also turn IPv4 and IPv6 connectivity on and off here for the network. Sometimes the configuration of a network, or its security, dictates that only one or the other are used.

FIGURE 3-8 Changing advanced network properties for a connection

Again in the Network Properties sheet, you can click the Details button to display useful information about the current network connection. This includes its IPv4 and—if relevant—IPv6 address, the subnet mask (useful to check whether you're connected to the right subnetwork), and the IP address of the DHCP server (see Figure 3-9).

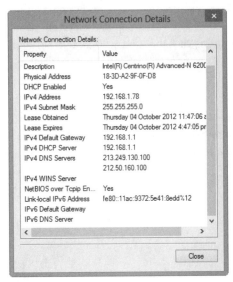

FIGURE 3-9 Viewing technical details of the current network connection

 EXAM TIP

The exam may test you whether you have the ability to configure networking settings via both the GUI and the commandline. The NETSH commandline tool is covered later in this chapter, allows you to display or modify the network configuration of your computer.

Resolving computer name, domain, and workgroup conflicts

Back in the days of Windows NT, computer name conflicts commonly caused problems. Even now they can cause connection difficulties if you connect the computers to a Windows Server and use the server to deploy apps and updates, and to manage group and security policies. When deploying Windows images, resolving the computer names is always important so that each computer has a specific ID. This means that those individual computers can be controlled, managed, and audited.

You can't always manage and audit laptops, tablets, and BYOD (bring your own device) computers, because these devices might have computer names that conflict with another computer on the network.

Problems with management and auditing are also the case with workgroups, another legacy feature in Windows that acts as a more user-friendly way to configure an equivalent of a subnet mask.

If you find that you can't connect to a computer on the network, or that the computer can't access network resources such as printers or file shares, check the computer name and workgroup for the PC. You can check the computer name and workgroup in the System panel from the main Control Panel. If you want to change these, click the Advanced System Settings link in the left pane of the window; in the dialog box that appears, click the Computer Name tab.

You can join a domain using a wizard interface by clicking the Network ID button, but if you need to change any of the settings manually, click the Change button. Any changes you make to the computer name, domain, or workgroup require you to log off or sometimes restart the computer before those changes will take effect (see Figure 3-10).

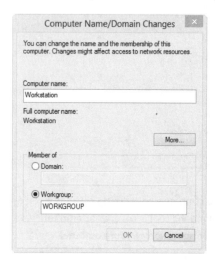

FIGURE 3-10 Changing the computer name, domain, or workgroup

Using the Windows 8 automatic network troubleshooter

The automatic network troubleshooter available in the Network and Sharing Center can be a genuinely useful tool to repair common network connection issues. However, it won't fix some problems.

All the automatic troubleshooters in Windows 8 work in the same way, by resetting components to their default state. In fairness, this will repair many common problems, especially where a problem has been caused by a network or other configuration file becoming corrupt.

You will find, however, that with more complex network setups and VPNs, the automatic troubleshooters either might not fix the problem or settings will need to be rebuilt afterward.

Thought experiment

Setting up a hidden wireless network

In the following thought experiment, apply what you've learned about this objective. You can find answers to these questions in the "Answers" section at the end of this chapter.

Employees need to connect to a hidden wireless network at a company location. The network is hidden to help maintain tight security.

Explain the details you need to set up the connection and where you would enter them in Windows 8.

Objective summary

- You can manage network connections in the Network and Sharing Center.
- Resetting faulty Wi-Fi connections is easy.
- You can connect to hidden wireless networks through the Network and Sharing Center.
- Setting up a VPN connection is simple, but some settings might need modification afterward.
- You can turn networking features on and off network by network.
- Conflicts can occur on a network if two computers have the same name or if a computer is set to the wrong domain or workgroup.
- The automatic network troubleshooter will reset network settings to their defaults.

Objective review

Answer the following questions to test your knowledge of the information in this objective. You can find the answers to these questions and explanations of why each answer choice is correct or incorrect in the "Answers" section at the end of this chapter.

1. You have set up a VPN and need to configure specific security settings provided by the network administrator. Where can you change these settings?

   A. The Network Connections panel, accessed from the Settings charm

   B. The Control Panel

   C. The Network and Sharing Center

   D. The network adapter settings

2. What settings do you select to connect to a VPN?

   A. Set Up A New Connection Or Network | Connect To The Internet

   B. Set Up A New Connection Or Network | Connect To A Workplace

   C. Set Up A New Connection Or Network | Set Up A New Network

   D. Set Up A New Connection Or Network | Manually Connect To A Network

3. In a business running entirely on IPv6, how can you turn off your IPv4 network settings?

   A. View Your Active Networks | *network name* | Details

   B. View Your Active Networks | *network name* | Wireless Properties

   C. View Your Active Networks | *network name* | Properties

   D. Network and Sharing Center | Change Adapter Settings

4. A laptop that has been brought into the workplace can't access the local file share, even though the user can still log on to the domain. What setting might need to be changed?

   A. The domain

   B. The adapter settings

   C. The computer name

   D. The workgroup

5. You need to check the current IP address, subnet mask, and DHCP server address for the current network connection. Where can you find this information?

   A. View Your Active Networks > *network name* > Details

   B. View Your Active Networks > *network name* > Wireless Properties

   C. View Your Active Networks > *network name* > Properties

   D. Network and Sharing Center > View Your Active Networks

Objective 3.3: Configure and maintain network security

Connecting to networks can sometimes cause people enough of a headache, but nothing is more important than keeping them secure. In a business environment, you will be trusted with personal data for clients and sensitive information about projects, as well as governed by data protection and privacy laws. The fines and penalties for breaching these laws can be steep enough to put a company out of business altogether—that is, if the negative publicity and ill feeling from current customers and colleagues doesn't do that for you.

Every so often you hear or read news stories of companies, sometimes even major corporations, that don't use strong enough network security who have sensitive information stolen by hackers. These cases are just a small proportion of the total overall number of cases worldwide. Everyone would probably be shocked and appalled if they really knew how often these types of security breaches occurred, but they are often covered up to avoid embarrassment. The main aim, then, is to ensure that your company won't suffer from such breaches, or that you can at the very least do everything possible to avoid them.

The information here won't give you a comprehensive guide to securing your networks because new flaws, hacks, and methods of penetrating computers are being developed and refined all the time. You must stay up-to-date with the latest information from Microsoft, your hardware and software vendors, and from "white-hat" hacking groups that regularly publish details of discovered vulnerabilities. The emphasis on the security aspect of your Microsoft Certification qualification, however, should never be understated. Security should always be foremost on your mind!

This objective doesn't look at internal threats such as file copying on USB flash drives, malware, and such (these are covered in Chapters 4 and 5). This objective looks at threats to the network itself.

Network threats fall into four main categories:

- **Eavesdropping** (also known as *sniffing*) occurs when data packets sent and/or received on your network are intercepted by a third party. This can compromise sensitive data, including usernames and passwords.

- **Denial of Service (DoS)** attacks are becoming increasingly common and aren't just the weapon of choice for criminals and blackmailers any more. In recent years, some political and activist groups deployed DoS attacks as a means of pressuring companies and even entire governments. A DoS attack typically cripples web services by flooding them with traffic.

- **Port scanning** has been around for so many years; it's hard to remember when it began. Hackers query communications ports on computers and computer networks that use the User Datagram Protocol (UDP) or TCP/IP to identify themselves. A port reply indicates that it is open and can be subject to attack and penetration.

- **Man-in-the-middle** attacks use a dummy computer to impersonate a legitimate host on the network that your computers communicate with. The attacker intercepts all the traffic intended for the destination host and can read, crack, or even modify the data.

Understanding defense in depth

Defense in depth is a security concept that approaches network security using a layered approach (see Figure 3-11). The reason for this is twofold:

- You have to consider many factors with security, many of which don't interact directly with one another.

- Many different things can be done, some of which you might not think of directly with network security.

Consider this scenario: Leaving your car in a parking garage involves all manner of security factors, some that you directly control and others that perhaps are out of your control. The factors you consider are the overall security of the parking garage, whether closed-circuit TV is present, how full the garage is, and how many people are coming and going. You also consider your car's own security, what might be on display in your car, and so on.

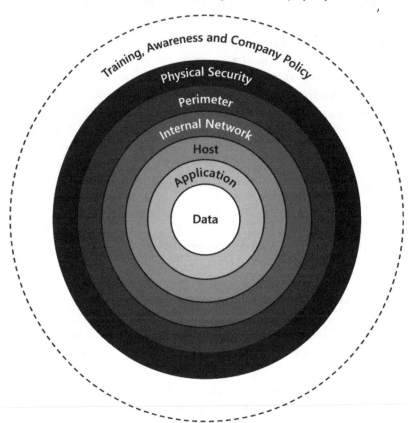

FIGURE 3-11 The seven areas of network security

The layers shown in Figure 3-11, in order, are as follows:

1. **Training, Awareness, and Company Policy** You should never assume that employees understand what's required to maintain good security, or what data protection rules and regulations might be. You should always make the best use of staff training to help raise awareness of not just security policies and practices, but also the need to maintain security and vigilance.

2. **Physical Security** You might not think of the physical security of your network, but this doesn't just include the external doors, windows, and other features of your building with regards to break-ins and extreme events such as fire or flood, but also the internal security that exists between the physical servers, computers containing sensitive data, and both staff and visitors.

3. **Perimeter** This is the security that exists between your own company network and other untrusted networks, such as the Internet, or the third-party hosting you use for your website that might, in turn, provide log-in facilities to your own network. You can use a reverse-proxy server to help isolate your corporate network from outside networks. Reverse Proxy-Servers enable you to publish services internally using email or web services without having to place the content on outside servers. This layer of security also includes firewalls and other dedicated security appliances in your premises.

4. **Internal Network** At this layer, you start configuring your own internal network security, including both local and wide area networks. Configuration can be done through the use of network address translation (NAT) or VPNs to implement encryption.

5. **Host** Getting down to the individual computers means looking at the security of the operating system. This includes not just antivirus and malware protection and an adequate firewall, but also any vulnerabilities that might exist in the operating system. This layer also includes the configuration of the operating system and user accounts to take into account any penetration points that might exist because of a specific configuration.

6. **Application** This layer gets down to the software itself—its installation, configuration, and any vulnerabilities and penetration points. You might be using custom software that's never gone through thorough security testing, or you might be forced to use software that has a history of wide attacks, such as macros in Microsoft Office documents or PDF documents created using not just Adobe's software but also a wide range of compatible applications.

7. **Data** Last but not least and (you hope) by now extremely secure under six layers of protection and security lies your data. This will need its own security, perhaps using BitLocker or another method of encryption, or perhaps using strict access permissions specified by active directory domain services. Having adequate security is still vital to prevent people within your organization, who will already be within the first few layers of security, from accessing data they shouldn't be allowed to.

Mitigating security threats

Previously, this objective defined the four main areas of network attack: eavesdropping, denial of service, port scanning, and man in the middle. This section looks at each of these to see how your company's network can defend against each one. Each is a very different type of attack and needs to be considered individually.

Consider the WikiLeaks story in which a US military employee at the Pentagon could copy data to which he shouldn't normally have received access. No doubt, this became not just an enormous worldwide news story, but it also gave rise to several international diplomatic incidents over both the content of leaked documents and the fate of WikiLeaks founder Julian Assange.

Unless your company deals with classified and sensitive military, medical, or other data, you're unlikely to ever be embroiled in a scandal the size of WikiLeaks, but in other high-profile cases in the last few years sensitive data has been stolen by current and former employees of an organization.

You should have the following methods and policies in place to prevent data theft within your organization:

- Consider whether the copying of data or files to removable storage such as USB flash drives and external hard disks or being burned to optical discs should be allowed. You can block all these methods in Group Policy.

- Should files and documents be allowed to be emailed? You can use various methods including configuration of your email server, document security policies in software such as Microsoft Office, and more to allow either documents to only be emailed to another internal email address or to prevent them from being forwarded or printed.

- You should have clear communication and policies regarding staff members who have been suspended, dismissed, or resigned that quickly blocks their file and email access.

- Be sure to have a clear misconduct policy regarding the misuse or transmission of sensitive company files and data. This works closely with staff training in which people might not be aware of data protection and other laws, or the sensitive nature of documents and how their leakage could result in fines or worse. Never assume that your employees understand the need for security and how their own actions can contribute to breaches.

Eavesdropping

Remember that with eavesdropping, data packets are intercepted en route between your company server and the host/destination server. You can use several security methods to prevent eavesdropping:

- **IPsec** (Internet Protocol Security) is built into the Windows Firewall and is widely supported across many operating systems and platforms. It provides a way to authenticate IP-based communications between two hosts and encrypt traffic where appropriate.

- **VPNs** can be used to allow remote workers to tunnel in securely to the corporate network. They provide end-to-end encryption and user/host authentication.
- **Dedicated intrusion detection systems** can be used on your network to monitor traffic for signs of attack and eavesdropping.

Denial of service (DoS) attacks

DoS or DDoS (distributed denial of service) attacks can cripple a company's servers and services by flooding them with traffic. They are commonly controlled from *botnets*, networks of individual computers that a criminal can remotely control to flood a server or website with traffic. Increasingly, however, individuals are deliberately installing botnets on their own computers that they then allow to be controlled by activist groups to attack companies and even governments for political reasons. You have several security methods available to prevent these types of attacks:

- **Firewall** You should always ensure that you have a firewall configured to block all unwanted and unsolicited traffic.
- **Perimeter networks** You can use these isolated areas of your network to segregate and manage traffic flow. You can defend your business from DoS attacks by placing a perimeter network between your workers and the Internet. As a result, the perimeter network takes the brunt of the attack while shielding the interior network from it.
- **IPsec** As explained in the preceding section, this feature built into the Windows 8 Firewall is also widely supported across other platforms and operating systems. It can be used to provide end-to-end authentication and encryption for data.
- **Server hardening** This method might sound like you're encasing your server in cement, but it means running only the services you really need on your servers and computers. This minimizes the area for attack on computers and servers. You can use tools such as the Microsoft Security Configuration Wizard or the Microsoft Baseline Security Analyzer to help with this.

Port scanning

With this means of attack, external computers are used to identify specific ports on your computers and your network to try and find any that are open and might be vulnerable to attack. The main methods of defense against port scanning are server hardening, as just described, and using external firewall appliances and routers that respond to outside requests only if they come through an approved method, such as a preconfigured VPN connection.

Man in the middle

Man-in-the-middle attacks use a dummy computer to simulate a real authenticated one. You have several methods of defense to use against this type of attack on your network:

- **IPsec**, as described previously, can be used to ensure that only properly authenticated traffic on your network is permitted.

- **Domain Name System Security Extensions (DNSSEC)** provides a facility in which DNS servers can use digital signatures to validate computers in a trusted zone. When a DNS server in the trusted zone—with the original copy of the signatures—queries an external computer, validation is performed on the received digital signature before access is granted.

Configuring the Windows 8 Firewall

So far this objective has focused on how the individual firewall settings on each host computer can contribute in a substantial way to the overall effectiveness of your company's security. This section looks at how you can configure the Windows Firewall itself.

When you open the Windows Firewall, either from the Control Panel or by searching for "firewall" at the Start screen, you see that it's fairly basic by default (see Figure 3-12). To access the full controls, you need to click the Advanced Settings link on the left, but for now you need to look at the basic controls.

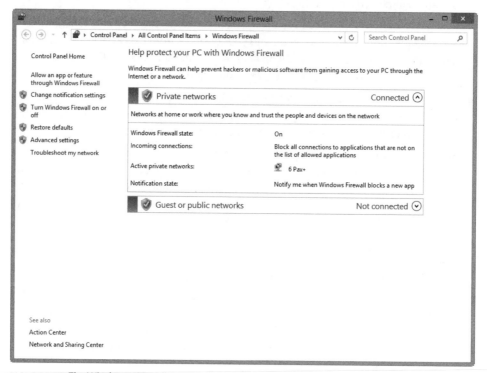

FIGURE 3-12 The Windows Firewall

In the main Windows Firewall window you should see your connected network types split into three different groupings: private networks, public networks, and domain networks. You can set sharing, security, and individual rules for each network type—allowing, for example, file and printer sharing only on a company domain network but not with private (home) or public networks. This can help prevent unauthorized printing and sharing of sensitive files.

You can perform other actions in the main Windows Firewall window, including allowing (or denying) an app or installed feature (this might be a Windows or a third-party feature) through the firewall.

The advanced firewall settings provide significantly more control over the inbound and outbound rules and the connection types allowed for each network (see Figure 3-13).

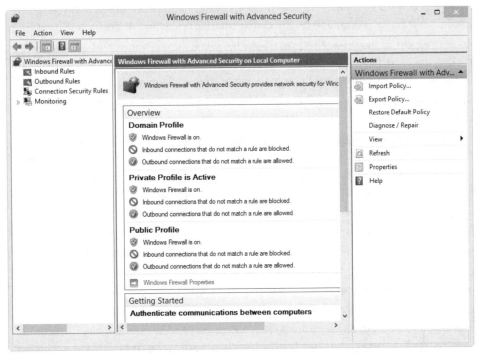

FIGURE 3-13 The advanced firewall security settings in Windows 8

The advanced firewall security window provides status information about your firewall and individual rules in the main central panel. The right panel, as with other Windows configuration and management tools, includes context-sensitive options; the left panel is the main tree containing each individual firewall control, enabling you to quickly switch from one to another.

The options that you can configure for each of the three network profiles (private, public, and domain) are as follows:

- **Firewall State** turns the firewall on or off for each profile.
- **Inbound Connections** blocks specific connections based on configurable rules. These can include blocking a program, port, or service.
- **Outbound Connections** is similar to Inbound Connections but blocks traffic from being broadcast from the computer.

- **Settings** can enable you to configure the display of notifications, unicast responses, local rules, and connection security rules.

- **Logging** enables you to configure how logs are kept and contain that information by the firewall for later review.

In the left panel is also a Monitoring option, which you can use to provide reporting on the rules that come preconfigured in the Windows Firewall and custom rules that you specify yourself. This includes information on the current status of rules and of the firewall itself.

You can export all the firewall rules as a .wfw file at the main advanced firewall window by clicking the Export Policy link on the right. The advanced rules can then be imported into other computers, thus simplifying the setting and porting of them across multiple machines.

When you create a new inbound or outbound rule, you can configure many settings throughout the process using a wizard interface:

- **Program Rules** can be set to determine firewall behavior for a specific piece of software. To set such rules, you must specify the .exe file for the program. Because of the way it's configured, this setting cannot be used to control new apps from the Windows Store or those that have been distributed through AppLocker.

- **Port Rules** can define connection rules for TCP or UDP port types. You can specify connection protocols that are permitted for different ports on the computer.

- **Predefined Rules** control connections for the Windows experience and can allow or block connections by selecting one of the programs or Windows services listed.

- **Custom Rules** cover everything that you might want to do with the firewall that's not covered by the first three rule types.

In addition to inbound and outbound rules, you can set Connection Security rules. These rules secure traffic by using the IPsec feature mentioned previously in this objective. You would use connection security rules to specify how and when authentication occurs between two computers. These include the following:

- **Isolation Rules** are for restricting connections based on an authentication criteria, such as membership of a specific domain or the health status of a computer (up-to-date antivirus, for example).

- **Authentication Exemption Rules** can be used to specify what connection types can be excluded from authentication. These rules can be used to grant access connections to and between specific computers and devices in an IP address range, subnet, or other connection and network types that don't require authentication. You might find granting unencrypted data communications between computers in a specific Active Directory domain group or connected to a specific DHCP server useful. These rules can also help with devices such as smartphones or tablets that might not support IPsec directly or might not be configurable for your specific network security protocols. In this last case, however, be aware of the security risks that permitting such devices on a network might incur.

- **Server-to-Server Rules** can protect connections between specific computers, such as accounts and payroll.
- **Tunnel Rules** can secure communications between two computers by using a tunnel mode in IPsec instead of the usual transport mode. This tunnel mode embeds the whole network packet into another for transportation between two defined endpoints.
- **Custom Rules** cover everything not in the main categories for connection rules.

Comparing communications ports in Windows 8

This objective has mentioned several times that ports can be attacked on your computer, but what are ports, which ones are used for which purpose, and which can be vulnerable? In short, the port numbers on your computer range from 0 to 65,535.

You can view the current TCP/IP port connections by using the *netstat –a* command at the Commmand Prompt, which can give you a good idea of what ports are currently open. Table 3-2 lists some of the most commonly used ports.

TABLE 3-2 Common communications ports

Port	Protocol	Usage
21	TCP	Commonly used by the File Transfer Protocol (FTP) though other ports can also be used by FTP
23	TCP	Telnet, providing access to command line interfaces on remote hosts
25	TCP	Simple Mail Transfer Protocol (SMTP) used to send email
53	UDP	Domain Name System (DNS)
53	TCP	DNS
80	TCP	Hypertext Transfer Protocol (HTTP) for Internet use
110	TCP	Post Office Protocol 3 (POP3) used for receiving email
143	TCP	Internet Message Access Protocol (IMAP) used for email synching
161	UDP	Simple Network Management Protocol (SNMP)
389	TCP	Lightweight Directory Access Protocol (LDAP)
443	TCP	Hypertext Transfer Protocol Secure (HTTPS)
3389	TCP	Remote Desktop Protocol (RDP) used to provide graphical control over other computers

EXAM TIP

Although many of the built in features will automatically configure the Windows Firewall rules correctly when you enable the feature, you should still learn the common port
numbers as they often can appear on the exam. You can use the netstat command with the
following switches:

- **-a** displays all the active TCP connections and UDP ports to which the computer is listening.

- **-e** displays Ethernet statistics, including the number of bytes and packets being sent and received. You can use this switch with the –s switch.

- **-n** displays the active TCP port numbers numerically rather than provides descriptive names.

- **-o** displays the active TCP connections with the process ID (PID) of each connection. The PID matches running applications in the Processes tab of Task Manager. You can combine this switch with –a, -n, and –p.

- **-p <protocol>** shows connections for the protocol specified. This can be tcp, udp, tcpv6, or udpv6. You can use this with the –s switch to display statistics by protocol, in which you can specify the protocols tcp, udp, icmp, ip, tcpv6, udpv6, icmpv6, or ipv6.

- **-s** displays statistics by protocol. By default, it shows statistics for TCP, UDP, ICMP, and IP protocols, but it can be combines with the –p switch to provide more specific infor-mation.

- **-r** displays the contents of the IP routing table, the equivalent of the route print com-mand.

- **<interval>** redisplays the information every specified number of seconds. You can press Ctrl+C to end the command.

Using IPsec to secure Windows 8

IPsec, as mentioned several times in this objective, is a set of industry-standard cryptographic services and protocols and is a requirement for IPv6 traffic. IPsec ensures that computers identify themselves when communication is established and ensures confidentiality by en-crypting data packets. IPsec has two modes:

- **Encapsulating Security Protocol (ESP)** encrypts data using one of several available algorithms.

- **Authentication Header (AH)** digitally signs data packets without encrypting them.

IPsec can be put to many uses, such as the following:

- **Enforcing logical networks** A *logical network* is a group of network nodes indepen-dent of the physical network topology. For example, you can use virtual local area net-works (VLANs) to create networks that group computers irrespective or their physical connections to routers, switches, or subnets.

- **Packet filtering** You can block inbound or outbound traffic by using IPsec with network address translation (NAT) and the basic firewall component of the Routing and Remote Access Service (RRAS).

- **Securing host-to-host traffic** You can use IPsec to encrypt data traffic between two specific computers.

- **Securing traffic between computers and servers** One of the most common uses of IPsec is to secure data flow between individual computers in the workplace and a server.

- **Site-to-site tunneling** You can use IPsec to provide encryption between end-to-end routers and other systems that don't natively support the L2TP/IPsec or Point-to-Point tunneling protocols. Site-to-site tunneling is also sometimes known as *gateway-to-gateway tunneling*.

- **Protecting wireless networks** You can use IPsec to protect traffic sent over 802.xx wireless networks, although using one of the standard wireless connection security systems, such as WPA or WPA2, is always better for encrypting data over wireless.

- **Using L2TP/IPsec to secure VPN connections** You can use the L2TP function with IPsec to secure tunneling for VPN connections.

You can configure IPsec on a Windows 8 computer in several ways:

- Through the Advanced Windows Firewall, by using the Connection Security Rules

- By using the Microsoft Management Console:

  - Search for "mmc" at the Start screen to open the Microsoft Management Console.

  - From the File menu, click Add/Remove Snap-In. From the list of available snap-ins, select IP Security Policy Management.

  - Click Add and then click OK.

- By using the *netsh* command from a command prompt:

  - Within the *netsh* command are two subcommands for configuring IPsec: ipsec and advfirewall.

  - You can use the *netsh ipsec static* or the *netsh ipsec dynamic* command with the *add*, *set*, or *delete* switches to perform the commands possible in the Microsoft Management Console.

MORE INFO THE NETSH IPSEC COMMAND

You can read more about the *netsh ipsec* command at *http://technet.microsoft.com/en-us/library/cc725926(v=WS.10).aspx.*

Configuring Windows Defender

Windows 8 is the first version of the operating system to come with built-in antivirus. If this is the antivirus you choose to use, you will want to know how to configure and administer it on Windows client computers. It's not to be confused with Windows Defender from Windows XP, Windows Vista, and Windows 7, which is a completely different product; Microsoft simply decided to adopt the name for the new antivirus package. In Windows 8, Windows Defender is a rebranded version of Microsoft Security Essentials.

Windows Defender offers a significant advantage over many other antivirus packages in that if you're busy using the computer, it won't tie up all the system resources performing scans. This feature makes it very suitable for business environments.

You can launch Windows Defender by searching for "defender" at the Start screen. The main configuration options can be found on the Settings tab (see Figure 3-14).

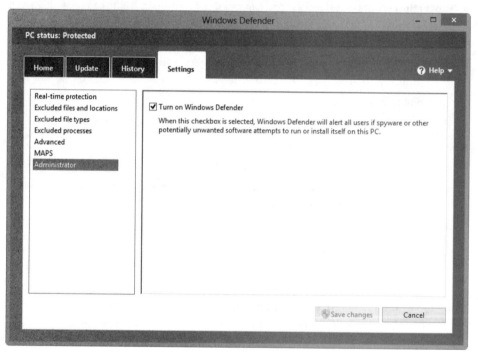

FIGURE 3-14 Windows Defender

The main configuration options in Windows Defender are as follows:

- **Real-Time Protection** enables you to turn constant scanning off, though doing so is almost never recommended.

- **Excluded Files And Locations** allows you to specify locations of the computer that are excluded from antivirus scans. This could include areas that regularly raise false-positive results.

- **Excluded File Types** allows you to specify certain file types. Again, that might raise false-positive results for exclusion from scans.
- **Excluded Processes** is possibly more useful in business because many companies use custom software, some of which might be incorrectly identified as malware. With this option, you can omit specific programs from scans.
- **Advanced** enables you to turn the following features on and off:
  - Scanning of archive files (zip, cab, rar, and so on)
  - Scanning of removable drives such as USB flash drives
  - Automatic creation of a system restore point before cleaning up infected items
  - Permitting viewing of the entire scanning and cleaning history
  - Removing quarantined items after a specified period, from 1 day to 3 months
- **MAPS** allows you to opt in or out of the Microsoft Active Protection Service, which helps identify malware with automatic reporting by Windows Defender. You might want to opt out to save network and Internet bandwidth.
- **Administrator** enables you to disable Windows Defender if you want to use a different antivirus product on your computers.

NOTE **WINDOWS RT AND TABLETS**

If you're administering Windows RT devices such as Surface tablets in your organization, this Administrator option is not available on those tablets.

EXAM TIP

Windows Defender could be easily overlooked when preparing for the exam because it has been included in previous versions of Windows. The Windows 8 version has been radically overhauled and includes many new components and administrative settings. Ensure you review the configuration tabs in detail.

Thought experiment
Deactivating authentication

In the following thought experiment, apply what you've learned about this objective. You can find answers to these questions in the "Answers" section at the end of this chapter.

You need to create secure network connections between computers connected to different routers and switches and connected to different subnets.

Describe what Windows 8 network security feature you would use to deactivate authentication for all the computers connected to a specific Active Directory Domain.

Objective summary

- The four types of network attack are eavesdropping, denial of service, port scanning, and man in the middle.
- Defense in depth is a strategy of ensuring that your network is protected at every level.
- You can mitigate many security threats through staff training and company policy.
- IPsec is an industry standard for providing end-to-end encryption of network communications.
- The Windows 8 Firewall can be configured with custom inbound, outbound, or communications rules.
- Three network types exist: private, public, and domain.
- Windows Defender—not to be confused with the old Windows Defender—is the new antivirus package in Windows 8.

Objective review

Answer the following questions to test your knowledge of the information in this objective. You can find the answers to these questions and explanations of why each answer choice is correct or incorrect in the "Answers" section at the end of this chapter.

1. Someone is using a dummy computer to impersonate a computer on your network in a man-in-the-middle attack. What methods can you use to block this?

   A. IPsec and DNSSEC

   B. Server hardening

   C. IPsec and Windows Firewall

   D. An external firewall appliance

2. What do you call the process of building an isolation area between your network and the Internet?

   A. Server hardening

   B. Perimeter network

   C. Firewall

   D. Tunneling

3. You want to grant unrestricted communications between computers in the workplace that are connected to different routers and switches. What type of rules would you specify?

   A. Inbound and outbound rules

   B. Authentication exemption rules

    C. Connection security rules

    D. Site-to-site tunneling rules

4. Which of the following is not a use for IPsec?

    A. Packet filtering

    B. Site-to-site tunneling

    C. Securing connections between computers and servers

    D. Specifying that only secure websites can be contacted

5. You have a custom business program that continually raises false-positive antivirus messages in Windows Defender. What feature in Windows Defender do you need to modify to allow the program to run properly?

    A. Excluded files and locations

    B. Excluded services

    C. Excluded file types

    D. Excluded processes

Objective 3.4: Configure remote management

As home and remote working become not just more popular, but also a more cost-effective way to operate a business, making remote desktop connections and remote management more simple becomes more important for companies such as Microsoft. Ensuring that desktop computers and laptops are correct configured for it and ready for any eventuality becomes more important for system administrators. Windows 8 comes with two remote facilities that enable control and management: Remote Desktop and Remote Assistance, both refined from earlier Windows versions.

Remote Desktop allows users to access files on a computer from another remote computer, such as a home PC, and to remotely run desktop programs and apps and access work files. This feature also allows system administrators to connect to several Windows Server sessions to facilitate remote administration.

Remote Assistance allows a trusted person to take control of a computer for the purposes of troubleshooting or performing maintenance or configuration.

> **This objective covers how to:**
> - Configure Remote Desktop
> - Configure Remote Assistance

Permitting remote sessions on the computer

By default, Windows 8 is configured to allow Remote Desktop and Remote Assistance sessions. You can change this setting in the Control Panel by clicking System and Security and then clicking System. In the main system panel, you then need to click the Remote Settings link in the top left of the window.

Whereas the main controls here are fairly straightforward, including being able to set the maximum amount of time a computer can be remotely controlled, you can also configure which users are allowed to use the Remote Desktop feature. This list, if configured, allows you to select users who already have an account on the computer.

Configuring Remote Desktop

You can find the Remote Desktop feature by searching for "remote" at the Start screen. By default, it asks you for the address of the computer to which you want to connect. This can be a web address, an IP address, or other common Windows address types. In the bottom left of the window is a Show Options button which, when clicked, displays the full Remote Desktop options (see Figure 3-15).

FIGURE 3-15 Configuring Remote Desktop

Now look at each tab in turn and the features that each one offers:

- **General** is where you specify the connection address of the computer on a local or remote network. You can also specify a username to log on with (you are automatically prompted for your password if the connection is successful). At the bottom of the page are options to save the current configuration options and open a saved options file.

This file can be a useful way for a network administrator to send configuration options to remote workers.

- **Display** enables you to change the graphics options for the connection, which can greatly reduce the overall bandwidth required. One important consideration with Remote Desktop is the amount of available network bandwidth and whether this cost can be changed for the business or the end user. For example, a remote worker might have to connect using a 3G or 4G mobile broadband data connection in which the total amount of data throughput allowed is limited, or a hefty charge is assessed per megabyte of data transferred.

- **Local Resources** allows you to specify whether sounds that play on the remote computer should also play on the host PC and whether they should even play on the remote computer at all. You can also choose whether you want to be able to use local printers with your remote computer and whether you want Windows key operations to apply to the local computer, the remote computer, or both.

- **Programs** enables you to set a program on the remote computer to automatically run when the Remote Desktop session begins. For example, you might want to specify that File Explorer opens so that you can copy files or a CRM package opens so that it can be updated.

- **Experience** deals with the overall quality of the network connection and, by default, adjusts the Remote Desktop experience depending on the type of connection it detects. You can set the experience manually, which might be useful if, for example, you want to either ensure that cost-per-megabyte bandwidth is minimized or that certain users who require a good graphical experience always get it.

- **Advanced** offers two important security options. First, if the authentication required to prove that you're connected to the correct computer fails, you can—if you want or if you work in a high-security environment—deny the connection altogether. Second, you can configure a Connect From Anywhere setting in which you can, at your discretion, specify that the computer connect through a dedicated Remote Desktop gateway server.

Configuring Remote Assistance

Remote Assistance works slightly differently from Remote Desktop in that it requires a user to sit physically at the remote computer when the session begins. This feature, first introduced with Windows XP, is a great way to be able to harness the power and flexibility of remote help and support. It also can significantly reduce the amount of time IT support departments waste having to visit a user at a desk only to determine that they'd opened the wrong window and hadn't followed your instructions.

A Remote Assistance request must be initiated by the user on the remote computer. To start a request, search for "remote" at the Start screen and in the Settings results click Invite Someone To Connect To Your PC And Help You, Or Offer To Help Someone Else. However, doing so can be complex and time consuming, and it's definitely a tool that you should pin to the Start screen so that employees can get quick access to it when they need it. Alternatively, you can get quick access to Remote Assistance by searching for "msra" at the Start screen.

You can send an invitation file in several ways, but note that the Use Email To Send An Invitation option works only if the computer has a software email client, such as Microsoft Outlook, installed and configured. If users are using a webmail system, perhaps Office 365 in a browser, they need to save the invitation file and attach it to an email manually.

When the Remote Assistance request file is opened, it asks for a connection password. This is displayed on the remote computer's screen and is normally intended to be read aloud over the phone to aid security. However, this can be copied and pasted into the body of the email, if required.

If you are taking remote control of a computer, two actions must be performed to do it properly, one by yourself and one by the person sitting at the remote computer.

The first of these is to click the Request Control link, which appears in the very top left of the Remote Assistance window (see Figure 3-16). If, however, you just want to be able to see what the user is doing (and in all probability how they're getting something wrong), you won't need to request control.

FIGURE 3-16 Requesting control of the remote computer

At this point, a dialog box opens on the remote computer for users to grant remote control. Here they must select the check box allowing the person providing the help to respond to user account control requests themselves (see Figure 3-17). Without this, both parties need to be in constant dialog, with the user at the remote computer being asked to click Yes on UAC prompts should they arise.

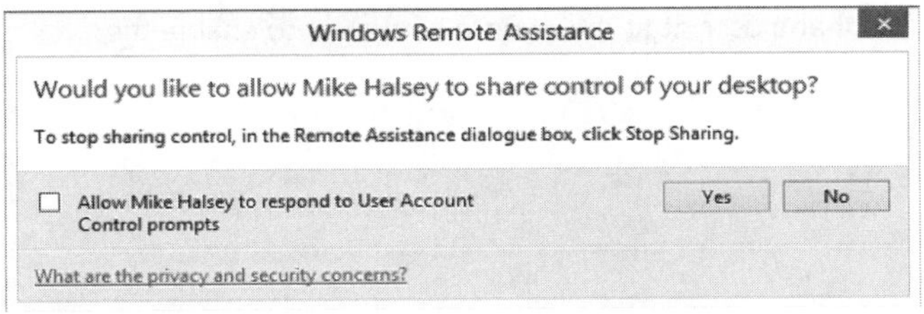

FIGURE 3-17 Granting remote control of the computer

At any time, both the person providing the assistance and the user receiving it can stop sharing by clicking the Stop Sharing button (see Figure 3-18). Also, the connection can be paused and the settings can be changed here to give the best possible experience based on your available network or Internet bandwidth.

FIGURE 3-18 Stopping sharing

Thought experiment

Establishing a secure Remote Desktop connection

In the following thought experiment, apply what you've learned about this objective. You can find answers to these questions in the "Answers" section at the end of this chapter.

You need to create a secure Remote Desktop connection from a home computer to one on the worker's desk.

What is the best and most secure way for that worker to connect to the computer in a remote session, and why?

Objective summary

- By default, remote sessions are enabled in Windows 8, and the Windows Firewall allows these connections.

- You can save and distribute Remote Desktop configurations to other users and computers.

- Windows detects the available bandwidth and adjusts the experience quality of Remote Desktop and Remote Assistance automatically. You can change the experience quality manually, however.

- Remote Assistance requires that a user sit at the remote computer to enable the session.

Objective review

Answer the following questions to test your knowledge of the information in this objective. You can find the answers to these questions and explanations of why each answer choice is correct or incorrect in the "Answers" section at the end of this chapter.

1. You need to find the full computer name of your PC so that you can later connect to it remotely. Where can you find this?

   A. In the Remote Desktop settings

   B. In the Control Panel, under System

   C. In the Devices and Printers panel

   D. You can discover this later when establishing a remote connection

2. You need to tell a user how to access Remote Assistance on her computer. What do you tell her to search for at the Start screen?

   A. Remote Assistance

   B. Remote

   C. MSR

   D. MSRA

3. What is very useful to explain to a user before he grants control of his computer?

   A. He should stay at the computer for the entire session.

   B. He must be prepared to click UAC prompts.

   C. He should make himself a coffee and be patient.

   D. He should allow the person helping to click the UAC prompts.

Chapter summary

- Whereas IPv4 is a 32-bit addressing system, IPv6 uses 128 bits, allowing for more information to be carried in the IP address itself.

- You can configure subnet masks on IPv4 networks to create subnetworks, allowing for more computers to be attached overall.

- You can use various command-prompt tools to troubleshoot and diagnose problems with network connectivity.
- The default gateway for a network is automatically configured by Windows 8 by default, although it can be set manually.
- You can manage network connections in the Network and Sharing Center.
- Resetting faulty Wi-Fi connections is easy.
- You need to connect to hidden wireless networks via the Network and Sharing Center.
- Setting up a VPN connection is simple, but some settings might need modification afterward.
- You can turn networking features on and off network by network.
- Conflicts can occur on a network if two computers have the same name or if a computer is set to the wrong domain or workgroup.
- The automatic network troubleshooter resets network settings to their default.
- The four types of network attack are eavesdropping, denial of service (DoS), port scanning, and man in the middle.
- Defense in depth is a strategy of ensuring that your network is protected at every level.
- You can mitigate many security threats through staff training and company policy.
- IPsec is an industry standard for providing end-to-end encryption of network communications.
- You can configure the Windows 8 Firewall with custom inbound, outbound, or communications rules.
- The three network types are private, public, and domain.
- Windows Defender—not to be confused with the old Windows Defender—is the new antivirus package in Windows 8.
- By default, remote sessions are enabled in Windows 8, and the Windows Firewall allows these connections.
- You can save and distribute Remote Desktop configurations to other users and computers.
- Windows detects the available bandwidth and adjusts the experience quality of Remote Desktop and Remote Assistance automatically. You can change the experience quality manually, however.
- Remote Assistance requires that a user sit at the remote computer to enable the session.

Answers

This section contains the solutions to the thought experiments and answers to the objective review questions in this chapter.

Objective 3.1: Thought experiment

The three different types of network class are designed to provide IP addressing that suited the needs of networks of different sizes. Class A networks allow for 16,777,214 hosts and Class C networks allow for only up to 254 hosts, so with 300 or 400 computers attached at any one time you would need a Class B network. This would mean you will use IP addresses in the range 128.x.x.x to 191.x.x.x, because IP addresses outside this range are used exclusively by the other class types or for Internet addressing.

Objective 3.1: Review

1. **Correct answer:** C

    A. **Incorrect:** Only IP addresses in the range 192.x.x.x (Class C), 172.x.x.x (Class B), and 10.x.x.x (Class A) are private address types associated with the local host.

    B. **Incorrect:** The address 255.255.255.0 is used for a subnet mask and not for a computer's IP address. IP addresses can only reach 223.x.x.x.

    C. **Correct:** The address 172.0.8.0 is a private address type for a Class B network.

    D. **Incorrect:** Only IP addresses in the range 192.x.x.x (Class C), 172.x.x.x (Class B), and 10.x.x.x (Class A) are private address types associated with the local host.

2. **Correct answer:** B

    A. **Incorrect:** An Anycast address type is used for sending information between networks or subnets using the nearest router.

    B. **Correct:** You would use a unicast address to send information directly between two individual computers on the same network or subnet.

    C. **Incorrect:** IPv6 doesn't have a singlecast address type.

D. Incorrect: A multicast address is used to send data to multiple computers on the same network or subnet.

3. **Correct answer:** A

   A. Correct: The boundary segments used in IPv4 and IPv6 addresses are 8-bit and 16-bit numbers displayed as decimal numbers for IPv4 and hexadecimal numbers for IPv6.

   B. Incorrect: Although the operating system translates decimal and hexadecimal numbers to binary, IP addresses aren't expressed in binary.

   C. Incorrect: IP addresses use 8-bit and 16-bit numbers, but IPv4 addresses are 32 bits in total length and IPv6 numbers are 128 bits in total length.

   D. Incorrect: IP addresses aren't classed in terms of the total numbers of characters in each segment because preceding zeros aren't required in a number.

4. **Correct answer:** B

   A. Incorrect: You can set two configurations for IPv4 addressing in Windows 8, but only one for IPv6.

   B. Correct: Windows 8 allows for a main and an alternate configuration for IPv4 networks, but only one for IPv6.

   C. Incorrect: You can set two configurations for IPv4 addressing in Windows 8, but only one for IPv6.

   D. Incorrect: You can set two configurations for IPv4 addressing in Windows 8, but only one for IPv6.

5. **Correct answer:** C

   A. Incorrect: You can use tracert to determine the route taken by a data packet, but the Pathping command provides much more detailed information on the route taken.

   B. Incorrect: You can use IPConfig to determine the overall status of network connections on the computer and to repair them. You can't use it to determine whether data sent from the computer has reached its destination.

   C. Correct: Pathping provides more information than the tracert command and is useful for troubleshooting network problems in Windows 8.

   D. Incorrect: The ping command can tell you only if your computer is successfully making contact with another computer or device. It can't provide more detailed information.

Objective 3.2: Thought experiment

You can set the connection settings for a hidden wireless network in the Network and Sharing Center by clicking the Set Up A New Connection Or Network link and then clicking Manually Connect To A Wireless Network.

In the Connection Wizard, you need to know the SSID for the network, the security and encryption types, and the security key (passphrase). You don't need access to the network to enter these details, meaning that the network team can set up computers in advance to auto-connect to hidden networks with the correct settings, saving users from having to enter settings in the Network and Sharing Center themselves, something they might not even be allowed access to by Group Policy settings.

Objective 3.2: Review

1. **Correct answer:** D

    A. **Incorrect:** Although the main network connections panel allows you to access a VPN, right-clicking this won't allow you to modify its settings.

    B. **Incorrect:** You can access the Network and Sharing Center from the Control Panel, but the Control Panel has no direct link for modifying the settings for a VPN.

    C. **Incorrect:** This is the main control center for networking on your computer, but it doesn't directly list all available networks, adapters, and VPNs. To access these, you need to also open the adapter settings.

    D. **Correct:** You can access the adapter settings from the Network and Sharing Center. Here, the VPNs are listed as network adapters. You can right-click a VPN (or any other adapter) to modify its properties.

2. **Correct answer:** B

    A. **Incorrect:** The Connect To The Internet option allows you to set up a wired, wireless, or dial-up connection to the Internet, but it won't allow you to connect to a VPN.

    B. **Correct:** Virtual private networks are used by businesses and, as such, the Connect To A Workplace settings is where you find the VPN connection options.

    C. **Incorrect:** If you choose the set up a new network, you are shown any available routers or access points that can be configured. These settings can't be used to access a VPN directly, however.

D. Incorrect: The Manually Connect To A Network settings are used only to access a wireless network that has a hidden SSID.

3. **Correct answer: C**

   A. Incorrect: The Details panel displays the current IPv4 and IPv6 settings, but it won't allow you to modify any settings.

   B. Incorrect: The Wireless Properties sheet is used to set up or modify settings for Wi-Fi networks, such as security keys and whether the computer should automatically connect to the network. It isn't used for turning network components on or off for the network.

   C. Correct: The Properties sheet is where you can turn specific networking features on or off for individual network connections. This includes the IPv4 and IPv6 settings.

   D. Incorrect: The Change Adapter Settings allow you to change the overall properties for a network adapter or a VPN, but you can't change the settings for an individual network.

4. **Correct answer: D**

   A. Incorrect: The user has already connected successfully to the domain, so this won't be the root cause of the problem.

   B. Incorrect: If the adapter settings on the computer were incorrect, the user couldn't connect at all to the company network or the domain.

   C. Incorrect: Having a computer name that also exists on another computer on the network might prevent the user from accessing a server share or getting updates from a server, but it would not prevent access to a printer because this is only one-way (outward) communications.

   D. Correct: The workgroup is like a subnet mask, a subnetwork on the domain. The printer is set up on a different workgroup, probably shared through another computer. A computer can see only other computers and network resources connected to the same workgroup.

5. **Correct answer: A**

   A. Correct: The Details panel is where you can find information about the currently active network connection.

   B. Incorrect: The Wireless Properties sheet is used only for setting automatic connection and security properties for a Wi-Fi network.

   C. Incorrect: The Properties sheet is where you can control what Windows networking features are switched on for the network. It doesn't provide specific information about the current status.

D. Incorrect: In the View Your Active Networks section of the Network and Sharing Center, you can see networks listed that you are now connected to, but this displays only the network names.

Objective 3.3: Thought experiment

If you have computers connected to different routers, switches, or even subnets in an office, you can use the authentication exemption rules in the Connection Security Rules of the Windows Firewall to deactivate the need for automatic authentication between different computers that are connected to the same Active Directory domain.

Objective 3.3: Review

1. **Correct answer:** A

    A. Correct: The IPsec and DNSSEC features are used to protect against a man-in-the-middle attack. IPsec encrypts data packets, while DNSSEC restricts communication to only computers that have a valid security certificate.

    B. Incorrect: Server hardening is the process of making sure that only the programs and services you need on your server or computer are running, minimizing the area for attack.

    C. Incorrect: You can configure the defense through the Windows Firewall and use IPsec as one of your tools, but the default firewall won't do the job on its own.

    D. Incorrect: An external firewall appliance has no way of knowing whether a computer communicating with it is a dummy. This is why DNSSEC is used to request a security certificate authenticating the computer.

2. **Correct answer:** B

    A. Incorrect: Server hardening minimizes the area for attack on a computer by running only the programs and services that are absolutely necessary. It doesn't isolate computers from the Internet.

    B. Correct: A perimeter network serves as a buffer zone between your company network and the Internet. It can be used to filter traffic and protect the network against DoS attacks.

    C. Incorrect: A firewall can be overrun with traffic during a DoS attack, causing the traffic on your company network to grind to a halt, so a perimeter network is needed to act as a buffer.

    D. Incorrect: Tunneling provides a method of communicating safely between two computers, but it does not isolate a network from the Internet.

3. **Correct answer:** B

    A. **Incorrect:** Inbound and outbound rules specify firewall rules per computer. They don't specify computer groups that can be bonded for communications.

    B. **Correct:** Authentication exemption rules allow you to specify groups of workplace computers, even ones on different routers and switches that can communicate unrestrictedly.

    C. **Incorrect:** Connection security rules specify overall secure and encrypted communications; authentication exemption rules fall under the banner of connection security Rules. This category has other rule types, however.

    D. **Incorrect:** Site-to-site tunneling rules are used when creating and using VPNs to ensure secure connections between two computers.

4. **Correct answer:** D

    A. **Incorrect:** Packet filtering is one of the uses for IPsec.

    B. **Incorrect:** Site-to-site tunneling can be performed using IPsec.

    C. **Incorrect:** Securing connections between computers and servers is one of the functions of IPsec.

    D. **Correct:** IPsec can't specify that only secure websites be contacted because this is a function of Group Policy and Internet rules.

5. **Correct answer:** D

    A. **Incorrect:** Excluded files and locations allow you to specify files and folders that regularly raise false-positive results. Although technically this can be used to specify the correct \Program Files folder, it isn't the correct option to use on this occasion.

    B. **Incorrect:** Excluded services isn't a feature of Windows Defender.

    C. **Incorrect:** Excluded file types exclude all file types based on a specific extension. For example, you would have to exclude all .exe files, which could include malware.

    D. **Correct:** Excluded processes are the correct part of Windows Defender to specify one program to be excluded from scanning.

Objective 3.4: Thought experiment

The best and most secure way for users to connect to a corporate network for the purposes of using Remote Desktop to access their work computers is via a virtual private network. A VPN provides the security and encryption needed to ensure that the connection won't be compromised.

Users need their own Internet connection and should connect to this first. Online, they can activate the VPN connection and then Remote Desktop. They will now have a secure Remote Desktop session.

Objective 3.4: Review

1. **Correct answer:** B

   A. **Incorrect:** The Remote Desktop settings won't provide any information about the addresses of computers that you can connect to, unless these have already been manually inputted by the user or imported from a save configuration file.

   B. **Correct:** The System page in Control Panel displays the Full Computer Name, which is required to use the Remote Desktop feature with that computer.

   C. **Incorrect:** The Devices and Printers panel allows you to change settings for the computer, but it won't display its full name.

   D. **Incorrect:** You will need to know the computer name before establishing a Remote Desktop connection because this information is required to make the connection.

2. **Correct answer:** D

   A. **Incorrect:** If users search for Remote Assistance, they still have to click in the Settings results to find the options they need from a selection. This option also isn't labeled as *Remote Assistance*, which can cause confusion.

   B. **Incorrect:** If users search for Remote, the first result is Remote Desktop, which could confuse them.

   C. **Incorrect:** MSR doesn't return any search results for Windows components in Windows 8.

   D. **Correct:** MSRA is the correct term to search for because it's the name for the Remote Assistance executable.

3. **Correct answer:** D

   A. **Incorrect:** Users don't have to stay at their PC during the entire session. They can leave after they grant control of the machine.

   B. **Incorrect:** If users are correctly informed that they don't need to click through UAC prompts, they can give permission to do this to the person providing the remote help.

   C. **Incorrect:** This is always good advice in the workplace, but with Remote Assistance it wouldn't help the person providing the remote help to get the control of the computer that they need.

   D. **Correct:** You should tell users when giving control to also check the UAC permission box. This allows the person providing the remote help to click through UAC prompts herself, thus freeing up the user receiving the help to go and have that cup of coffee.

CHAPTER 4

Configure access to resources

Files and folders are probably the most important assets on your computer. Chapter 7, "Configure backup and recovery options," covers backing up and restoring files, but this chapter focuses on how to ensure that your information remains safe, secure, and accessible.

Have you ever been locked out of your home, lost your car keys, or arrived at the store after it's closed? When you lose access or "control" over something, you might experience many unwanted feelings. It can be very frustrating if you can't access one of your documents such as a media file, or the project on which you have been working. Windows resource access works in both directions: It allows you to access your resources and it can be used to prevent unauthorized access to the same resources from another user.

Ever since Windows was first released more than 20 years ago, the process of sharing has constantly evolved, making sharing easier for users to implement while at the same time ensuring that the security and integrity of the user files is maintained.

Starting with Windows Vista, Microsoft added several new features to simplify access to resources. These features have matured in Windows 8 to include libraries and HomeGroups. This chapter explores some new features, including SkyDrive and Secure Boot. You will learn the terminology of certificates, biometrics, New Technology File System (NTFS), and quotas, and how to implement best practices in sharing resources across your network.

Objectives in this chapter:

- Objective 4.1: Configure shared resources
- Objective 4.2: Configure file and folder access
- Objective 4.3: Configure local security settings
- Objective 4.4: Configure authentication and authorization

Objective 4.1: Configure shared resources

Because Chapter 3, "Configure network connectivity," covered networking, you should now understand that modern computing expectations include being able to access resources (such as a file share, a printer, or a web page) across an internal network or over an external network such as the Internet.

The Internet has become second nature to most users; it's seen as "always on" and requires little in the way of authentication, passwords, or access control. In some respects, this simplification has resulted in many users not realizing that a real threat of data theft still exists, especially if access to resources isn't configured effectively.

This objective covers the following topics:

- Configuring HomeGroup settings
- Configuring file libraries
- Configuring shared printers
- Setting up and configuring SkyDrive
- Configuring Near Field Communication (NFC)
- Configuring shared folder permissions

Configuring HomeGroup settings

HomeGroups—introduced with Windows 7—are the recommended way for home users to share their media (music, pictures, videos, and so on) and other files between computers on a home network. The reason for using a HomeGroup is because it's straightforward to use after it's set up and helps make sharing trouble-free for home users. This is a good thing: Your average home user shouldn't have to worry about NTFS file-level access control lists (ACLs) and similar technical issues. As long as the HomeGroup has been created and the PC is part of that same network, any user of the PC can access the resources being shared across the network.

This simplicity comes with some limitations. First, you can create only one HomeGroup. That HomeGroup can be created from any of the PCs on the network, and then other PCs join that HomeGroup.

To create a HomeGroup, type **HomeGroup** into the Start screen and then select the HomeGroup item on the left. As part of the process, you select which types of files are to be shared, as shown in Figure 4-1. You would reopen this window if you wanted to change the settings later.

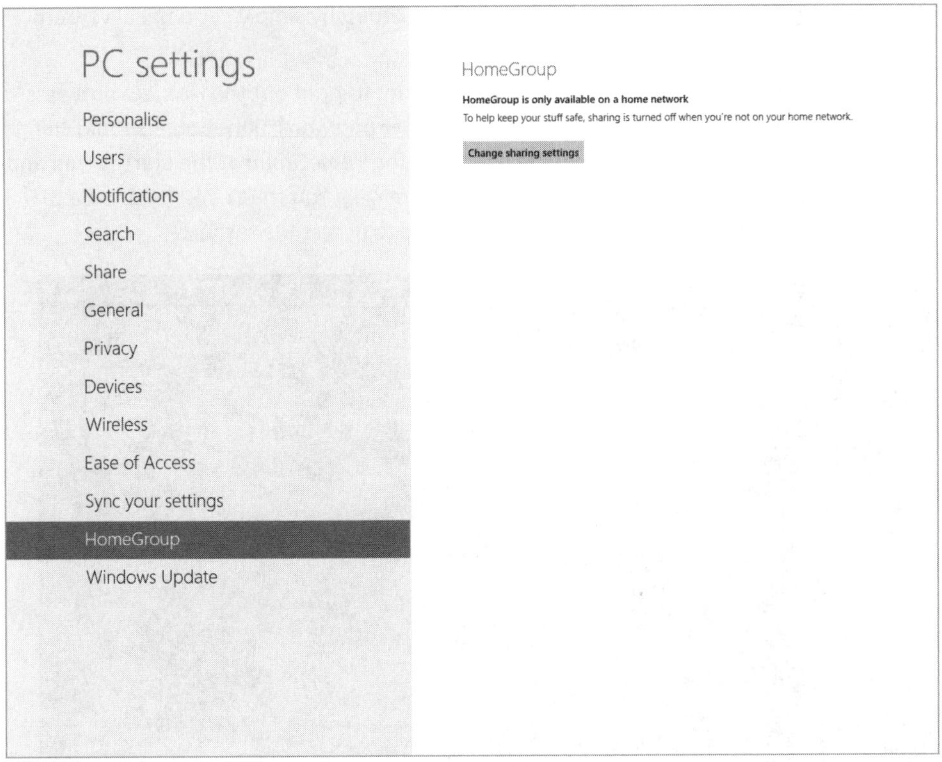

FIGURE 4-1 Accessing HomeGroup settings in the PC settings panel

> **NOTE HOMEGROUPS WORK ONLY AT HOME**
>
> If your Windows 8 device joins another network outside your home—for example, a work or public network—the HomeGroup and configuration options are unavailable until you rejoin your home network.

After creating your home network, as described in Chapter 3, and your HomeGroup, you can start to add client devices to the network. By default, when connected to the home network, Windows 8 can recognize whether a HomeGroup has been configured. No other Windows 8 computers can have access to the resources until they "join" the HomeGroup, which is achieved by entering the system-generated "membership" key—a random secure password. Although Windows 8 can detect the presence of a HomeGroup when connecting to the network, it doesn't automatically join any Windows 8 device to the HomeGroup.

> **NOTE KEEPING HOMEGROUPS SECURE**
>
> Even though you might believe your home network is safe, always securing access to your resources is a best practice. HomeGroup within Windows 8 achieves this security by ensuring that *only* devices that have been configured with the HomeGroup password can gain access.

At any point, you can have a device leave the HomeGroup by simply clicking Leave from the PC Settings HomeGroup page.

If you have many devices to configure, you might want to print out the HomeGroup password or alternatively change it to an easier-to-remember password (although it should still be secure). You can change the password by searching for *HomeGroup* at the Start screen and then selecting Change Homegroup Password (see Figure 4-2). You then need to change the password on all other devices so that they can continue to access the resources.

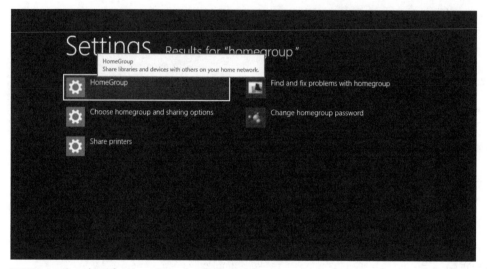

FIGURE 4-2 Searching for HomeGroup in Windows 8

Because HomeGroups were introduced prior to Windows 8, computers running Windows 7 can also join your Windows 8 HomeGroup. Even domain-joined computers can join a HomeGroup and access shared resources; however, they themselves can't host or create the HomeGroup.

> **NOTE THE HOMEGROUP TROUBLESHOOTER**
>
> If you run into difficulties and need some help, you could consider starting the wizard-based HomeGroup troubleshooter to resolve your problem. This wizard can be found by searching Settings for *HomeGroup* and then selecting the Find And Fix Problems With HomeGroup item on the right (refer to Figure 4-2). The wizard checks for the presence of an existing HomeGroup, whether IPv6 is enabled, and whether the required services (as explained in the preceding exam tip) are running.

Configuring file libraries

Introduced in an earlier Windows version, libraries are useful for organizing your documents, photos, music, and most common files. They are powerful but often underutilized and misunderstood by users.

The concept of libraries is a good one: A library—just like a real-world book library—keeps a record/index of all files "stored" in it so that they can be located, indexed, and searched very quickly by the operating system. The files "appear" in the library but continue to be stored in their original locations. The actual library folder is simply an XML file that contains metadata connecting the link to the actual file location.

Libraries are links that provide a single "folder" for the user to interface with in which they store and locate all their files.

Windows 8 gives you five default libraries:

- Documents
- Music
- Pictures
- Podcasts
- Videos

> **NOTE PODCAST LIBRARIES AND ZUNE**
>
> Podcast libraries are available in previous versions of Windows if Microsoft Zune software is installed.

You can easily create an additional library. Suppose that you want to add a new library for "website development" to store files relating to a web development project. Navigate within Windows Explorer to the Library location and right-click the Libraries icon, select New, and then select Library. Rename the default New Library label to *Website Development*, as shown in Figure 4-3. If you select the library and select the properties (right-click the library), you can even change the default library icon for your new library.

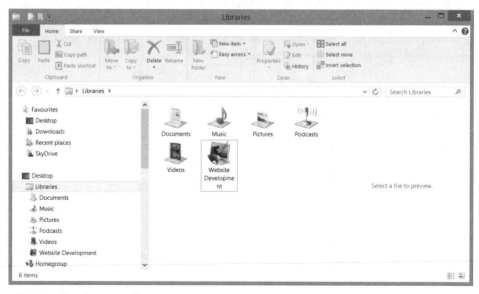

FIGURE 4-3 Creating a new library

Whether you create your own custom libraries or simply use the existing libraries, you might want to include additional folders in your libraries. Including your own folders is where the power of libraries really takes effect. For example, you might have several years' worth of family photographs and need to archive them for backup purposes. If you back up all your photos up to a shared drive or USB drive and add this to the Photos library, all these photos will be indexed and quickly searchable. You could also create a new folder and designate it to the default save location for current photos.

To add a new folder and modify the display order and default save options, follow these steps:

1. Select the Library folder.

2. Choose the Manage tab in the File Explorer ribbon (this additional menu appears as soon as you select a library folder).

3. Select Manage Library.

4. Click Add to include more folders in the library. Folders added to the library are displayed as library locations.

5. To change the default save location for the library, right-click the folder displayed in the Manage Library dialog box and select Set Default Save Location.

6. Click OK to close the Library Locations dialog box.

> **NOTE CHANGING THE DEFAULT DISPLAY ORDER**
>
> Two or more folders must be present for the option to reorder the display and to make the folder the default save location. The default save location options described here can be applied to both the default save and the default public save location.

Configuring shared printers

Despite the prediction that everyone would all have moved over to a paperless office by now, this utopia is still unrealistic in nearly all cases. With a few exceptions, such as e-book readers and e-boarding passes, many people still want to hold and read from a piece of paper.

Printer technology continues to advance, although the days of parallel ports and dot-matrix printers are now limited primarily to museums.

Only a few years ago, connecting to a printer meant connecting using a cable via a parallel or USB port. Today, printers have built-in networking support and even Wi-Fi connections. Emerging technologies such as Bluetooth and Near Field Communications (NFC) all aim to take the pain out of printing by allowing people access to shared printers from any Windows 8 device. NFC is discussed later in this objective.

Automatically sharing a printer

If HomeGroups aren't already one of your favorite features, this factoid might convince you: Any printer connected to a PC that is part of a HomeGroup is automatically shared to all other member devices of the HomeGroup.

Of course, both the "sharing" PC and the printer need to be turned on and connected to the network for you to print. If the PC or printer regularly turns itself off, you might want to review and make changes to the power setting of the PC and/or the printing device.

Manually sharing a printer

You might want to manually configure printer sharing and grant access to the printer user by user. To share an installed printer, search for *print* in the Start screen and select Devices And Printers. Locate and right-click the printer that you want to share and select Printer Properties. On the Sharing tab, select Share This Printer.

If you have multiple devices on your network, you can mix 32-bit (x86) and 64-bit (x64) processors. If this is the case and you plan to share printers between these PCs, you need to ensure that you've obtained the additional drivers for both processor types. This functionality is useful because it allows Windows to automatically install the drivers required without asking users to self-source the drivers themselves. When you have these drivers, you can optionally add them to the shared printer by clicking the Additional Drivers option on the Sharing tab.

EXAM TIP

Because this additional driver functionality hasn't changed over the last few versions of the Windows, it might not appear on the examination.

Manually connecting to a shared printer

Windows 8 can find most local network shared printers automatically and offer to connect to them for you. You can add a print device to your PC manually in several ways. One new way in Windows 8 is via the Devices section of PC Settings. Press Windows+I, select Change PC Settings, and then select Devices. The resulting screen lets you add new devices or remove an existing device. You can't change the properties or share the device from this screen.

After installing a printer, you can manually configure printer sharing and grant access to that printer user by user.

EXAM TIP

Standard users can add new printers to their PC. However, if a suitable driver isn't available—meaning, the driver must be downloaded and installed—adding the printer will require administrative privileges.

Using the Print Management console

If you want greater control over your printing environment, Windows 8 offers a single comprehensive console called *Print Management* that allows you to administer multiple printers and print servers (see Figure 4-4). Part of Administrative Tools, the Print Management console is available in Windows 8 Pro and Windows Enterprise editions.

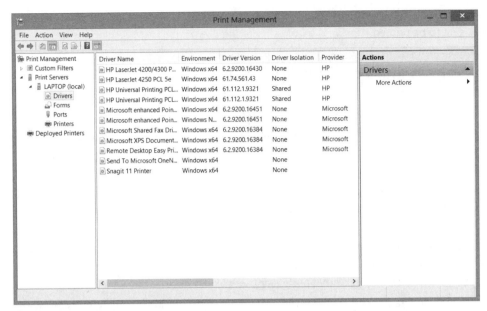

FIGURE 4-4 The Print Management console

To open the Microsoft Management Console (MMC) snap-in for Print Management, click Administrative Tools in Control Panel and then click Print Management. You also can search for *printmanagement.msc* in the Start screen. If you prefer to use the command line, you can type **Run** followed by printmanagement.msc.

In addition to allowing you to view and manage the printers, print servers, and drivers on your machine, the Print Management console allows you to view and manage the following Print Management tasks related to the Print Queue:

- View
- Pause
- Re-order
- Cancel (all print jobs or an individual job)

EXAM TIP

If you are encountering repeated crashing or failure of a printer driver, you could configure it to be used by Windows 8 in isolation from other drivers. (The default Windows 8 status for printer drivers is that they are used in shared mode.) To change the status of a printer driver, right-click it and change the Driver Isolation status.

Within the Print Management console you can configure print servers. Often, users get confused when they encounter the term "server" on a client machine. A print server is a device that connects printers to client computers across the network. Print servers take the workload from the client machine; they can act as dedicated print server machines, be an embedded part of the printer itself, or serve as a task that runs on the client PC after the print job is sent to be printed.

Setting up and configuring SkyDrive

SkyDrive offers PC users a new way of working with files. In some ways, SkyDrive offers a fundamental change on how PC users should think about file management.

Imagine a scenario in which a user has multiple devices—PC, tablet, smartphone, and an office laptop—all connected to the Internet. This isn't really imagination; this is becoming quite common.

SkyDrive provides a mature service that allows users to keep all their devices synchronized in relation to files and folders. When using SkyDrive, you can save documents into a private or public store that can then be shared with anyone you choose.

SkyDrive is Microsoft's cloud-based file management service. Having a Microsoft account is a key component to allowing this synchronization. The account provides the "glue" that associates the files and settings with a particular user's SkyDrive.

Although an Internet connection is required to host and transport the files, tools are available through which you can access the files locally from your Windows 8 PC rather than via the SkyDrive website:

- SkyDrive app for Windows 8
- SkyDrive desktop app

Both tools offer local control over your files. Any changes you make to the files are then synchronized to the SkyDrive storage in the cloud. Similarly, changes you make to the SkyDrive files are synchronized to your local computer.

SkyDrive is supported natively within Windows 8 and app developers are enabling direct access to SkyDrive so that you can access, create, and save files easily to your online SkyDrive area.

In addition to Windows 8, you can access SkyDrive in the following ways:

- Directly via the website at *http://www.skydrive.com*
- From a Windows PC running Windows Vista Service Pack 2 or newer via the Desktop app
- From a Windows PC running Windows 7 Desktop app
- From Windows Server 2008 Service Pack 2 or newer via the Desktop app
- From the Windows Phone SkyDrive app
- From the MAC OS X 10.7 (Lion) SkyDrive app
- From the iPhone SkyDrive app
- From the iPad SkyDrive app
- From an Android device using the SkyDrive app

You can download the SkyDrive desktop app at *http://windows.microsoft.com/en-gb/sky-drive/download.*

When you start the SkyDrive app for the first time, SkyDrive takes a few moments to prepare and then the app logs on with your Microsoft account. If you haven't already signed into your Microsoft account on your computer or created a Microsoft account, you're prompted to do so to using SkyDrive. You can create a new account if you don't have an existing account.

During the preparation, the SkyDrive app creates a new folder in the user profile folder (%userprofile%\SkyDrive) with subfolders that sync to the SkyDrive cloud.

You configure the SkyDrive app via the SkyDrive system tray icon. Choose Settings (see Figure 4-5) to configure these items:

- Allow SkyDrive to autostart after logon
- Allow files to be available to other SkyDrive-enabled devices
- Allow Microsoft Office 2013 to sync the files to SkyDrive automatically as a background process as you work on them
- Allow the unlinking of SkyDrive to this computer, which stops the checking, processing and synchronizing files to the device but doesn't remove any files

FIGURE 4-5 Opening SkyDrive settings

After the SkyDrive app fully synchronizes all files and folders between the local computer and SkyDrive cloud, the transfer activity stops and the system tray icon reports that SkyDrive Is Up To Date (see Figure 4-6).

FIGURE 4-6 The SkyDrive system tray icon pop-up notification

> **NOTE SYNC FILES WITH SKYDRIVE**
>
> For SkyDrive to be able to sync files and make them available to other devices, you must sign into the SkyDrive service with the same SkyDrive account that you used when the SkyDrive was created.

If you no longer want to use the SkyDrive service on your device, click the Unlink SkyDrive button, which is found on the SkyDrive Settings dialog box. This stops checking, processing, and synchronizing files to the device but doesn't remove any files. To re-enable the SkyDrive sync functionality, you must repeat the initial preparation phase as outlined previously.

Currently, SkyDrive provides users with 7 GB of cloud storage for free, but you can increase your SkyDrive capacity by purchasing more storage via annual subscription according the following table.

Annual SkyDrive paid storage options

7 GB	Add 20 GB	Add 50 GB	Add 100 GB
Free	$10*	$25*	$50*

* Prices are for illustration purposes only and were correct at time of this writing.

Configuring Near Field Communication (NFC)

Windows 8 supports Near Field Communication (NFC). However, at the time of this writing, no user-configurable options were available. Windows 8 shipped with the application pro-gramming interface (API) capability to support NFC, and as devices emerge with built-in NFC requirements, drivers and applications can take advantage of the NFC code within Windows 8.

NFC is a technique similar to radio-frequency identification (RFID), whereby a device can be used to read or perform a function based on the content of the NFC transponder. Unlike Bluetooth devices, which require a form of energy such as a battery, NFC devices require no power supply and are "awakened" when the NFC device is in close proximity to a reader.

EXAM TIP

Because no user configuration is currently available regarding NFC within Windows 8, NFC is unlikely to play a large part on the 70-687 exam, except for awareness and appreciation of the concept. Because NFC is an emerging technology, new devices will find their way onto the market. By that time, you can probably expect questions relating to NFC to ap-pear on the exam.

Configuring shared folder permissions

In the preceding sections, you saw that Windows 8 attempts to make the process for ac-cessing your files, folders, and other resources as painless as possible by using HomeGroups, libraries, and SkyDrive. However, if you have computers on your network that are running an operating system older than Windows 7, some of these options won't be available. If you require fine-tuning of the permissions on shared folders, you might prefer to eschew the "new" tools and use the built-in file and folder tools described next.

This section focuses on the folder-sharing enhancements found in Windows 8, whereas the advanced sharing section covers permissions that deliver even more granularity-file level permissions.

In this section, you will discover several different ways to share folders on the network, including the following:

- Through Network and Sharing Center
- Through File Explorer
- Through the command line
- Via the Shared Folders MMC snap-in
- Through Computer Management
- Via PowerShell version 3 cmdlets

Using the Network and Sharing Center

You should be familiar with the Network and Sharing Center from Chapter 3. This section focuses on the network sharing aspect of the Network and Sharing Center.

Because you are intending to share files and folders across your network, this section assumes that you have connected your computer to a network and have enabled File and Printer Sharing within the Network and Sharing Center. This setting allows Windows 8 to enable file and printer shared traffic through the firewall. If you have any doubt, review the "Configuring the Windows 8 Firewall" section in Objective 3.3 of Chapter 3.

To review your current network settings, open the Network and Sharing Center, using one of the following methods:

- Right-click the network icon in the taskbar notification area and then click Open Network and Sharing Center.
- Press the Windows key and then type **sharing** in the Start screen Search box.
- Open File Explorer, right-click the Network icon, and select Properties.

After opening the Network and Sharing Center, you can ensure that file and printer sharing has been turned on by selecting Change Advanced Sharing Settings to display the options as shown in the Figure 4-7.

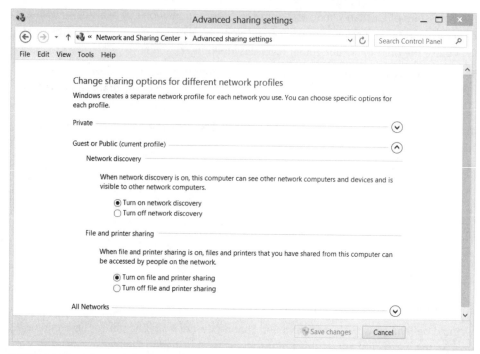

FIGURE 4-7 The Advanced sharing settings window

EXAM TIP

The Network and Sharing Center is a key tool you need to be familiar with for the examination. It provides all the required networking and sharing tools in one central location.

You might have noticed that whenever you join your Windows 8 computer to a new network, you are prompted to choose a network location that can be Private, Guest or Public, or Domain. After you make your choice, Windows sets the appropriate firewall, security, and sharing settings for the type of network you specified.

To protect your computer and your information and to reduce the likelihood of being hacked, you should choose carefully when Windows alerts you. Accidently setting a coffee shop Wi-Fi connection to the Private setting would leave your computer open to potential attack.

Each of the three options is described here in more detail:

- **Private** This setting indicates that your computer is inside a trusted private network. Don't choose this network location for public places such as coffee shops and airports. Network discovery and file and printer sharing are turned on for private networks, allowing you to see and access other computers and devices on the network, and allowing other network users to see and access your computer.

- **Guest or Public** If you don't recognize the computers on the network (for example, you are in a coffee shop or airport), this is a public network and should never be trusted. Selecting this location helps keep your computer from being visible to other computers around you, and helps to protect your computer from any malicious software from the Internet. Network discovery, and file and printer sharing, are turned off.

- **Domain** Select the location for domain networks such as those in corporate workplaces. The corporate network administrator typically controls this type of network location via Group Policy.

If you incorrectly set the wrong location for the network location, you can edit this through the Change Advanced Sharing Settings link, which you can find in the Network and Sharing Center. This link lets you enable, disable, and change the settings that influence how the network services behave.

Sharing folders via File Explorer

Windows File Explorer offers two options for sharing a folder:

- Using the Share With Wizard from the context menu or ribbon
- Through the Sharing tab on the Properties sheet

You should have noticed that the File Explorer has been treated to a ribbon makeover in Windows 8. A Share tab now appears on the top of the ribbon interface. This Share With Wizard is also available as a context menu if you right-click the folder.

If you select a folder that you want to share and then click the Share tab, you see several options to consider how to share the folder and its contents. The ribbon is context sensitive and therefore some options are unavailable for the selection made.

In the Share With section, you can share a folder with named individuals or computer users, or remove sharing completely by clicking Stop Sharing. You can also fine-tune the sharing by selecting the option to share with specific people and adding or removing user accounts there.

Alternatively, you can use the Sharing tab on the Properties sheet. To do that, right-click the folder you want to share, select Properties, and then click Share on the Sharing tab (see Figure 4-8). You can then share the folder and indicate which user accounts you want to share the folder with. By using the wizard, you can share the folder in a couple of clicks, and the share is given the same name as the actual folder.

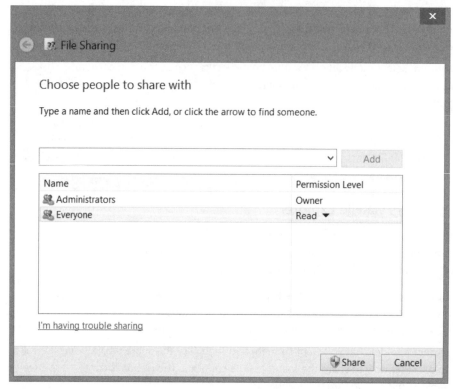

FIGURE 4-8 Changing folder sharing settings

By default, the user account sharing the folder is designated as an owner with full control. That user can give other users access to the folder; those users receive only read access unless you explicitly change the access to read/write permissions for that folder.

To encourage use of the shared folder that you have just created, at the end of the wizard, you can choose to email and/or copy the shared folder link so that you can share it with others on your network.

> **NOTE BASIC SHARING SYSTEM FOLDERS**
> You can't share system folders using basic sharing. If you try, the wizard will become the Advanced Sharing Wizard.

As you can see, basic sharing has some limitations, such as changing the share name, or fine-tuning the level of access permissions, which you can take care of by using Advanced Sharing instead.

Using Advanced Sharing

If you require more customization than basic folder sharing offers, you can use Advanced Sharing. By default, when using the File Explorer ribbon, Windows offers basic folder sharing for all the files and folders that you create. For system folders such as Program Files, Users, and Windows, basic sharing is replaced by the Advanced Sharing option visible on the File Explorer ribbon. To configure advanced sharing, select the folder you want to share, right-click and select Properties, and then click the Sharing tab. From there you can click the Advanced Sharing button (which requires elevated permissions to access).

With the Advanced Sharing settings visible, select the Share This Folder option so that you can configure the remaining options.

Unlike basic folder sharing, which uses the folder name as the share name, using the advanced configuration options enables you to create a different name (or even multiple names) for the shared folder. You also can configure share permissions for users and groups on each of these shares. By default, Advanced Sharing also sets the share name the same as the folder name. You can specify share permissions per user as Full Control, Change, or Read (see Figure 4-9).

FIGURE 4-9 Changing the Advanced Sharing settings for a folder

Figure 4-9 shows a Caching option to configure folder caching. The default behavior when sharing a folder is that all files and programs are made available offline, but you can modify this setting.

Offline files and folders are still present in Windows 8 despite the emergence of SkyDrive as a credible alternative. You can access from Control Panel an administrative console for these files and folders. Called *Sync Center*, it maintains a local cached copy of shared folders and files. By using Sync Center, you can initiate a manual synchronization, stop in-progress synchronizations, see the status of current synchronization activities, and help resolve sync conflicts.

EXAM TIPS

Because both Offline Files and the Sync Center were available in previous Windows versions, I would expect the focus of the exam to be forward looking, rather than backward.

Previous Windows versions limited the number of simultaneous users who could access the share to 10, but in Windows 8, the default limit has been raised to 20 users.

SHARING THROUGH THE COMMAND LINE

Many users still like to configure Windows via the command line. You can share a folder through the command line by using the net share command. The following example shows the syntax of a net share command that creates a simple share, using the share name that you specify, and that grants all users the read permission:

```
Net Share name=drive:path
```

Additional options when using Net Share include the following:

Option	Description
/Grant:user permission	Allows you to specify Read, Change, or Full share permissions for the specified user
/Users:number	Allows you to limit the number of users who can connect to the share
/Remark:"text"	Allows you to add a comment to the share
/Cache:option	Allows you to specify the caching options for the share
sharename /Delete	Allows you to remove an existing share

USING THE SHARED FOLDERS MMC SNAP-IN

The Computer Management tool is a collection of MMC snap-ins that includes the Shared Folders snap-in. You can open the Computer Management tool in several ways:

- Press Windows+X, and then select Computer Management.
- Open File Explorer, right-click Computer, and select Manage.
- Open Control Panel | System and Security | Administrative Tools, and then double-click the Computer Management shortcut.

Within Computer Management is the Shared Folder MMC snap-in, as shown in Figure 4-10.

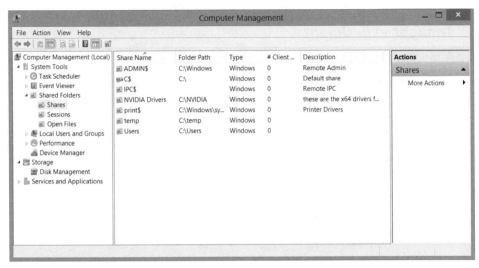

FIGURE 4-10 The Computer Management console, showing the Shared Folders MMC snap-in

EXAM TIP

The Shared Folders snap-in functionality within Computer Management hasn't changed over the last few versions of the Windows, so it might not appear on the examination.

USING POWERSHELL 3.0 CMDLETS

You've already used PowerShell cmdlets in earlier chapters of this book, so you should be relatively familiar with them. PowerShell 3.0 introduced several new cmdlets you can use to manage shares.

The new command for creating a share using PowerShell 3.0 is

```
New-SmbShare -Name ShareName -Path C:\LocalFolder
```

Additional options when using PowerShell 3.0 for managing shares include the following:

Command	Description
Get-SmbShare	Gets a list of the existing shares on the computer
Set-SmbShare	Modify an existing share
Remove-SmbShare	Removes an existing share
Get-SmbShareAccess	Retrieves the share permissions for a share
Get-Acl	Retrieves the NTFS ACL
Grant-SmbShareAccess	Used to set share permissions on a share
Set-Acl	Used to set the NTFS ACL for a specified resource

Thought experiment
A musical family

In the following thought experiment, apply what you've learned about the objective. You can find answers to these questions in the "Answers" section at the end of this chapter.

You need to configure a new home network with four family members, each of whom want to access shared files, including music, over the network. All four computers have either Windows 7 or Windows 8 installed and are currently connected via a Wi-Fi router.

Explain how you would enable sharing of the family MP3 collection with minimum configuration, yet still allow additional clients computers to join as required.

Objective summary

- The improved HomeGroups and libraries enable users to simplify the sharing of resources on home networks.

- Only Windows 7 and later computers can create HomeGroups. Users establishing this feature require little networking knowledge, although in the background it uses IPv6.

- Through its strong integration in Windows 8, SkyDrive is emerging as *the* Windows tool for synchronizing files between devices and keeping them in the cloud.

- Advanced Folder sharing is still available for those users who need to fine-tune them, whereas the new Share With Wizard offers simplification for most users.

- Printing continues to evolve and offer easier ways for users to connect and print, including Wi-Fi connections and automatic printer publishing through HomeGroups.

Objective review

Answer the following questions to test your knowledge of the information in this objective. You can find the answers to these questions and explanations of why each answer choice is correct or incorrect at the end of this chapter.

1. To install a new driver for an unsupported printer, what user account should you use?

   A. Standard user

   B. Power user

   C. Administrator

   D. Service account

   E. Built-in administrator

2. Which of the following represents the five default libraries provided by Windows 8?

A. Videos, Podcasts, My Documents, Pictures, and Music

B. Videos, Podcasts, Documents, Pictures, and Music

C. Movies, Podcasts, My Documents, Pictures, and Videos

D. Movies, Podcasts, Documents, Pictures, and Music

3. Which of the following are characteristics of the HomeGroup feature in Windows 8?

A. Printers are automatically installed.

B. No networking knowledge is required.

C. The password must be at least 10 characters in length.

D. The HomeGroup password must be changed every 90 days.

E. You must remove all shared folders before configuring HomeGroup.

4. SkyDrive users can connect to their files in the cloud through which of the following ways?

A. SkyDrive app

B. Library plug-in

C. SkyDrive desktop app

D. iPad Windows Plus app

E. Windows Phone SkyDrive app

5. Which PowerShell 3.0 command would you use configure a shared folder on your home network?

A. Net Share LocalFolder=C:\LocalFolder

B. New-SmbShare –Name ShareName –Path C:\LocalFolder

C. Grant-SmbShareAccess –Path C:\LocalFolder

D. Net Use LocalFolder=C:\LocalFolder

Objective 4.2: Configure file and folder access

Computers became far more widespread and popular when they became networked, letting people share resources with others in a workgroup. Networking allowed businesses to gain economy of scale by sharing printers and centralizing expensive resources such as backup, Internet provision, and file servers.

Chapter 3 discussed networking; this objective focuses on how to take advantage of the network not only to share files and folders, but also how to protect and secure networked resources so that only authorized access is permitted.

All the gold in the bank wouldn't be there very long if the door to the vault was left open. Similarly, if a corporation allowed unauthorized access to its Wi-Fi network, it wouldn't be long before hackers found their way in and snooped around for information from which they could profit.

Network security has been discussed in general already, and one area is related to the concept of defense in depth—having more than one layer of defenses that an intruder must break through to gain access.

One of the biggest sources of industrial espionage comes not from external hackers trying get into the network, but rather from disgruntled or inquisitive employees sniffing around inside the network. Unless the network has been set up to provide protected internal zones, an employee could potentially have full access to all the files and folders on the company servers.

Therefore, your network needs to undergo a risk assessment, and you need decide what levels of internal security must be implemented for each group of users and for each level of seniority. Thankfully, the tools and processes that this section covers are available to help prevent unauthorized access to resources.

> ***NOTE*** **PLEASE BE CAREFUL!**
>
> **Some processes in this section can seriously affect your ability to access files and folders. You could be locked out of your own files. If possible, you should carry out your practical learning in a virtualized lab environment. If that's not possible, please be careful.**

> **This objective covers the following topics:**
> - Configuring NTFS permissions
> - Encrypting files and folders by using EFS
> - Configuring disk quotas
> - Configuring object access auditing

Configuring NTFS permissions

Windows NTFS file-system and folder permissions have been at the leading edge of file access management for more than 20 years and remain a key weapon in preventing unauthorized access to resources.

Before getting started with NTFS, you need to clearly establish what you are trying to protect. Everything that can have access-based permissions set on it is referred to as an *object*. These objects are what you are seeking to protect. Some examples of objects include files, folders, printers, and registry keys.

Because NTFS isn't a new topic, this section provides only a quick review of NTFS highlighting areas that have changed in Windows 8 compared to previous versions.

To protect files and folders, Windows 8 offers both access control–based permissions and encryption. Although both offer protection, you should know which to choose and the characteristics of each. A later section covers the Encrypting File System (EFS).

In most cases, the default settings work well; Windows 8 is configured to work out of the box, and most permissions don't need modification. Only if restricting access to specific users or groups of users is required, you might need to change permissions. In a corporate environment, NTFS permissions are carefully designed and documented to carefully control and minimize the risk of data theft or unauthorized access. Another NTFS tool, object auditing, is covered later in this objective. Object auditing keeps a record of any security breaches or attempted attacks.

A common mistake when reviewing access-based permissions within Windows 8 is to forget that the first account created on the computer is an administrator. The account with administrator-level privileges is the most powerful user on your computer; anyone with access to that account often can cut straight through any permission-based restrictions in place.

> **NOTE SPLIT PERSONALITY?**
>
> Always create a standard user account to use daily. Use the administrator account only for administrative tasks and then revert back to your standard user account.

With shared folder permissions, users feel the effect of older permissions only if they access the shared resources from across the network. Therefore, if a user has local access to the server or PC, the shared folder permissions won't have any effect on that user. To address this potential limitation, Windows provides NTFS settings, which are always in effect whether the user is local or accessing resources across the network.

Working with access control lists (ACLs)

Unlike FAT32 or older file systems, NTFS maintains a special record known as an *access control list (ACL)* for each object (such as a file or folder) on the computer. The ACL documents the list of users and groups that have been assigned permissions to the object. You can envision an ACL as having a similar role to a doorman or a nightclub bouncer.

Access to an object is either allowed, denied, or not set. Be careful not to use the deny setting unless it is absolutely necessary because deny nearly always takes precedence and "trumps" an allow setting that might apply from elsewhere. I have consulted with corporations that have thousands of users and millions of files and advised that they have no deny permissions in effect. Deny permissions add a level of complexity to the authorization policy and can often create unexpected errors.

Using NTFS permissions

NTFS has two types of permissions: standard and special. During normal operations, the standard permissions are used most of the time.

STANDARD FILE AND FOLDER PERMISSIONS

The following table lists the standard NTFS file and folder permissions. You can choose whether to allow or deny each permission.

File permission	Description
Full Control	Provides complete control of the file/folder and control of permissions
Modify	Provides read and write access
Read and Execute	Enables files to be read, and programs to be started
Read	Enables read-only access
Write	Enables file content to be changed, and deletion of files.
Special permissions	Custom configuration

EXAM TIPS

Where groups or users are granted Full Control permission on a folder, they can delete any files in that folder, regardless of the permissions protecting the file.

The owner of a file or folder can modify NTFS permissions; otherwise, to make modifications you need to have the Full Control permission. Administrators can take ownership of files and folders to make modifications to NTFS permissions.

SPECIAL FILE AND FOLDER PERMISSIONS

Special permissions give you a deeper granular approach to the control of files and folders. However, special permissions are more complex to manage than standard permissions and, as a result, should be used by experienced administrators only.

Table 4-1 outlines the special permissions and a brief summary of each permission.

TABLE 4-1 Special permissions

File permission(s)	Description
Traverse Folder/Execute File	The Traverse Folder permission applies only to folders. This permission allows or denies users from moving through folders to reach other files or folders, even if a user doesn't have permissions for the traversed folders. The Execute File permission allows or denies the running of program files and must be set on files to have effect.
List Folder/Read Data	The List Folder permission allows or denies users from viewing filenames and subfolder names in the folder. The List Folder permission applies only to folders and affects only the contents of a particular folder. The Read Data permission applies only to files and allows or denies users from viewing data in files.

File permission(s)	Description
Read Attributes	This permission allows or denies users from viewing the attributes of a file or folder, such as read-only and hidden attributes. NTFS defines the attributes.
Read Extended Attributes	This permission allows or denies users from viewing the extended attributes of a file or folder. Extended attributes are defined by programs, and they can vary by program.
Create Files/Write Data	The Create Files permission applies only to folders, and allows or denies the user from creating files in the folder. The Write Data permission applies only to files and allows or denies the user from making changes to the file and over-writing existing content by NTFS.
Create Folders/Append Data	The Create Folders permission applies only to folders and allows or denies users from creating folders in the folder. The Append Data permission applies only to files and allows or denies users from making changes to the end of the file but not from changing, deleting, or overwriting existing data.
Write Attributes	This permission allows or denies users from changing the attributes of a file or folder, such as read-only or hidden. NTFS defines the attributes. The Write Attributes permission doesn't imply that you can create or delete files or folders. It includes only the permission to make changes to the attributes of a file or folder.
Write Extended Attributes	This permission allows or denies users from changing the extended attributes of a file or folder. Programs define the extended attributes, which can vary by program. The Write Extended Attributes permission doesn't imply that you can create or delete files or folders. It includes only the permission to make changes to the attributes of a file or folder.
Delete Subfolders and Files	This permission applies only to folders and allows or denies users from deleting subfolders and files, even if the Delete permission isn't granted on the subfolder or file.
Delete	This permission allows or denies users from deleting the file or folder. If you haven't been assigned Delete permission on a file or folder, you can still delete the file or folder if you are granted the Delete Subfolders and Files permission on the parent folder.
Read Permissions	This permission allows or denies users from reading permissions about the file or folder, such as Full Control, Read, and Write.
Change Permissions	This permission allows or denies users from changing permissions on the file or folder, such as Full Control, Read, and Write.
Take Ownership	This permission allows or denies users from taking ownership of the file or folder. The owner of a file or folder can change permissions on it, regardless of any existing permissions that protect the file or folder.

UNDERSTANDING NTFS PERMISSION INHERITANCE

NTFS permissions inheritance saves you a lot of time when configuring your NTFS permissions. Enabled by default, inheritance of NTFS permissions allows permissions configured on any parent object, such as a folder, to be automatically propagated to their child objects, such as subfolders. Whenever new subfolders are created at a later date, these folders also are applied with the same NTFS permissions as the parent.

You can also set additional permissions at any point in the folder structure without need-ing to modify the original permissions assigned.

NTFS permissions come in two types:

- **Explicit permissions** These set on objects when they are created or by action directly on the object.

- **Inherited permissions** These are applied to the object by virtue of permissions given to their parent object. Inherited permissions flow from parent to child objects and ease the task of managing and setting permissions on structured object hierarchies.

An explicit permission takes precedence over inherited permission and is always enforced. Even an inherited Deny permission can't prevent access to an object if the object has an ex-plicit Allow permission entry.

You can tell when permission has been inherited because the check box is selected and dimmed when you look at the ACL. An explicit permission always has the check box either selected or cleared, but not dimmed.

EXAM TIP

NTFS permissions inheritance helps administrators and home users by reducing admin-istrative overhead. Examinations often ask you to perform a specific task with the least administrative effort.

DISABLING NTFS INHERITANCE IN WINDOWS 8

Although NTFS inheritance is generally a good thing, you might want to stop inheritance from propagating, especially if you want to set new NTFS permissions on any child object manually (see Figure 4-11). When you disable inheritance for child objects, you can choose to retain the currently inherited NTFS permissions or remove them completely. You must then create your own permissions for the object.

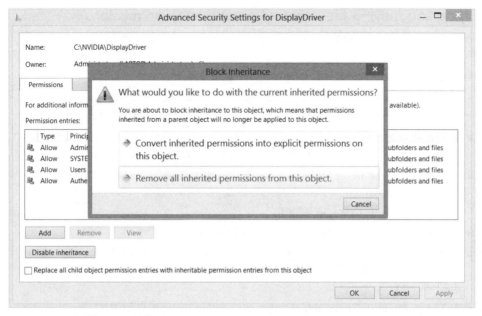

FIGURE 4-11 Disabling NTFS inheritance

To disable NTFS inheritance, follow these steps:

1. Log onto your Windows 8 computer with an administrator account and open File Explorer.

2. Select the folder on which inheritance is to be blocked.

3. Right-click the folder and from the context menu click Properties.

4. Click the Security tab and then the Advanced button.

5. In the Permissions tab of the Advanced Security Settings dialog box, click Disable Inheritance.

6. In the Block Inheritance dialog box, click Convert Inherited Permissions Into Explicit Permissions On This Object option to remove all inherited permissions while retaining the permissions on the object.

7. To allow child objects to inherit the new NTFS permissions that you are setting on this object, select the Replace All Child Object Permissions With Inheritable Permissions From This Object check box.

8. Click OK twice to save the changes.

Copying and moving files and folders with NTFS permissions

Whenever you copy or move files with NTFS permissions set, you should be aware of certain implications.

For copying files and folders, consider the following:

- When you copy a file or folder to another location on the same NTFS partition, the copied files and folders inherit the permissions of the destination folder.

- When you copy a file or folder to another location on a different NTFS partition, the copied files and folders inherit the permissions of the destination folder

- When you copy a file or folder to a non-NTFS partition—for example, a FAT32 partition—the copied files and folders lose all NTFS permissions because they aren't supported on non-NTFS partitions.

When moving files and folders, consider the following:

- When you move a file or folder to another location on the same NTFS partition, the moved files and folders retain the explicit permissions and inherits the new parent folder permissions.

- When you move a file or folder to another location on a different NTFS partition, the moved files and folders inherit the permissions of the destination folder.

- When you move a file or folder to a non-NTFS partition, for example a FAT32 partition, the moved files and folders lose all NTFS permissions, because they aren't supported on non-NTFS partitions.

> **NOTE MOVING REQUIRES MODIFY AND WRITE PERMISSIONS**
>
> When you move a file or folder within an NTFS partition or across NTFS partitions, you must have the Write permission for the destination and the Modify permission on the source location because Windows 8 deletes the original after moving it to the new destination.

Using Effective Permissions

When files and folders have multiple permissions set on them—perhaps because a user has membership of several groups—Windows 8 needs to calculate the effective (that is, resulting) permissions for that user. Windows determines the effective permissions based on the following criteria:

- User and Group permissions are combined.

- Deny permissions override allow permissions.

For example, if a user named *John* is assigned Read permission but is also a member of the Sales Team group, which has Modify permission, John will have the effective permissions of Modify.

For more complicated scenarios, Windows 8 provides the Effective Permissions feature, which determines the permissions that a user or group has set on an object. This feature allows you to modify the focus of the tool so that it can evaluate other users and groups and not solely the logged-on user.

> **NOTE REVIEWING YOUR PERMISSIONS**
>
> This feature is particularly useful to verify that you have set NTFS permissions correctly.

To view Effective Permissions, navigate to the Advanced Security Settings For <folder> dialog box, which you can locate by clicking the Advanced button on a folder's Security tab on the Properties sheet.

Understanding self-healing NTFS

Since Windows Vista, NTFS has been able to monitor and self-heal itself, thereby detecting and repairing file system corruption while the operating system is still running. In most cases, this takes place without informing users. Despite this self-healing happening in the background, the user should benefit from an improved reliability with Windows 8.

If Windows 8 detects corrupted metadata on the file system, it tries to self-heal and invokes ChkDsk to rebuild the metadata. Previously, ChkDsk could be run only at Startup; however, in Windows 8 some problems can be fixed while the system drive is still online.

Although some data can still be lost, Windows marks the area of the disk as "dirty" until it can run a full repair, using ChkDsk at the next startup. This prevents other data being written to the bad areas, thus preventing further data loss.

Self-healing NTFS is enabled by default and requires no user interaction.

To see the ChkDsk results of an automatic scan, look in the following Windows event log: Event Viewer\Windows Logs\Application.

To start Chkdsk, click Find on the Action menu and search for *chkdsk*.

> **MORE INFO WHEN NTFS GOES WRONG**
>
> If you have been experimenting with NTFS and end up getting frustrated and locked out of folders on your drives due to NTFS permissions, all is not lost. You can use the command line to instruct Windows 8 to reset all NTFS permissions for all objects and restore them back to their default settings. Open an elevated command prompt, navigate to the drive or folder which is giving you the headache, and then type the following commands:
>
> ```
> icacls * /RESET /T /C /Q
> ```
>
> ```
> Syntax: ICACLS name /reset [/T] [/C] [/L] [/Q]
> ```
>
> This replaces ACLs with default inherited ACLs for all matching files. This could take a few minutes, but it could save you from having to reinstall the operating system.

Using EFS to encrypt files and folders

NTFS permissions go a long way to prevent unauthorized access to files and folders on our systems. However, if a hacker really wanted to access the files, he could by starting the computer from a non-Windows operating system. Of course, this means that he must have physical access to the system to do this.

Encryption has been used for decades and still provides an excellent way to prevent unauthorized access to information. During World War II, much secrecy surrounded the messages sent over the radio waves between high command and their troops in the field. Only when the Allies captured a working encryption/decryption device (known as the *Enigma machine*) was there any real progress in breaking the encryption codes being used at that time.

> **MORE INFO** **A QUICK HISTORY LESSON ON ENCRYPTION**
>
> For more information about the Enigma machine and code breaking during World War II, visit *http://www.bletchleypark.org.uk/edu/archives/machines.rhtm*.

A huge amount of progress has been made since the first encryption mechanisms were invented, and today the Encrypting File System (EFS) built into the Windows 8 Pro and Enterprise versions is extremely secure and can be trusted to protect the contents of your files.

EFS works by using a unique key to encrypt files. Only with this key can the operating system decrypt the files and allow you to read them in their unscrambled form. A user who doesn't have the key receives an Access Denied message in response to any attempt to open, copy, move, or rename the encrypted file or folder.

> **NOTE** **THE WEAKEST LINK**
>
> When you log onto Windows 8, EFS is still enforced, but each file is automatically decrypted as you access them. The weakest part of EFS is your logon username/password.

Safeguarding the EFS key that's created when you encrypt your first file should prevent any unauthorized access to your files. Moreover, users should be fully aware that the decision to use EFS should be taken seriously. What follows are real-world examples of how users have lost access to every EFS protected file:

- Don't store the EFS key (which is stored in a certificate) on the PC on which it's used. Back it up to a separate, secure location.

- On re-installation of Windows, a user realized that all his EFS files were still encrypted, but the decrypt key was on the old system.

- If EFS protection is no longer required, decrypt the files.

- Deleting your user account causes you to lose your access to the EFS-protected files until you grant your "new" user account access with the EFS key.

- A user forgot his password and asked an administrator to reset it for him. This caused the EFS files to be unreadable until the EFS key was assigned to the user account.

EFS supports industry-standard encryption algorithms, including Advanced Encryption Standard (AES). AES uses a 256-bit symmetric encryption key and is the default EFS algorithm.

Because you are guaranteed 100 percent that the security of EFS won't be cracked in your lifetime, if you use EFS, you must make a backup of the key. Windows offers some help here: After you encrypt a file the first time, Windows 8 prompts you to back up your EFS key to removable storage. You should store the EFS key in more than one secure location, and clearly label it.

Deciding between BitLocker and EFS

EFS was introduced with Windows 2000 Professional, and many of you might believe that because BitLocker is newer, it must therefore be a better choice for securing your computer. Fundamentally, the two tools are different: EFS encrypts non-system volumes, or just the files and folders that you require encrypting, whereas BitLocker offers whole-disk encryption. The current version of EFS still offers enterprise-class encryption for files and folders.

EXAM TIP

EFS can't be used to encrypt system files. If you are asked to encrypt the system drive, this can be done only with BitLocker.

Chapter 5, "Configure remote access and mobility," covers BitLocker (and BitLocker To Go) in more detail.

Encrypting a file or folder with EFS

To encrypt a file or folder, right-click it in File Explorer and then choose Properties. On the General tab, click the Advanced button to display the Advanced Attributes. Here, you can select the Encrypt Contents To Secure Data option, and then click OK twice to encrypt both subfolders and files (see Figure 4-12).

FIGURE 4-12 Encrypting the contents of a folder

 EXAM TIP

The file system must be NTFS for EFS to encrypt files. If you don't see the option to encrypt your file, check the Windows version and whether the file system is NTFS.

During the process of using EFS for the first time, Windows 8 generates a self-signed certificate with an encryption key and assigns it to the logged-on user account. Windows prompts you to make a backup of the EFS key (a best practice), offering the following choices:

- Backup now (recommended)
- Back up later
- Never back up

Previous Windows versions were more subtle, and users could miss the notification tray reminder.

You can test that you have successfully encrypted a file in a number of ways:

- The color of the file in File Explorer changes to green.
- In the Advanced Attributes dialog box, the Encrypt Contents To Secure Data option is selected.

- If an unauthorized user tries to open the file, the operation fails.

Recovering your EFS-encrypted files

If you followed the prompt to back up your EFS key and now need to recover your EFS-protected files (for example if you have a new PC or are using a different computer), follow the steps:

1. Search for *certmgr.msc* on the Start screen and select Certmgr.
2. Select the Personal folder.
3. On the Action menu, click All Tasks and then click Import. The Certificate Import Wizard should appear.
4. Click Next.
5. On the File To Import page, click Browse.
6. Locate your EFS certificate backup, click Open, and then click Next.
7. On the Private Key Protection page, type the password you used to protect the certificate, and select the check box to Mark This Key As Exportable.
8. Click Next.
9. Click Next on the Certificate Store page, and then click Finish.

The import is complete, and you should now be able to access and open your EFS protected files.

> **NOTE USING EFS AT WORK**
> In corporate environments, either EFS is often disabled, or the network administrator enforces the backup of EFS recovery keys to a safe location.

Configuring disk quotas

Disk quotas are a useful tool to monitor and control how much of a disk volume a single user can fill with files. This is typically performed in client/server environments; however, Windows Server 2012 has advanced monitoring tools that outperforms disk quotas.

For the home network, disk quotas are still useful to implement when multiple users store their data in the following locations:

- Single shared computer
- A single volume
- A storage pool

Using disk quotas for a storage pool would help prevent a single user from completely filling a volume, thereby preventing other users from saving files.

By default, disk quotas are disabled. When enabled, the system tracks all file and folder generation and ownership.

EXAM TIP

The administrator account is exempt from any warnings or disk space limits.

To configure disk quotas on a single computer, follow these steps:

1. Press Windows+X and open Disk Management.

2. Right-click the drive on which you want to enable disk quotas and then click Properties.

3. Click the Quota tab.

4. Select the Enable Quota Management check box.

The following options are available when you have enabled quota management:

- Deny Disk Space To Users Exceeding Quota Limit
- Do Not Limit Disk Usage
- Limit Disk Space To
- Set Warning Level To
- Log Event When A User Exceeds Their Quota Limit
- Log Event When A User Exceeds Their Warning Level

By selecting the Quota Entries button, you can review the current quota usage level for all users.

Disk quotas, originally introduced in Windows 2000, are difficult to manage and use in any real practical environment. Although Microsoft hasn't deprecated disk quotas, the company has stated that the reduction of prices and increased capacities of hard drives since the introduction of this feature renders the tool outdated.

Configuring object access auditing

Auditing is the process of checking to see whether a task or event has occurred. Windows 8 has implemented some enhancements to assist you with monitoring, troubleshooting, and enforcing security compliance in a network. You can find most of this reporting within the Windows Event logs—a useful source of information, especially when troubleshooting a problem.

Object access auditing in Windows 8 is concerned with whether a user has accessed or tried to access some type of object. As mentioned previously, an object can be a file, folder, printer, registry key, or other resource on the computer. If you've configured your system with shared folders, NTFS, and maybe even EFS, you should be well protected from unauthorized access.

However, consider a scenario in which, in preparation for your summer vacation, you lock all the doors and windows and then leave for your trip. Assuming that when you came back nothing was broken and all the doors and windows were still locked, how could you be certain that no one had been into your home, or how many times someone had tried to turn to door handle on the back door? You couldn't be sure, unless you had installed CCTV, set your alarm, or asked a friend or family member to house sit for you. The point is, you can always do more to ensure that you are secure.

With object access auditing, you keep an eye on the security from the inside to make sure that it is doing its job. It can also alert you to failed attempts, such as when someone tried to gain access to that file marked *For CEO eyes only*. Configuring auditing on a limited set of resources is far more appropriate, as is configuring alerts to inform you when those defenses have been breached or tested.

One key goal of security audits is to verify regulatory compliance. Increasingly, security breaches are often in the spotlight. New regulatory compliance measures and industry standards are now in force and require enterprises to follow a strict set of rules related to data security.

> **REAL WORLD AUDITING CAN PAY DIVIDENDS**
>
> Think about which resources in your computer system you would want or need to audit. I recall several years ago enabling an Object Access audit policy to monitor a particular high-cost, large format color laser printer. The office worked around the clock, and we couldn't account for the high running costs of the color printers, especially when our daytime usage was quite low. After setting up the auditing on the printer, we soon found the culprit: One employee had been printing off his favorite pop idols onto large posters during his evening shift.

Enabling object access auditing

Auditing is a two stage process: First we must enable object access, and then we need to point the auditing at an object, such as a folder or file(s). Follow these steps:

1. Log on with an administrator account (policies can be configured only with administrator privileges).

2. Search for *gpedit.msc* on the Start screen.

3. Navigate to the Computer Configuration | Windows Settings | Security Settings.

4. Expand Local Policies and click Audit Policy.

5. In the right pane, double-click Audit Object Access (see Figure 4-13) and then select the Success and Failure check boxes.

6. Click OK and close the Local Group Policy Editor snap-in.

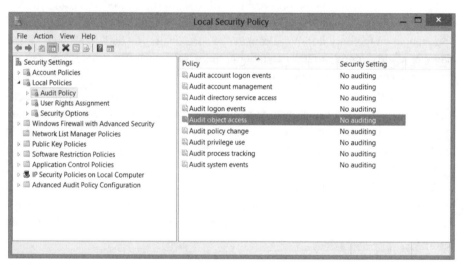

FIGURE 4-13 The Local Group Policy Editor snap-in

After you experience auditing, you might want to change the scope of the logging to focus just on successful or failed attempts. For the purpose of this demonstration, you configured both success and failure object access in the preceding steps.

Now that auditing is enabled, you need to specify which objects (files or folders) should be audited. Choose a file or folder of your choice to review the logs as soon as you access them.

Enabling object access auditing on a folder

After you enable the auditing within group policy, you can implement the second stage—to select specific objects and define the types of access you want to monitor with auditing. You can make these selections in the object's audit settings:

1. Open File Explorer and navigate to the folder that contains the files that you want have audited.

2. Right-click the folder, select Properties, and then select the Security tab.

3. Click the Advanced button to open the Advanced Security Settings dialog box.

4. On the Auditing tab, click Continue and allow User Account Control (UAC) to process the request, if required.

5. Click Add.

6. Click Select A Principal and type the name of the user or group you want to monitor.

7. Modify the object's Type, Applies To, and Basic Permissions settings, if required, and then click OK. Auditing is now enabled for the selected folder and user.

> *NOTE* **FINDING AUDIT ENTRIES**
> Audit entries are written to the Security Event log, which you can view in the Event Viewer. The Event Viewer is discussed in detail in the next section.

EXAM TIP

Windows 8 now provides audit capability for organizations to track the use of removable storage devices. If you enable the new Audit Removable Storage policy, an event is generated each time a user attempts to access a removable storage device. Success audits (Event 4663) record successful attempts to write to or read from a removable storage device. More importantly, this event log records the filenames being copied to the removable drive.

This audit policy appears under Computer Configuration\Windows Settings\Security Settings\Advanced Audit Policy Configuration\System Audit Policies\Object Access.

Viewing audit log entries in Event Viewer

Auditing can add an important component to the overall security of your system. It allows you to proactively monitor that your security intentions are working and that hackers or nosy employees aren't gaining access to your resources.

One of the most useful troubleshooting and reporting tools in Windows is the Event Viewer. This MMC snap-in underwent some significant improvements in Windows 7 that you can take advantage of in Windows 8. Whether you are looking for audited events taking place or working on specific problem solving, you should first check the Event Viewer to see any errors or warnings that might help reveal what the problem is.

You can open Event Viewer in a number of ways:

- In Control Panel, select Administrative Tools, and then open Event Viewer.

- In Computer Management (Windows+X), select System Tools, and then open Event Viewer.

- Search for *Event* on the Start screen and select View Event Logs.

- Type **eventvwr.exe** or **eventvwr.msc** at an elevated command prompt.

Previously, you saw how to enable auditing on a folder. To view the Event Viewer and look for the entries made by Windows relating to the audited activity, follow these steps:

1. To open the Event Viewer, search for *Event* into the Start screen and select View Event Logs.

2. Navigate to the Windows Logs and then Security Logs. You should see Audit Success log events in the Event Viewer.

3. Minimize the Event Viewer and open File Explorer.

4. Navigate to the folder on which you have configured auditing, double-click it, and then open one of the files within the folder.

5. Return to the Event Viewer and refresh the Security Log screen. The top most events logged should have recorded object access activity based on the recent file opening.

6. Review the event log properties to locate the Object Name and confirm that this is the object that you are auditing (see Figure 4-14).

> *NOTE* **TRY THIS EXPERIMENT**
>
> Navigate to the audited file or folder resource in File Explorer and then open, modify, and save the resource. Then return to the Event Viewer and see how many new security log entries were generated as a result of your File Explorer actions.

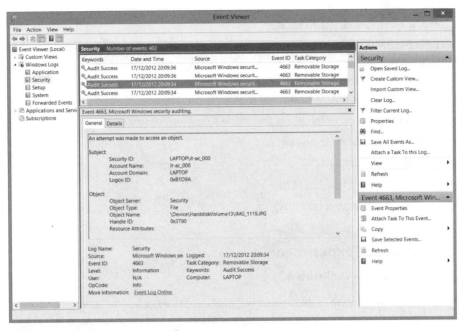

FIGURE 4-14 The Windows 8 Event Viewer

> **NOTE AUDITING SPRAWL**
>
> If you apply auditing too liberally—for example, you set the auditing on every file within a folder rather than on the key file that needs to be monitored—you might find that the system generates thousands of audit entries whenever the file location is accessed. To use auditing effectively, you should target a specific risk and then fine-tune the only file actions, such as read or modify, that need to be monitored.

Attaching an action to an event occurrence is a simple task in the new Event View. You might want to fine-tune what is being audited so that you're not inundated with email message alerts, but hopefully by the time you have received the first email, you will be out the door trying to apprehend the culprit anyway. Follow these steps to attach an action to an event occurrence:

1. Right-click the Event Log entry and select Attach Task To This Event.

2. The Create a Basic Task Wizard opens. Follow the wizard pages to create the desired action, such as to send an email alert.

3. After you set your "trap," test it. Create a temporary user account and then try to access the audited file.

Event Viewer can open saved event logs for archiving, analysis, and incident reporting. You can save an event log using any of the following formats:

- Event log (.evtx) file (the default)
- XML (.xml) file
- Tab-delimited text (.txt) file
- Comma-separated text (.csv) file

 Thought experiment

Operation lockdown

In the following thought experiment, apply what you've learned about the objective. You can find answers to these questions in the "Answers" section at the end of this chapter.

You need to set up an audit system to ensure that your company's credit card details are safe. The company collects credit card data from customers who place orders online. Only members of the finance management team should have access to the details, and all access must be monitored. The data is downloaded from the web server every hour and stored on a computer running Windows 8.

Explain the key tools and processes that you should implement to comply with the requirements.

Objective summary

- Always in force, NTFS remains the primary access control mechanism for files and folders in Windows 8.
- Shared Folders permissions are effective only when accessed across the network.
- NTFS inheritance is enabled by default and can ease the task of managing and setting permissions.
- The EFS recovery key should be stored separately from the computer.
- Object access auditing provides you with a powerful tool to monitor and report breaches of object-based security.
- New audit policies in Windows 8 allow monitoring of file activity to removable devices.

- Event Viewer provides enhanced reporting and can trigger action-based notifications in response to alerts.

Objective review

Answer the following questions to test your knowledge of the information in this objective. You can find the answers to these questions and explanations of why each answer choice is correct or incorrect at the end of this chapter.

1. Which of the following are examples of objects?

   A. File

   B. Partition

   C. Folder

   D. Registry key

2. When you combine various Allow and Deny permissions, which of the following NTFS access-based permissions takes precedence?

   A. Inherited Deny

   B. Inherited Allow

   C. Explicit Deny

   D. Explicit Allow

3. When you move a folder configured with NTFS permissions from one disk to another disk partition that's configured with NTFS, what happens to the original NTFS permissions?

   A. The copied files and folder retain the explicit permissions and also inherit the new parent folder permissions.

   B. The moved files and folder inherit the permissions of the destination folder.

   C. All permissions are retained.

   D. The moved files and folder lose all the NTFS permissions.

4. How can you test that you have successfully encrypted a file?

   A. You can't open the file.

   B. The file color is green in File Explorer.

   C. The Encrypt Contents To Secure Data check box is selected.

   D. You can open the file.

5. Security auditing of files can help identify what types of activity on your computer?

    A. Deletion of files

    B. Unauthorized file access

    C. When files are renamed

    D. Files deleted from an ExFAT USB drive

Objective 4.3: Configure local security settings

Security is a big deal. Everyone wants freedom but at the same time wants to feel secure and know that what is theirs remains safe. Computer security is no different—nobody wants their PC hacked or their credit card details stolen. Over the years, we have come to rely so much on our computers that we need to keep abreast of the emerging trends in computer security so that we don't become complacent.

Thankfully, new security considerations are built into Windows 8 that most users are unaware of, such as Secure Boot to help reduce rootkit attacks and built-in but dormant functionality. You need to wait for the original equipment manufacturers (OEMs) and in-dependent software vendors (ISVs) to release hardware and software to take advantage of emerging technology. For example, Near Field Communication (NFC) for Windows 8 is ready, as explained previously in this chapter, but very few applications of NFC are available as of this writing.

Releasing a new operating system that addresses today's security concerns is difficult, but building an operating system that can mature with age and adapt to the changing security landscape is quite an achievement.

Chapter 3 showed how the Local Security Policy (secpol.msc) has been extended to include new policy settings for auditing usage of removable drives. In earlier chapters you read that you aren't restricted to logging on with a password, but with Windows 8 we can also log on by using a PIN or a picture password.

> **This objective covers the following topics:**
> - Configuring Secure Boot
> - Configuring SmartScreen Filter
> - Configuring Local Security Policy
> - Configuring User Account Control (UAC) behavior

Configuring Secure Boot

The prevalence of *malware* (a broad term that encompasses viruses, worms, Trojan horses, and rootkits, as well as spyware and other potentially unwanted software) has soared, and so has the cost to the PC user and corporate helpline in having to resolve these infections. One of the biggest computer threats in the last five years has been the emergence of malware known as *rootkits*—clever pieces of software that manage to get loaded before the operating system and sits "underneath" Windows, which is then completely unaware of its existence.

Windows Vista offered new features that would prevent software from writing to areas of the computer in which could be used to hide rootkit code. The next chapter shows that BitLocker, introduced in Windows 7, helps protect system integrity by ensuring that critical Windows startup files are checked to see whether they've been modified (which might occur if a rootkit or other malware has infected the system).

Combining UEFI and Secure Boot

With the introduction of Windows 8, Microsoft is trying to regain the initiative, at least regarding rootkits. By adopting and embracing Unified Extensible Firmware Interface (UEFI)—the new international standards–based replacement for PC BIOS—Microsoft is implementing a feature that seeks to prevent possible rootkits loading during the startup process. This feature is known as *Secure Boot*.

At present, UEFI is still emerging, and only recently manufactured motherboards feature the new bootstrap standard. The vast majority of PCs still use traditional PC BIOS, whether or not they have Windows 8 installed. Microsoft through its Windows 8 Logo program can force OEMs to enable Secure Boot on all new Windows 8 devices.

> *NOTE* **DIY SECURE BOOT**
>
> DIY and hobbyist PC builders can buy UEFI-based motherboards and implement Secure Boot themselves. To support Secure Boot, the BIOS must be UEFI compliant and be able to be flashed to support the Windows 8 Secure Boot extensions and embedded Microsoft certificates.

Windows 8 PCs ship with Microsoft's certificate registered in UEFI, and this is verified each time as the boot loader starts to ensure that both the boot loader and certificate are digitally signed by Microsoft. If a rootkit or another malware program manages to replace your boot loader, because the rogue software won't pass the integrity check, UEFI prevents it from booting. This prevents malware from taking over your boot process and hiding itself from Windows 8. If tampered code is detected during the startup, Windows attempts an automatic repair of the startup process.

Secure boot requires that your disk be configured in GUID Partition Table (GPT) mode and not the legacy Master Boot Record (MBR). The conversion process is painless; the Windows 8 installer provisions both the GPT disk and creates the four custom partitions on the disk required for Secure Boot (see Figure 4-15).

Where do you want to install Windows?

Name	Total size	Free space	Type
Drive 0 Partition 1: Recovery	300.0 MB	79.0 MB	Recovery
Drive 0 Partition 2	100.0 MB	71.0 MB	System
Drive 0 Partition 3	128.0 MB	128.0 MB	MSR (Reserved)
Drive 0 Partition 4	97.6 GB	83.3 GB	Primary
Drive 0 Unallocated Space	134.8 GB	134.8 GB	

Refresh   Drive options (advanced)
Load driver

FIGURE 4-15 Installing Windows 8 in GPT mode

Windows 8 PowerShell 3.0 provides a new cmdlet to confirm that Secure Boot is functioning properly. After you configure Secure Boot and install Windows 8, type the following at an elevated PowerShell command prompt:

```
confirm-SecureBootUEFI
```

If Secure Boot has been enabled and is functioning properly, the cmdlet should return a value of True, as shown in Figure 4-16.

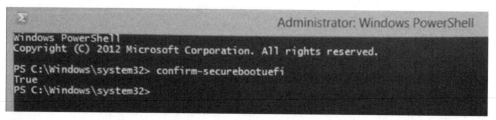

FIGURE 4-16 Using PowerShell to check Secure Boot

Disabling Secure Boot

Currently, with x86 (Intel) based Windows 8 PCs and tablets you can enter the UEFI and control Secure Boot. If you decide to disable Secure Boot entirely, you need to reconfigure your hard disk and reinstall Windows 8. Secure Boot prevents "unauthorized" operating systems from loading during the startup process; if you wanted to install an operating system other than Windows 8 (such as Linux), you need to disable Secure Boot first.

EXAM TIP

If you install Windows 8 to a PC BIOS and then upgrade your motherboard to allow UEFI, you can't convert Windows 8 over to use UEFI without reinstalling the operating system.

Understanding x86 and ARM

Although x86 (Intel) Windows PCs and tablets are still available, you can choose whether to allow Secure Boot to protect your system. However, with the release of ARM-based machines running Windows RT, users can't modify or even enter the UEFI configuration. For these devices and future ARM-based Windows laptops, ultrabooks, and desktops, you can't modify the boot loader—it will be locked. Microsoft has stated that every ARM device with Windows RT installed won't allow you to disable Secure Boot. This is, of course, safe for the user, but highly frustrating for the hacker, hobbyist, and rootkit author.

EXAM TIP

Systems certified for Windows 8 must allow Secure Boot to start in a custom mode, or Secure Boot must be disabled. However, UEFI Secure Boot can't be disabled in Windows 8 RT edition.

Configuring SmartScreen filter

SmartScreen is a feature, taken from Internet Explorer 8 and 9, that has been integrated into Windows 8. SmartScreen is a security enhancement that actively watches for unknown apps and malicious websites trying to start and stops them from running, thereby protecting the operating system and user. The user is given the warning shown in Figure 4-17 if Windows believes the app to be malicious.

FIGURE 4-17 The Windows SmartScreen in action

Depending on the user awareness of the application, if the user clicks OK, the app or website won't start. To enable the app to start, the user must click More Info and then click the option to allow the app to run. As is to be expected with this type of tool, it occasionally might prevent a legitimate application from running.

To keep itself up to date and to learn of new threats, SmartScreen routinely connects to Microsoft and reports app startup behavioral information back to Microsoft.

Although the tool is enabled by default, it can be modified or even disabled by searching for *Smart* on the Start screen and selecting Change SmartScreen Settings. Then choose a setting from the options shown in Figure 4-18.

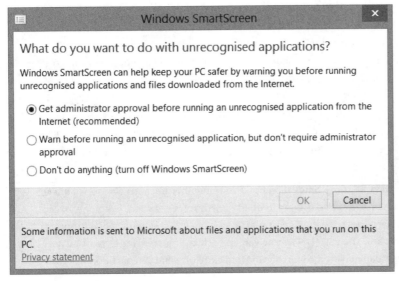

FIGURE 4-18 Administering Windows SmartScreen

The following options are available:

- Get Administrator Approval Before Running An Unrecognized Application From The Internet (Recommended) (default)
- Warn Before Running An Unrecognized Application, But Don't Require Administrator Approval
- Don't Do Anything (Turn Off Windows SmartScreen)

Configuring User Account Control (UAC) behavior

Would considering any negatives about Windows XP be considered useful, or would that be seen as poor form? Its Internet browser was pretty poor, it needed a lot more RAM than before, its roaming profiles would keep getting corrupted, and you had to log off from your standard user account and then back on again with an administrator account if you wanted to install software (because RUNAS wasn't ideal for installing).

A few years ago, as a replacement to Windows XP, Microsoft introduced Windows Vista, and with it came User Account Control (UAC). Most users complained very loudly about both and although Vista has been replaced, UAC has persisted. The key purpose for UAC is to make protecting their computers from malicious attacks easy for average users.

Understanding how UAC works

Whether or not you log onto Windows 8 as a standard user or through an administrator account, the system allows you to run applications in the security context of a standard user. It's estimated that 95 percent of all computer tasks are designed to run under a standard user. If you try to start a program that could cause harm or affect other users on the computer (such as install a program, change the time, or open an elevated command prompt), the system knows that it must run the task by using a full administrative access token. To run with administrative access, the system offers you one of two prompts:

- If you are logged on as a standard user, it prompts you for administrative credentials. This way, a standard user can easily perform an administrative task by entering valid credentials for a local administrator account.

- If you are logged on as a user who's a member of the Administrators group, you are presented with a consent prompt, asking you for approval. This process is referred to as *Admin Approval Mode*.

As soon as the system has administrative "permission," it continues with the task. If approval isn't received, the task is discarded and no changes are made.

In Figure 4-19 you can see an example of the UAC credential prompt.

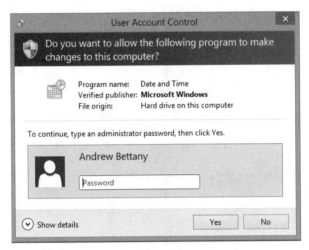

FIGURE 4-19 A UAC credential prompt

Figure 4-20 shows an example of the UAC consent prompt.

FIGURE 4-20 A UAC consent prompt

Both prompts require you to provide an explicit action—either a password or an acknowledgement for the task to be carried out. UAC doesn't work passively; you can't simply ignore UAC and expect Windows or the applications to make the actions for you.

UAC SHIELD

Some built-in Control Panel applications, such as Date and Time, contain a combination of administrative and standard user operations. Standard users can view the clock and change the time zone, but only administrators can change the local system time. The shield icon on the Change Date And Time button (see Figure 4-21) indicates that the process requires administrative permission and will display a UAC elevation prompt.

FIGURE 4-21 Adjusting the date and time

UAC ELEVATION PROMPTS

UAC elevation prompts are color coded—to help users differentiate the meaning of each—and relate to the application they are attempting to start. Applications are separated into three categories based on the status of the executable file's publisher:

- Windows 8 (Microsoft)
- Publisher is verified (signed)
- Publisher not verified (unsigned)

The UAC elevation prompt color coding is as follows:

- **Red background with a red shield icon** The application is blocked by Group Policy or is from a blocked publisher.

- **Blue background with a blue and gold shield icon** The application is a Windows 8 administrative application, such as a Control Panel item.

- **Blue background with a blue shield icon** The application is signed by using Authenticode and is trusted by the local computer.

- **Yellow background with a yellow shield icon** The application is unsigned, or signed but not yet trusted by the local computer.

UAC SECURE DESKTOP FEATURE

The elevation process is further secured by forcing the elevation prompt to display the secure desktop. This feature switches the user desktop to the secure desktop, which is a dimmed version of the user desktop displaying an elevation prompt that you must respond to before continuing. When you click Yes or No, the desktop switches back to the user desktop.

The consent and credential prompts are displayed on the secure desktop by default in Windows 8.

> **NOTE PROTECTING SECURE DESKTOP**
>
> By design, only Windows 8 processes can access the secure desktop. This prevents malware from invoking or disabling the UAC prompt.

Malware can try to imitate the look of the secure desktop, but even if you click prompts on the malware-imitated secure desktop screen, the system won't have granted the required elevation and therefore the malware won't benefit.

IMPROVEMENTS TO UAC IN WINDOWS 8

UAC has been available now for several years, and Microsoft has listened to feedback. One main complaint about UAC has been that the process was too "noisy"—that Windows prompted users too many times, which actually lessened the security because users would begin to ignore the messages and elevate the requests regardless.

Windows 8 UAC has been made less "noisy." Also, you can now configure the notification level and even set UAC to never notify, effectively disabling the prompts (see Figure 4-22). To review and, if necessary, change the UAC notification level, search for *UAC* on the Start screen and then open Change User Account Control Settings.

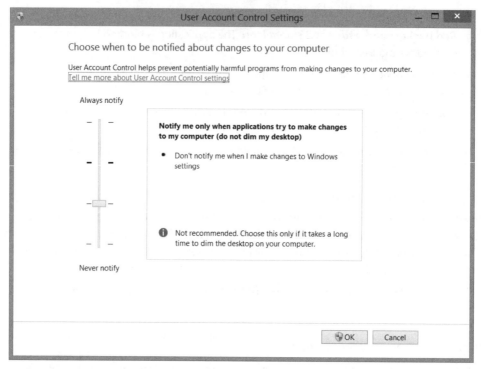

FIGURE 4-22 The UAC control slider

You can see from Figure 4-22 that UAC now has four levels of notification to choose from, and a slider to use to select the notification level. These levels are explained as follows:

- **High** If the slider is set to Always Notify, the system checks whether the secure desktop is enabled and notifies the user when the following occurs:
    - Applications try to install software or make changes to the user computer
    - The user makes changes to the Windows settings
- **Medium (default)** If the slider is set to Medium, the system notifies the user only when applications try to make changes to the computer. It doesn't notify the user when the user makes change to Windows settings.
- **Low** If the slider is set to Low, the system will do the following:
    - Notify the user only when programs try to make changes to the computer; it doesn't dim the desktop
    - Don't notify the user when the user makes changes to Windows settings
- **Never Notify** If the slider is set to Never Notify, the system never notifies the user when the following occurs:
    - Applications try to install software or make changes to the computer
    - The user makes changes to Windows settings

The notification slider might give you the impression that UAC becomes disabled if Never Notify is selected. However, anyone modifying the slider position can never turn UAC completely off. With the slider set to Never Notify, Windows does the following:

- Keeps the UAC service running
- Causes all elevation requests initiated by administrators to be auto-approved without showing a UAC prompt
- Automatically denies all elevation requests for standard users

EXAM TIP

To fully disable UAC, you must disable the following policy setting: User Account Control: Run all administrators in Admin Approval Mode.

Using Local Security Policy to configure UAC behavior

You can configure and fine-tune the behavior of UAC by modifying the settings found in Local Security Policy. Ten settings relating to UAC can be seen in Figure 4-23 and are listed here with a brief description:

- **User Account Control: Admin Approval Mode for the Built-In Administrator Account** This is disabled by default.
- **User Account Control: Allow UIAccess applications to prompt for elevation without using the secure desktop** This is disabled by default.
- **User Account Control: Behavior of the elevation prompt for administrators in Admin Approval Mode** By default, this is set to Prompt For Consent For Non-Windows Binaries.
- **User Account Control: Behavior of the elevation prompt for standard user** By default, this is set to Prompt For Credentials On The Secure Desktop.
- **User Account Control: Detect application installations and prompt for elevation** This is enabled by default on Windows 8 and disabled by default on Windows 8 Pro and Enterprise editions.
- **User Account Control: Only elevate executables that are signed and validated** This is disabled by default
- **User Account Control: Only elevate UIAccess applications that are installed in secure locations** This is enabled by default.
- **User Account Control: Run all administrators in Admin Approval Mode** This is enabled by default.
- **User Account Control: Switch to the secure desktop when prompting for elevation** This is enabled by default.
- **User Account Control: Virtualize file and registry write failures to per-user locations** This is enabled by default.

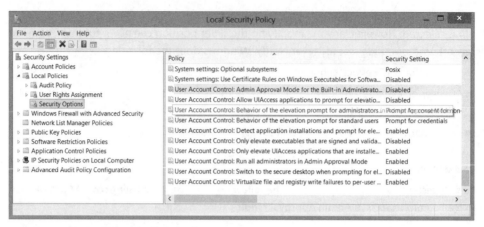

FIGURE 4-23 The Local Security Policy editor

EXAM TIP

You should review the User Account Control policy settings thoroughly for the exam.

The next section shows you how to configure UAC behavior by using the Local Security Policy snap-in (Secpol.msc) or Group Policy. (gpedit.msc).

Configuring Local Security Policy

Most of the time, you can configure Windows 8 from the standard user interface, which is designed for standard users to use. However, you might want to enforce some security settings that aren't available in the user interface (UI).

Consider the following changes that you might want to make on your system:

- Enforce complex user passwords
- Users should change their password every 90 days
- Turn off UAC for Administrators
- Configure auditing on a private folder

Viewing and modifying Local Security Policy

Follow these instructions to view the Local Security Policy on your computer:

1. Log onto Windows 8 with administrative privileges.

2. Search for Secpol.msc. Click it to open the Local Security Policy Editor.

3. Expand both Account Policies and Local Policies. Your window should be similar to the one shown in Figure 4-24.

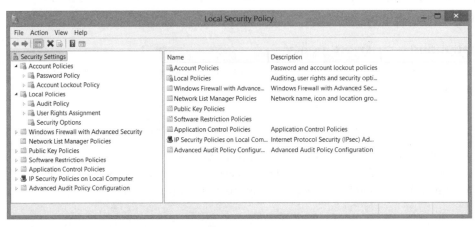

FIGURE 4-24 Configuring a Local Security Policy

The following sections can be configured within Local Security Policy:

- **Account Policies** Include Password Policy and Account Lockout Policy. Enable you to configure password history, maximum and minimum password age, password complexity, and password length, as well as to define settings related to the action that you want Windows 8 to take when a user enters an incorrect password at logon. These settings apply only to local accounts.

- **Local Policies** Include Audit Policy, User Rights Assignment, and Security Options. Enable you to enable/disable auditing, configure user rights (including the ability to log on locally), access the computer from the network, and shut down the system. You also can configure many security settings, including interactive logon settings, User Account Control settings, and shutdown settings.

- **Windows Firewall with Advanced Security** Enable you to configure the firewall settings.

- **Network List Manager Policies** Enable you to configure user options for configuring new network locations.

- **Public Key Policies** Include settings for Certificate Auto-Enrollment and the Encrypting File System (EFS) Data Recovery Agents.

- **Software Restrictions Policies** Enable you to identify and control which applications can run on the local computer.

- **Application Control Policies** Enable you to configure AppLocker.

- **IP Security Policies** Enable you to create, manage, and assign Internet Protocol Security (IPsec) policies.

- **Advanced Audit Policy Configuration** Enable you to provide greater granularity and control over audit policies.

You are now ready to make some security setting changes to your system via Local Security Policy Editor.

Configuring a password policy

If you want to make sure that all users of your computer have secure passwords and that passwords are changed after a set number of days, you can configure a password policy as follows:

1. With Local Security Policy still open, expand Account Policies and click Password Policy.

2. Double-click Enforce Password History. This setting determines the number of unique new passwords that a user account must have used before an old password can be reused. This is useful to prevent frequent reuse of passwords.

3. Enter 5 and click OK to set this policy.

4. Double-click Maximum Password Age. The default is 42, which specifies that a user can use her password 42 times before she's forced to change it.

5. Enter 90 and click OK to set this policy.

6. Double-click Minimum Password Age. The default is 0, meaning that users can change their passwords whenever they like. A setting of 14 would be appropriate. This setting is intended to prevent users from changing their password in rapid succession to bypass the password history setting.

7. Enter 14 and click OK to set this policy.

8. Double-click Minimum Password Length. The default is 0. A setting of 8 would state that a password must be at least 8 characters long.

9. Enter 8 and click OK to set this policy.

10. Double-click Password Must Meet Complexity Requirements. This is disabled by default. Set it to Enabled ould force all passwords to be "complex" in nature (see following note).

11. Double-click Store Passwords Using Reversible Encryption. The default is disabled. If you enable this policy, all passwords are stored in a way that's easier for hackers to crack.

12. Close the Local Security Policy editor.

The changes relating to local passwords become effective immediately; however, users' existing passwords remain until they are aged by 90 days, and then they need to be changed. The next time a user changes her password, the change must be in accordance with the settings in the Password Policy.

Configuring an account lockout policy

A strong password is an excellent step toward good security. However, your account can still be threatened despite a strong password. Password-cracking tools are available that can attempt thousands of passwords every hour in the hope that they succeed.

By default, nothing can stop a hacker from attempting to guess your password any number of times on your computer. Such behavior is called a *brute-force attack*. The following steps define an Account Lockout Policy that monitors incorrect attempts to log in to your computer, and then locks the account if the attempts continue. This type of deterrent is extremely useful and will foil hackers, who would then typically move their focus to another, "easier" target. So, follow these steps to define that lockout policy:

1. Open the Local Security Policy snap-in.

2. Expand Account Lockout Policy, which is located in the Account Lockout Policy subtree.

3. Double-click Account Lockout Threshold (this setting defines how many times a password can be entered incorrectly).

4. Enter 3 and click OK to set this policy.

5. In response to setting the Account Lockout Threshold, Windows offers default settings for Account Lockout Duration and Reset Account Lockout Counter After. These settings specify for how long, in minutes, a user account stays locked after entering a wrong password and after which period of time the count of wrong passwords entered is set back to zero. Leave these settings as suggested and click OK.

Your Account Lockout Policy is now effective on this computer.

Importing and exporting security settings

If you've created a set of policies that you want applied to other computers within your home network, you can export the settings as a Security Template and then import them onto each of the other computers. The following steps describe this process:

1. Open the Local Security Policy snap-in and right-click Security Settings.

2. Select Export Policy.

3. Enter a meaningful name for the .inf Security Template and click Save (you also might want to make a backup copy of this file to your HomeGroup or onto a removable drive).

4. To import the security settings onto another computer, repeat step 1 and then click Import Policy in step 2. Navigate to the location where you stored the .inf file and then click Open.

5. Close the Local Security Policy snap-in.

 Thought experiment
Local lockdown

In the following thought experiment, apply what you've learned about the objective. You can find answers to these questions in the "Answers" section at the end of this chapter.

You don't have a domain, but you need to configure your computers so that they are secure. You want to configure a local security policy and then distribute it to 15 computers on your network. Your new policy must include the following requirements:

■ Passwords must be complex and minimum of six characters long.

■ Only authenticated users can access computers remotely and shut down the computers.

What must you do to meet these requirements?

Objective summary

■ UEFI-enabled Secure Boot protects Windows 8 against rootkit infiltration.

■ Windows 8 takes advantage of the SmartScreen filter to prevent unsigned apps and bad websites from starting on your computer.

■ Retail Windows 8 devices have Secure Boot enabled.

■ Only Windows processes can access the secure desktop.

- Local Security Policy is used to configure local security settings on a computer.
- You can export and import security policies onto another computer.

Objective review

Answer the following questions to test your knowledge of the information in this objective. You can find the answers to these questions and explanations of why each answer choice is correct or incorrect at the end of this chapter.

1. Which of the following types of security threats are mitigated by Secure Boot?

   A. Phishing attacks

   B. Trojan Horse attacks

   C. Rootkit infection

   D. Virus infection

2. Which two features are required by Secure Boot?

   A. UEFI

   B. GPT

   C. MBR

   D. PC BIOS

   E. TPM 1.2

3. Windows SmartScreen protects against which two of the following?

   A. Rootkit infection

   B. Unrated apps

   C. Unsigned apps

   D. Phishing websites

4. UAC is designed for what purpose?

   A. To monitor your computer activity

   B. To prevent malware from infecting your computer

   C. To prevent you from installing software

   D. To provide an audit trail of installed software

5. Which command provides you with the Local Security Policy snap-in?

   A. gpedit.msc

   B. certmgr.msc

   C. regedit.msc

   D. secpol.msc

Objective 4.4: Configure authentication and authorization

Hackers and writers of malicious code are determined to infiltrate your systems and, at the same time, you expect Windows 8 to stand firm and defend your computer from those bad guys. Two terms are often used to describe how Windows 8 controls the users of the system and network resources: authentication and authorization.

Returning to the nightclub analogy in the section "Working with access control lists (ACLs)," *authentication* checks to see that you are who you say you are and that you are on the club's entry list; you then are accepted into the club. *Authorization* is the mechanism that lets the bouncers inside the club know whether you are a very important guest with privileges.

A user through his initial logon is authenticated, and then the system needs to check that she has the appropriate authorization to access resources that she needs. This chapter has already discussed how NTFS controls access to resources or—more correctly—to objects through access control technologies.

The access control model used for Windows is well established and robust. Windows tracks each and every resource on the system, and when a user or group (known also as a *security principal*, which is allocated a unique security identifier, or SID) requests access to these resources, the permissions allocated to the resource is examined to determine whether access should be agreed.

Security principals can perform actions, such as Read, Write, Modify, or Full Control, on objects. As mentioned previously, objects can include files, folders, printers, registry keys, and Active Directory Domain Services (AD DS) objects.

Ultimately, all this checking of the security principal and the resource access control lists (ACLs) results in one of two outcomes in relation to the resource:

- Deny access to unauthorized users and groups
- Provide access to authorized users and groups

> **This objective covers the following topics:**
> - Configuring rights
> - Managing credentials
> - Managing certificates
> - Configuring smart cards
> - Configuring biometrics
> - Configuring picture password
> - Configuring PIN
> - Setting up and configuring a Microsoft account

Configuring rights

The key difference between a user right and a permission is the user's ability to perform a task. User rights are applied to users and groups, whereas permissions are attached to objects.

Administrators assign specific privileges rights to groups or users. These rights authorize users to perform specific actions, such as logging onto a system interactively or shutting down a system.

Because users can travel around the network and log onto various computers, their rights must follow them. This is fundamentally different to an object permission, which is typically static, like a network share, and is hard coded into the object ACL. Two types of user rights are available:

- **Privileges** For example, the right to back up files and directories
- **Logon rights** For example, the right to log onto a system locally

Objective 4.3 discussed Local Security Policy. One of the components of Local Policy is User Rights Assignment, which is where you can configure user rights. Figure 4-25 shows the User Rights Assignment section of Local Policy.

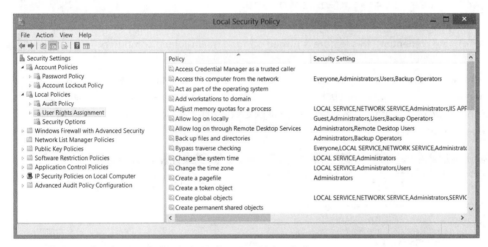

FIGURE 4-25 Configuring a Local Security Policy User Rights Assignment

If you look at the user right for Change The System Time and Change The Time Zone, notice that the Users group doesn't have the right to perform any tasks of changing the system time. This should explain why users are prompted by the UAC to provide administrator credentials.

Popular user rights that can be applied to user accounts and groups include the following:

- Allow log on locally
- Change the system time
- Change the time zone
- Deny log on through Remote Desktop Services

- Shut down the system
- Take ownership of files or other objects

Managing credentials

Roaming of user profile information has been a Windows feature for many years, as has the Credential Manager, which saves usernames and passwords. In Windows 8, Credential Manager has a new, improved component: Credential Locker, a secure storage area located within the user profile that stores usernames and passwords that the user has saved from websites and Windows 8 apps.

The best part of the enhanced Credential Manager is that the Credential Locker "roams" with the user, as long as the user logs onto his device by using his Microsoft account. Now, not only do Windows 8 users automatically get the same look, feel, and settings as before, they also get stored usernames and passwords for websites and Windows 8 apps across all their devices.

> **NOTE** **TAKING YOUR CREDENTIALS WITH YOU**
>
> **Credential roaming is enabled by default on non-domain joined computers. To protect corporate credentials, this feature is turned off for domain-joined computers.**

Credential Locker is the secure storage component of Credential Manager, which is found in the Control Panel or via the Windows search. To open Credential Manager, search for *credential* on the Start screen and then click Credential Manager. Figure 4-26 shows the Credential Manager.

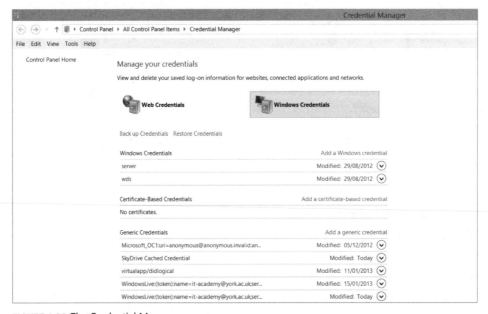

FIGURE 4-26 The Credential Manager

Credential Manager is carefully locked down so that the feature releases stored credentials only under the following conditions:

- To Windows 8 apps that support the Credential Manager APIs
- To websites that the user chose to store that credential on when the browser supports the Credential Manager APIs

The Credential Manager allows you to manage two types of credentials:

- **Web Credentials** For supported websites that uses credentials
- **Windows Credentials** For Windows credentials, certificate-based credentials, and generic credentials

Only Windows Credentials (not Web Credentials) have the functionality to back up and restore your stored credentials.

> *NOTE* **BACKING UP CREDENTIALS FROM CREDENTIAL MANAGER**
>
> You should back up your Credential Locker to non-local storage—for example, to your SkyDrive. The file extension for the Credential Locker is .crd.

EXAM TIP

Remember that you can back up and restore only Windows Credentials with the Credential Manager, not Web Credentials. Web Credentials can be synchronized between devices when you use a Microsoft account to log on.

Managing certificates

Previously this chapter covered Encrypting File System and explained that EFS uses certificates to ensure that the data that is being encrypted is secure. This section demonstrates how to manage the certificates on your computer and to safeguard them by being able to export and import your personal certificates. Should your primary computer fail, you can recover your certificates and any data encrypted with them.

Exporting personal certificates

To prevent being unable to access an encrypted file, you can export your personal certificate. Certificates are stored as files, and you can copy or move the encrypted file to another computer and still access it by importing the certificate you exported with it. (Later, this section covers importing certificates.)

To export your personal certificate, follow these steps:

1. Open File Explorer and select one of your encrypted files.

2. Right-click the file and then select Properties.

3. Click Advanced on the General tab.

4. Click Details on the Advanced Attributes tab to open the User Access dialog box.

5. Select your user name and then click Back Up Keys to open the Certificate Export Wizard.

6. Click Next. Select the .PFX container format to store the certificate.

7. Click Next, enter a password to protect the key, and then click Next again.

8. Save the file to a location of your choice, and then click Next.

9. Click Finish to export the certificate, and then click OK.

> *NOTE* PFX AND CER FILE TYPES
>
> To back up both the self-generated EFS certificate and the user private key, you should choose the Personal Information Exchange (PFX) file type. This is password-protected during the export process. However, if you want to distribute only your public key, you can export the client EFS certificate to a Canonical Encoding Rules (CER) file.

Importing personal certificates

After you encrypt files, you might want to share them with your coworkers or family via the Certificate Manager (see Figure 4-27). To be able to share files, you need to obtain the certificate for the other user and then import that certificate into your certificate store on your computer. Finally, you can then add that user name to the list of users who are permitted access to the encrypted file.

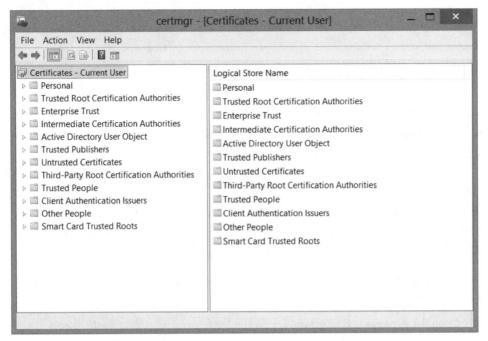

FIGURE 4-27 The Certificate Manager

To import a user certificate, follow these steps:

1. Search for *mmc* on the Start screen, click mmc.exe, and consent to the UAC prompt to open a blank Microsoft Management Console (MMC).

2. Click File and then click Add/Remove Snap-in.

3. Select Certificates and click Add. Select My User Account and click Finish. Click OK to close the dialog box.

4. Click Certificates Current User and then double-click Trusted People.

5. Under Trusted People, right-click Certificates. On the All Tasks menu, click Import to open the Certificate Import Wizard.

6. Click Next and then browse to the location of the certificate you want to import.

7. Select the certificate and then click Next.

8. Type the password for the certificate and then click Next.

9. Click Next to place the certificate in the Trusted People store.

10. Click Finish to complete the import.

11. Click OK to acknowledge the successful import and then close the MMC.

Granting users access to an encrypted file

Now that you have another user's certificate in your trusted people certificate store, you can add that user to the list of users who have access to an encrypted file.

To add a user whose certificate you have imported to the users who can access a file, follow these steps:

1. Open File Explorer and select the encrypted file to which you want to share access.

2. Right-click the file and then choose Properties.

3. Click Advanced on the General tab.

4. Click Details on the Advanced Attributes tab to open the User Access dialog box.

5. Click Add to open the Encrypting File System dialog box, and then select the user you want to use the encrypted file.

6. Click OK to add the user to the list of users who have access to the encrypted file.

7. Click OK to exit the dialog box.

Configuring smart cards

Smart cards continue to prove very popular in medium-security to high-security environments for a number of reasons. First, they are reliable, cost effective and easy to use and, second, they are very well suited to high level of security, such as the following:

- Authentication for scenarios such as remote access and IT administration

- Data integrity for scenarios such as document signing
- Data confidentiality for scenarios that require encryption

Whereas a security breach of any user account is never acceptable, account types that are particularly sensitive should be afforded every effort to protect them.

> **NOTE SMART TWO-FACTOR AUTHENTICATION**
>
> Smart cards are examples of two-factor authentication, in that the user must have the smart card and also know the PIN to gain access to network resources.

Windows Vista first introduced support for smart cards, which allowed the following to use without additional software:

- Unlocking BitLocker-encrypted drives with a smart card
- Logging onto the domain with a smart card
- Signing XPS documents and email messages
- Using smart cards with custom applications that use Cryptography Next Generation (CNG) or the older Cryptographic Application Programming Interface (CryptoAPI) to enable the application to use certificates

Some laptops have built-in smart card readers, and external USB smart card readers are available for desktop and server computers.

Windows 8 continues to support smart cards and offers new updated smart card functionality, including the following:

- Virtual smart cards
- Changes to the smart card logon experience
- Smart Card Service start and stop behavior
- Smart card transactions

Virtual smart cards

A virtual smart card doesn't require a physical smart card reader or card. The reader effectively is the computer, which takes advantage of the security capabilities of a Trusted Platform Module (TPM) chip that's commonplace on motherboards. The user then emulates the smart card and selects the correct smart card account on the screen and then enters his PIN to authenticate.

> **NOTE NO VIRTUAL CARD SPRAWL**
>
> Each user must have a unique virtual smart card per computer. Shared computers can host multiple virtual smart cards, one for each user.

Changes to the smart card logon experience

For end users, the logon experience on Windows 8 has improved. The system detects the most recent experience—as in whether a smart card or a password was used to log on or unlock the computer the last time.

For potential new smart card users, if the user selects the smart card logon icon, the system requests that the user to connect a smart card. Only after a card is connected does the smart card PIN dialog box appear. An additional message on the logon screen also allows the user to select from different logon options.

Smart Card Service start and stop behavior

Smart card reader detection logic has been added in Windows 8 so that the Smart Card Service runs only when appropriate. The Smart Card Service (SCardSvr.exe) automatically starts when the user connects a smart card reader and automatically stops when a user removes a smart card reader.

If a smart card reader has never been connected to the computer, the service won't start automatically.

Smart card transactions

Usually, smart card processing is nearly instantaneous. In an effort to prevent spoofing or eavesdropping of the card transactions, Windows 8 monitors the transaction duration, and if it's delayed and more than 5 seconds elapse with no operations happening on the card, the card is reset. The user is then required to restart the logon process.

> **NOTE SMART CARD RESTRICTIONS WITH WINDOWS RT**
>
> Windows RT support for smart card readers is restricted to USB devices that support the USB Chip/Smart Card Interface Devices (CCID) specification. Windows RT support for smart cards is also restricted to those that support the Generic Identity Device Specification (GIDS) or the Personal Identity Verification (PIV).

Configuring biometrics

Windows 7 introduced the Windows Biometric Framework (WBF), which provides a technology stack for supporting fingerprint biometric devices by independent hardware vendors (IHVs). Windows 8 continues to support the WBF and allows developers to leverage the Windows Biometric Framework API.

> **NOTE BIOMETRICS SERVICE**
>
> Ensure that the Windows Biometric service is running (set to start up manually by default) if you are using biometrics.

The Windows Biometric service provides the following functionality:

- Captures biometric samples and uses them to create a template
- Securely saves and manages biometric templates
- Maps each biometric template to a unique identifier, such as a GUID or SID
- Enrolls new biometric templates

In addition to the functionality, the WBF offers the following features built into the operating system:

- A Biometric Devices item on the Control Panel that allows users to manage device settings
- Device Manager support for managing drivers for biometric devices
- Credential provider support to enable the use of biometric data to log onto a local computer or domain
- Group Policy settings
- Windows Update support for downloading biometric device driver software

> **NOTE INSTALLING BIOMETRIC DEVICES**
>
> Only after a biometric device driver is installed will it appear in Device Manager and the Control Panel.

You might want to modify the behavior of biometrics on the system by configuring the Group Policy settings (see Figure 4-28). One setting allows the disabling of biometrics.

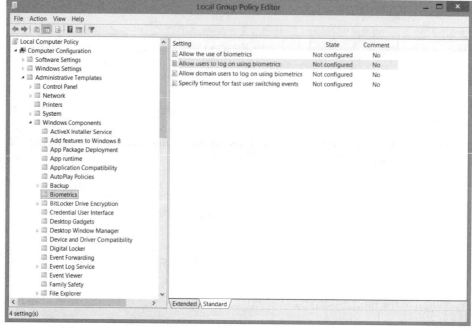

FIGURE 4-28 Configuring biometrics policies

Configuring picture password

Previously, this objective discussed how passwords can now follow the Windows 8 user from device to device. This should afford users greater security because they can configure complex passwords for websites and know that Windows is storing them safely in the Credential Locker. You can retrieve the passwords from Credential Manager at any time simply by providing your Windows logon password.

Windows 8 is designed to be used on both touch-enabled devices and as a traditional desktop operating system. Touch screens allow typing, but typing a complex password using touch can be a little clumsy. Windows 8 now introduces gesture or picture password as a logon option, which is far more intuitive, especially for touch devices. You can use a picture password in Windows 8 and Windows RT.

Of course, traditional mouse and keyboard users can also use picture passwords because you can perform the task with the mouse. You can select a picture of your own to be used or chose a sample picture that ships with Windows. The best picture types to use are those that have multiple points of interest—that is, points on the picture that you can choose to touch or select that forms your unique password.

In addition to these gestures, you can draw a line between two points of interest on your picture.

Follow these steps to enable picture passwords:

1. Press Windows+I and select Change PC Settings.

2. Select Users.

3. Click Create a Picture Password.

4. Browse and select a picture to use, and then select Open.

5. Drag the picture to position it within the screen.

6. Click Use This Picture (see Figure 4-29).

FIGURE 4-29 Choosing a photo for a picture password

7. Add your gestures. Windows then prompts you to re-enter them (see Figure 4-30).

8. Click Finish.

FIGURE 4-30 Configuring a picture password

 EXAM TIP

When trying to log on, Windows 8 locks you out after five failed attempts and asks you for your current text-based password to unlock.

If you think that using a picture password isn't as secure as a complex password, you are probably correct. Picture passwords are convenient and they are much better than no password (and also better than a PIN).

You can remove a picture password within the User section, and click Remove next to the Change Picture Password.

> **NOTE DISABLING THE PICTURE PASSWORD**
>
> A Group Policy setting is available to disable the use of picture password logon. You can find the Turn Off Picture Password Logon setting in Computer Configuration\Administrative Templates\System\Logon.

Configuring PIN

This option is similar to the picture password option described in the preceding section. Personal identification number (PIN) logon offers users a simple four-digit numeric password. When configured on a touch device, such as Windows RT, the system provides a numeric keypad for the user to input the PIN.

Using a PIN password isn't as secure as a complex password or picture password. However, PIN passwords are convenient and better than no password at all.

Follow these steps to enable PIN passwords:

1. Press Windows+I and select Change PC Settings.

2. Select Users.

3. Click Create a PIN.

4. Provide your usual logon credentials.

5. Type and confirm your four-digit PIN.

6. Click Finish (see Figure 4-31).

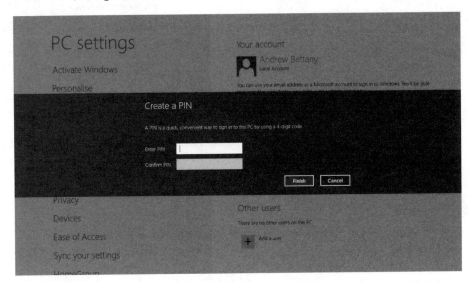

FIGURE 4-31 Creating a PIN number

Domain users are prevented from using PIN logons. Within Group Policy an administrator can override this (see Figure 4-32).

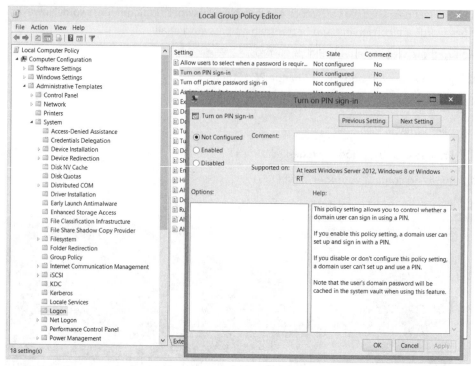

FIGURE 4-32 Configuring PIN sign-in

EXAM TIP

One Group Policy setting enables the use of PIN password logon for domain users. Called Turn On PIN Sign-In, it can be located in this container: Computer Configuration\Administrative Templates\System\Logon. Enabling this option increases security risk because the user's domain password is cached in the system vault (because the PIN and logon password are associated with each other).

Setting up and configuring a Microsoft account

The default method of logging onto Windows 8 has changed from previous versions of Windows. Windows 8 introduces the ability to log onto a computer by using a Microsoft account rather than a local account. Formerly known as a *Windows Live ID account*, a Microsoft account uses a Microsoft cloud-based authentication service to validate your logon and to synchronize your settings across multiple devices.

Although the logon is now cloud based, you need to be connected to the Internet only during the initial account creation stage. If you don't have a Microsoft account, an Add A User wizard walks you through the process of getting one. After the account is created, your details and password are securely cached locally, thereby allowing you to still log onto your computer, even if the Internet isn't available.

Using a Microsoft account provides user personalization through roaming settings and also roaming credentials, which were discussed previously.

To set up a new Microsoft account, follow these steps:

1. Click Windows+I, and then select Change PC Settings.

2. Select Users.

3. Select+Add A User.

4. Complete the Add A User wizard, shown in Figure 4-33.

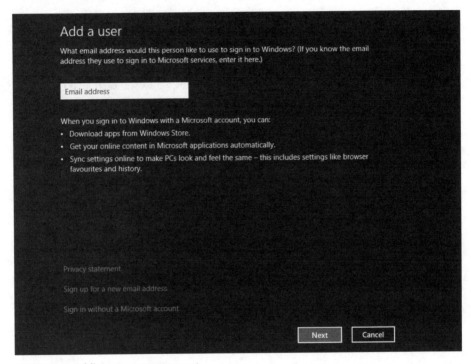

FIGURE 4-33 Adding a new user account

5. If this account is the first one that you've created after the Windows 8 installation, it becomes a member of the Administrators group.

6. Close the wizard when complete.

> **NOTE ENABLING FAMILY SAFETY**
>
> If you are creating an account for a child (ideally every user of the computer should have their own account), you can select the Family Safety check box, which can help safeguard the child while she uses the computer.

Microsoft accounts are required if you plan to download or purchase apps from the Windows Store. The Microsoft account keeps a record of your purchases (including free apps) so that you aren't charged again if you download them onto another device.

EXAM TIP

Be aware that the Microsoft account was formerly known as a *Windows Live ID* account and that the old term could still be present in the exam.

Thought experiment
Configuring authentication

In the following thought experiment, apply what you've learned about the objective. You can find answers to these questions in the "Answers" section at the end of this chapter.

You need to configure the most appropriate authentication methods for four distinct groups of users. Your financial services company has 16 staff members, all using a shared file server but not on an Active Directory domain. During a recent upgrade, everyone has been allocated a new Windows 8 device, as follows:

- **Sales team** Five Windows RT tablet devices
- **Marketing** Five high-specification desktop PCs
- **Accounting and Finance** Three standard desktop PCs
- **Management** Three laptops

Decide which authentication methods you would use for each group and explain why.

Objective summary

- Authentication is the method of checking that you are who you say you are, whereas authorization is used to ensure that you gain access to only the resources that you are authorized to access.
- The updated Credential Manager includes a Credential Locker, which stores your Windows and web credentials.
- Windows 8 synchronizes the Credential Locker across devices when the user logs on using their Microsoft account.
- EFS certificates can be backed up using the Personal Information Exchange (PFX) file format, which includes the certificate and key
- Smart cards can unlock BitLocker-enabled computers.

- Picture and PIN passwords, introduced in Windows 8, offer a convenient alternative logon experience for users.
- Microsoft accounts are the default method for a user to log onto Windows 8.

Objective review

Answer the following questions to test your knowledge of the information in this objective. You can find the answers to these questions and explanations of why each answer choice is correct or incorrect at the end of this chapter.

1. Which two of the following are characteristics of Credential Manager?

    A. Credential Locker is used to store passwords.

    B. Web credentials can't be backed up.

    C. It synchronizes credentials when using a Microsoft account.

    D. It saves passwords for Internet Explorer 9 and 10.

2. Which of the following isn't a user right?

    A. Log on locally

    B. Change the time zone

    C. Manage auditing and security log

    D. Access this computer from the network

    E. Allow the use of biometrics

3. You want to give a colleague access to your EFS encrypted files. Which file do you give him?

    A. .docx

    B. .cer

    C. .pfx

    D. Certificate

4. Which of the following isn't a Windows 8 logon option?

    A. Use an eight-digit PIN

    B. Smart card

    C. Microsoft account

    D. Picture password

    E. Local password

5. After how many failed attempts does Windows 8 lock the computer?

   A. 3

   B. 4

   C. 5

   D. 10

   E. Never

Chapter summary

- The improved HomeGroups and libraries enable users to simplify the sharing of resources on home networks.
- Only computers with Windows 7 and later can create HomeGroups.
- Through its strong integration in Windows 8, SkyDrive is emerging as *the* Windows tool for synchronizing files between devices and keeping them in the cloud.
- Always in force, NTFS remains the primary access control mechanism for files and folders in Windows 8.
- Shared Folders permissions are effective only when accessed across the network.
- The EFS recovery key should be stored separately from the computer.
- Object access auditing provides you with a powerful tool to monitor and report breaches of object-based security.
- Event Viewer provides enhanced reporting and can trigger action-based notifications in response to alerts.
- UEFI-enabled Secure Boot protects Windows 8 against rootkit infiltration.
- Windows 8 takes advantage of the SmartScreen filter to prevent unsigned apps and bad websites from starting on your computer.
- Local Security Policy is used to configure local security settings on a computer.
- Windows 8 synchronizes the Credential Locker across devices when users log on using their Microsoft accounts.
- Smart cards can unlock BitLocker-enabled computers.
- Picture and PIN passwords, introduced in Windows 8, offer a convenient alternative logon experience for users.

Answers

This section contains the solutions to the thought experiments and answers to the objective review questions in this chapter.

Objective 4.1: Thought experiment

The most appropriate configuration in this situation would be to configure a HomeGroup on one of the Windows 8 computers. Optionally during initial configuration, the password could be changed to a more recognizable passphrase that the family can recognize. All other client computers could then be connected to the HomeGroup with the password. Subfolders within the Music folder for each family member could also be provided.

Additional family members or new clients could be added at any time if they join the HomeGroup and provide the password key.

Objective 4.1: Review

1. **Correct answer:** C

   A. **Incorrect:** A standard user can't install downloaded drivers.

   B. **Incorrect:** The power user is deprecated in Windows 8.

   C. **Correct:** An administrator has the appropriate privileges to install the downloaded drivers.

   D. **Incorrect:** The service account isn't suitable because it doesn't interface with the user.

   E. **Incorrect:** The built-in administrator is incorrect because it's disabled by default after installation.

2. **Correct answer:** B

   A. **Incorrect:** My Documents is stored in the user profile in Windows 8, but not in the library.

   B. **Correct:** Videos, Podcasts, Documents, Pictures, and Music are the default library folders.

   C. **Incorrect:** Movies and My Documents aren't valid library folders.

   D. **Incorrect:** Movies isn't a valid folder.

3. **Correct answers:** A and B

   A. **Correct:** Printers automatically installed

   B. **Correct:** Requires no networking knowledge

   C. **Incorrect:** No such requirement that the password must be at least 10 characters long

   D. **Incorrect:** No such requirement that the password be changed every 90 days

   E. **Incorrect:** No such requirement that you must remove all shared folders before configuring HomeGroup

4. **Correct answers:** A, C, and E

   A. **Correct:** SkyDrive app is a valid method of connecting to SkyDrive.

   B. **Incorrect:** No Library plug-in exists.

   C. **Correct:** SkyDrive Desktop app is a valid method of connecting to SkyDrive.

   D. **Incorrect:** No iPad Windows Plus app exists.

   E. **Correct:** Windows Phone SkyDrive app is a valid method of connecting to SkyDrive.

5. **Correct answer:** B

   A. **Incorrect:** Net Share LocalFolder=C:\LocalFolder isn't a PowerShell command.

   B. **Correct:** New-SmbShare –Name ShareName –Path C:\LocalFolder is the correct syntax.

   C. **Incorrect:** Grant-SmbShareAccess –Path C:\LocalFolder wouldn't create a new share.

   D. **Incorrect:** Net Use LocalFolder=C:\LocalFolder isn't a PowerShell command.

Objective 4.2: Thought experiment

The corporation should physically protect the Windows 8 computer from theft, ensure that strong passwords are used, and ensure that communication between the web server and computer is secured by using a VPN or IPsec. The data stored should be encrypted by using EFS, access to the data protected by NTFS, and read-only access permissions given only to members of the Finance Management Team. Auditing should be enabled for this folder and its contents so that any unauthorized access (other than the Finance Team Management group) is alerted immediately to the compliance officer.

Objective 4.2: Review

1. **Correct answers:** A, C, and D

    A. **Correct:** A file is a valid computer object.

    B. **Incorrect:** A partition isn't a valid computer object.

    C. **Correct:** A folder is a valid object.

    D. **Correct:** A registry key is a valid object.

2. **Correct answer:** C

    A. **Incorrect:** Explicit always wins over implicit.

    B. **Incorrect:** Explicit always wins over implicit.

    C. **Correct:** Explicit Deny will win in all situations.

    D. **Incorrect:** The explicit Deny will always win over explicit Allow.

3. **Correct answer:** B

    A. **Incorrect:** The question asks about moving files, not copying them.

    B. **Correct:** The moved files inherit the permissions of the destination folder.

    C. **Incorrect:** This wouldn't be the outcome if the files are moving to another partition.

    D. **Incorrect:** This would be correct if the new partition wasn't NTFS; however, the drive is formatted NTFS.

4. **Correct answers:** B and C

    A. **Incorrect:** This is unreliable; the file might be corrupt.

    B. **Correct:** The default color for encrypted files is green.

    C. **Correct:** The check box would be selected.

    D. **Incorrect:** You could open the file, but this isn't a reliable indicator of the file being encrypted.

5. **Correct answers:** A, B, and C

    A. **Correct:** Deletion of files can be tracked by auditing.

    B. **Correct:** Unauthorized file access is tracked by auditing.

    C. **Correct:** Auditing can track when files are renamed.

    D. **Incorrect:** Auditing is available only on NTFS volumes.

Objective 4.3: Thought experiment

This exercise requires the use of a custom Local Security Policy template to be created, exported, and then imported on all the other computers. When complete, each computer has the same security and protection.

Specific areas of the Security Policy to be configured include the following:

- Enable: Account Policy |Password Policy | Password must meet complexity requirements

- Configure: Account Policy | Password Policy | Minimum password length = 6

- Configure: Local Policies | User Rights Assignment | Shut down the system = Authenticated Users

- Configure: Local Policies | User Rights Assignment | Access this computer from the network = Authenticated Users

Objective 4.3: Review

1. **Correct answer:** C

   A. **Incorrect:** Phishing attacks trick users into visiting websites to dupe them into revealing personal or confidential information that's valuable to the scammer.

   B. **Incorrect:** A Trojan horse typically runs within the operating system.

   C. **Correct:** Rootkit is the correct answer.

   D. **Incorrect:** A virus typically runs within the operating system.

2. **Correct answers:** A and B

   A. **Correct:** UEFI is required for Secure Boot.

   B. **Correct:** GPT is used with Secure Boot.

   C. **Incorrect:** MBR isn't used with Secure Boot.

   D. **Incorrect:** PC BIOS doesn't support Secure Boot.

   E. **Incorrect:** TPM 1.2 is required for BitLocker, not Secure Boot.

3. **Correct answers:** A and D

   A. **Correct:** Windows SmartScreen helps protect you from malware/rootkit infection.

   B. **Incorrect:** SmartScreen doesn't help against unrated apps.

   C. **Incorrect:** SmartScreen doesn't help against unsigned apps.

   D. **Correct:** SmartScreen helps protect you from phishing websites.

4. **Correct answers:** C and D

   A. **Incorrect:** Smart Screen is designed to prevent rogue apps and websites.

   B. **Incorrect:** Smart Screen doesn't review the app rating.

   C. **Correct:** Smart Screen warns you if an app is unsigned.

   D. **Correct:** Smart Screen doesn't allow potentially harmful websites to open.

5. **Correct answer:** B

   A. **Incorrect:** UAC monitors which applications are started but not your activity.

   B. **Correct:** UAC is designed to prevent malware from infecting your computer.

   C. **Incorrect:** UAC allows the installation of software if administrative permission is given.

   D. **Incorrect:** UAC doesn't maintain a record of installed software.

Objective 4.4: Thought experiment

This exercise requires the most appropriate use of authentication methods that Windows 8 supports:

Team	Form Factor	Authentication	Reason
Sales team	Windows RT	Picture	Touch enabled
Marketing	Desktop	Local	Basic required
Accounting	Desktops	Smart card	Financial data
Management	Laptops	Smart card	Responsibility

This answer is a guide only.

Objective 4.4: Review

1. **Correct answers:** B and C

   A. **Incorrect:** Credential Locker stores the passwords.

   B. **Correct:** Only Windows credentials can be backed up.

   C. **Correct:** A Microsoft account enables synchronization.

   D. **Incorrect:** Only Internet Explorer 10 allows passwords to be saved to the Credential Manager.

2. **Correct answer:** E

    A. **Incorrect:** Log on locally is a user right.

    B. **Incorrect:** Change the time zone is a user right.

    C. **Incorrect:** Manage auditing and security log is a user right.

    D. **Incorrect:** Access this computer from the network is a user right.

    E. **Correct:** This is a GPO found in Administrative Templates, not a user right.

3. **Correct answer:** B

    A. **Incorrect:** .docx is a Microsoft Word file extension.

    B. **Correct:** You can export the client EFS certificate without the private key to Canonical Encoding Rules (CER).

    C. **Incorrect:** This would export the certificate and private key to a Personal Information Exchange (PFX) file.

    D. **Incorrect:** This isn't a value file type.

4. **Correct answer:** A

    A. **Correct:** PINs must be four digits long.

    B. **Incorrect:** A smart card is a valid Windows 8 logon option.

    C. **Incorrect:** A Microsoft account is a valid Windows 8 logon option.

    D. **Incorrect:** Picture password is a valid Windows 8 logon option.

    E. **Incorrect:** Local password is a valid Windows 8 logon option.

5. **Correct answer:** C

    A. **Incorrect:** Windows 8 allows five attempts, not just three.

    B. **Incorrect:** Windows 8 allows five attempts, not just four.

    C. **Correct:** Windows 8 allows five attempts

    D. **Incorrect:** Windows 8 allows five attempts, not 10.

CHAPTER 5

Configure remote access and mobility

More computer users are working outside the traditional office environment, and this trend is expected to continue. Advances in technology continue to enable employees to be more productive and achieve more while they are away from the office, while at the same time ensuring that their mobility doesn't compromise issues such as data security, social interaction, and teamwork.

Windows 8 certainly continues to deliver strong opportunities for mobile users by helping them to connect to enterprise resources more easily and more reliably than ever. New and improved features in Windows 8 and Windows 2012 help create a more productive environment. New and improved technologies such as VPN Reconnect, BitLocker, and Remote Desktop are helping both users and IT professionals consume and deliver services to end users that are driving forward the mobile landscape.

Objectives in this chapter:

- Objective 5.1: Configure remote connections
- Objective 5.2: Configure mobility options
- Objective 5.3: Configure security for mobile devices

Objective 5.1: Configure remote connections

One major frustration for the IT support helpdesk (and users when they are working from home) is that occasionally the Internet connection is lost for no apparent reason. The first thing every user should do, of course, is restart the computer and then log back on to see whether the problem has gone away. What typically happens is that users start making random changes to the networking or VPN connection settings in an attempt to fix the problem, which they have decided must be on their computer.

One thing desktop support technicians need to ask their users is whether the system was working fine before the problem occurred. This single piece of knowledge is a powerful troubleshooting tool. If the answer is yes (and it invariably is), the problem very likely is upstream and lies either with the ISP or the office, but most probably not with the end user. Despite the best advice, users will still try to fix the problem themselves and when an IT professional is called to actually fix the problem, that person typically finds the problem has become worse.

Windows 8 provides two excellent ways for the IT professional to remotely connect with a user's machine over the Internet: Remote Assistance and Remote Desktop. If you are configuring a new system for a remote worker or unraveling a failed attempt to fix a broken system, this section is aimed at providing you with a deeper understanding of the protocols, concepts, and technologies that Windows 8 offers for remote working.

> **This objective covers the following topics:**
> - Configuring remote authentication
> - Configuring Remote Desktop settings
> - Establishing VPN connections and authentication
> - Enabling VPN Reconnect
> - Managing broadband connections

Configuring remote authentication

Security—and especially security failures—makes headline news and is a topic that's continually evolving. Wherever possible, you should ensure that your systems are protected and using the most up-to-date security possible.

As is often said, the overall security of any system rests with the lowest level of protection. For example, if an enterprise spent a huge amount of money provisioning and securing a brand new in-house private cloud server room and then gave janitors daily access to that room to empty the trash, the weakest point could be this unsecured server room access. As an IT professional, you should review the security implemented and wherever possible raise the level across all your systems to ensure that you don't leave a weak or unprotected attack vector. One area that occurs as planned is the upgrade and removal of legacy operating systems that no longer support current security standards.

Look, for example, at virtual private networks (VPN), covered later in this section. Four common, well-known VPN technologies are available today, and Windows 8 supports all four. However, two of these—Secure Socket Tunneling Protocol (SSTP) and Internet Key Exchange (IKEv2)—have been mainstream only in the last few years. Windows XP and Windows Server 2003 were released more than 10 years ago, have had their last service packs, and have no built-in support for SSTP or IKEv2. In most cases, a modern operating system reverts to a less-secure protocol if necessary, but you can appreciate that this significantly lowers the security of the whole system.

One recent advance in authentication has been the emergence of Network Level Authentication (NLA). Windows 8 supports this new enhanced authentication protocol, and it's also incorporated in the latest version of Remote Desktop (also referred to as *RDP* or *Remote Desktop Connection*), which uses the Remote Desktop Protocol version 8.0.

Remote Desktop allows the choice of using NLA or the built-in RDP authentication. NLA offers a more secure method of establishing a remote connection with a distant server; disabling NLA allows for RDP connections to be accepted from legacy versions of Windows, such as Windows XP and Windows Vista. With NLA, the client and server can negotiate a secure channel for exchanging data before allocating resources for the session. Only after this process has successfully taken place does RDP attempt to establish the remainder of the remote desktop connection where the logon screen appears. Not only is this more secure, but it also reduces spoofing and man-in-the middle attacks as well as server overhead when establishing RDP connections.

Configuring Remote Desktop Connection

Remote Desktop was first introduced in Windows NT 4.0, Terminal Server Edition. Remote Desktop Protocol (RDP) allows a user to connect to a single or multiple computers over the network, typically for remote administration purposes. With the increased demand and drive for server virtualization and remote management, Remote Desktop is now seeing something of a revival. Each new upgrade of the protocol supporting Remote Desktop heralds increased performance, reliability, and capabilities that help RDP remain a key tool for IT professionals and administrators.

Enabling Remote Desktop

Before launching Remote Desktop, you should ensure that Remote Desktop connections are allowed on each machine. This also creates the required firewall rules to allow Remote Desktop traffic.

Remote Desktop is disabled by default in Windows 8. To enable Remote Desktop connections, follow these steps:

1. Press Windows+X and select Control Panel.

2. Open System from the Control Panel (if System isn't visible, click View By Large Icons).

3. On the Remote tab of the System Properties sheet, select the Allow Remote Connections To This Computer setting in the Remote Desktop section (see Figure 5-1).

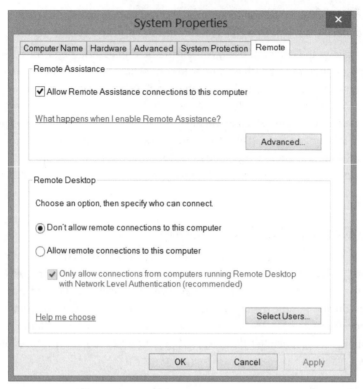

FIGURE 5-1 Enabling Remote Desktop

EXAM TIP

Enabling Remote Desktop requires administrative credentials, because inbound rules must be enabled in Windows Firewall.

NOTE HELLO, IS ANYBODY THERE?

You can't use Remote Desktop to connect to a PC that's in Sleep mode or hibernating.

Two options are available in the Remote Desktop section:

- **Don't Allow Remote Connections To This Computer** This is the default.
- **Allow Remote Connections To This Computer** If you chose to allow remote connections, you can then select the optional check box to Only Allow Connections From Computers Running Remote Desktop With Network Level Authentication (Recommended). This option is more secure and should be selected in most cases.

To launch the Remote Desktop connection, type **mstsc.exe** or search for *remote* using Windows 8 Search, and then select Remote Desktop Connection.

> **NOTE** **REMOTE DESKTOP FIREWALL CONSIDERATIONS**
>
> If Remote Desktop is enabled, Windows 8 automatically configures the necessary settings to allow Remote Desktop traffic through the Windows Firewall.

EXAM TIP

You can use a PC running any edition of Windows XP, Windows Vista, Windows 7, or a PC running Windows 8 or Windows RT to initiate a Remote Desktop connection. However, you can connect to only PCs that run these Windows operating systems:

- Windows 8 Enterprise
- Windows 8 Pro
- Windows 7 Professional
- Windows 7 Enterprise
- Windows 7 Ultimate
- Windows Vista Business
- Windows Vista Ultimate
- Windows Vista Enterprise
- Windows XP Professional

With the Remote Desktop Connection dialog box open, select Show Options and configure the following connection settings so you can successfully connect to the distant computer (see Figure 5-2):

- **General** Specify remote host, username, and password (or wait to be prompted, after connected).
- **Display** Choose the screen size/resolution; the default is set to show full screen.
- Local Resources Configure printers, Clipboard, smart card, drives, audio, and keyboard settings.
- **Programs** Specify whether a script or program is executed after you are logged on.
- **Experience** If your connection is fast, you can specify a better experience (fast rendering/see wallpaper background/font smoothing). For a slower connection, try reducing the visual overhead.
- **Advanced** Specify Remote Desktop gateway settings and action to be taken if server authentication fails (the default is set to warn).

After you configure these settings, you can save them for future connections.

FIGURE 5-2 Configuring Remote Desktop Connection settings

Group Policy has more than 75 GPOs relating to Remote Desktop services that you can use to configure and fine-tune your connections. A few GPO settings are as follows:

- Do not allow passwords to be saved
- Allow users to connect remotely by using Remote Desktop Services
- Do not allow drive redirection
- Allow remote connections to this computer

> *NOTE* **MULTIPLE LOGON REQUESTS**
>
> When a Remote Desktop session is active, it locks the target computer so that only one user at a time can be connected. If another user tries to log on to the target computer while the connection is in force, the active connection will display a 30-second notice that warns that the connection will be terminated. The logged-on user can cancel this warning and continue to remain connected or, if the current logged-on user provides no response, the connection is disconnected and the other user can complete his logon.

Working with new Remote Desktop functionality

To assist users who use Remote Desktop Connection to connect to Windows 8 or Windows Server 2012 computers, Microsoft has added new functionality to the current version of Remote Desktop to allow users to access the Charms and other features.

A new menu called the *Remote Commands* has been added to the Remote Desktop client connection menu, which you can access by right-clicking the Remote Desktop icon when in window mode. If the session is in full screen, click the down arrow to the left side of the connection bar at the top of the screen. This menu allows you to use special features, such as the following:

- Start menu
- Windows 8 and Windows Server 2012 Charms
- Switch apps
- Snap apps
- App commands

Establishing VPN connections and authentication

A virtual private network (VPN) allows your network to be extended across the Internet by establishing a secure encrypted "tunnel" in which only your network traffic can transmit. Typically, VPNs are used to connect branch offices to the head office, or a home-based employee to his office server. A home user can also establish a secure connection back to his home computer via a VPN from a remote location.

VPNs have continued to be a popular method of connecting networks. With the increase of speed of the Internet and desirability in some situations to work from anywhere an Internet connection exists, VPNs are currently a popular topic. Through its continued development of VPN technologies, Microsoft first introduced first Direct Access with Windows 7 and Windows Server 2008 R2, and more recently VPN Reconnect with Windows 8 and Windows Server 2012.

At the heart of a VPN are the protocols used to create the secure tunnel. Two types of VPN connections are available:

- **Remote Access** Also referred to as a point-to-point connection, this is the most common VPN. Typically, a user connects to a home network or accesses an office server over the public Internet.
- **Site-to-Site** This VPN connects branch offices together over the public Internet. Also referred to as a *wide-area network (WAN) link*, it's commonly known as a *router-to-router VPN connection*. Site-to-site VPNs create the tunnel infrastructure only; the traffic originates at the client or server machines.

Using tunneling protocols in VPN connections

Windows 8 supports four types of VPN connections that use tunneling protocols:

- **Point-to-Point Tunneling Protocol (PPTP)** Based on the original Point-to-Point Protocol (PPP), Point to Point Tunneling Protocol (PPTP) is now considered to have weak encryption and authentication; therefore, L2TP with IPsec is typically preferred.

- **Layer 2 Tunneling Protocol (L2TP)/IP security (IPsec)** L2TP is the next-generation tunneling protocol partially based on PPTP. To provide encryption, L2TP acts as a Data Link layer (Layer 2 of the Open Systems Interconnection [OSI] model) protocol for tunneling network traffic between two peers over an existing network (usually the Internet). L2TP tunnels commonly carry PPP sessions. L2TP doesn't provide confidentiality or strong authentication by itself; IPsec is often used to secure L2TP packets by providing confidentiality, authentication, and integrity across public networks. The combination of these two protocols is generally known as *L2TP/IPsec*. IPsec consists two different protocols: AH (Authentication Header) is responsible for authenticity and integrity, whereas ESP (Encapsulating Security Payload) encrypts the payload. L2TP/IPsec is supported on Windows XP, Windows Vista, Windows 7, Windows 8, Windows Server 2003, and Windows Server 2008.

- **Secure Socket Tunneling Protocol (SSTP)** Introduced in Windows Vista, SSTP uses the Hypertext Transfer Protocol Secure (HTTPS) over TCP port 443 to pass traffic through firewalls and web proxies that might block PPTP and L2TP/IPsec traffic. SSTP provides a mechanism to encapsulate PPP traffic over the Secure Sockets Layer (SSL) channel of the HTTPS protocol. The use of PPP allows support for strong authentication methods, such as Extensible Authentication Protocol-Transport Layer Security (EAP-TLS). SSL provides transport-level security with enhanced key negotiation, encryption, and integrity checking. SSTP is supported on Windows Vista, Windows 7, Windows 8, Windows Server 2008R2, and Windows Sever 2012.

- **Internet Key Exchange (IKEv2)** Introduced in Windows 7, this tunneling protocol uses the IPsec tunnel mode protocol over User Datagram Protocol (UDP) port 500. An IKEv2 VPN is useful when the client moves from one wireless hotspot to another or when it switches from a wireless to a wired connection. The use of IKEv2 and IPsec together provide strong authentication and encryption methods. IKEv2 is supported on Windows 7, Windows 8, Windows Server 2008R2, and Windows Server 2012.

These four VPN connections have the following properties:

- **Encapsulation** Private data is encapsulated with a header that contains routing information, which allows the data to navigate the network.

- **Authentication** This can take three different forms:

  - User-level authentication by using Point-to-Point Protocol (PPP) authentication

  - Computer-level authentication by using Internet Key Exchange (IKE)

  - Data origin authentication and data integrity

- **Data encryption** This ensures that sent data remains confidential as the sender encrypts the data, it travels within the shared or public network, and the receiver decrypts it. The encryption and decryption processes depend on both the sender and the receiver using a common encryption key.

The following table summarizes the encapsulation and data encryption methods for the four VPNs supported by Windows 8.

VPN Protocol	Encapsulation	Data encryption
PPTP	TCP/IP	MS-CHAPv2 or EAP-TLS
L2TP/IPsec	L2TP/UDP + IPsec	Advanced Encryption Standard (AES) or Triple Data Encryption Standard (3DES)
SSTP	TCP/IP 443	HTTPS SSL
IKEv2	ESP/AH	AES256 or 3DES

The following authentication methods are in common use today:

- **Password Authentication Protocol (PAP)** The least secure authentication protocol; uses plain-text passwords. Typically used if the remote access client and remote access server can't negotiate a more secure form of validation. PAP doesn't protect against replay attacks, remote client impersonation, or remote server impersonation. It's not enabled by default for Windows 8 and isn't supported by remote access servers running Windows Server 2008 and later.

- **Challenge-Handshake Authentication Protocol (CHAP)** Uses a three-way handshake in which the authentication agent sends the client program a key to be used to encrypt the user name and password. CHAP uses the Message Digest 5 (MD5) hashing scheme to encrypt the response. CHAP is an improvement over PAP in that the password isn't sent over the PPP link. It requires a plain-text version of the password to validate the challenge response. CHAP doesn't protect against remote server impersonation. Although remote access servers running Windows Server 2008 don't support this protocol, it's enabled by default for Windows 8 VPN connections accessing legacy VPN connections.

- **Microsoft CHAP version 2 (MS-CHAP v2)** Supports two-way mutual authentication. The remote access client receives verification that the remote access server that it's dialing in to has access to the user's password. MS-CHAP v2 provides stronger security than CHAP.

- **EAP-MS-CHAPv2** Allows for arbitrary authentication of a remote access connection through the use of authentication schemes, known as *EAP types*. EAP offers the strongest security by providing the most flexibility in authentication variations. This protocol requires the installation of a computer certificate on the VPN server.

> ***NOTE*** **AUTOMATIC VPN PROTOCOL NEGOTIATION**
>
> Just like the VPN protocols, by default, Windows first tries to use the most secure authentication protocol that's enabled, and then it falls back to less secure protocols if they are supported.

EXAM TIP

Always try to recommend the most secure VPN connection and authentication methods possible.

Configuring VPN connections

Windows 8 has optimized the VPN client for touch devices. This should allow creating a VPN connection, and connecting to a corporate network, faster and easier. The VPN connection icon now appears in View Available Networks, along with other network connections.

Creating a VPN profile requires only the server information. Windows 8 then tries to auto-discover the correct authentication methods and tunnels while connecting, making the VPN experience seamless.

CREATING A NEW VPN CONNECTION

To create a new virtual private network (VPN) in Windows 8, follow these steps:

1. Type **vpn** in the Settings screen, as shown in Figure 5-3.

FIGURE 5-3 Creating a VPN connection, starting at the Settings screen

2. Select Set Up A Virtual Private Network (VPN) Connection. The Create A VPN Connection wizard appears, as shown in Figure 5-4.

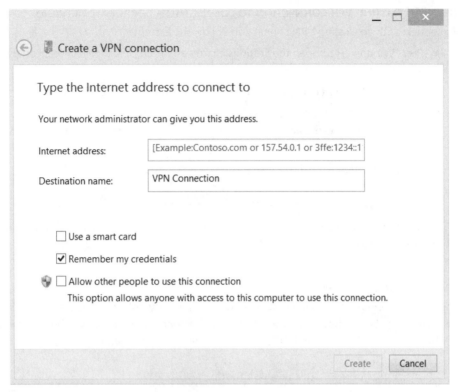

FIGURE 5-4 Create a VPN connection wizard

3. Provide the Internet address of the Remote Access VPN server to which you want to connect. This can be an IP address or the fully qualified domain name (FQDN) of the Remote Access server.

4. Provide a name in the Destination Name text box. This is the text used for the VPN connection name (profile name).

5. Click Remember My Credentials to save your credentials on the first successful connection attempt.

You have created a new Discovery Profile, which Windows 8 will use to connect to VPN.

> **NOTE NEGOTIATING PROTOCOLS**
>
> The authentication and tunneling protocols are negotiated and configured during the first successful connection attempt for username/password based VPNs. After the protocols are negotiated, you can edit the settings in Connection Properties.

USING AN EXISTING VPN CONNECTION TO CONNECT TO A CORPORATE NETWORK

To connect with an existing VPN connection, follow these steps:

- Press Windows+I to open the Settings charm, and then click the Network icon displayed in the lower right corner.

- Click the VPN connection that you want to use and then click Connect.

- A new connection is negotiated with the server using the saved credentials. If the VPN cannot use the saved credentials or they aren't valid, you are asked to provide them again.

The VPN connection wizard completes and you are connected.

> **NOTE** **CLEARING CACHED CREDENTIALS**
>
> You can clear the cached credentials by right-clicking the connection and selecting Clear Cached Credentials.

EDITING CONNECTION PROPERTIES

You can edit a connection that you've already configured by right-clicking the connection and then selecting View Connection Properties. The VPN connection properties sheet (see Figure 5-5) has five tabs: General, Options, Security, Networking, and Sharing.

FIGURE 5-5 Configuring VPN properties

Here's an explanation of each tab:

- **General** Change the VPN server hostname or IP address. Also, configure an optional interface connection to the public network.

- **Options** Configure PPP Settings and enable/disable caching of credentials.

- **Security** Configure specific tunnel type (or leave to automatic), authentication, and data encryption settings, as shown in Figure 5-6.

- **Networking** Configure transport protocols. The most common protocols are TCP/IPv4 and TCP/IPv6.

- **Sharing** Allow other network users to share this VPN connection.

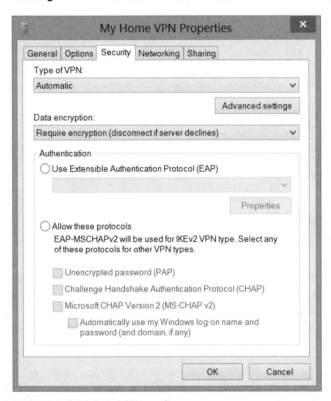

FIGURE 5-6 Setting up VPN security

DELETING A CONNECTION

To delete an existing VPN connection, follow these steps:

1. Type **vpn** in the Settings screen.

2. Click View Network Connections.

3. Right-click the VPN connection you want to remove and then click Delete (see Figure 5-7).

4. Close the Network Connections window.

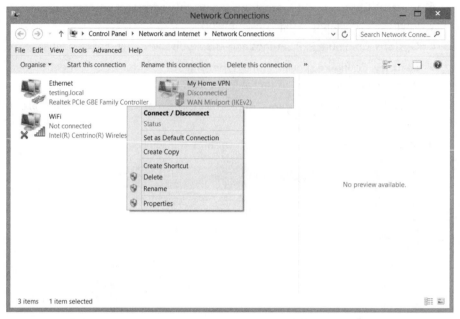

FIGURE 5-7 Deleting a VPN

Enabling VPN Reconnect

As you've seen, VPNs can be either *site-to-site* or *remote* access. Traditionally, these connections were over fixed-line broadband. In recent years, the speed and availability of Wi-Fi has become mainstream; as a result, VPNs are now commonly connecting via Wi-Fi. One frustration of using VPN over Wi-Fi is that VPN requires a reliable connection; otherwise, the connection drops out and the VPN needs to be reinitiated. VPN Reconnect is a feature introduced in Windows 7 that uses IKEv2 and automatically reestablishes a VPN connection whenever the Internet connection is temporarily lost.

> **REAL WORLD VPN RECONNECT INCREASES PRODUCTIVITY**
>
> I have used the VPN Reconnect feature while on a metered connection such as mobile broadband traveling on a train. VPN Reconnect managed to keep me connected throughout the journey, whereas without VPN Reconnect previously, I have been frustrated by the end of the journey because of losing the VPN connection whenever the train passed through a tunnel, which would necessitate that I reconnect manually each time.

VPN Reconnect is automatically enabled for VPN connections in Windows 8. You can configure the Network Outage Time from 30 minutes (default) up to a maximum of 8 hours. This period specifies how long the VPN connection can be in a disconnect state before the system stops trying to reconnect.

To disable VPN Reconnect or configure the Network Outage Time for an existing VPN connection, follow these steps:

1. Type **vpn** in the Search screen.

2. Click View Network Connections.

3. Right-click the VPN connection you want to configure and then click Properties.

4. On the Security tab, click Advanced Settings.

5. On the IKEv2 tab, clear the Mobility check box (shown in Figure 5-8) to disable VPN Reconnect.

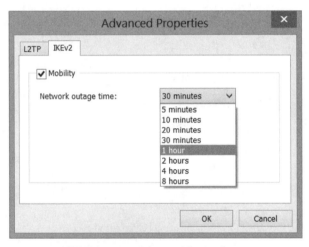

FIGURE 5-8 VPN Reconnect Advanced Properties

6. To specify the Network Outage Time, select the required time from the drop-down list.

7. Click OK twice to exit the VPN properties.

Managing broadband connections

Not all Internet service providers (ISPs) provide "always on" broadband. If your ISP requires you to connect to the Internet each time, you need to create an icon on your desktop to facilitate this.

Windows 8 provides a wizard to create a broadband connection. Follow these steps to create a new broadband connection if you aren't connected to the Internet:

1. On the Windows 8 Desktop, right-click the Network icon in the Notification area and select Open Network And Sharing Center.

2. In the Network and Sharing Center, click Set Up A New Connection Or Network.

3. In the Set Up A New Connection Or Network dialog box, select Connect To The Internet. Choose the VPN connection that you want to use and then click Connect.

4. Choose Broadband (PPPoE).

5. Type the information provided to you by your ISP. You can also share your broadband connection through your computer to allow other users access to the Internet (as shown in Figure 5-9).

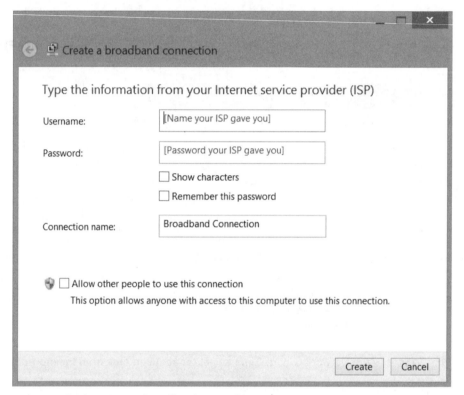

FIGURE 5-9 Setting up a new broadband connection

After you create this broadband connection and then modify the settings, you get additional options to modify authentication protocols, IPv4/IPv6 settings, Internet connection sharing, hang-up settings, PPP settings, and service name.

Working with Windows 8 Remote Assistance

Previously, this chapter explained that Remote Desktop is the enterprise remote support tool and is used extensively for remotely connecting to virtual servers and controlling computers where physical access would be challenging (such as inside a secure datacenter). Remote Assistance is in no way inferior to Remote Desktop. Both have different roles and purposes, but they also share a lot of technology—particularly the Remote Desktop Protocol (RDP), which is at the heart of both tools. Remote Assistance allows support staff to connect to a remote computer and optionally can take remote control of a computer with full visibility to the user at the remote station.

Remote Assistance is a graphical support tool that helps users when their computers misbehave or when they are working from home and need you to show them how to configure BitLocker or Offline Files. Remote Assistance empowers both participants by visually displaying what's going on and allows (if the user is interested) rapid comprehension and learning of the planned solution.

Remote Assistance allows a user to seek help and support from a remote support technician or administrator. It can be beneficial under the following scenarios:

- Diagnosing hard-to-explain or hard-to-reproduce problems.
- Remotely viewing the computer so that the user can visually show you the problem.
- Guiding a user to complete a set of instructions under supervision.
- Taking control of the computer and completing the tasks in view of the user.

Remote Assistance also offers the following capabilities:

- It allows a user to invite help from a remote support technician.
- You can offer to help someone who needs support.
- You can text chat with a remote user.

Remote Assistance was first introduced as a feature of Windows XP and has proven to be a popular tool with both helpdesk operators and users. It has been improved in each subsequent Windows version, and Windows 8 provides the following high-level changes:

- RDP improvements ensure that Remote Assistance is more bandwidth-optimized and efficient.
- Improvements in network address translation (NAT) traversal using IPv6 and Teredo tunneling ensures that the connection is now more reliable and allows multiple Remove Assistance sessions over a shared network.
- The primary executable, msra.exe, supports PowerShell scripting.
- Initial connection time is faster.

New Group Policy settings have also been added for improved manageability, including the following:

- Allow only Windows Vista or later connections
- Configure Offer Remote Assistance
- Configure Solicited Remote Assistance
- Customize warning messages
- Turn on bandwidth optimization
- Turn on session logging

The new Easy Connect feature for requesting Remote Assistance provides another level of simplicity for the end users.

Enabling Remote Assistance

Remote Assistance is enabled by default in Windows 8. To revoke or confirm this, follow these steps:

1. Open System from the Control Panel.

2. Open Remote Settings.

3. On the Remote tab, select or clear the Allow Remote Assistance Connections To This Computer check box. Figure 5-10 shows the Remote Assistance check box enabled.

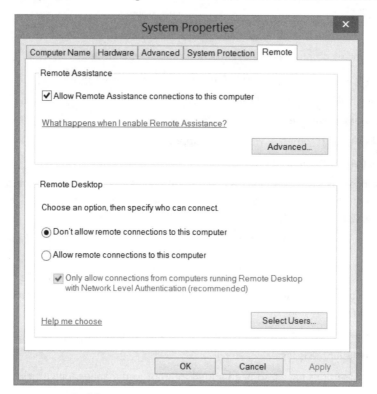

FIGURE 5-10 Enabling Remote Assistance

> **NOTE** **REMOTE ASSISTANCE FIREWALL CONSIDERATIONS**
>
> If Remote Assistance is allowed, the necessary settings within Windows Firewall to allow Remote Assistance traffic through the Windows Firewall are automatically configured by Windows.

Requesting and initiating Remote Assistance

In the following example, a remote user calls you (the helper) to ask for assistance. You decide that it would be beneficial to initiate a Remote Assistance connection. You explain this to the remote user and then follow these steps:

1. Ask the remote user to search for Remote Assistance (or msra.exe) in the Windows 8 search.

2. The remote user needs to select the item Invite Someone To Connect To Your PC And Help You Or Offer To Help Someone Else.

3. From the Windows Remote Assistance dialog box, the remote user needs to select Invite Someone You Trust To Help You.

4. The wizard offers the remote user three methods of creating the invitation that needs to be sent to the helper. Depending on how you will connect, you should advise the remote user which option is the most appropriate from the following options:

   - Save this invitation as a file
   - Use email to send an invitation
   - Use Easy Connect

5. Choose Save the invitation as a file. Instruct the user then to share this file either by email, VPN, SharePoint, or SkyDrive to the helper. (The file is called *Invitation. msrcIncident* but can be renamed.)

6. When the file is saved, the Remote Assistance tool provides a unique complex password that's needed to "open" the remote connection. Ask the remote user to inform you of the password.

7. At this point, the user should remain connected to the Internet and maintain the telephone call to the helpdesk.

8. You (the helper) receive the file and double-click it to open Remote Assistance.

9. Remote Assistance requests the password relating to the incident. You need to request remote control access and await acknowledgement.

10. The remote user is prompted to give remote control and can then watch as you (the helper) take control of his system.

11. When the help has been given, the user can close the Remote Assistance session to terminate access.

Using Easy Connect

Windows 8 has improved the Easy Connect tool for simplifying remote assistance. Now, the experience is more reliable and even quicker. In the background, Easy Connect uses Peer Name Resolution Protocol (PNRP) to create a direct peer-to-peer transfer, using a Microsoft Hosted service on the Internet to establish the connection. PNRP uses IPv6 and Teredo tunneling to create a private tunnel between the two computers for the duration of the Remote Assistance session.

Thought experiment
Connecting to the office network from home

In the following thought experiment, apply what you've learned about the objective. You can find answers to these questions in the "Answers" section at the end of this chapter.

One of your remote staff members, Jenny, works from her home office, using Windows 8 Professional on a corporate laptop. She has being trying, unsuccessfully, to connect remotely to her office PC, which uses Windows 7 Home Premium by using Remote Desktop Connection.

Identify potential issues to investigate what could prevent her from connecting.

Objective summary

- Remote Desktop is a proven method to allow a home-based worker to connect to his office-based computer via the Internet.

- Windows 8 supports four common, well-known VPN technologies: SSTP, IKEv2, PPTP, and L2TP.

- The VPN Reconnect feature automatically reestablishes a VPN connection whenever a connection is temporarily lost.

- Remote Assistance allows a helpdesk support operator to connect to a remote computer interactively and offer assistance to the end user across the Internet.

- Windows 8 includes an improved version of Easy Connect, which uses Peer Name Resolution Protocol to assist the establishment of a Remote Assistance session.

Objective review

Answer the following questions to test your knowledge of the information in this objective. You can find the answers to these questions and explanations of why each answer choice is correct or incorrect at the end of this chapter.

1. Easy Connect makes Remote Assistance connections easier to establish. Which two of the following are components of Easy Connect?

   A. Internet Connection Sharing

   B. Broadband (PPPoE)

   C. Peer Name Resolution Protocol (PNRP)

   D. IPv6 and Teredo tunneling

2. Which of the following is used to launch Remote Desktop from the command line?

   A. *mstsc.exe*

   B. *netsh*

   C. *tsclient*

   D. *net use*

3. Your network technician calls and asks you which port number he needs to open on his firewall router to allow Remote Desktop traffic. Which port number do you give him?

   A. 443

   B. 25

   C. 110

   D. 3389

4. Which of the following isn't a VPN tunneling protocol supported by Windows 8?

   A. IKEv2

   B. SSL

   C. PPTP

   D. SSTP

   E. L2TP

5. Which of the following is the strongest authentication method supported by Windows 8?

   A. EAP-MS-CHAPv2

   B. PAP

   C. CHAP

   D. MS-CHAP v2

Objective 5.2: Configure mobility options

Windows 8 is designed to support a new generation of mobile computer users who expect to always be connected to the Internet, be fully synchronized with all their data, and not have to worry about when the laptop or tablet battery runs out.

> **This objective covers the following topics:**
> - Configuring power policies
> - Configuring offline file policies
> - Configuring Windows to Go
> - Configuring sync options
> - Configuring Wi-Fi Direct

Using the Windows Mobility Center

Mobile devices are growing in popularity, especially for teenagers and young adults. Portability is the expected standard for this generation and is unlikely to reverse. Where perceived weaknesses are identified in mobile computing, new opportunities emerge to service them; for example, portable battery boosters, detachable keyboards, and folding Bluetooth mice have all emerged within a short period of time.

The following devices currently make up the mobile landscape:

- Laptops and notebooks
- Netbooks
- Ultrabooks
- Touch-enabled laptops and ultrabooks
- Tablet devices
- Smartphones

Already you've seen just in the last few years notebooks and netbooks fading in popularity and smartphones, tablets, and ultrabooks becoming the "must-have" devices.

The Windows Mobility Center offers users an easy-to-use portal, which brings together key mobility settings that you can quickly configure without needing to locate each setting in the Control Panel. To launch the Mobility Center, press Windows+X. The portal includes settings for the following:

- Display brightness
- Volume
- Battery status and current power plan
- Wireless networking (if you are currently connected to Wi-Fi)

- External display
- Sync Center
- Presentation settings

Items developed by independent software vendors can also appear in the Windows Mobility Center.

Configuring power policies

As users become more mobile, they demand greater portability, quicker startup, and longer battery life. Users have always had to balance performance and battery life. The power options in Windows 8 allow users to carefully fine-tune the most appropriate power settings that match their lifestyles. When those settings are perfected, users can export the power profile and import it to other devices easily.

Windows 8 inherited several excellent power-management tools and features from Windows 7 and also made some improvements. One new feature is a battery meter found by default in the notification tray, which tells you at a glance how much battery life is remaining. It also allows you to quickly switch power plans to meet your needs.

Using the Power Options utility in Control Panel

Power plans let you adjust and fine-tune your computer's performance and power consumption. You can define separate power plans for when a mobile device is plugged into the power supply or if it's using the device battery. Notice that the power plan console has not changed significantly from previous Windows versions.

All power-related items are available via Power Options, which can be accessed in a variety of ways:

- In the Control Panel, choose Power Options.
- Search for *power* and select Power Options.
- On the desktop, right-click the Battery icon in the notification area and select Power Options.
- In the Windows Mobility Center, choose Battery Status.
- On the command line, type **powercfg.exe**.

By default, three pre-configured power plans are available, as shown in Figure 5-11:

- **Balanced** Default and recommended, this setting offers good performance when needed while trying to conserve battery life.
- **Power Saver** This setting reduces system performance whenever possible with the aim of maximizing the duration of the battery.
- **High Performance** This setting uses the full performance of the device, which uses the most battery power.

A common misconception is to think that Power Options only relate to laptops when drawing power from the internal battery. You can set your desktop, laptop, and tablet to the High Performance setting and make it the default for whenever the device is connected to the power supply. The device reverts automatically to the balanced power plan after it's unplugged and becomes mobile again.

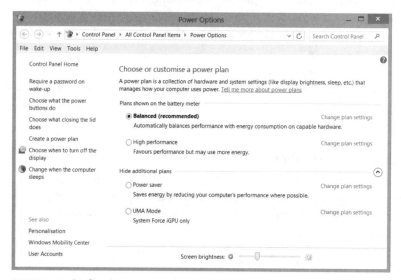

FIGURE 5-11 Configuring power options

Later, this section explains how to use Group Policy to configure power plans. After you create the desired power plan within the user interface, you can then export it by using the powercfg.exe command-line tool with the /IMPORT and /EXPORT switches. The power configuration data file has a .pow file extension.

Each power scheme is labeled with the unique Globally Unique Identifier (GUID) of the computer. A GUID is a 128-bit integer (16 bytes) that is unique to each computer and is used as a unique identifier.

Within the Power Options tool are many other options that you can configure. For example, you could configure your laptop to hibernate whenever you close the laptop lid.

You should also know the standard settings for turning a computer on and off:

- **Shut down** Clears the page file, closes all open applications, logs out the active user, and turns off the computer.

- **Hibernate** Saves the system state and system memory contents to a file on the hard disk and powers off the computer. The file, hiberfil.sys, is the same size as the physical memory contained on the computer and is typically located in the root of the system drive.

- **Sleep** Saves work and open programs to RAM, which provides fast resume capability (typically several seconds). This setting consumes a small amount of power. By default, Windows 8 goes into Sleep mode when you press the on/off button on the computer. If the computer's battery power runs low, the system switches to Hibernate mode.

To add hibernation to the Power menu, follow these steps:

- Search for *power* on the Start screen and select Power Options.

- Click Choose What The Power Buttons Do.

- On the System Settings page, click Change Settings That Are Currently Unavailable (see Figure 5-12).

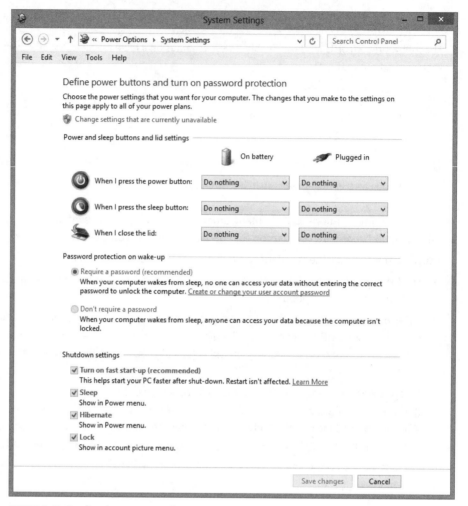

FIGURE 5-12 Configuring power options

- Items that were greyed out before are now changeable. Select the Hibernate: Show In Power Menu check box.

- Restart the computer if prompted.

Using Group Policy to configure Power Management

You can use Group Policy to configure Power Management policy settings separately in Windows 8 for when the computer is plugged in or running on battery power (see Figure 5-13):

- **Button Settings** Used to configure the behavior of pressing the following:

  - Power and sleep buttons

  - Start menu power button

  - Lid switch on laptops

- **Hard Disk Settings** Used to specify the period of inactivity after which the hard drive turns off
- **Notification Settings** Used to specify low and critical battery levels and behavior
- **Sleep Settings** Used to specify sleep and hibernation timeouts and behavior
- **Video and Display Settings** Used to configure the display timeout, which controls the length of inactivity before the display automatically turns off

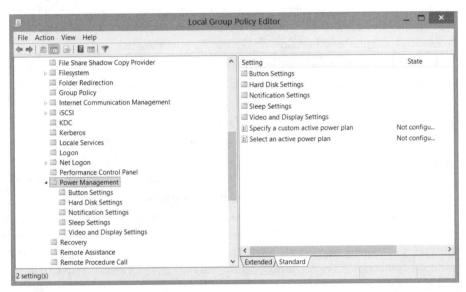

FIGURE 5-13 Group Policy settings for power management

> **NOTE CORPORATE POWER SAVINGS**
>
> If your organization uses a server and Active Directory Directory Services, you also can modify all the power settings via the Group Policy Preferences within Group Policy Management. This will allow an administrator to create centralized power configurations that can be applied to selected computers and users within the organization.

Group Policy settings for Power Management are found in the following location: Computer Management/Administrative Templates/System/Power Management.

> **NOTE VIEWING POWER MANAGEMENT SETTINGS**
>
> Powercfg.exe exposes all power management settings, including those that aren't available in the UI or from Group Policy.

Working with offline files

One benefit of working in an office is that you have all your resources available, such as your filing cabinet, draw full of pens, and a fast networked printer across the hall. Those days of the office being the "norm" is changing, and the Offline Files feature was an initial enabler for allowing office-based staff to start worrying less about if and how the IT infrastructure worked and allowed them to focus on the actual workload itself.

Offline files allow staff to continue working, even if they are away from the office or the network goes down. The Offline Files feature has been built in since Windows 2000 Professional and provides the following benefits for enterprise users:

- Users can continue working with files shared on the corporate network, even when those file servers become unavailable because of network issues or some other problem.
- Users in remote or branch offices or home offices can continue working with files stored on file servers at corporate headquarters, even when the Internet or WAN link between the remote office and headquarters is unavailable or slow.
- Remote workers can continue working with files stored on network shares when they are traveling and can't connect to the remote corporate network.

Offline files are the locally cached files available to remote users, even if they aren't connected to the corporate file server. When mobile users work with offline files, they simply use them just as they were working on the actual files on the file servers. In the background, the Windows operating system keeps both sets of files fully synchronized and up to date whenever the data connection is restored.

The Offline Files feature isn't enabled by default. Users select which network shared files and folder they require to be made available offline. Local cached copies of the files on their portable devices have the same "look and feel" as the online files. As soon as they reconnect to the file servers, the files are automatically synchronized according to the timestamp, and the most up-to-date versions of the files are copied over to the file servers and marked as the latest versions.

Enabling offline files

Settings for the Offline Files feature can be made from either the server side, or the client side.

CONFIGURING SERVER-SIDE OPTIONS

Administrators can configure the following options from the server side:

- Only The Files And Programs That Users Specify Are Available Offline
- No Files Or Programs From The Shared Folder Are Available Offline
- All Files And Programs That Users Open From The Shared Folder Are Automatically Available Offline

To set options for Offline Files from the server side for users on a network share, follow these steps:

1. Open File Explorer, or the Shared Folders snap-in within Computer Management (press Windows+X).

2. Navigate to a network share and right-click the shared folder to access the properties.

3. Click the Offline Settings button.

4. Choose one of the three options for the shared folder Offline Settings, as shown in Figure 5-14, and then click OK.

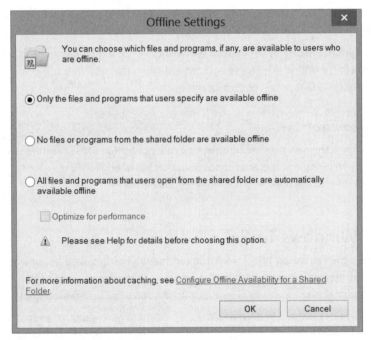

FIGURE 5-14 Configuring offline files from the server

CONFIGURING CLIENT-SIDE OPTIONS

On the client (user) side, you can choose to make a file or folder offline by following these steps:

1. Open File Explorer.

2. Navigate to the network file or folder that you want to make available offline.

3. Right-click the file or folder, and then click Always Available Offline.

Windows now synchronizes a locally cached copy onto your computer. The next time you try to access this file or folder, you can open it from the same network location, even if the network version is unavailable.

> **NOTE DISABLING OFFLINE FILES AND FOLDERS**
>
> If you no longer want a network file or folder to be available offline, simply right-click it and then click Always Available Offline to clear the check mark on the context menu.

Configuring offline file policies

Thirty Group Policy settings directly affecting Offline Files can be found in the following sub-tree location: Local Computer Policy/Administrative Templates/Network/Offline Files.

Windows 8 introduced two new Group Policies for working with Offline Files:

- **Remove "Work Offline" Commands** This policy removes the Work Offline option in File Explorer.
- **Enable File Synchronization On Costed Networks** Disabled by default, this policy doesn't synchronize offline files in the background when the system is using Global System for Mobile (GSM) or cell phone roaming.

> **NOTE METERED CONNECTIONS**
>
> Windows 8 introduced the new terminology *metered connections* for when a feature uses 4G mobile network roaming or a metered connection that has bandwidth usage limits. Some settings still refer to the legacy terminology: *costed networks*.

Configuring Windows To Go

In all the prerelease hype regarding Windows 8, the top feature being talked about was Windows To Go. Even though no one had seen the feature live, everyone seemed to be an expert on it. No wonder everyone was talking about it; Windows To Go sounded great.

Now that Windows 8 is released and Windows To Go has hardware support, everyone can now use it. With Windows To Go, you can bring together the whole cloud-based story into one 3-inch-long removable USB flash drive. I was recently on vacation and even tried it on a PC at an Internet café and it worked great; the owner was stunned that I had Windows 8 in my pocket.

Windows To Go offers users and administrators a unique feature, but you need to be aware of some considerations regarding its use:

- **Hibernate and Sleep are disabled** Disabling them helps protect Windows To Go from data corruption. They can be re-enabled by Group Policy.

- **Internal disks are offline** This is to segregate the two operating systems—that is, the host and Windows To Go.

- **Windows To Go USB drive doesn't appear in File Explorer** Again, this is to segregate the two operating systems. You can allocate a drive letter in Computer Management to see the contents of the USB drive.

- **BitLocker TPM isn't used** The Trusted Platform Module (TPM) chip is tied to the computer's motherboard and therefore can't travel with the Windows To Go USB drive. A BitLocker password can be used instead of TPM.

- **Windows Recovery Environment isn't available** If your USB drive becomes corrupt, you need to reimage it.

- **Push Button Reset isn't available** This feature isn't supported.

- **It's available only for Windows 8 Enterprise users** Only the Windows 8 Enterprise version is licensed to create a Windows To Go drive.

EXAM TIP

Windows To Go is licensed only for Microsoft Software Assurance customers who have Windows 8 Enterprise edition.

When each new computer that uses Windows To Go is started, to use hardware such as webcams, printers, and so on, Windows 8 needs to detect all the new hardware that it finds and install the necessary drivers and restart. Subsequent visits to the same "host" computer load the correct drivers as Windows To Go starts, and no delay should occur.

The requirements for Windows To Go are as follows:

- 32 GB or larger USB removable drive formatted with NTFS
- A computer that fulfills the minimum hardware requirements for Windows 8
- Microsoft Software Assurance Windows Enterprise 8 license

Here are some best practices for using Windows To Go:

- Purchase verified USB drive hardware that has been certified to work with Windows To Go.
- Always shut down Windows and wait for shutdown to complete before removing the Windows To Go drive.
- Don't insert the Windows To Go drive into a running computer.
- Don't start the Windows To Go drive from a USB hub. Always insert the Windows To Go drive directly into a port on the computer.
- Use a USB 3.0 port with Windows To Go wherever possible.
- Don't pull out the Windows To Go USB drive while it's in use.

Remember that Windows To Go doesn't replace your standard PC or laptop; moreover, it should be seen as an additional offering whenever the opportunity arises. Imagine working away from the office without your laptop; with your Windows To Go workspace device, you could use another computer that supports starting from USB. (Most PCs manufactured in the last five years support USB startup.)

By leveraging cloud services such as SkyDrive and using a Microsoft account to sign into Windows 8, your "desktop" will be available on your Windows To Go workspace, and your working files will be synchronized securely into your SkyDrive.

Configuring Group Policy settings for Windows To Go

If you want to control Windows To Go settings via Group Policy, the following settings are available in the subtree Local Computer Policy/Computer Configuration/Administrative Templates/Windows Components/Portable Operating System:

- **Allow hibernate (S4) when starting from a Windows To Go workspace** Specifies whether the PC can use the Hibernate sleep state (S4) when started from a Windows To Go workspace.

- **Disallow standby sleep states (S1-S3) when starting from a Windows To Go workspace** Specifies whether the PC can use Standby sleep states (S1-S3) when starting from a Windows To Go workspace.

- **Windows To Go Default Start-up Options** Controls whether the PC starts to Windows To Go if a USB device containing a Windows To Go workspace is connected. Also controls whether users can make changes using the Windows To Go Start-up Options Control Panel item.

- **Allow Store to install apps on Windows To Go workspaces** Allows or denies access to the Store application on Windows To Go workspaces. (Note that this policy is located in the /Windows Components/Store subtree.)

Creating a Windows To Go Workspace

To create a portable Windows To Go workspace, you should use the built-in wizard that's available as part of Windows 8 Enterprise edition.

> **NOTE WINDOWS TO GO BEFORE RTM**
>
> Before the Release to Manufacturing (RTM) version of Windows 8 Enterprise, you could create a Windows To Go workspace using ImageX and BCDBoot, but this wasn't supported.

Follow the steps to create a Windows To Go workspace:

1. Insert your USB drive into your PC.

2. In Windows 8 Enterprise edition, perform a search for *windows to go* (see Figure 5-15).

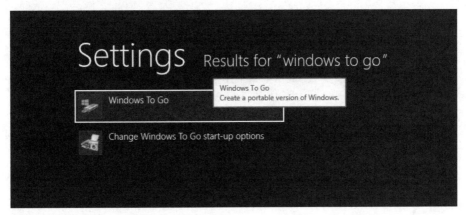

FIGURE 5-15 Searching for *Windows To Go*

3. Start the Create A Windows To Go Workspace Wizard.

4. On the Choose The Drive *You* Want To Use page, select the drive that represents the USB drive you inserted in step 1 (see Figure 5-16).

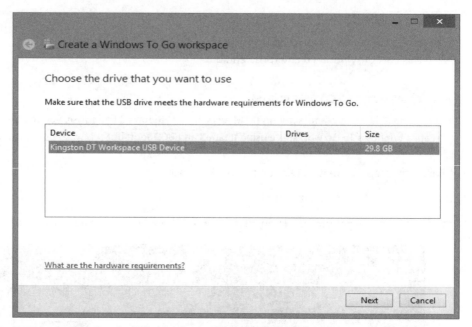

FIGURE 5-16 Selecting the USB drive for the Windows To Go workspace

5. On the Choose A Windows 8 Image page, click Add Search Location and then navigate to the file folder location that contains your sysprep generalized .wim file image that you will use for your Windows To Go workspace (see Figure 5-17).

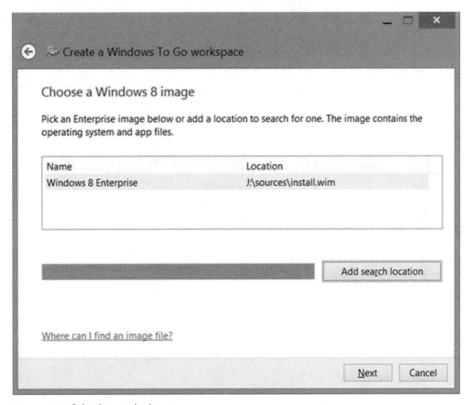

FIGURE 5-17 Selecting a .wim image

6. Optionally, on the Set A BitLocker Password (Optional) page, select Use BitLocker With My Windows To Go Workspace to encrypt your Windows To Go drive.

7. Optionally, if you chose to use BitLocker to protect your drive, your recovery password is saved in the documents library of the computer used to create the workspace automatically.

8. Click Create to start the Windows To Go workspace provisioning process (see Figure 5-18).

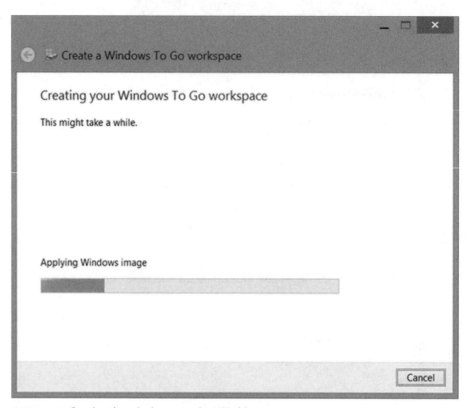

FIGURE 5-18 Copying the .wim image to the USB drive

Wait for the process to complete. A completion page appears (see Figure 5-19) when your Windows To Go workspace is ready to use. You can now enable the Windows To Go startup options and restart into your Windows To Go device.

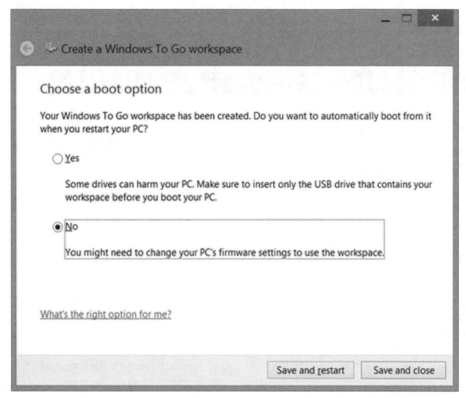

FIGURE 5-19 Choosing a startup option

Configuring sync options

This section focuses on the new options relating to the cloud-based synchronizing of user profile information for users whom use a Microsoft account (formerly known as a *Windows Live ID*) when they log in into Windows 8.

For users upgrading from previous versions of Windows, using Windows 8 means somewhat of a fundamental change in functionality. For example, you can have all your settings synced with each other across multiple Windows 8 devices.

As you will soon see, you are in complete control of the sync options. For example, you can choose whether to sync your home laptop and your Windows RT tablet but not your office desktop computer. The choice is yours.

Windows 8 syncs only devices that you sign into with your Microsoft account *and* if you confirm that the PC is "trusted" (see Figure 5-20). As an added measure of control, even if you sign in with your Microsoft account and the PC is trusted, you can still turn off sync.

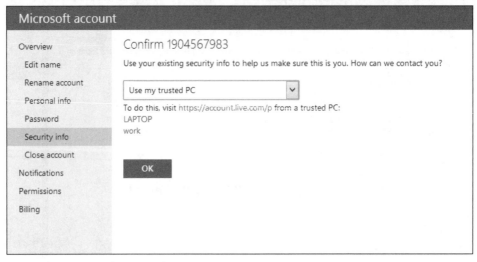

FIGURE 5-20 Trusting the Microsoft account

If you are using a Microsoft account, the following settings are synced automatically by default:

- **Sync Settings On This PC** Enabled by default. If turned off, Windows overrides all the following settings.

- **Personalize** If enabled, Windows syncs colors, lock screen, background, and account picture settings.

- **Desktop Personalization** If enabled, Windows syncs your themes, taskbar, high contrast, and more.

- **Passwords** If enabled, Windows syncs passwords for websites, networks, HomeGroups, and some apps.

- **Ease Of Access** If enabled, Windows syncs high-contrast Narrator, Magnifier, and more.

- **Language Preferences** If enabled, Windows syncs keyboards and other input methods, the display language, and more.

- **App Settings** If enabled, Windows syncs certain settings in your apps.

- **Browser** If enabled, Windows syncs settings and info such as history and favorites for Internet Explorer 10.

- **Other Windows Settings** If enabled, Windows syncs File Explorer, mouse settings, and more. You also can choose to limit sync when you are using a metered connection.

If you want to limit or turn off any of these above settings, follow these steps:

1. Press Windows+I and chose Change PC Settings.

2. Click to open the Sync Your Settings app.

3. Make your choices (as shown in Figure 5-21) and then close the app.

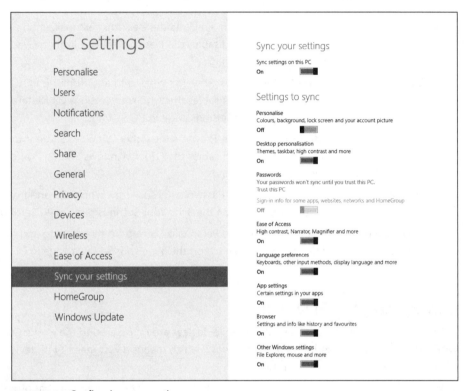

FIGURE 5-21 Configuring sync options

> **NOTE USING SYNC ON A DOMAIN-JOINED PC**
>
> Even if you are part of a corporate domain, you can still sync your details. To do so, you
> need to connect your domain account to a Microsoft account in PC Settings | Users, and
> then confirm the machine as a trusted PC on the Microsoft account.

If you want to control these settings via Group Policy so you can then configure syncs
across several machines, all the settings are available in the subtree Local Computer Policy/
Computer Configuration/Administrative Templates/Windows Components/Sync your settings.
The following policy settings are available:

■ **Do not sync** Prevents syncing to and from this PC. This also disables the Sync Your
Settings On This PC switch on the Sync Your Settings page in PC Settings.

- **Do not sync app settings** Prevents the App Settings group from syncing to and from this PC and disables the App Settings switch on the Sync Your Settings page in PC settings.

- **Do not sync browser settings** Prevents the Browser settings from syncing to and from this PC and disables the Browser switch on the Sync Your Settings page in PC Settings.

- **Do not sync desktop personalization** Prevents the Desktop Personalization settings from syncing to and from this PC and disables the Desktop Personalization switch on the Sync Your Settings page in PC Settings.

- **Do not sync on metered connections** Prevents syncing to and from this PC when on metered Internet connections and disables the Sync Your Settings On Metered Connections switch on the Sync Your Settings page in PC Settings.

- **Do not sync other Windows settings** Prevents the Other Windows Settings group from syncing to and from this PC and disables the Other Windows Settings switch on the Sync Your Settings page in PC Settings.

- **Do not sync passwords** Prevents the Passwords group from syncing to and from this PC and disables the Passwords switch on the Sync Your Settings page in PC Settings.

- **Do not sync personalize** Prevents the Personalize group from syncing to and from this PC and disables the Personalize switch on the Sync Your Settings page in PC Settings.

Configuring Wi-Fi Direct

Approximately 1.2 billion Wi-Fi–enabled mobile devices are in use around the world. Current Wi-Fi devices require a fixed topology framework, which means a vast majority of devices can talk to each other only if a router is present.

Wi-Fi Direct is a new and emerging point-to-point connectivity technology that offers secure high-bandwidth connections between two devices over a private peer-to-peer Wi-Fi network without the need for additional hardware such as routers or access points. (On previous Windows versions, you might have come across the name *ad hoc Wi-Fi*. This term has been replaced with Wi-Fi Direct in Windows 8.)

What makes Wi-Fi Direct very exciting is that you can connect two Wi-Fi devices and transfer files with very high bandwidth without the need for additional hardware. The following provides a high-level overview:

- Provides a secure, wireless connection between two devices

- Allows consistent pairing experience using "Find + Pair + Connect"

- Uses the new 802.11 device discovery protocol

- Pairs with found device via PIN or direct push button.

- Automatically detects and installs the PlayTo Device after Wi-Fi Direct pairing

When you use Wi-Fi Direct, you need to keep the following considerations in mind:

- Devices need to be paired to communicate. (Pairing is similar to Bluetooth pairing.)

- Bandwidth is sufficient for media streaming because of single hop & 802.11n.

- Devices can use IPv4 or IPv6.

- Wi-Fi Direct is designed to fit the Wi-Fi Alliance Industry Standard specification.

- For a Windows 8 to Windows 8 connection, a maximum of two devices is allowed.

- Wi-Fi Direct uses built-in WPA2 security with no user configuration.

- No additional hardware is required to take advantage of Wi-Fi Direct.

- You can use the PlayTo feature to stream video, music, or picture files stored on your computer to a PlayTo device.

Windows 8 offers built-in support within the networking stack for Wi-Fi Direct, which is accessed either directly via a Wi-Fi Direct–enabled app, or via *netsh* command-line option using an elevated prompt.

Use the following command to create a Wi-Fi Direct network:

```
netsh wlan set hostednetwork mode=allow ssid=wifidirect key=passphrase
```

You can start Wi-Fi Direct by running this command:

```
netsh wlan start hostednetwork
```

To stop Wi-Fi Direct, run this command:

```
netsh wlan stop hostednetwork
```

The Windows 8 machine now broadcasts this SSID and allows connections without an Access Point, as shown in Figure 5-22.

MORE INFO **CONFERENCE SESSION ON WI-FI DIRECT**

The Microsoft BUILD conference for developers showcased Wi-Fi Direct in a session titled "Understanding Wi-Fi Direct in Windows 8." You can find it at *http://channel9.msdn.com/ Events/BUILD/BUILD2011/HW-329T.*

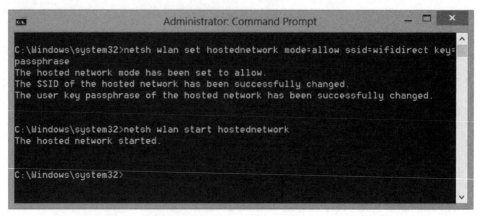

FIGURE 5-22 Using *netsh* to configure Wi-Fi Direct

Thought experiment

Privacy concerns using Sync

In the following thought experiment, apply what you've learned about the objective. You can find answers to these questions in the "Answers" section at the end of this chapter.

You want to implement the Windows 8 sync options for users of Windows 8 devices. One member of your staff, Hilary, is uncomfortable sharing personal information.

Indicate which areas can be synced and how you can reassure Hilary's concerns for privacy.

Objective summary

- Windows 8 offers three preconfigured power plans; Balanced, Power Saver, and High Performance.
- Power schemes can be imported and exported on a system using the configuration settings saved in a .pow file.
- Locally cached offline files are synchronized and kept up to date each time Windows 8 restores a network connection to the original files.
- Windows To Go is a Windows 8 Enterprise feature that enables a fully working version of Windows 8 to run from a removable USB drive.
- Signing into a Windows 8 trusted computer with a Microsoft account allows Windows to sync profile settings, including passwords, desktop personalization, and browser settings between shared devices.
- Wi-Fi Direct offers high-bandwidth wireless networking.

Objective review

Answer the following questions to test your knowledge of the information in this objective. You can find the answers to these questions and explanations of why each answer choice is correct or incorrect at the end of this chapter.

1. Choose three standard choices for the Power Off button in Windows 8.

    A. Hibernate

    B. Hybrid Sleep

    C. Restart

    D. Sleep

    E. Shut Down

2. Which of the following files is created during Sleep mode?

    A. Hiberfil.sys

    B. Pagefile

    C. Dumpfile

    D. BCDBoot

3. You want to export the current customized power options. Which command-line option would you use??

    A. *powercfg -import C:\customscheme.pow <<GUID>>*

    B. *powercfg –L*

    C. *powercfg -export C:\customescheme.pow <<GUID>>*

    D. *powercfg -getactivescheme*

4. Which of the following isn't a valid Offline Files caching option in Windows 8?

    A. Encrypt Offline Files

    B. No Files Or Programs From The Shared Folder Are Available Offline

    C. All Files And Programs That Users Open From The Shared Folder Are Automatically Available Offline

    D. Only The Files And Programs That Users Specify Are Available Offline

5. Windows To Go has which of the following considerations?

    A. If the USB drive becomes corrupt, you can run the Windows Recovery Environment.

    B. BitLocker can't be used.

    C. Windows 8 Enterprise and Professional editions support Windows To Go.

    D. Hibernate and Sleep are disabled.

6. Sync offers to synchronize which of the following settings?

    A. Password

    B. Language Preferences

    C. Spelling Dictionary

    D. Shared pictures

7. You can enable Wi-Fi Direct via the command line using the *netsh* command. What is the correct syntax?

    A. `netsh wlan start hostednetwork`

    B. `netsh wlan set hostednetwork mode=allow ssid=wifidirect key=passphrase`

    C. `netsh wlan start hostednetwork mode=allow ssid=wifidirect key=passphrase`

    D. `netsh wlan stop hostednetwork`

Objective 5.3: Configure security for mobile devices

Some of you know from experience or know of someone whose laptop or tablet was lost or stolen. Losing anything can be a traumatic experience, especially a computer. Although I've never lost a laptop, I've inserted plenty of those little removable USB sticks and forgot to pull them out again, leaving them behind. Losing your corporate confidential information to an opportunist thief on the subway or leaving USB stick with your internal sales pricing spread-sheet on a customer's PC can be career limiting as well as potentially very damaging for the organization.

Thankfully, Windows 8 can encrypt all your removable USB external data drives or thumb drives and every laptop in your organization or home, without the need for additional hardware. All you need is either Windows 8 Pro or Windows 8 Enterprise edition. (BitLocker is supported only on these two Windows versions.)

To encrypt the volumes on your computer BitLocker, you can, if one is present, use a Trusted Platform Module (TPM) chip—a dedicated security hardware microchip built onto your motherboard, which holds the keys used in the encryption. If your device doesn't have a TPM 1.2 (or later), BitLocker can alternatively use a USB flash drive to store the startup key used to encrypt/decrypt the volumes.

Chapter 4, "Configure access to resources," discusses Encrypting File System (EFS) and how that tool encrypts files and folders. BitLocker, unlike EFS, can encrypt entire volumes, includ-ing the page file, hibernation file, registry, and temporary files (which might hold confidential information). EFS can encrypt only user files, not system files.

Recall the discussion in Chapter 4 of rootkits and their invisibly to Windows. BitLocker, when used with TPM hardware, can help protect against rootkits by ensuring that Windows startup files haven't been modified, thus protecting your system integrity.

In the days before BitLocker, one common way to bypass Windows New Technology File System (NTFS) security was to remove the hard drive and place it inside another computer as a second drive. A thief could then access all the data without ever needing to know a single password. Of course, if the files were protected with EFS, they would be safe. BitLocker prevents a thief from extracting data from a stolen hard disk by forcing the user to enter a recovery password before gaining access to the protected volumes.

This objective covers the following topics:

- Configure BitLocker and BitLocker To Go policies
- Configuring startup key storage
- Configuring remote wipe
- Configuring location settings (GPS)

Understanding how BitLocker works

BitLocker-encrypted drives can be decrypted only by someone with access to the decryption key, known as the *Full Volume Encryption Key (FVEK)*. Windows 8 actually stores the FVEK in the volume metadata of the drive. This metadata then is also encrypted using the Volume Master Key (VMK). Both the FVEK and the VMK use maximum-strength Advanced Encryption Standard (AES) 256-bit encryption, whereas the cipher strength for the volume encryption uses 128-bit AES with Diffuser. (AES256 bit can be used, but this affects performance). In essence, as long as Windows 8 has access to the Full Volume Encryption Key (FVEK), Windows can encrypt and decrypt data on the volume on the fly as required.

At startup, the system checks to see whether all components are in the right place and haven't been modified. Only then, if everything is correct, can the TPM chip provide Windows Boot Manager with the decrypted Volume Master Key it needs to unlock the Full Volume Encryption Key and read the drive contents.

The stages of BitLocker startup are as follows:

1. System integrity is verified if a TPM is present.

2. (Optional) User authentication collects a key from USB storage or a PIN from the user.

3. The VMK is retrieved, and the Windows Boot Manager requests that the TPM decrypt the VMK.

4. The operating system starts.

5. The VMK is passed to the operating system loader.

6. Windows uses the VMK to decrypt the FVEK.

7. Windows uses the FVEK to decrypt the BitLocker encrypted volume.

The volume and its data will be still encrypted and unreadable if any of the following states changes:

- The TPM is disabled in BIOS.
- The TPM is corrupted.
- The disk is moved to another computer.
- The Windows boot files are changed.
- A PIN or USB flash drive isn't provided.

If the drive is locked, the recovery key must be entered to allow Windows to access the data. If no recovery key is provided, the disk remains encrypted.

Since Windows Vista first introduced BitLocker, Microsoft has added a number of improvements, as shown in the following table. You can see from this table that BitLocker continues to improve:

Operating System	BitLocker Improvement
Vista	Encrypt only one volume
Vista SP1	Encrypt data volumes
Windows 7	BitLocker To Go
Windows 8	BitLocker pre-provisioning Used disk space–only encryption Standard user PIN and password selection Network Unlock Extended Storage Support

NOTE BETTER SAFE THAN SORRY

You are recommended to save your recovery password to multiple locations or a USB flash drive to ensure that you can recover it in case the BitLocker drive becomes locked. Keep the recovery keys safe and separate from the protected computer.

This section focuses on the improvements and then walks you through the configuration of BitLocker and BitLocker To Go. These new features and enhancements in Windows 8 are as follows:

- BitLocker pre-provisioning
- Used disk space–only encryption
- Standard user PIN and password selection

- Network Unlock
- Extended storage support

BitLocker pre-provisioning

In Windows 8, administrators can enable BitLocker for a volume even before installing the operating system. This saves both the user and administrators a huge amount of time and simplifies the deployment of BitLocker. In Windows Vista and Windows 7, users had to wait until Windows had been fully installed, BitLocker had been enabled, and the entire encryption process finished.

During pre-provisioning, Windows generates a random "temporary" encryption key that Bit-Locker uses to encrypt the volume. After Windows is finished deploying, users can fully protect their system by activating BitLocker on the volume and selecting a BitLocker unlock method.

Administrators can enable BitLocker pre-provisioning from the Windows Pre-installation Environment (WinPE) by using the manage-bde BitLocker command-line utility. For example, to pre-provision BitLocker on your D drive, type the following command at a WinPE command prompt:

```
manage-bde -on d:
```

> **NOTE** **INCLUDING MANAGE-BDE WITH WINPE**
>
> You need to create a customized WinPE image to make manage-bde work in WinPE, because a standard WinPE image won't include manage-bde or the WMI tools.

As soon as BitLocker is pre-provisioned, you must select a BitLocker unlock method. You can choose one of the following BitLocker unlock methods to unlock the operating system volume:

- Trusted Platform Module (TPM) only
- TPM plus PIN
- TPM plus startup key
- TPM plus PIN plus startup key
- Startup key only

If the volume was a data drive or a removable drive, you can choose one of the following BitLocker unlock methods:

- Password
- Smart card
- Automatic unlock

> **MORE INFO** **A GOOD BITLOCKER REFERENCE**
>
> The Microsoft article, "How Strong Do You Want the BitLocker Protection?" is a useful comparison of the unlock methods. You can find it at *http://w1n.in/Wqla*.

Used disk space–only encryption

Windows 8 BitLocker supports a new encryption option that encrypts only the used space on a protected volume. Used disk space–only encryption makes the encryption of volumes much faster, as shown in Figure 5-23. In previous Windows versions, BitLocker would encrypt every sector on the disk—that is, the data as well as all free space.

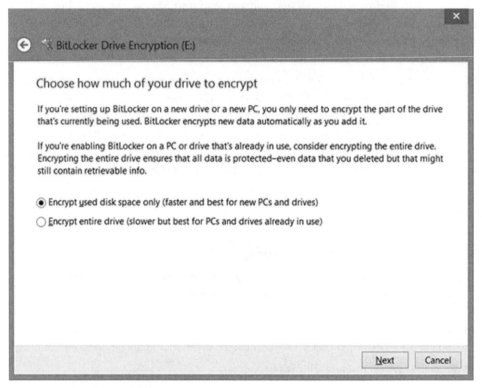

FIGURE 5-23 BitLocker used disk space

Microsoft recommends that you use the used disk space–only encryption method only on new PCs and new volumes. Full encryption is the recommended option for volumes that already have data present because the free space on a previously used volume might still hold user data. In these cases, only full encryption can ensure that everything is encrypted and therefore protected.

When you enable BitLocker from the command-line by using manage-bde with the *-on* switch, BitLocker uses full encryption. If you require BitLocker to use the used disk space–only encryption option, you must add the *-usedspaceonly* switch after the *-on* switch, as shown in Figure 5-24.

FIGURE 5-24 Using the used disk space–only encryption method

Standard user PIN and password change

Another much-welcomed BitLocker addition is the ability to allow a standard user to change the following:

- BitLocker unlock PIN for system drives
- BitLocker unlock password for fixed data drives

With this new ability, an administrator can more easily set a default initial personal identification number (PIN) or password value on all deployed PC images. When deployed, users can be told to change the initial values to ones that they can choose. Windows 8 now allows users to change their BitLocker PIN or password as required without contacting the helpdesk to perform the task on their behalf. The helpdesk retains the ability to reset a forgotten password or PIN, however.

> **NOTE** **CHANGING BITLOCKER PASSWORDS OR PINS**
>
> Standard users can change the password or PIN only if they know the current PIN or password. A user has five attempts to enter the correct current PIN or password before she's blocked from further attempts. The retry count can be reset to zero when an administrator resets the volume PIN or password or when the system is restarted.

Using Network Unlock

Network Unlock is a new unlocking method for BitLocker-protected system volumes. Network Unlock allows for the automatic (that is, no user intervention) unlocking of a BitLocker-protected system volume whenever a Windows domain-joined desktop or server starts.

This new feature should ease the administrative burden on IT professionals and support because it allows BitLocker-protected devices to be treated just like other corporate machines in that they can also be forced to restart and automatically install software and security patches on these machines. Previously, these machines would halt at the password or PIN stage of startup.

Network Unlock still secures the volume by use of the TPM but instead of obtaining the startup key from a USB drive, Network Unlock uses an unlock key that's tied to the machine's TPM chip and a key that's received from a Windows Server 2012 Windows Deployment Services server on the trusted network. If the Windows Deployment Services server is unavailable, BitLocker reverts back to the standard startup key unlock screen.

The key exchange between the client and the Windows Deployment Services server uses DHCP. The Windows Deployment Services server role must have the optional BitLocker Network Unlock feature installed to allow the server to service the incoming Network Unlock DHCP requests.

On the client side, Network Unlock requires the client hardware to have a DHCP driver implemented in Unified Extensible Firmware Interface (UEFI), which is found on modern motherboards. Finally, the Windows Deployment Services server and clients need to trust each other, which is achieved by installing a special X.509 certificate and associated private key.

Extended storage support

Windows 8 BitLocker supports a new type of disk drive that provides hardware-based encryption: Encrypted Hard Drives (EHDs). You can manage EHDs and BitLocker through the same BitLocker Drive Encryption Control Panel applet. EHDs and BitLocker each use a different approach for encryption, as follows:

- **BitLocker** Protects system and data volumes by using volume-level and software-based encryption.
- **Encrypted Hard Drives** Provides Full Disk Encryption (FDE) and hardware-based encryption. FDE occurs on the disk level; hardware-based encryption is offloaded to the drive's storage controller, making encryption operations more efficient.

In Windows 8, Device Manager identifies EHDs and integrates them into the operating system.

MORE INFO **MICROSOFT BITLOCKER FAQ**

You can find this FAQ at *http://technet.microsoft.com/en-us/library/hh831507.aspx.*

NOTE **PAUSING BITLOCKER DURING DRIVE ENCRYPTION**

After encryption starts, you are told not to remove the removable drive during encryption process, although you can pause the process and resume later.

Configuring BitLocker

Windows 8 BitLocker allows any volume to be encrypted. The system drive and data volume are recommended to be encrypted to secure the data. If your computer doesn't have a TPM, you can still use BitLocker, but you will be using the Startup key–only authentication method and will need to have enabled the Group Policy setting (discussed in the next section) to allow BitLocker to be used without a TPM chip. Follow these steps to enable BitLocker:

1. Log on to a Windows 8 computer with an account that has administrative privileges.

2. Search for *bitlocker* and select BitLocker Drive Encryption.

3. Next to the C: BitLocker Off icon, click Turn BitLocker On.

4. Click Next in the next three windows (if your system has a TPM chip).

5. Choose how to unlock your drive at startup in the next window.

6. If your system doesn't have a TPM, you are presented with two choices as shown in Figure 5-25. Choose Enter A Password and then enter a complex password.

7. You will be prompted to back up your recovery key. You are offered four different options to store the recovery key:
   - Save To Your Microsoft Account
   - Save To A USB Flash Drive
   - Save To A File
   - Print It.

8. Choose Save To A File and save the file in a safe location.

9. Choose how much of your drive to encrypt window and click Next.

10. In the Are You Ready To Encrypt Disk Drive? window, leave everything as default and click Continue.

11. Click Restart Now to restart the computer.

12. After the computer restarts, enter the BitLocker password specified previously and start Windows 8.

After logging onto Windows 8, BitLocker begins encrypting the drive. This can take several minutes or hours, depending on the amount of data on your drive. You can continue to use your system during this process.

NOTE USING A USB DRIVE TO UNLOCK BITLOCKER

If you want to store the BitLocker startup key on a USB flash drive, you need to provide the USB flash drive during the initial encryption of your drive, as shown in Figure 5-25. BitLocker then copies the unlock key to the USB drive. You must then present the USB flash drive at each startup to allow the system to be started.

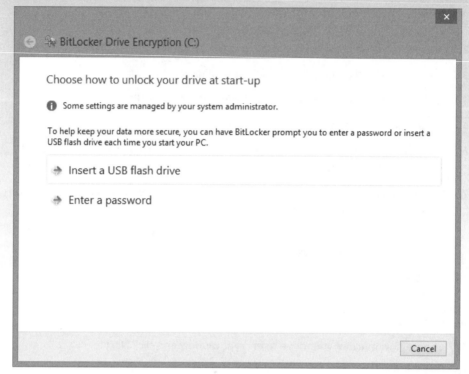

FIGURE 5-25 Unlocking with BitLocker drive encryption

EXAM TIP

BitLocker and TPM initialization must be performed by a user who's a member of the local administrators group.

If your system doesn't have a TPM chip, you can still use BitLocker. You need to enable the Group Policy object called *Require Additional Authentication At Startup* and check the box Allow BitLocker Without A Compatible TPM (see Figure 5-26). This setting can be found in the following location: Local Computer Policy\Computer Configuration\Administrative Templates\Windows Components\BitLocker Drive Encryption\Operating System Drives.

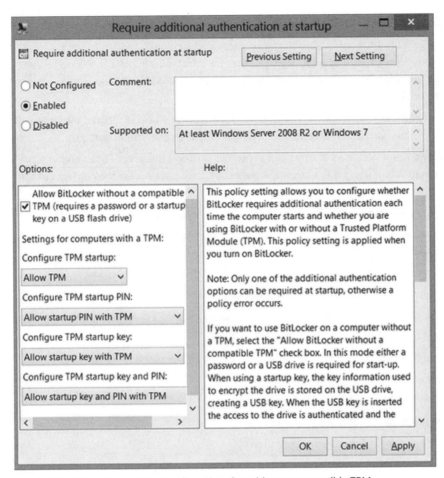

FIGURE 5-26 Using Group Policy to allow BitLocker without a compatible TPM

NOTE **SUSPENDING BITLOCKER DURING MAINTENANCE**

If BitLocker is enabled and you need perform any maintenance to the BIOS or perform a hardware upgrade, you should use the Suspend Protection option before implementing the changes.

Using BitLocker To Go

BitLocker To Go is used for removable storage devices and includes a hidden driver for Windows 8 (discovery drive) and an AutoPlay viewer for Windows XP SP3 and Windows Vista with SP1. The BitLocker To Go reader is required by Windows XP SP3 so that you can copy the files from the drive.

You don't need a TPM chip to use BitLocker to Go. BitLocker To Go is secured by the use of a password or smart card and then encrypted via the BitLocker encryption software.

On Windows 7 and Windows 8, users can choose to unlock a BitLocker To Go encrypted volume automatically. If users don't know the password, they can't access the contents of the removable drive.

The following are some useful BitLocker To Go Group Policy settings:

- Allow access to BitLocker-protected removable data drives from earlier versions of Windows
- Do not install BitLocker To Go Reader on FAT formatted removable drives
- Deny write access to removable drives not protected by BitLocker
- Choose drive encryption method and cipher strength
- Control use of BitLocker on removable drives
- Enforce drive encryption type on fixed data drives
- Allow network unlock at startup
- Require additional authentication at startup
- Configure minimum PIN length for startup
- Allow Secure Boot for integrity validation

Configuring startup key storage

The BitLocker startup key is a useful alternative on devices that don't have (or support) TPM. When enabled, the startup key is saved on USB storage and can be formatted with an NTFS, FAT32, or FAT file system. Every time that you start your system, you need to have the flash drive with the startup key inserted.

Don't leave the USB drive permanently in the computer. You can purchase small, discreet thumb drives that you can clip to a key ring.

EXAM TIP

Be careful when using BitLocker on devices without a keyboard. Don't enable user authentication with a password or PIN, because the onscreen keyboard won't be loaded during the BitLocker startup at the time the PIN is required.

Configuring location settings (GPS)

It seems only a few years ago that devices that rely on the Global Positioning Service (GPS) such as vehicular navigation systems had a monopoly regarding location-aware services and devices. Nowadays, smartphones and tablet devices have caught up and are expanding far beyond the scope of navigation systems.

Mobile devices now contain location-aware software, which receives location positioning data from the GPS network. Windows 8 has built-in support for a location-provider service so that apps from the Microsoft Store can take advantage of location. Windows can harness built-in GPS hardware as well as data from a connected or teamed GPS device.

Much of the functionality comes directly from the apps and associated driver, which simply call the Windows Location Provider API that interfaces with the GPS enabled chipset. You can configure some settings in Group Policy that enable you to turn on or off the Windows Location platform (it's on by default) and each app that requires location information is required to request user approval so that the use of location services is allowed. To modify the Windows Location platform settings, follow these steps:

1. Search Windows 8 for location.

2. Click Location Settings.

3. Select the Turn On The Windows Location Platform check box if you want users to decide to allow, app by app, whether to use Windows Location (see Figure 5-27).

4. Click Apply and provide administrative approval or credentials to apply.

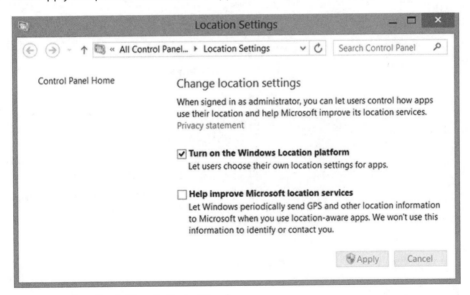

FIGURE 5-27 Location Settings in Control Panel

You can configure four Group Policy settings relating to the Windows Location Provider:

- Turn off location
- Turn off location scripting
- Turn off sensors
- Turn off Windows Location Provider (within the \Windows Location Provider subtree), as shown in Figure 5-28

You can find these settings in this subtree: Computer Configuration\Administrative Templates\Windows Components\Location and Sensors.

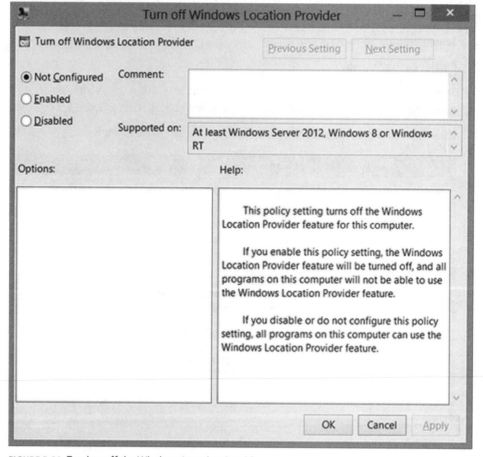

FIGURE 5-28 Turning off the Windows Location Provider

> ### *Thought experiment*
> #### Performing a BitLocker recovery
>
> In the following thought experiment, apply what you've learned about the objective. You can find answers to these questions in the "Answers" section at the end of this chapter.
>
> You have deployed BitLocker on your laptop. Today when you switch on your laptop, you see the following message:
>
>   BitLocker Drive Encryption Password Entry. Please enter the
>   recovery password for this drive.
>
> Explain what might have happened and a possible solution.

Objective summary

- BitLocker uses a Trusted Platform Module (TPM) version 1.2 or higher, a dedicated security hardware microchip built onto your motherboard.
- BitLocker is supported only on Windows 8 Pro and Windows 8 Enterprise editions.
- BitLocker pre-provisioning allows you to enable BitLocker for a volume even before the operating system is installed.
- Use manage-bde from the command line to configure BitLocker
- Users can now change BitLocker PINs and passwords.
- Windows 8 provides Windows Location platform support for apps.

Objective review

Answer the following questions to test your knowledge of the information in this objective. You can find the answers to these questions and explanations of why each answer choice is correct or incorrect at the end of this chapter.

1. Which Windows 8 versions support BitLocker?

   A. Windows RT

   B. Windows 8 Home

   C. Windows 8 Pro edition

   D. Windows 8 Enterprise edition

2. Which level of encryption does BitLocker use for volume encryption?

   A. AES 256 bit

   B. AES 128 bit

   C. AES 256 bit with Diffuser

   D. AES 128 bit with Diffuser

3. Which of the following options isn't a valid BitLocker unlock method?

   A. Startup key only

   B. TPM plus PIN

   C. PIN only

   D. Trusted Platform Module (TPM) only

4. Which of the following isn't a valid method of unlocking a BitLocker-enabled removable drive option in Windows 8?

   A. PIN

   B. Automatic unlock

   C. Password

   D. Smart card

5. Which of the following does BitLocker with TPM 1.2 helps protect against?

   A. Malware

   B. Hard-drive theft

   C. RootKits

   D. Online hacking

6. What are some BitLocker enhancements in Windows 8?

   A. Used disk space–only encryption

   B. Network Unlock

   C. AES 256 bit encryption

   D. WinPE support

Answers

This section contains the solutions to the thought experiments and answers to the objective review questions in this chapter.

Objective 5.1: Thought experiment

Several factors could be affecting this situation. The primary issue is that Windows 7 Home Premium doesn't allow Remote Desktop Connection. She would need to upgrade to an operating system such as Windows 8 Pro, which supports inbound Remote Desktop Connections.

If the problem remains after she upgrades her operating system, other potential issues would include the following:

- The office computer is turned off, or in Sleep or Hibernate state.
- Firewall port 3389 might not be allowing RDP traffic on either side.
- She might have an incorrect FQDM or public IP address for the office computer.
- She might have incorrect credentials.

The status of the Allow RDP Connections check box within the Remote Properties sheet on the office computer isn't valid because the Windows edition used in the office doesn't support Remote Desktop Connections.

Objective 5.1: Review

1. **Correct answers:** C and D

   A. **Incorrect:** Internet Connection Sharing isn't part of Easy Connect.

   B. **Incorrect:** Easy Connect can use any Internet connection type.

   C. **Correct:** Easy Connect uses PNRP.

   D. **Correct:** To navigate the Internet securely, Easy Connect uses both IPv6 and Teredo tunneling.

2. **Correct answer:** A

   A. **Correct:** *mstsc.exe* is the Remote Desktop executable.

   B. **Incorrect:** *netsh* is the command-line tool used for testing and configuring networking.

   C. **Incorrect:** *tsclient* is the legacy Terminal Services executable.

   D. **Incorrect:** The *net use* command can be used at the command-line to map network shares.

3. **Correct answer:** D

   A. **Incorrect:** 443 is used by the Secure Sockets Layer (SSL).

B. Incorrect: 25 is used by the Simple Mail Transport Protocol (SMTP).

C. Incorrect: 110 is used by the Post Office Protocol (POP).

D. Correct: 3389 is used by the Remote Desktop Protocol (RDP).

4. **Correct answer:** B

A. Incorrect: IKEv2 is a supported VPN tunnel protocol.

B. Correct: SSL isn't a VPN tunnel protocol.

C. Incorrect: PPTP is a supported VPN tunnel protocol.

D. Incorrect: SSTP is a supported VPN tunnel protocol.

E. Incorrect: L2TP is a supported VPN tunnel protocol.

5. **Correct answer:** A

A. Correct: EAP-MS-CHAPv2 is the strongest authentication method supported by Windows 8.

B. Incorrect: PAP is weaker than EAP-MS-CHAPv2.

C. Incorrect: CHAP is weaker than EAP-MS-CHAPv2.

D. Incorrect: MS-CHAP v2 is weaker than EAP-MS-CHAPv2.

Objective 5.2: Thought experiment

The primary issue is that Hilary doesn't want her personal details to be synchronized. The following items are usually synced. Boldfaced items are potentially personal.

Setting	Description
Personalize	**Colors, background, lock screen, and your account picture**
Desktop personalization	Themes, taskbar, high contrast, and more
Passwords	**Sign-in info for some apps, websites, networks, and HomeGroup**
Ease of Access	Settings for Narrator, Magnifier, and more
Language preferences	Keyboards, other input methods, display language, and more
App settings	**Certain settings in your apps, but not all**
Browser settings	**Internet Explorer history and bookmarks/favorites**
Other Windows settings	Windows Explorer, mouse settings, and more

You could explain to Hilary that if she wants to keep some of her personal settings private, she can turn off syncing for specific settings.

Objective 5.2: Review

1. **Correct answers:** C, D, and E

   A. **Incorrect:** Hibernate requires enabling.

   B. **Incorrect:** Hybrid Sleep isn't an option on the Power Off menu.

   C. **Correct:** Restart is a Power Off menu item.

   D. **Correct:** Sleep is a Power Off menu item.

   E. **Correct:** Shut Down is a Power Off menu item.

2. **Correct answer:** A

   A. **Correct:** hyberfil.sys is the file created.

   B. **Incorrect:** pagefile is created by Windows under the usual circumstances.

   C. **Incorrect:** dumpfile isn't a valid file.

   D. **Incorrect:** BCDBoot is a valid file but is used to modify boot entries.

3. **Correct answer:** C

   A. **Incorrect:** powercfg -import C:\customscheme.pow <<GUID>> is used to import the exported power plan

   B. **Incorrect:** powercfg –L lists the current plans.

   C. **Correct:** powercfg -export C:\customescheme.pow <<GUID>> is the correct syntax.

   D. **Incorrect:** powercfg –getactivescheme obtains details about the currently loaded power scheme.

4. **Correct answer:** A

   A. **Correct:** Although encrypting files is possible (and advisable), this isn't a valid Offline Files caching option.

   B. **Incorrect:** This is a valid Offline Files caching option.

   C. **Incorrect:** This is a valid Offline Files caching option.

   D. **Incorrect:** This is a valid Offline Files caching option.

5. **Correct answer:** D

   A. **Incorrect:** Windows Recovery Environment isn't enabled.

   B. **Incorrect:** BitLocker can be used, just not with a TPM.

   C. **Incorrect:** Only Windows 8 Enterprise Edition supports BitLocker to Go.

   D. **Correct:** To prevent possible corruption, both Hibernate and Sleep are disabled.

6. **Correct answers:** A and B

   A. **Correct:** Passwords can be synchronized.

B. Correct: Language preferences can be synchronized.

C. Incorrect: Spelling dictionaries is currently an option.

D. Incorrect: Shared pictures are currently an option.

7. **Correct answer:** B

A. Incorrect: This command is used to start Wi-Fi Direct broadcasting.

B. Correct: This command configures Wi-Fi Direct.

C. Incorrect: The start command must be sent after the network is configured.

D. Incorrect: This command is used to stop the Wi-Fi Direct broadcasting.

Objective 5.3: Thought experiment

The BitLocker encryption key is unavailable. BitLocker enters recovery mode if one of the following occurs:

- One of the boot files is modified.
- The BIOS has been modified and the TPM is disabled.
- The TPM is cleared or corrupt.
- Someone has tried to start without the TPM, PIN, or USB key being available.
- The BitLocker-encrypted disk has been moved to a new computer.

Possible solutions could involve:

- Restart and enter the PIN.
- Plug in the USB key.
- Enter the recovery password.
- Format and reinstall Windows.

Objective 5.3: Review

1. **Correct answers:** C and D

A. Incorrect: Windows RT is a consumer device and doesn't support BitLocker.

B. Incorrect: Windows Home edition doesn't support BitLocker.

C. Correct: Windows 8 Pro edition supports BitLocker.

D. Correct: Windows 8 Enterprise edition supports BitLocker.

2. **Correct answer:** D

A. Incorrect: BitLocker doesn't use AES 256 bit encryption by default.

B. Incorrect: BitLocker doesn't use AES 128 bit encryption by default.

C. Incorrect: Windows 8 supports AES 256 with Diffuser, but this isn't enabled by default.

    D. **Correct:** Windows 8 uses AES 128 bit with Diffuser by default for BitLocker encryption.

3. **Correct answer:** C

    A. **Incorrect:** Startup key only is a valid unlock method.

    B. **Incorrect:** TPM plus PIN is a valid unlock method.

    C. **Correct:** PIN isn't valid unless used with a TPM.

    D. **Incorrect:** TPM only is a valid unlock method.

4. **Correct answer:** A

    A. **Correct:** PIN is used to unlock fixed drivers, not removable drives.

    B. **Incorrect:** Automatic unlock is a valid method of unlocking a removable drive.

    C. **Incorrect:** Password is a valid method of unlocking a removable drive.

    D. **Incorrect:** A smart card is a valid method of unlocking a removable drive.

5. **Correct answers:** A, B, and C

    A. **Correct:** Rootkits are a form of Malware.

    B. **Correct:** Because BitLocker-enabled hard drives remain encrypted if removed from the computer, BitLocker could be a deterrent to physical theft.

    C. **Correct:** BitLocker with TPM protects against rootkits.

    D. **Incorrect:** Using BitLocker doesn't prevent online hacking. As soon as a hacker has control of Windows, the drive is already decrypted on the fly.

6. **Correct answers:** A and B

    A. **Correct:** Windows 8 introduces used disk space–only encryption.

    B. **Correct:** Network unlock is a feature introduced with Windows 8 and Windows Server 2012.

    C. **Incorrect:** AES 256-Bit encryption has always being part of BitLocker.

    D. **Incorrect:** WinPE doesn't have built-in support for BitLocker.

CHAPTER 6

Monitor and maintain Windows clients

When it comes to my car, I just drive it; I'm not really a maintenance type of guy. Sure, I take care of the basics, such as put gas in the tank and make sure that the tires have air, but little else. I take my car to the garage regularly for a checkup and service. The mechanics change the oil, add antifreeze, and check the essentials to ensure that my car stays roadworthy.

When I was in my late teenage years, I tweaked and fixed up motorcycles. A group of friends and I would strip down little (50cc) two-stroke engines and file away at the ports to make them minutely bigger, clean away all the burnt carbon deposits to make the pistons shine, and change the ratios on the sprocket gears to aim for either a sprint start or top-end speed. Then we would head out on the road to test our "tuned" motorcycles. I still have a motorcycle today, except now I would never dream of tweaking and tuning my big Honda like I used to do.

Only a few years ago you might remember that you needed to fine-tune and tweak Windows to get the best performance possible. Over the years users seem to have become more like consumers and, a bit like me and my car, they just want to use their computers, not work on them. Although I still consider myself as a bit of a Windows 8 mechanic, I know many people who really don't think about what happens "under the hood"; they prefer that the computer just works. Does that sound familiar to you? Do you act as a Windows "mechanic" for some of your coworkers or family and friends?

One reason I don't try to speed up my motorcycle or my computer anymore is because they are fast enough. My bike has a 1000cc engine and all the power I need in a motorcycle; I don't need to tweak it to try to get more. Similarly, my current laptop has a quad core, 16 GB RAM, 256 GB SSD drive and a full HD display. Sure, it would be nice to have it weigh half as much (thankfully, my laptop bag has wheels), and to be touch-enabled. The point is that although I could still tweak this computer a little to get a little more speed, I believe that we are fast approaching a time where our PCs are fast enough "as they are." As long as the devices "work," we're becoming less interested in what's "under the hood" or how to tweak performance.

Objectives in this chapter:

- Objective 6.1: Configure and manage Windows updates
- Objective 6.2: Manage local storage
- Objective 6.3 : Monitor system performance

Objective 6.1: Configure and manage Windows updates

Over the years, you've probably seen new Windows versions as well as hundreds, if not thousands, of updates from Microsoft. Updates can offer new functionality, fix problems, plug security holes, and update drivers. Of course, at times you might have had an update mess up your system—maybe an updated driver didn't work properly and you needed to perform a driver roll back or system restore.

Updates have been a part of Windows for many years and, quite honestly, Microsoft is getting pretty good at it.

You can be sure that when Microsoft released Windows 8, its developers made the operating system as secure and reliable as possible for the day it was released. However, within days of any release, new security threats, expiring certificates, and patches would have been identified that would threaten the ongoing security of Windows.

Thankfully, Windows has a reliable, proven, and regular updating infrastructure. Overall, allowing Microsoft to update Windows 8 will improve the security, efficiency, and overall well-being of the operating system.

EXAM TIP

Windows 8 allows a standard user to install updates from Windows Update without receiving a User Access Control (UAC) prompt.

NOTE **BACK UP, BACK UP, BACK UP!**

Please ensure that you have a valid, up-to-date, and verified backup of your system. This is especially useful whenever making updates to your drivers, hardware, firmware, and BIOS. Refer to Chapter 7, "Configure backup and recovery options," for detailed guidance.

Configuring update settings

Microsoft has two primary ways to distribute updates: the Windows Update client and Windows Server Update Services (WSUS). Depending on the organization's size and how many computers are on the network, Microsoft provides the following guidance:

Update Method	Network Size	Remarks
Windows Update	50	No management or infrastructure needed. Doesn't allow for testing or approval of each update.
WSUS	Any	Allows testing and approval of each update. Requires an infrastructure server.

Updates in Windows Update come in four different types, each with a particular focus:

- **Security updates**, by the Microsoft Security Response Center (MSRC), resolve security vulnerability. Security updates are accompanied by two documents: a security bulletin and a Microsoft Knowledge Base article.

- **Critical updates** are important updates relating to the operating system.

- **Windows Defender definitions** keep Windows Defender as up to date as possible. Regular updates of antimalware signatures and definitions are required.

- **Service Packs** provide a cumulative set of all the updates created for a Microsoft product. A service pack also includes fixes for other problems that have been found by Microsoft since the product's release. A service pack can contain customer-requested design changes or new features. Like security updates, service packs are available for download and are accompanied by Knowledge Base articles.

> **NOTE WINDOWS UPDATE IS AUTOMATIC**
>
> For home users and small businesses, Windows 8 is configured to retrieve updates automatically and directly from Microsoft.

EXAM TIP

By default, the Windows Update service is configured for Delayed Start, which prevents the service from running as soon as Windows 8 starts, so that startup isn't slowed down. Instead, it runs a few minutes after Windows 8 has successfully loaded.

Configuring Windows Update settings in Windows 8

If you can't remember the permissions that you gave Windows 8 the first time you turned on the device, or if you want to make changes, you can follow these steps to review and, if necessary, make changes to your settings:

1. Search the Start screen for *Windows Update*, as shown in Figure 6-1.

FIGURE 6-1 Windows Update settings in Windows 8

2. Click Turn Automatic Updating On Or Off to open the full Windows Update panel.

3. On the Choose Your Windows Update Settings page, use the drop-down list to select one of the four choices, as shown in Figure 6-2, to modify the update settings.

4. Click OK to confirm your choices.

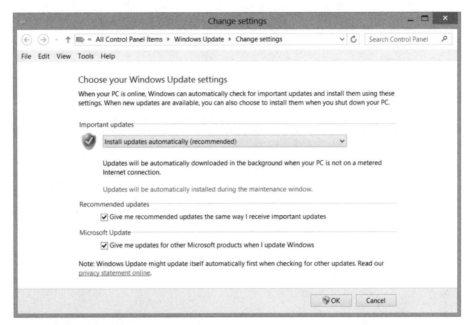

FIGURE 6-2 Modify Windows Update settings

The following table contains a brief description of each option.

Option	Description
Install Updates Automatically (Recommended)	Updates are automatically downloaded in the background when your PC isn't on a metered Internet connection.
Download Updates But Let Me Choose Whether To Install Them	You receive notifications about new Windows 8 updates.
Never Check For Updates (Not Recommended)	This option effectively disables automatic updates completely.

EXAM TIP

Windows 8 allows a standard user to install drivers that are downloaded from Windows Update or included with the operating system without receiving a UAC prompt.

By default, if you leave the automatic updates as the default, your updates are downloaded and automatically installed at 3 A.M. local time (just like with Windows 7). You can change this to another time in the Run Maintenance Tasks Daily At option, as shown in Figure 6-3.

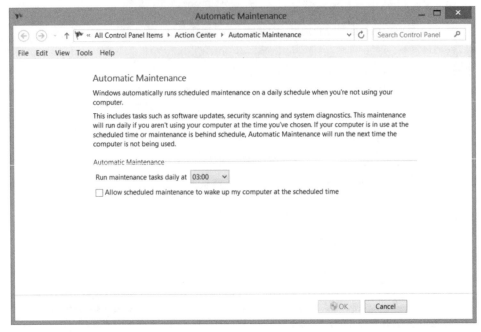

FIGURE 6-3 Windows Update maintenance window

Even if everything is set to automatic, your computer might not have installed all the updates. Occasionally using the option Check for Updates is useful.

> **NOTE INSTALLING UPDATES WHILE YOU'RE AWAY**
>
> Plan your updates. If I see that Windows has some optional updates to install, I usually start them just before I leave for lunch or a meeting. One of the most computer-related frustrations is waiting for Windows to complete a cycle of updates.

Previous versions of Windows have allowed users to decide to postpone or cancel the installation of updates, via notification area alerts. Microsoft has changed the default behavior in Windows 8 so that users are only notified of updates on the logon screen.

This effectively reduces the amount of "chatter" to the desktop during normal operations while maintaining the operational security of Windows.

> **NOTE AUTOMATICALLY INSTALLING DRIVERS**
>
> Windows 8 always searches Windows Update for the latest compatible drivers when a new device is connected to the computer.

Configuring Windows Server Update Services (WSUS)

Windows Server Update Services version 3.0 SP2 is the supported patch-management tool available for Windows Server administrators to authorize, publish, and distribute updates within their networked environment that contains Windows 8 devices.

Micromanaging any tasks that include hundreds or thousands of items generally isn't a best practice within any environment, and a busy IT department is no exception. Administrators have a diminishing amount of time in which to perform maintenance tasks. WSUS, which was introduced with Windows Server 2000, significantly helps with the process of ensuring that administrators keep their networks safe and secure.

Rather than have each workstation manually connect to Microsoft Update, administrators can use WSUS to centrally download updates to an internal server. They then can authorize and deploy each update internally to specific workstations or computer groups based on hardware or function. This allows administrators to exert a greater level of control over which updates are deployed within the organization.

EXAM TIP

For the workstation to automatically check and download updates from WSUS, the wuauserv service must be running. You can find this service on the Task Manager Processes tab under Service Host: Local System.

Updating Windows Store applications

To ensure that only apps that run in the new Windows 8 interface have been thoroughly checked to work, Microsoft insists that all apps need to be downloaded from the Windows Store to be installed on your device.

The developers who built and published the app most likely have an update release schedule during which they might have a number of new features, enhancements, bug fixes, and so on. After they develop these changes, they upload a new version of the code to the Windows Store. After this update is thoroughly tested by a Microsoft app engineer, the new version is approved and appears in the Windows Store as a more up-to-date replacement. All updates available via the Windows Store will have been verified via the same quality-control procedures as the original application.

> **NOTE THE INS AND OUTS OF SIDE-LOADING**
>
> An organization can bypass the wait for new updates by *side-loading* an app. This is the process of installing apps that haven't been approved by the Windows Store. An app must be digitally signed and the PC must be configured to allow the installation of trusted apps before the app can be side-loaded (use the PowerShell 3.0 command Add-AppxPackage.)

As part of the Microsoft update service, the apps installed on your device are checked, by default, to see whether the store has a newer version. If it does, the Store tile indicates the number of updates available. In Figure 6-4, the number shown in the lower right corner indicates 12 updates are available.

FIGURE 6-4 Live Store tile indicating updates available

To install the updates, click the Store tile to open the Windows Store. In the upper-right corner of the Store should be the option to install available updates, as shown in Figure 6-5.

Updates (12)

Games >

FIGURE 6-5 Store app indicating 12 updates available

After you click Updates, Windows 8 verifies the updates available and then displays a screen, shown in Figure 6-6. If you are on a metered Internet connection, you might want to clear any non-essential updates; you can choose which updates to install.

> **NOTE** **UPDATING THE CORE APPS AFTER INSTALLATION**
>
> On a fresh installation, Windows 8 requires 15 app updates. This updating is by design and ensures that the core apps included with the operating system are the latest versions available.

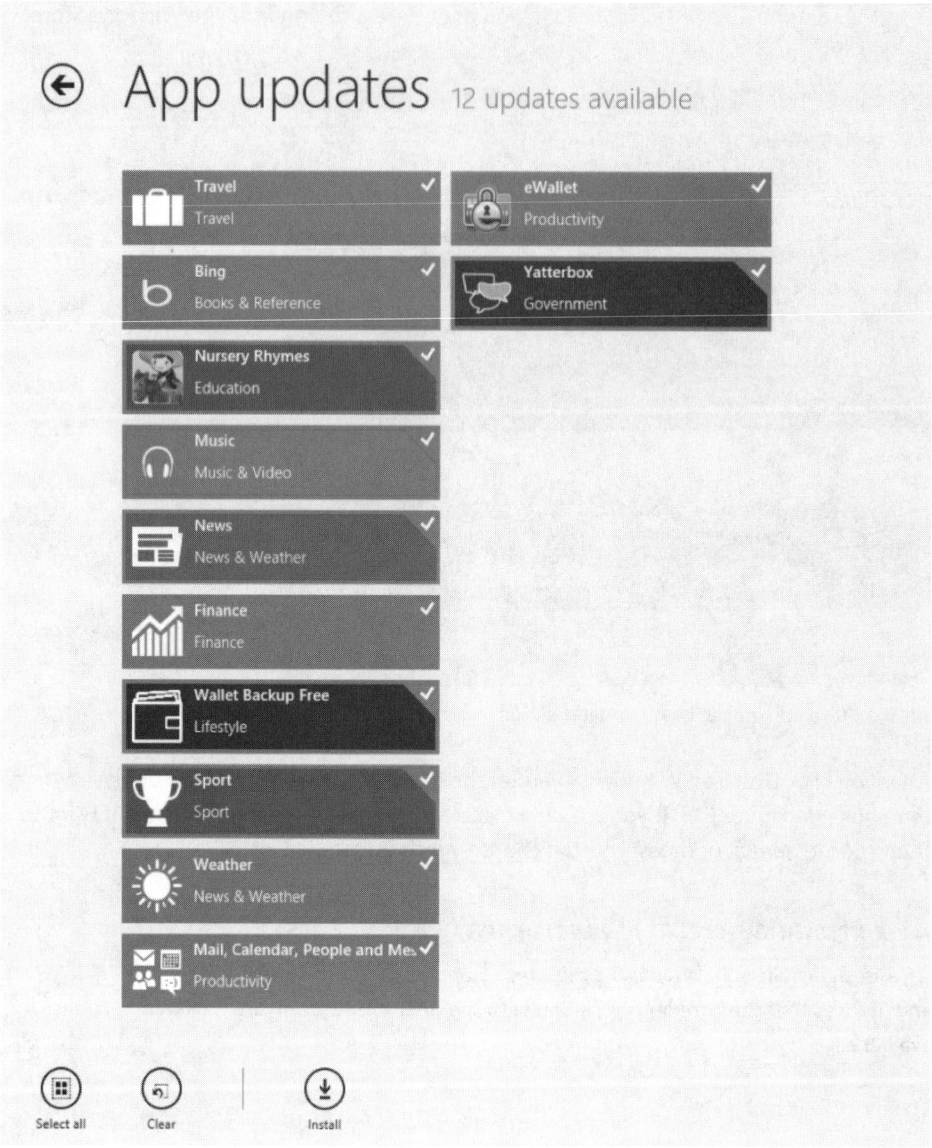

FIGURE 6-6 Current app updates available

By default, Windows notifies you when app updates are available. If you don't see any updates, you can check to identify whether the default setting has been changed by following these instructions:

1. Ensure that your computer is connected to the Internet.

2. From the Start screen, click the Store tile to open the Windows Store.

3. Open the Store charms bar and select Settings.

4. Choose App Updates. (If requested, you might need to sign in to the Windows Store before proceeding.)

5. Ensure that the automatic setting is configured to yes, as shown in Figure 6-7.

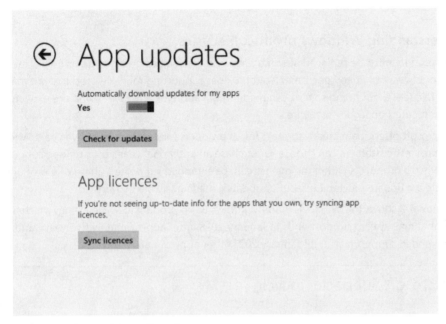

FIGURE 6-7 App update configuration

Removing Windows 8 apps

Often apps are installed, tried once or twice, and then quickly ignored and never used again. If you find that several of the apps that require updating aren't familiar to you, they might no longer be required and could be removed.

To uninstall an app, right-click the app from the Start screen and then click Uninstall, as shown in Figure 6-8.

FIGURE 6-8 Uninstalling an App

> ***NOTE* UNINSTALLING DESKTOP APPS**
>
> **If the app is a desktop variety, you would use the Programs and Features Control Panel applet to uninstall a desktop app.**

Understanding Windows product lifecycles

Every product must be replaced at some time, and often a business maintains only a set number of versions at any one time. Not only does supporting multiple products not make economic sense, but doing so also can hinder motivation for employees who are expected to remain focused on legacy software.

Microsoft offers mainstream support for its products for a minimum of five years. After this time, business customers can choose to purchase an additional year's of extended support. Only while a product is within the mainstream or extended supported phase of a product lifecycle are updates, including security updates, made available by Microsoft.

Figure 6-9 shows the Windows 8 and Windows 8 Pro product lifecycle listing, which indicates that mainstream support ends in January 2018, after approximately five years, and that the extended support lasts until January 2023, after approximately 10 years.

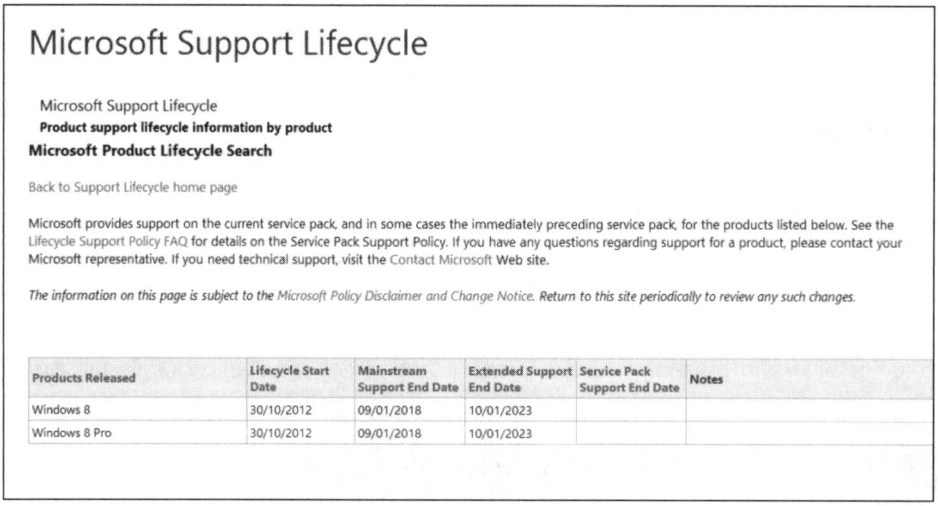

Microsoft Support Lifecycle

Microsoft Support Lifecycle
Product support lifecycle information by product
Microsoft Product Lifecycle Search

Back to Support Lifecycle home page

Microsoft provides support on the current service pack, and in some cases the immediately preceding service pack, for the products listed below. See the Lifecycle Support Policy FAQ for details on the Service Pack Support Policy. If you have any questions regarding support for a product, please contact your Microsoft representative. If you need technical support, visit the Contact Microsoft Web site.

The information on this page is subject to the Microsoft Policy Disclaimer and Change Notice. Return to this site periodically to review any such changes.

Products Released	Lifecycle Start Date	Mainstream Support End Date	Extended Support End Date	Service Pack Support End Date	Notes
Windows 8	30/10/2012	09/01/2018	10/01/2023		
Windows 8 Pro	30/10/2012	09/01/2018	10/01/2023		

FIGURE 6-9 Windows 8 product lifecycle

> ***MORE INFO* PRODUCT LIFECYCLE**
>
> **For more information on the Windows 8 product lifecycle, see *http://support.microsoft.com/gp/lifeselectwin.***

Managing Installed Updates

Although all updates are thoroughly tested by Microsoft, guaranteeing that they will work for every PC and possible combination of installed software is impossible. For example, if you recently noticed that Windows updated your system but now a specific app freezes or fails to work properly, you could try to remove an update if you have diagnosed an incompatibility.

To remove an installed update, follow these steps:

1. Search the Start screen for *Windows Updates*.

2. Select View Installed Updates.

To remove an update, select the installed update that's causing the problem and select Uninstall, as shown in Figure 6-10.

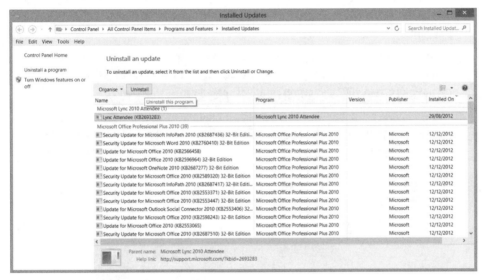

FIGURE 6-10 Uninstalling a Windows update

Testing updates

Larger organizations with hundreds and thousands of users must dedicate significant resources to ensure that Microsoft updates work on their computers. Suppose that a banking enterprise has 20,000 employees, and the majority of them have a computer. Because the potential for disaster is huge, that bank must create an update process that involves planning, discussion, testing, and then finally installing the update.

Within an organization, every piece of software is inventoried and accounted for. Each update undergoes testing to ensure that the Line of Business (LOB) software and the update are compatible. Only when the process is complete can the rollout begin. This is performed in controlled phase deployments based on risk and need. If any problems are encountered during the rollout, the process can be halted and investigated.

In large organizations, this process can be continual because updates are received from not only Microsoft, but also the following:

- Software vendors
- Vendors that build customized software
- Antivirus software vendors
- Hardware drivers

Thought experiment
Upgrading your company laptops

In the following thought experiment, apply what you've learned about the objective. You can find answers to these questions in the "Answers" section at the end of this chapter.

You have recently started working for Contoso, Inc., a rapidly expanding nationwide insurance corporation. Growth over the last few years has meant that the company now has more than 400 sales representatives spread across the country.

Expansion plans will continue, and you need to submit a proposal to your manager for upgrading some of the older laptop computers used by the field sales representatives. You have taken an inventory, which shows the following installed operating systems:

Operating System	Quantity
Windows XP SP3 Professional	193
Windows Vista Enterprise	70
Windows 7 Ultimate	110
Windows 8 Enterprise	47

What recommendations would you suggest in your report to your manager?

Objective summary

- Windows Update is enabled by default.
- Standard users can install updates from Windows Update without UAC restrictions.
- Updates can be categorized as Security, Critical, Service Packs and Windows Defender Definitions.
- Windows 8 checks automatically for app updates in the Store.

- Windows Server Update Services (WSUS) is the preferred enterprise solution for managing and deploying updates to a networked environment of 50 or more workstations.

- Microsoft offers mainstream support for products for a minimum of five years.

Objective review

Answer the following questions to test your knowledge of the information in this objective. You can find the answers to these questions and explanations of why each answer choice is correct or incorrect at the end of this chapter.

1. You need to configure your network to receive Windows Updates. Currently, the network has 73 Windows, 7 workstations, 32 Windows RT devices, and 34 Windows 8 workstations. Which tool would you use?

    A. Windows Update

    B. Microsoft Baseline Security Analyzer (MBSA) version 2.2

    C. Windows Server Update Services (WSUS)

    D. Software Update Services

2. You need to restart the Windows automatic updating feature. Which command would you use?

    A. services.msc

    B. net stop wuauserv

    C. net start wuauserv

    D. svchost.exe -k netsvcs

3. Which of the following are types of updates that are released by Microsoft for Windows 8?

    A. Security updates

    B. Viruses

    C. Malware

    D. Service packs

4. You've noticed that your Microsoft Windows 8 laptop is occasionally freezing. You think the cause might be a conflict with your biometric fingerprint reader, for which you installed a new security update yesterday. What should you do?

    A. Contact the vendor support center

    B. Reapply the update and reboot the laptop

    C. Reset your PC

    D. Reinstall the latest software from the vendor website

    E. Uninstall the update

5. You notice that 23 app updates are ready to install. You don't recognize many of the apps. What should you do?

   A. Install all the updates

   B. Install updates for only the apps you recognize

   C. Uninstall the apps that you don't recognize

   D. Turn off automatic app updates

Objective 6.2: Manage local storage

All this talk about cloud storage makes overlooking just how important local storage is easy. All computers have some local storage, and the technology for local storage keeps advancing.

Just a few years ago, USB 2.0 (High Speed) was considered the most sought-after item regarding data transfer speeds, especially compared to USB 1.0. In addition to providing a huge performance gain, USB 2.0 flash drives offered new functionality such as Windows Ready-Boost, which uses the USB storage device as an additional cache to speed up a Windows PC.

With USB 3.0 (Super Speed) now on the market, earlier versions of the USB standard are looked at as inferior. Released in late 2008, USB 3.0 offers up to a massive 5 Gbit/s (625 MB/s) data transmission speed, almost 20 times the speed of USB 2.0.

Another phenomenon has been the emergence of solid-state drives (SSDs), which offer extremely fast data transfer rates. SSDs are fast becoming the standard local storage media for the tablet form factor due to weight savings, zero moving or mechanical parts, and data transfer speed. Although prices for SSD technology continues to fall, solid-state drives are still around 10 times more expensive when comparing traditional magnetic hard disk drives (HDDs).

As cloud technologies become more commonplace, local storage becomes less important as most services, data, and even applications become accessible only via the Internet. Ultimately in the consumer-driven arena, the device ultimately becomes the interface. Many tablet devices don't allow the end user to modify or upgrade the internal components. Customization of these sealed devices isn't permitted except for limited choices, such as the ability to choose the amount of RAM, size of the SSD, or color of cover at the point of purchase.

This objective covers the following topics:

- Managing disk volumes
- Managing file system fragmentation
- Managing Storage Spaces

Managing disk volumes

Whether or not you use HDD or SSD to store your local files, Windows 8 provides various tools that you can use to configure, troubleshoot, and tune your system. Because this book focuses on the Windows 8 exam, this discussion is limited to new features introduced with this release; it will skim over the changes introduced with previous releases.

Two main tools are available to manage your PC disk volumes: the Disk Management MMC Snap-In component and the DiskPart command-line tool. Both have been included since Windows 2000. Other often overlooked tools include the Computer location in File Explorer, as shown in Figure 6-11, and fsutil, covered later. The fsutil tool allows advanced configuration of both FAT and NTFS file systems, such as managing reparse points, managing sparse files, or dismounting a volume.

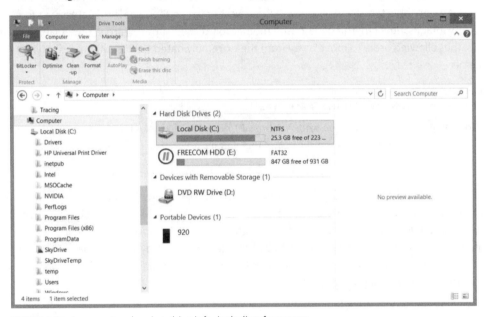

FIGURE 6-11 A computer showing drive info, including free space

EXAM TIP

You must be logged on as an administrator or be a member of the Administrators group to use fsutil.

Although Windows 8 RTM didn't benefit from the new Resilient File System (ReFS) implemented in Windows Server 2012, Windows 8 has introduced several new features for handling ever-increasing disk capacity. Windows 8 supports the following file-system formats.

File System	Max Volume Size
FAT	4GB
FAT32	32GB
exFAT	256TB
NTFS	256TB

Windows 8 continues to support both Master Boot Record (MBR) and GUID Partition Table (GPT) partition table types and allows you to convert between the two. This enables you to take advantage of the emerging EFI-based motherboards that support large-format GPT disks, thus allowing users to move away from the extremely dated (1980s) MBR partitioning scheme.

NOTE SWITCHING PARTITION TABLE TYPES

To change partition table types from MBR to GPT or revert, the disk must have no partitions or data. Therefore, you should ensure that you have a backup of any data you want to keep.

Hard disk drives have traditionally been based on 512-byte sectors. Hard disk vendors have introduced a new larger sector size of 4,096 bytes (4 KB). These are generally known as an Advanced Format disk. Support for both the Standard and Advanced Format hard drives continues in Windows 8, allowing drives to exceed the legacy 512-byte sector-based hard disk specification and allowing for 512e and 4k Advanced Format drives, which allow very large (that is, multi-terabyte) hard drives.

To verify the kind of drive that you have, follow these steps and view the results as shown in Figure 6-12:

1. Search the Start screen for *CMD* and open an elevated command prompt, or use Windows+X and choose Command Prompt (Admin).

2. Type the following command:

    ```
    Fsutil fsinfo ntfsinfo C:
    ```

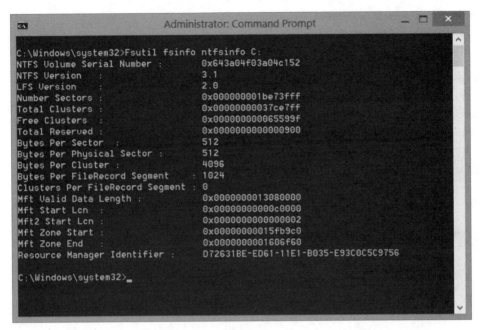

FIGURE 6-12 Using the Fsutil tool

If the "bytes per sector" is greater than 512, you have an Advanced Format disk:

Bytes Per Sector value	Bytes per Physical Sector value	Drive type
4096	4096	4K native
512	4096	Advanced Format (also known as 512E)
512	512	512-byte native

> **MORE INFO ADVANCED FORMAT DISKS**
>
> For more information on Advanced Format disks, see *http://support.microsoft.com/kb/2510009*.

Using Disk Management

Disk Management offers support for many features already covered in previous releases of Windows, including the following:

- Extend and shrink a volume
- Create, delete, and format a volume
- Convert a basic disk to a dynamic disk or vice-versa

- Add or change a drive letter
- Convert an MBR disk to a GPT disk or vice-versa
- Mark a partition as active

The Virtual Hard Disk (VHD) format, also known as a *disk-in-a-file abstraction*, is a useful way to conceptualize the actual files and disks on a PC, offering new opportunities for trans-porting, virtualizing, and deploying systems for both developers and IT Professionals. Every file on a computer system can now be stored in and accessed via one single VHD file, which is fully transportable.

In addition to the VHD support introduced in Windows 7, Windows 8 now provides the support of virtual hard disks with the VHDX format. VHDX allows VHD files to be up to 64 TB in size—significantly larger than the 2,040 GB limit of VHDs (see Figure 6-13).

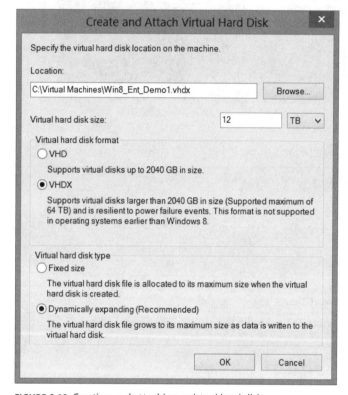

FIGURE 6-13 Creating and attaching a virtual hard disk

> **NOTE** **VHDX ENABLES LARGER VHDS**
>
> Using the VHDX format requires that the disk type be dynamically expanding. It also allows virtual hard drives to be up to a maximum of 64 TB in size, significantly larger than the VHD format.

To create a VHDX, follow these steps:

1. Open the Disk Management MMC by typing Windows+X and selecting Disk Management.

2. Click the Action menu item and select Create VHD to display the Create and Attach VHD dialog box.

3. Provide the name and location of the VHDX file and the required size.

4. Select the virtual hard disk format as VHDX.

5. Choose the virtual hard disk type, or leave the default setting.

6. Click OK.

> **MORE INFO** **VHDX SPECS**
>
> For a more detailed description of the VHDX virtual hard disk format released by Microsoft, read the specification at *http://www.microsoft.com/en-us/download/details. aspx?id=34750*.

Using DiskPart for disk operations

Although Disk Management offers users a GUI to configure disks and volumes, the command-prompt tool DiskPart.exe offers more options and the scripting ability to automate the process using simple batch files.

DiskPart offers the following commands:

- **active** Marks the selected partition as active
- **add** Adds a mirror to a simple volume
- **assign** Assigns a drive letter or mount point to the selected volume
- **attributes** Manipulates volume or disk attributes
- **attach** Attaches a virtual disk file
- **automount** Enables and disables automatic mounting of basic volumes
- **break** Breaks a mirror set
- **clean** Clears the configuration information or all information from the disk
- **compact** Attempts to reduce the physical size of the file
- **convert** Converts between different disk formats
- **create** Creates a volume, partition, or virtual disk
- **delete** Deletes an object
- **detail** Provides details about an object
- **detach** Detaches a virtual disk file
- **exit** Exits DiskPart
- **extend** Extends a volume
- **expand** Expands the maximum size available on a virtual disk

- **filesystems** Displays current and supported file systems on the volume
- **format** Formats the volume or partition
- **gpt** Assigns attributes to the selected GPT partition
- **help** Displays a list of commands
- **import** Imports a disk group
- **inactive** Marks the selected partition as inactive
- **list** Displays a list of objects
- **merge** Merges a child disk with its parents
- **online** Marks as online an object that's currently marked as offline
- **offline** Marks as offline an object that's currently marked as online
- **recover** Refreshes the state of all disks in the selected pack, attempts recovery on disks in the invalid pack, and resynchronizes mirrored volumes and RAID 5 volumes that have stale plex or parity data
- **rem** Means nothing; used to comment scripts
- **remove** Removes a drive letter or mount point assignment
- **repair** Repairs a RAID 5 volume with a failed member
- **rescan** Rescans the computer looking for disks and volumes
- **retain** Places a retained partition under a simple volume
- **san** Displays or sets the SAN policy for the currently booted operating system
- **select** Shifts the focus to an object (you can also type sel)
- **setid** Changes the partition type
- **shrink** Reduces the size of the selected volume
- **uniqueid** Displays or sets the GUID partition table (GPT) identifier or master boot record (MBR) signature of a disk

To use DiskPart, follow these steps:

1. Search the Start screen for *CMD* and open an elevated command prompt, or use Windows+X and choose Command Prompt (Admin).

2. Type **DiskPart** and press Enter.

3. After DiskPart loads, the cursor changes to shw DISKPART>. Type the commands list disk and sel disk 0 (or the correct disk number), and then detail disk, as shown in Figure 6-14.

4. To obtain detailed help with examples of a command, type **HELP** followed by the command. For example, HELP LIST provides the syntax that DiskPart uses.

5. To exit DiskPart, type **EXIT** and press Enter.

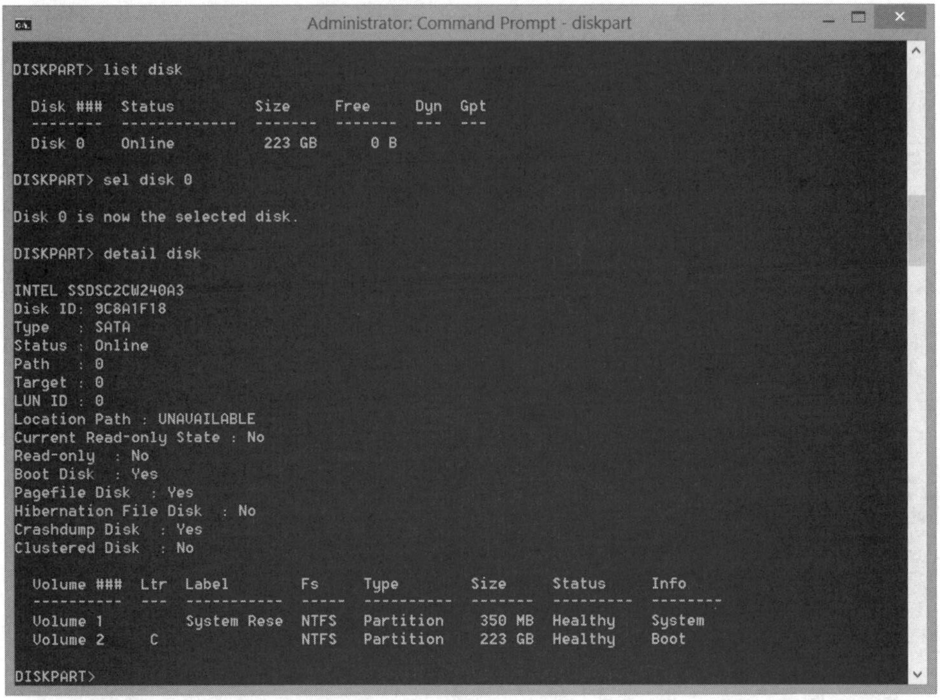

FIGURE 6-14 Using DiskPart to retrieve disk information

NOTE **ABBREVIATING DISKPART COMMANDS**

You can abbreviate many, but not all, commands within DiskPart. For example, you can use SEL instead of SELECT or PART instead of PARTITION. REM cannot be used in place of REMOVE, however, because the REM command is already used for REMARK when commenting out commands.

Performing disk management with PowerShell 3.0

When you need to produce more complex scripts or to run them remotely or in simultaneous operations, PowerShell is the tool of choice. PowerShell 3.0—included in both Windows 8 and Windows Server 2012—introduces for the first time native disk management commands. The most basic commands include Get-Disk and Get-Partition, as shown in Figure 6-15.

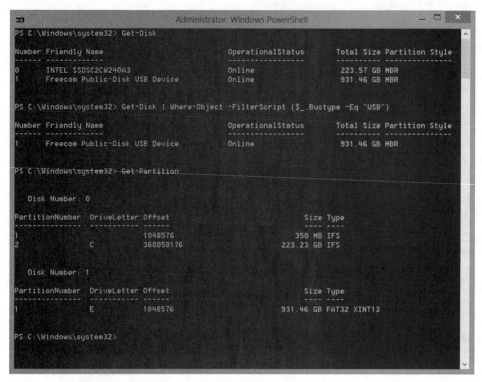

FIGURE 6-15 Using PowerShell to retrieve disk information

Other useful disk-related PowerShell 3.0 commands include the following:

- Format-Volume
- Remove-Partition
- New-Partition
- Set-Disk
- Set-Partition
- Repair-Volume

Using the Check Disk tool

As mentioned previously, Windows 8 has introduced feature enhancements to NTFS, such as self-healing abilities. To further reduce the need for users to perform manual maintenance on disk drives, Windows also includes automatic scheduling of disk maintenance utilities.

A system exhibiting strange behavior or suffering from frequent file or disk errors typically indicates the likelihood of disk problems or possible drive failure. Drives do fail, and the only safe way to protect your data is to use (and verify) regular backups.

Each morning at 3 A.M. local time, Windows 8 performs an automated scan of your disk drives using the Check Disk tool (chkdsk.exe), which fixes errors and inconsistencies in NTFS volumes and files on your disks.

> **NOTE USING CHKDSK**
>
> You can use Chkdsk.exe to check for and optionally repair issues found on FAT, FAT32, exFAT, and NTFS volumes.

The chkdsk tool within Windows 8 provides an enhanced scan and repair (for NTFS volumes) compared to previous versions of the chkdsk tool, and can even take the volume offline temporarily while the repair takes place. Boot and system volume repairs are performed at the next system restart.

EXAM TIP

The computer must be running on AC power for the 3 A.M. automated maintenance to take place. Otherwise, the task is carried over until the next time that the PC is running on AC power and the operating system is idle.

To run the chkdsk.exe tool manually to check whether your C: drive has any problems, open an elevated command prompt and type the following command, as shown in Figure 6-16:

```
chkdsk /scan C:
```

If the tool finds errors, you can attempt to repair errors on drive C: by typing this command:

```
chkdsk /spotfix C:
```

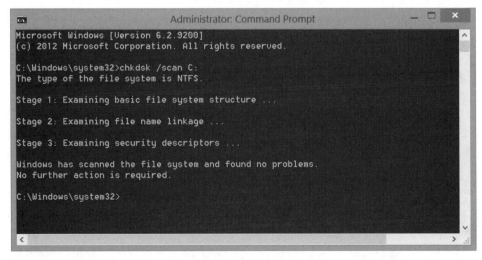

FIGURE 6-16 Using chkdsk /scan to scan a disk for errors

Managing file system fragmentation

Ever since hard drives were invented, some form of file fragmentation has existed, as has the need to defragment or maintain the status of how files are kept on disk. Windows performance can be adversely affected through severe fragmentation of the files on your disk.

Each new file saved to your disk might need to be "broken" into smaller fragments to be stored in the free spaces. This greatly adds processing and I/O overhead when reading/writing to disk and slows down your computer. Defragmenting your hard disk can recover some of the lost speed.

Defragmentation

Windows continues to provide support tools, such as Disk Defragmenter, to defragment your hard disk. By using the improved Task Scheduler, Windows automatically runs the Optimize Drives utility, which examines your disk drives and then defragments them weekly.

To manually launch the Optimize Drives utility, use the command prompt and type **defrag**, or follow these steps to invoke the GUI version:

1. Search the Start screen for *drive* and select Defragment and Optimize your Drives from the Settings Search results. Alternatively press Windows+X, select Run, type **dfrgui.exe**, and then press Enter.

2. In the Optimize Drives utility, you can select the hard disk drive that you want to defragment and then click Optimize (see Figure 6-17).

Using this utility to optimize your drive can take several hours, depending on the size and level of fragmentation. If the defragmentation process is stopped and then restarted before completion, Windows automatically continues from the last position. This feature is known as *cyclic pickup defragmentation*.

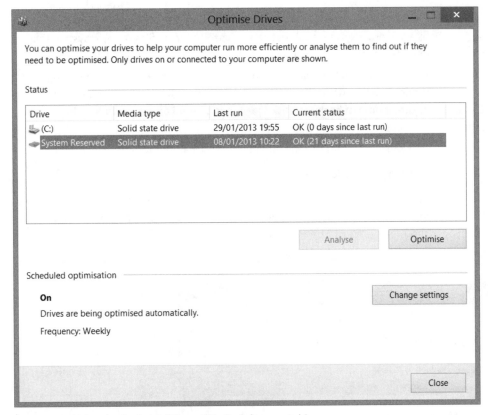

FIGURE 6-17 Using the Optimize Drives utility to defragment drives

Newer drives such as SSD don't need to be defragmented because files aren't accessed mechanically. If an SSD, thumb drive, or flash drive was to become defragmented, defragmenting the drive would result in only an infinitesimal speed benefit, because files on the drive are accessed at a uniform high speed regardless of the location or drive fragmentation.

NOTE DON'T DEFRAGMENT SSDS AND FLASH DRIVES

Defragmenting a solid state or a flash drive can significantly decrease the life span of the drive.

Disk Cleanup

Disk Cleanup is a Windows system tool that can be used to locate files on your system that are no longer needed, such as temporary files or temporary Internet download files.

Just how many files are built up over time that can be safely deleted from your computer is amazing. Deleting the files not only provides you with more free space, but also reduces the size and length of time of backups. Disk Cleanup is a useful tool to consider when "spring cleaning" your computer.

To launch Disk Cleanup, either use the command-line cleanmgr tool or follow these steps:

1. Search the Start screen for *cleanmgr* and open Disk Cleanup.

2. If you need to choose a hard drive to clean, select the one you want and click OK. Disk Cleanup analyzes the selected drive for files that can be deleted and presents them to you in a summary report (see Figure 6-18).

3. To delete the files or pages, click Clean Up System Files.

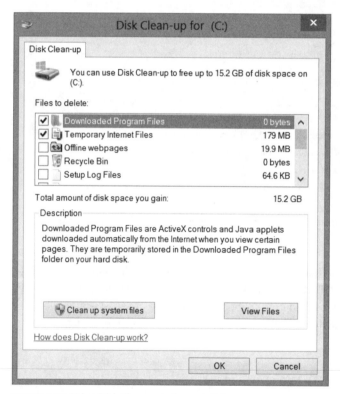

FIGURE 6-18 Using Disk Cleanup to free up disk space

The file categories that Windows reports for possible deletion include the following:

■ Downloaded Program Files

- Temporary Internet Files
- Offline Files
- Temporary Offline Files
- Offline Webpage Files
- Debug Dump Files
- Recycle Bin
- Setup Log Files
- System error memory dump files
- Hibernation File Cleaner
- Temporary Files (including Microsoft Office Temp Files)
- Thumbnails
- Windows Error Reporting Archive and Queue
- Files Discarded by Software Upgrades (including Windows Upgrade Files)

In many of these file categories, you can view the files or pages before permanently deleting them.

EXAM TIP

Windows Upgrade creates a hidden folder where the previous Windows installation files are saved: %SystemDrive%\Windows.old.

If you want to show the Disk Cleanup utility on the Start screen, select the option to Show Administrative Tools on the Tiles menu (see Figure 6-19). You can display the Tiles menu on the Charms bar by pressing Windows+C from the Start screen and then clicking Settings and Tiles.

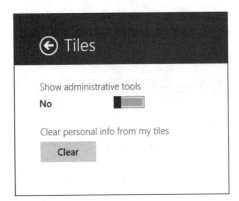

FIGURE 6-19 Showing administrative tools

Managing Storage Spaces

Storage Spaces is a new feature built into both Windows 8 and Windows Server 2012 that allows you to add storage to your system and pool existing drives without needing to purchase traditionally expensive storage area network (SAN) devices.

Within a Storage Space, you create a storage pool, which can span multiple physical disks. One nice feature of storage pools is the ability to add and remove disks from a pool as your capacity demand changes. Windows allows you to provision storage from the pool as a number of virtual disks that behave exactly like a physical disk. A virtual disk is sometimes referred as a *LUN (Logical Unit Number)*.

> **NOTE** USE ONLY BLANK DRIVES WITH STORAGE SPACES
>
> When creating or adding a drive to a Storage Space, Windows 8 formats it and any data is lost.

EXAM TIP

LUNs are generally used with SAN technology. Windows 8 supports LUNs with the Storage Spaces feature.

To configure Storage Spaces, you need first to attach your storage, which can be a mix and match type/size/interface, such as internal/external drives, USB drives, Serial ATA (SATA), Serial Attached SCSI (SAS), and so forth. Any existing data on a drive can't be integrated into the storage pool; when drives are added, they are specially formatted and then configured to be part of the pool. You should ensure that any existing data is removed, backed up, or transferred to the existing pool; otherwise, it's permanently lost.

Storage Spaces allows Windows 8 users to configure volume-level resiliency, which helps protect the data while it's stored in the storage pool. Depending on how many drives the storage pool contains, you can configure volume mirroring or parity volume levels of redundancy.

Windows offers the following types of redundancy:

Type	Description
Simple (none)	No mirroring; data is lost if the drive fails.
Two-way mirror	Every file in the pool is stored on at least two different physical drives, "mirroring" your data.
Three-way mirror	Every file in the pool is stored on at least three different physical drives. This allows you to lose two out of the three drives.
Parity	At least three drives are required for parity. Data is stored across at least two different physical drives and the parity information is saved on another disk. This method uses less disk space but can be higher on disk I/O overhead as the parity information needs to be calculated.

After your drives are connected, follow these steps to configure Storage Spaces:

1. Search the Start screen for *Storage Spaces* and open Storage Spaces from the Settings search.

2. Select Create A New Pool And Storage Space, as shown in Figure 6-20.

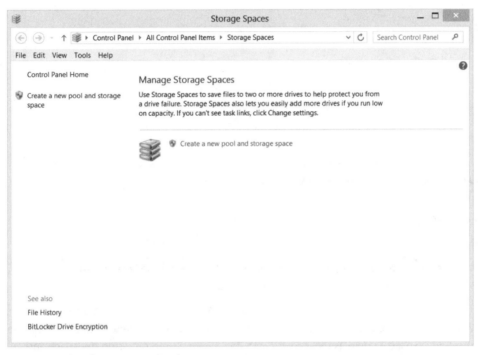

FIGURE 6-20 Creating a new pool and storage space

3. If requested, accept the UAC prompt.

4. Storage Spaces identifies available drives to create the Storage Pool. Select the drive(s) you want to add, as shown in Figure 6-21. (If a drive isn't formatted, it is automatically selected.)

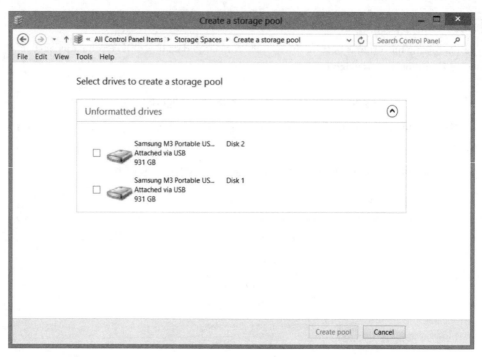

FIGURE 6-21 Selecting drives to create a storage pool

5. Click Create Pool.

6. Name the storage space and select the drive letter you want to use.

7. Use the drop-down list, as shown in Figure 6-22, to select the level of resiliency that you require, and then click Create Storage Space.

Your storage pool is now created and is ready to use.

Windows allows you to specify a maximum size larger than the current amount of available physical drive space. Known as *thin provisioning*, this allows you to provision the space and then add drives as they are required. The system prompts you as the physical limit is reached to add more drives. You can also increase the maximum size of an existing storage space at a later stage.

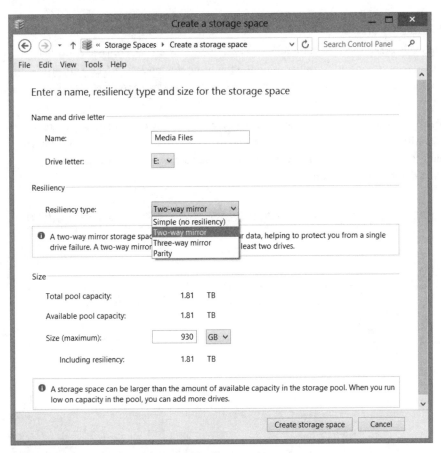

FIGURE 6-22 Selecting the storage space resiliency type

MORE INFO POWERSHELL STORAGE SPACES MODULE

A module is available for PowerShell users who want to script Storage Spaces. Details can be found here: *http://www.microsoft.com/en-us/download/details.aspx?id=30125*.

NOTE MOVING STORAGE POOL DISKS TO A NEW PC

Drives configured as part of a storage pool must be kept together if the pool is moved to a different Windows 8 PC. If a disk is removed, it needs to be reformatted before it can be reused in another PC.

After you create a storage pool, it can be managed using the Manage Storage Spaces console (see Figure 6-23). You can create additional storage spaces, add drives, and delete or rename both the storage space and the name of each physical drive.

Most drives have a warranty for one, three, or five years. If for any reason one of your disk drives fails within the warranty period, you should be able to obtain a replacement from the manufacturer. Marking the drive with your purchase date and warranty expiry date could be useful in a few years' time.

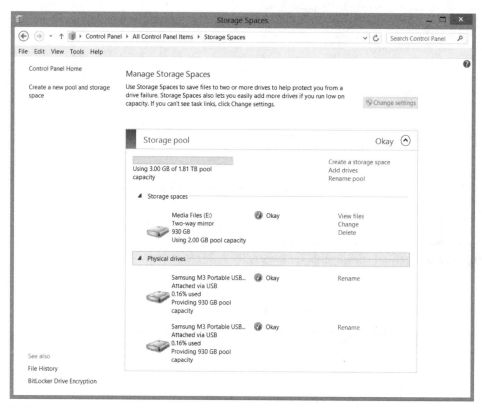

FIGURE 6-23 Managing your Storage Spaces

One potential downside to the use of Storage Spaces is that the system (Windows) drive can't be included as part of the pool. To provide resiliency for the system drive, you should consider other options such as RAID.

Thought experiment
Auditing Storage Spaces

In the following thought experiment, apply what you've learned about the objective. You can find answers to these questions in the "Answers" section at the end of this chapter.

You are a support technician working for Contoso Inc., which has approximately 2,000 employees working across four sites around the country. Your manager has been reading about Storage Spaces and wants you to audit each PC within the company so that he can consider implementing the feature.

You've taken an inventory that shows the following installed operating systems and drive configurations:

Operating System	Quantity	Disk Drives
Windows 7 Ultimate - PC	1100	2
Windows 7 Ultimate - Laptop	200	1
Windows 8 Enterprise - PC	470	2
Windows 8 Enterprise - Laptop	200	1

Compile an audit for your manager, detailing which of the current computers could be configured to use the Storage Spaces feature.

Objective summary

- DiskPart provides a command-line tool for disk and volume management, which can also be scripted.
- The fsutil tool allows advanced configuration of both FAT and NTFS file systems.
- Disk Management is the Windows GUI tool that allows you to perform many disk-related tasks.
- The VHDX format allows VHDs to be created up to 64 TB in size.
- Disk Defragmenter is updated and renamed to the Optimize Drives utility, which is scheduled to run weekly.
- The Disk Cleanup tool enables users to free up disk space by deleting unwanted files.
- Storage Spaces is a new feature in Windows 8 that allows the pooling of drives and offers volume-level resiliency.

Objective review

Answer the following questions to test your knowledge of the information in this objective. You can find the answers to these questions and explanations of why each answer choice is correct or incorrect at the end of this chapter.

1. You need to format four new 3 TB external USB drives to use with Windows 8. Which of the following file system format could you use?

   A. FAT

   B. NTFS

   C. exFAT

   D. FAT32

2. You need to check whether a new batch of disk drives is of the Standard or Advanced Format Disk type. Which of the following commands would you use?

   A. Fsinfo fsutil C:

   B. Fsinfo C:

   C. Fsutil fsinfo ntfsinfo C:

   D. Fsutil fsinfo C:

3. Which of the following options are available within Disk Management?

   A. Convert MBR disk to GPT disk or GPT to MBR

   B. Extend and shrink a volume

   C. Convert dynamic disk to basic disk

   D. Mark a drive as hidden

   E. Repair a disk

4. You've noticed that your Windows 8 laptop is operating slowly and occasionally freezing. You think your SSD drive could be fragmented or lack free space. What should you do?

   A. Use the Optimize Drives utility only.

   B. Run the Disk Cleanup tool only.

   C. Run the Disk Cleanup tool and then run the Optimize Drive utility.

   D. Run the command chkdsk /spotfix C: dfrgui.exe.

   E. Run the command dfrgui.exe.

5. Your Windows 8 PC has two internal hard drives and one external USB drive. You want to configure Storage Spaces and need to ensure that if one of the drives in the storage pool fails, no data will be lost. Which of the following volume-level resiliency type(s) could you chose?

   A. Parity

   B. Simple

   C. Three-way mirror

   D. Two-way mirror

Objective 6.3: Monitor system performance

For many years I was a techie guru that wanted to always squeeze more speed out of my PC. I would buy more RAM, faster processors, and (most recently) SSD drives to speed up my PC. Nowadays I buy the best that my budget will allow, but I no longer delve into obscure places such as tweaking swap file sizes and visual effects found on the performance options (as shown in Figure 6-24) to optimize my computers like I used to. Why? Because Windows 8 is fast, and remains fast, even after months of normal use.

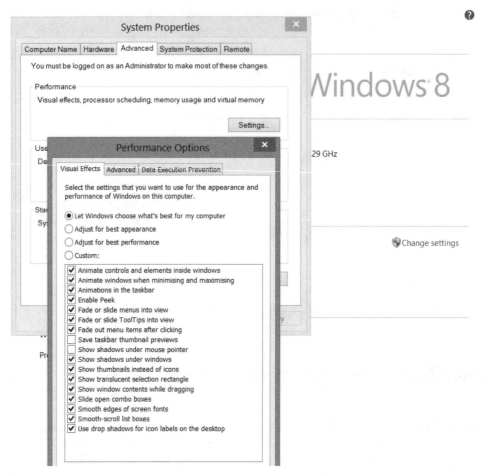

FIGURE 6-24 Windows 8 Performance Options

At the first hint of Windows 8 beginning to slow down or even crashing, you should know exactly which tools, logs, and events to investigate to find out what's going on and hopefully get the system working again. Many have been part of the Windows operating system for years, but some great enhancements and new additional tools are also available. This objective covers many of these tools and shows you how to monitor, optimize, and configure your system for performance.

Configuring Task Manager

Task Manager has been, for many years, one of the most useful Windows techie tools that you can use to investigate and monitor performance-related issues. Windows 8 has overhauled Task Manager significantly, and you should be impressed with the enhanced functionality. Microsoft announced that it was incorporating the following capabilities into Task Manager during the engineering phase of building Windows 8:

- Clearer relationship between apps and processes
- Easy-to-read performance metrics per process
- Expanded PC performance information, similar to Resource Monitor default view
- App performance history
- List of Startup programs, with option to disable

To open Task Manager, follow these steps and view the results for your system, which should be similar to those shown in Figure 6-25:

1. Search the Start screen for *task* and open Task Manager (or press Windows+X and choose Task Manager).

2. Click More Details or Fewer Details to expand or contract the view.

3. Explore the Task Manager tabs: Processes, Performance, App history, Start-up, Users, Details, and Services.

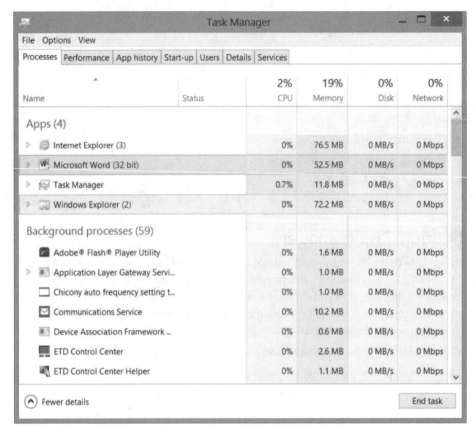

FIGURE 6-25 The new Task Manager in Windows 8

The End Task option at the lower right of the Task Manager screen is useful to stop an app that might not be responding. You can also stop a running app or running process by right-clicking the item and then selecting End Task.

The Performance tab is particularly informative and shows detailed results for CPU, memory, disk activity, and Ethernet and Wi-Fi networking. If you highlight one of the items on the left side, such as the CPU, you can see even more information. The CPU information shown in Figure 6-26 displays useful information on whether the computer supports virtualization, the number of cores/processors, and even the speed and family of processor that's installed.

EXAM TIP

For another example of the wealth of information gleaned from the performance tab within Task Manager, click the Ethernet or Wi-Fi area and notice the currently allocated IPv4 and IPv6 addresses.

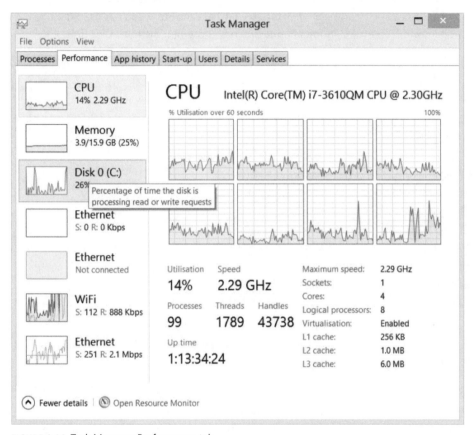

FIGURE 6-26 Task Manager Performance tab

Task Manager now can modify which apps automatically run when Windows 8 starts. If your PC remains unresponsive after you have logged on, you might find that the computer is busy executing the startup conditions of several installed programs that are configured to run in the background. You could safely disable many of these apps to free up resources and speed up your computer. Previously, this utility was contained within the msconfig.exe tool.

EXAM TIP

Msconfig.exe is still present within Windows 8; however, the redundant Start-Up tab now informs you to open the Task Manager to configure startup items.

Many applications won't be offended if the automatic startup status is set to disable, and changing the setting with Task Manager can significantly speed up computer responsiveness, especially during the period immediately after you log on.

Another useful addition to the Task Manager is the App History tab, which also shows a *heat map*—a graphically appealing way in which the items with the largest values are highlighted. This can be clearly seen in Figure 6-27, where the Store app has used the most network bandwidth and the Windows Phone app has consumed the most CPU time.

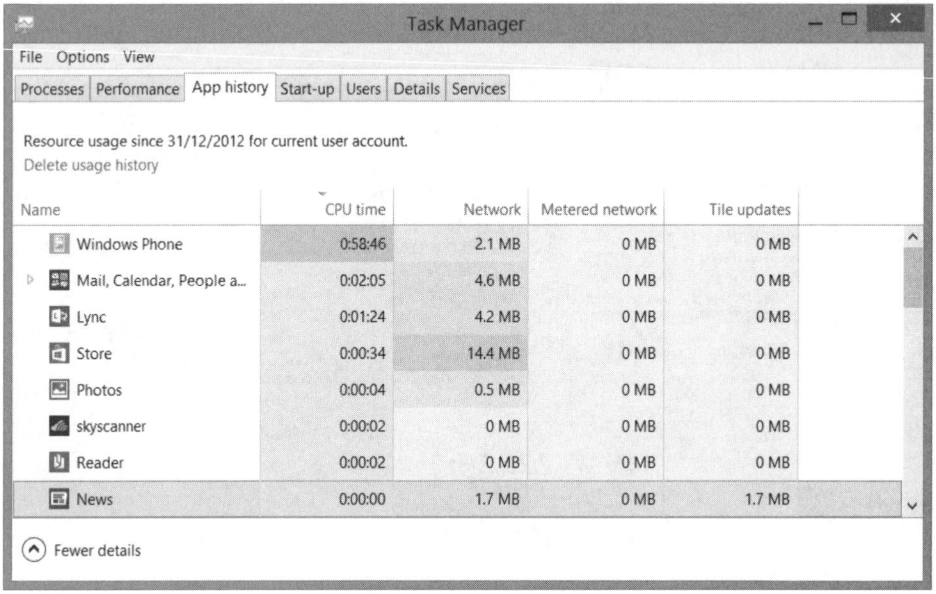
Task Manager
File Options View
Processes Performance App history Start-up Users Details Services
Resource usage since 31/12/2012 for current user account.
Delete usage history
Name CPU time Network Metered network Tile updates
Windows Phone 0:58:46 2.1 MB 0 MB 0 MB
Mail, Calendar, People a... 0:02:05 4.6 MB 0 MB 0 MB
Lync 0:01:24 4.2 MB 0 MB 0 MB
Store 0:00:34 14.4 MB 0 MB 0 MB
Photos 0:00:04 0.5 MB 0 MB 0 MB
skyscanner 0:00:02 0 MB 0 MB 0 MB
Reader 0:00:02 0 MB 0 MB 0 MB
News 0:00:00 1.7 MB 0 MB 1.7 MB
Fewer details

FIGURE 6-27 Task Manager Performance tab, showing heat map

The Details tab includes comprehensive information relating to running and suspended processes on the computer. When you are troubleshooting a system and find an unfamiliar process or one that's exhibiting strange behavior, the details section of Task Manager can be extremely useful. Right-clicking a running process (as shown in Figure 6-28) allows you to select one of many useful tools, such as to end the task, open the file location of the process, and even search online for additional details of the process.

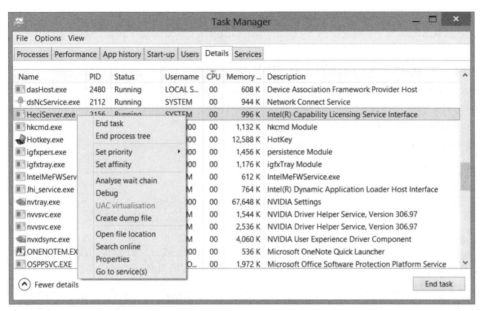

FIGURE 6-28 Using the Task Manager Details tab to troubleshoot a suspicious process

---

MORE INFO **WINDOWS 8 TASK MANAGER**

For information from the Windows engineering team regarding the Windows 8 Task Manager, see *http://blogs.msdn.com/b/b8/archive/2011/10/13/the-windows-8-task-manager.aspx*.

Monitoring system resources

In addition to the Task Manager, Windows 8 provides users with several other tools in relation to monitoring system resources. You should review each one and understand how each tool varies slightly in their level of detail and usefulness.

Resource Monitor, introduced with Windows 7, is retained in Windows 8. It can be accessed directly from within the Task Manager, as shown at the bottom of the screen in Figure 6-26, or from within the Performance Monitor console.

EXAM TIP

You can run the Resource Monitor directly from the Start menu or Run command. The executable is resmon.exe.

Although the Resource Monitor hasn't noticeably changed from Windows 7, it still offers a very granular and detailed method of viewing how the system resources on your computer are performing in real time. With all the enhancements made to the Task Manager in Windows 8, whether the Resource Monitor tool is used in practice will be interesting to see.

Using the Windows Experience Index

Windows 8 continues to offer users the ability to measure the computer's "overall" performance. The Windows Experience Index (WEI) allows users to see the relative subsystem scores of five key aspects of the computer hardware:

- Processor
- Memory (RAM)
- Graphics
- Gaming graphics
- Hard disk

The WEI calculates an overall score determined by the lowest score of the five individual scores that are indexed on a range from 1.0 to 9.9, as shown in Figure 6-29.

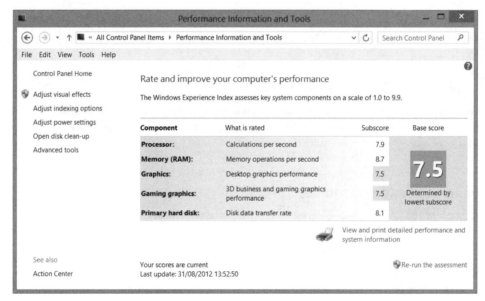

FIGURE 6-29 Windows 8 WEI assessment

If the computer was recently upgraded or a new driver has been installed, you should be able to rerun the WEI assessment from the assessment screen. Running the assessment won't produce any performance gain, but it might result in a change to the base score.

Performance Monitor

Ever since the early days of Windows, the Performance Monitor tool has allowed IT professionals to monitor—at a very low level—the activity of their computers, either in real-time monitoring or by building collector sets that are designed to store a configuration and be rerun at defined times. The tool allows the monitoring of one or several of the hundreds of available performance counters. Examples of performance counters that can be monitored include the following:

- CPU Busy Time
- Hard disk read speed
- Hard disk read time
- Hard disk write time
- Memory idle space

To open Performance Monitor, follow these steps:

1. Search on the Start screen for *perfmon* and then select perfmon.exe to open the Performance MMC.

2. Click the Performance Monitor subtree to display the console (see Figure 6-30).

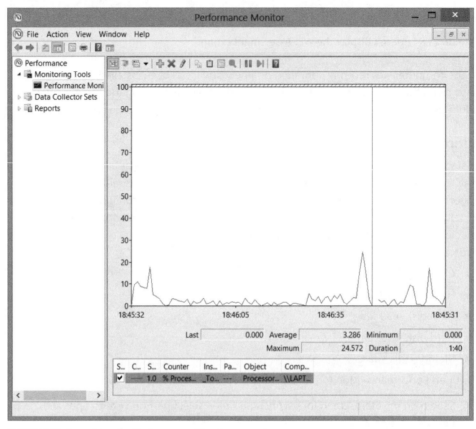

FIGURE 6-30 Launching the Performance Monitor console

The default real-time performance graph displays a red colored line that represents the % Processor time, with the actual values shown in a table at the bottom of the window. You can add or delete additional counters to be monitored by using the green plus and red X buttons on the console's tool bar.

By default, counters are selected from the local computer; however, you also can add a counter from another computer on your local network by selecting the remote computer, as shown in Figure 6-31.

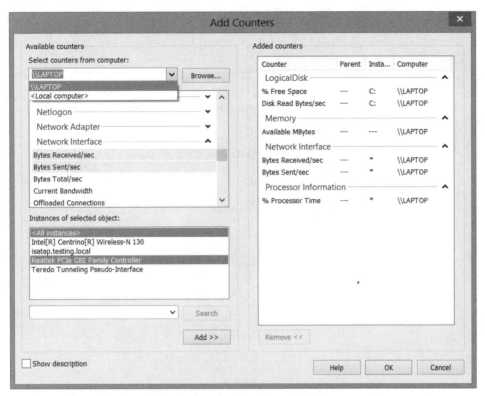

FIGURE 6-31 Adding counters from a remote computer to be monitored

Because Performance Monitor results are shown in real time, the PC might suffer slight overhead from the data collection process. Also, the configuration is lost when the console is closed. To create and preserve a predefined monitoring configuration, you can create your own custom Data Collector Set or use one of the many built-in system-defined sets.

The Data Collector Set is a wizard that requires a name, which counters are to be monitored (and on which computer), and the storage location where to save the collected data log file. To create a custom Data Collector Set, right-click the User Defined node, select New, and then select Data Collector Set, as highlighted in Figure 6-32.

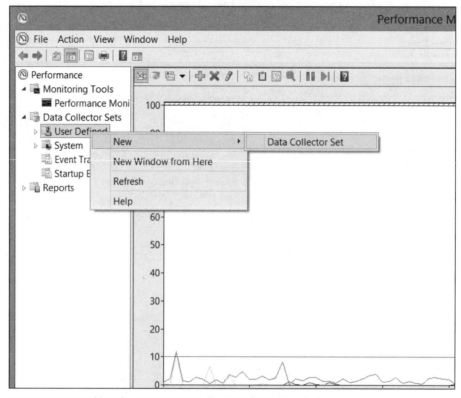

FIGURE 6-32 Launching the custom Data Collector Set Wizard

To begin collecting data from either the custom Data Collector Set or a built-in system set, right-click the desired Data Collector Set from the subtree in the left pane and select Start. The collection begins, and you should see the Collector Set icon change to indicate that the process is running.

After you run the collector for the desired amount of time (the minimum is 60 seconds), you can stop the collection and then navigate to the reports section, where you can see a report with the same name as your collector set and a corresponding date to the time that the data was collected.

> **NOTE CATEGORIZING REPORTS**
>
> Reports are categorized into User Defined and System reports in the tree pane.

Open the report by selecting it in the subtree. The report should open in the central pane of the MMC, and you should be able to drill into the data or view the performance graph if you created a user defined set without using a template.

Performance counters and bottlenecks

If you're investigating a performance issue on a computer, the following counters and their respective values and behavior could be useful in your diagnosis and suggested remediation.

Performance Counter	Bottleneck
%Processor Time	Measures how busy the processor is. Apart from bursts of activity, constant operation at greater than 80 percent is a sign of an overworked or under-powered processor. Consider upgrading the processor to a faster unit or adding additional processors/cores.
Page faults/sec	If memory isn't available when the processor calls for it, page faults can occur. If the page/sec is great than 20, add more memory to the system.
Page/sec	Increase the memory available if the value is above 1.5.
%Avg. Disk Queue Length	Some queuing is acceptable, but if the average value is 2 or higher, consider installing a faster disk drive such as an SSD.
Interrupts/sec	Interrupts relate to the requests that the processor is responding to. A figure less than 1000/sec is acceptable; otherwise, investigate potential hardware failure or driver issues.

Action Center

The Action Center was initially called the *Security Center in Windows XP SP2*, and in each Windows release since it has been expanded and improved. Now the Action Center provides a centralized comprehensive location to track and troubleshoot problems, which your Windows 8 computer might encounter.

Specific Windows 8 Action Center additions include support for new features, including the following:

- Windows SmartScreen
- Microsoft account and Trust this PC
- File History
- Drive Status
- Startup apps
- Storage Spaces
- Advanced recovery tools

In addition to being the centralized location for the various tools and settings, the primary aim of the Action Center is to trigger alert notifications when something goes wrong with Windows 8 for the user to act on.

Even if a user disables a setting or fails to complete a task that could make the system less safe, the Action Center flags the issue as still being a concern. For example, Windows 8 prompts users to trust their PC with a Microsoft account. This allows users to benefit fully from added functionality, such as password and website synchronization, that a trusted Microsoft account can provide. Another unresolved Action Center issue could be if a virus or malware alert occurred or the user ignored an available driver update.

Users need to be made aware that a red-flag warning in the Action Center indicates important messages for the user and that the system is potentially vulnerable and needs action. It would be wise to visualize the Action Center similarly to the warning lights that appear on a motor vehicle dashboard. To see which items are to be resolved within the Action Center, the user should click the flag icon in the system tray, as shown in Figure 6-33.

FIGURE 6-33 Action Center red flag warning of a problem

Reliability Monitor

Computers can take a lot of abuse. They are nearly constantly connected to the Internet, apps are installed and uninstalled frequently, regular maintenance is forgotten (although Windows 8 takes care of most maintenance tasks automatically), and often the slowing down of the computer is gradual as you allow them to "clog up" over time.

One of the best ways to establish whether your system, network, disk, or Internet speed is becoming slower is to refer to a benchmark that you might have recorded previously. This could be created by using the Performance Monitor console referred to previously or another benchmarking tool. Windows 8 includes an app called *Reliability Monitor*, which is contained within the Action Center, and keeps a record of each time your computer crashes or when software or a driver fails and presents the history in a graphical representation that provides a visual confirmation of the problems and aids in diagnosis (see Figure 6-34).

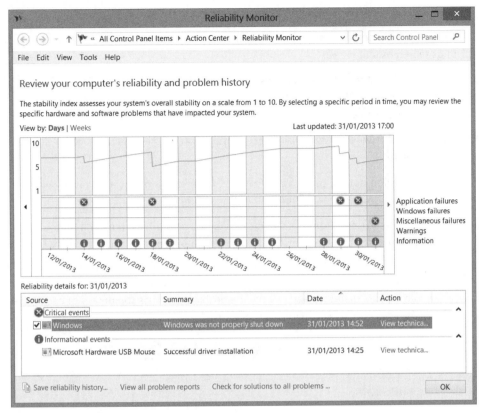

FIGURE 6-34 Viewing the reliability history for your computer

Showing results either weekly or daily on a graph, Reliability Monitor provides you with an overall stability index on a scale from 1 to 10. This index is based on hardware and software problems that have had a detrimental effect on the computer, such as the following recorded events:

- Application failures (severe)
- Windows failures (severe)
- Miscellaneous failures (severe)
- Warnings
- Informational events (not necessarily issues)

You can see from the graph that prolonged use of your computer without a failure actually causes the stability index to increase as your PC becomes more reliable. After you establish a stable benchmark for the system, creating a restore point or backing up the system can be useful at this time. You can also save the status of the reliability history by clicking the save option, shown at the bottom left of Figure 6-34.

To open and view Reliability Monitor, follow these steps:

1. Search on the Start menu for *reliability* and select View Reliability History in the settings search results.

2. The tool collects the data and then dispalys a record of the reliability history of your computer, similar to the history shown in Figure 6-34. You view the history in days or weeks and you can scroll the history backward in time.

3. Highlight a day, week, or event, and you should be able to see the detail of each problem.

4. Under the Action option, select View Technical Details. This opens a new window—part of the Action Center—displaying the problem details.

5. The information gained from the technical details should enable a technician to diagnose and remediate the problem. Click OK to close the problem details.

The tool is extremely useful for helpdesk technicians when troubleshooting an unreliable computer. By viewing the problem details relating to an event, as shown in Figure 6-35, a technician should be able diagnose and resolve the problem because the details of each issue is recorded in one easy-to-use, consolidated tool.

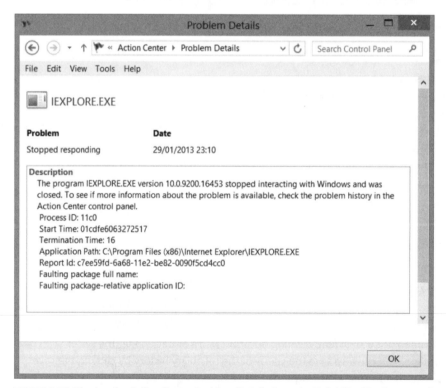

FIGURE 6-35 Viewing the Action Center Problem Details from the Reliability Monitor console

Optimizing networking performance

With the continued growth of cloud computing and the demand for "always on" online services, the speed and reliability at which computers access these resources will be under ever greater scrutiny. Internet outages that hinder connecting to cloud-based services such as SkyDrive or productivity suites such as Office 365 can leave users frustrated during a time when general expectation is that these services are just as reliable as their locally installed legacy counterparts.

In this decade, 100 percent uptime and accessibility to connected services is required by every user and, thankfully, in most cases this is indeed achievable. Issues relating to networking typically falls into three clear categories: working, broken, or intermittent.

Most network equipment such as routers, switches, and access points are hardware-based appliances that require some initial configuration and then only a power supply to operate "forever," typically without a hitch. For the Wi-Fi router, performing a backup of the configuration is essential (ideally to both the cloud and a local backup, because you might not have access to the cloud backup if the router has failed). Remember, these devices commonly last five to ten years and, during that time, you'll probably lose or misplace the initial correspondence from your ISP regarding setup. Nowadays, most of the configuration and setup is automatic or, in some cases, the initial URL/admin passwords are stenciled to the underside of the device. (Don't forget to change them, especially if the unit is located in a publically accessible place.)

> **REAL WORLD** **CAN OLDER HARDWARE CAUSE ISSUES?**
>
> I recently needed to upgrade one of my Wi-Fi routers—it was suffering from intermittent failures. I soon realized that the intermittent nature of the fault affected only Windows 7 and Windows 8 devices and not some legacy or non-Windows devices on my network, such as my TV and Network Attached Storage (NAS) box. It seemed that although my 54 Mbps Wi-Fi router is pretty old, it works fine with devices built during the same time period it was manufactured. One potential issue with devices that happily keep working for 10 years is that newer technology (such as Windows 8–enabled devices) expects to operate at much higher speeds than the legacy hardware was designed for.
>
> I replaced the Wi-Fi router and now have three antennae on top of the router. I'm enjoying my 300 Mbps Dual Band Wireless N Router, which has increased speed, longer range, and—because of the extra antennae—supports the increase in the number of connected devices that I fear was beginning to cripple the old router through interference or throughput bottlenecks.

Key pointers for achieving the reliability and optimal networking that a modern computer expects include the following:

- Keep the drivers of the network card or Wi-Fi card up to date.
- Flash the router or modem with the most recent ROM available.

- If applicable, use good quality Ethernet cabling and route it away from energy sources, such as power transformers.
- Consider updating your Wi-Fi router each decade.

Troubleshooting your network

A whole book could be written, or at least a chapter, to explain networking and the protocols and addresses used to transport data around your network. Many of the networking protocols, including TCP/IP, were invented more than 40 years ago and are still in operation today. However, thankfully much protocol processing is hidden beneath the user interface away from users, as it should be—after all, this is Windows 8, not UNIX.

> **NOTE THE NEW WINDOWS NETWORKING STACK**
>
> Several core services within Windows, including the TCP/IP networking support, have been completely rewritten by Microsoft in recent years and now offer increased performance and reliability while retaining backward compatibility to earlier Windows versions.

Because Windows 8 has been designed to support this generation of cloud users, it comes with excellent networking support, proven reliability, and troubleshooting tools that should be given respect, because they work really well.

At the first sign of trouble with your network, such as the exclamation mark over the system tray networking icon (see Figure 6-36), you should right-click the networking icon and select Troubleshoot Problems.

FIGURE 6-36 System Tray networking icon indicating that a problem has occurred

The Network Diagnostics wizard attempts to diagnose the problem thoroughly and, in most cases, will fix the problem. The first point of reference in troubleshooting in Windows 8 should be the built-in, wizard-driven troubleshooting tools.

Suppose that a problem develops with the network adaptor and the TCP/IP stack needs to be reset. Without the wizard diagnosing and fixing this problem, you would probably need to consult the helpdesk via the telephone (because the network is unavailable, you can't search the Internet for a remedy, nor can the helpdesk be able to remote assist to your PC). After several minutes and possible several misspelled ipconfig /release or similar commands in the command prompt, the helpdesk technician will diagnose that the TCP/IP stack needs to be reset. To fix this, the technician will tell you to open an elevated command prompt and type **netsh int ip reset c:\resetlog.txt** to use the *netsh.exe* utility to reset the registry keys for the TCP/IP and DCHP parameters. (Alternatively, they might ask you to reboot your PC, which also resets the TCP/IP stack, but that could inconvenience you.)

With the Windows 8 Network Diagnostics wizard, the system diagnoses and attempts the reset fix without you needing to call the helpdesk or rebooting your machine as shown in Figure 6-37.

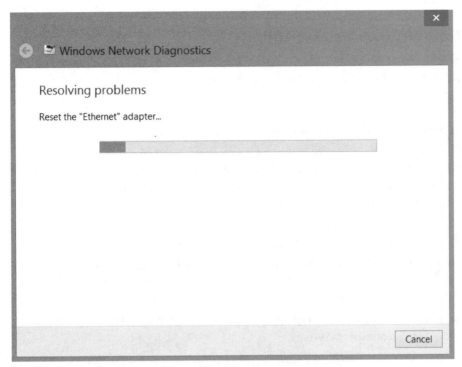

FIGURE 6-37 Windows 8 Network Diagnostics wizard resolving a problem

Where a network becomes slow or very unresponsive for no apparent reason, most users automatically assume that the problem is with their PC and start making changes. My advice is to do nothing immediately, or perhaps try to reboot your PC. Most Internet problems result from a temporary failure of one of the millions of components that make up "the Internet" and not you or your computer. If the problem becomes intermittent or a regular occurrence, the problem is more likely to be internal, such as one of the following:

- A failing component
- A broken or loose cable
- Virus/malware infection
- A corrupt driver
- Interference (power source) or obstacle
- Security settings not configured properly
- Wi-Fi antenna issues, such as misalignment

Potentially, the issue could be outside your direct influence, such as one of the following:

- Increased volume of Internet-enabled users in your local neighborhood/home/office
- Changes to the service provision or contention ratio from your ISP
- Congestion/traffic overload on the external network

Configuring event subscriptions

If you need to dig a little deeper into the system to find answers to problems, you should probably look at the Event Viewer console. You've seen from the various tools mentioned already that the source of the reporting is generated and stored by Windows 8 recording events in the Event Logs. Event Viewer was significantly overhauled in Windows Vista and provides easier access to hundreds of system and custom logs.

The key task of a log is to record important events that have occurred on the computer. You can use Event Viewer to view logs from the local computer or from a remote networked computer. An administrator can also create an event subscription, which allows the collection of specific events from other computers on the network.

The type of events that Windows 8 stores include events generated by processes, services, applications, and hardware devices. Windows 8 uses two main types of logs:

- **Windows logs** These logs record system events related to applications, security, setup, and system components. The Windows logs folder contains the following logs: Application, Security, Setup, System, and Forwarded Events.

- **Applications and services logs** These logs are generated by specific applications or services to record specific events.

> **NOTE THE SYSTEM LOG**
>
> The System log is the primary Windows 8 operational log. Typically, this is the first log that you view when you are diagnosing system problems.

A log entry can be afforded a specific warning or severity level, as follows:

Level	Meaning
Information	An informational event
Audit Success	An event related to the successful execution of an audit-related action
Audit Failure	An event related to the failed execution of an audit-related action
Warning	An event that warns that problems are occurring on the computer
Error	An error, such as the failure of a service or application
Critical	An event that warns of a significant loss of functionality or data

Following an incident or action, the system typically records an event log. To view the Event Logs, open Event Viewer by searching the Start screen for *event* and open View Event Logs (or press Windows+X and choose Event Viewer). The Event Viewer MMC snap-in appears, as shown in Figure 6-38.

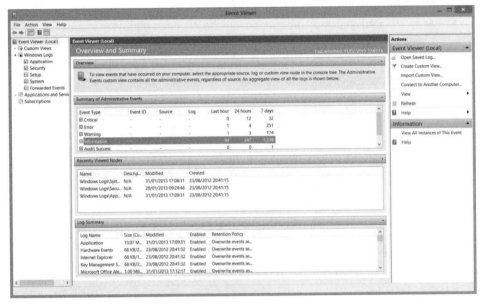

FIGURE 6-38 Viewing the Event Viewer console

Even with the new Event Viewer and the enhanced ability to create filters, custom views, and even connections to remote computers, the sheer volume of event-related information can be overwhelming. If you plan to use Event Viewer regularly, you should use the custom view capability or create alerts and triggers for specific events. Both approaches allow you to refine the results and create exception-based results.

Typically, administrators want to collect data from a computer or a group of computers that alerts them to a specific event or type of event occurring. Event subscriptions enable you to configure subscriptions of events that are then collected and displayed on a single Event Viewer console. Windows 8 supports two types of event subscriptions:

- **Collector initiated** Subscriptions receive events from the source computer. Each computer must be configured manually to participate.

- **Source computer initiated** In this model, each source computer sends events to the collector. The configuration details can be distributed by Group Policy, allowing this type of subscription to be suitable on large networks.

To create subscriptions, you need to ensure that all computers in the scope of the subscription can communicate with each other and that Windows Remote Management (on the source computers) and Windows Event Collector service (on the collector computer) are running.

To configure the necessary services to run, follow these steps:

1. On the collector computer, open an elevated command prompt and type the following command: **wecutil qc**.

2. On each source computer, follow these steps:

   A. At an elevated command prompt, enable the Windows remote management by typing the following command: **winrm quickconfig**.

   B. Add the computer account for the collector to the local Administrators group in the Local Users and Groups snap-in of the Computer Management console. (This gives the collector sufficient privileges to collect the events.)

EXAM TIP

You need to be an administrator or member of the Event Reader group to configure event subscriptions.

With the necessary configuration in place, you can now create an event subscription by following these steps to configure a collector-initiated subscription:

1. Log onto the computer that will act as the collector.

2. Search the Start screen for *event* and open View Event Logs (or press Windows+X and choose Event Viewer).

3. When the Event Viewer MMC snap-in appears, click the Subscriptions node and select Create Subscription.

4. Provide a name for your subscription.

5. Choose Collector Initiated, click Select Computers, and specify the name of one or more computers on your network from which you want to collect events.

NOTE **GROUP POLICY AND SUBSCRIPTIONS**

If you are using Group Policy on your network, you should create and deploy your subscription settings by using a GPO. To enable this method, choose a Source Computer Initiated subscription in Step 5 and then configure the source computers to forward events to your collector computer.

6. Click Select Events. The Query Filter dialog box appears, allowing you to select which events you want to collect.

7. Click Advanced to choose delivery settings and to choose HTTP or HTTPS.

8. Click OK to create the subscription.

EXAM TIP

Event subscriptions are communicated via HTTP or HTTPS across the network using TCP port 5985 for HTTP or TCP port 5986 if HTTPS.

Optimizing the desktop environment

As this chapter nears the end, some of the tools included with Windows to help improve performance are summarized here. These tools are found the Performance Information and Tools screen, which is shown in Figure 6-39.

Tool	Description
Adjust visual effects	Visual effects can sometimes slow down other tasks on your PC. You can turn these effects on and off and view more options.
Adjust indexing options	You can fine-tune indexing and searching to focus on the files and folders that you most commonly use.
Adjust power settings	Power settings on your PC can significantly affect its performance. You can change settings to balance your PC the way you want to between higher performance and longer battery life.
Open Disk Cleanup	Freeing up space on your hard disk can increase performance, especially if the disk is quite full.
Advanced tools	This option (as shown in Figure 6-39) displays additional system tools, such as System Information, Task Manager, and Event Logs.

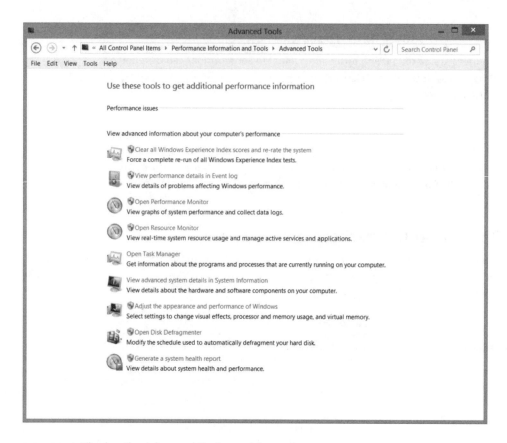

FIGURE 6-39 Viewing the Advanced Tools used for performance

Configuring Indexing Options

Windows 8 maintains an index of all the files, folders, and documents on your computer. This speeds up searches and helps maintain quick access to files in libraries. To manually manage this index and get a significant amount of control over it, search for *Index* at the Start screen, where you will find it in the Settings search results. Figure 6-40 shows the Indexing Options window, which lists all the currently indexed locations on your computer. You can use the Modify button to add or remove locations from the index and the Advanced button to manage the index itself.

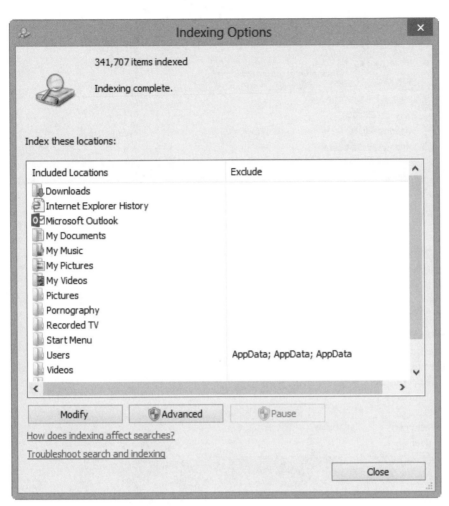

FIGURE 6-40 The Indexing Options window in Windows 8

Clicking Modify displays a list of all available locations that can be indexed (see Figure 6-41). The bottom list displays all the currently selected locations; if you click Show All Locations, this list expands to display all system and hidden locations that are also indexed by default.

> **NOTE ADDING NETWORK LOCATIONS TO THE INDEX**
>
> Various methods are available—some are official and some aren't—for adding network storage to your index and to libraries. A non-indexing workaround for libraries is the MKLINK command, which won't be detailed here because it's not official (although it does work). Some people suggest making a network drive available offline on your computer, although this will copy the network files over to your PC, taking up huge volumes of space.

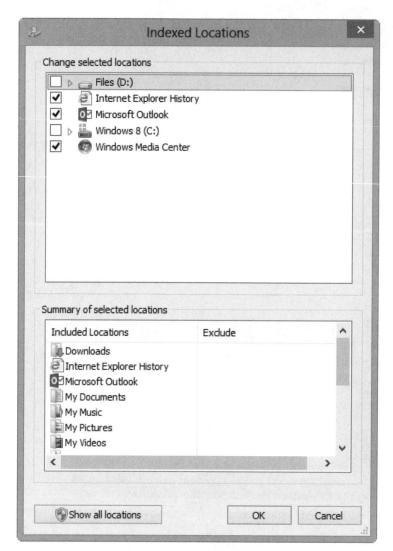

FIGURE 6-41 Selecting what locations are indexed

Clicking the Advanced button gives you fine control over the indexing options themselves (see Figure 6-42). The resulting window has two tabs across the top:

- Index Settings allow you to fine-tune the index and includes options for adding or excluding encrypted files, using natural language search with the index, moving the index completely to a different folder or hard disk, and even completely dumping the index and starting again, perhaps if it has become corrupt.

- File Types allow you to manually include or exclude any of the hundreds of file types Windows 8 knows or that are associated with software on your computer. If, for example, your company uses custom software that has its own file extension and file format, Windows 8 won't know to add it to the index. You can manually add those files to the index on this tab, and choose whether you want to index just the file properties or also its contents.

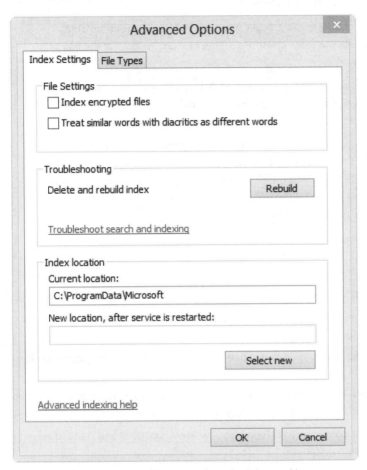

FIGURE 6-42 Managing indexing options from the Advanced button

Thought experiment
Managing weekly maintenance

In the following thought experiment, apply what you've learned about the objective. You can find answers to these questions in the "Answers" section at the end of this chapter.

You are a support technician working for a small charity with 43 computers and four servers. Each client computer is running Windows 8, and the servers run Windows Server 2012 Enterprise.

You want to complete a weekly maintenance checklist for each computer and server to detail such items as the amount of free space on the primary hard disk, logon attempts outside office hours, and the number of running tasks that each computer is running. You want to perform this task with the minimum amount of effort and without incurring any additional costs.

How would you accomplish this?

Objective summary

- The Windows Experience Index (WEI) allows you to "rate" your system, using an index on a range from 1.0 to 9.9.
- Start-up conditions for installed apps has been moved from the msconfig.exe tool to the Task Manager.
- Resource Monitor offers a rich and detailed graphical view of system resources and can be launched from the Performance tab of Task Manager.
- Performance Monitor continues to offer a very low-level reporting and benchmarking tool for troubleshooting system performance.
- Action Center is further enhanced in Windows 8 and now offers even greater integration and support to protect the computer.
- Event Viewer provides an indispensable tool for monitoring the health of your system and troubleshooting issues when they arise.
- Event subscriptions enable administrators to collect events from computers within their network automatically.

Objective review

Answer the following questions to test your knowledge of the information in this objective. You can find the answers to these questions and explanations of why each answer choice is correct or incorrect at the end of this chapter.

1. Which of the following items affect the WEI score of a Windows 8 computer?

   A. Edition of Windows 8 installed

   B. Free Disk Space

   C. Amount of RAM installed

   D. Processor speed

2. Task Manager includes which tabs?

   A. Processes, Performance, Apps, Start-Up, Users, Details, and Servers

   B. Processes, Performance, App History, Start-Up, Users, Details, and Services

   C. Processes, Perfmon, App History, Start-Up, Users, Details, and Services

   D. Processors, Performance, App history, Start-Up, Users, Details and Services

3. A user reports a lot of disk activity on her computer. You investigate, using Performance Monitor, and notice that the %Avg Disk Queue Length is 2.3. What do you recommend?

   A. Convert the disk to a GPT disk

   B. Upgrade the processor so that the queue can be processed more quickly

   C. Increase the size of the swap file on the disk

   D. Replace the disk with SSD-type storage

4. Which new Windows 8 feature(s) are supported within the Action Center?

   A. Trust this PC

   B. Storage Spaces

   C. Location Settings

   D. Family Safety

5. Windows 8 Event Viewer provides extensive logging. Which of the following logs can be found in the Windows Logs folder?

   A. Windows

   B. Auditing

   C. Forwarded Events

   D. Security

Answers

This section contains the solutions to the thought experiments and answers to the objective review questions in this chapter.

Objective 6.1: Thought experiment

Managing four different operating systems across a distributed network could cause you and your manager a headache. You should recommend to your manager that you want to rationalize the inventory during this growth phase of the enterprise to maintain only the currently mainstream supported operating systems. This would require the replacement or upgrade of the laptops, which currently use Windows XP Professional and Windows Vista.

You can justify this recommendation because you can obtain significant savings in many areas of IT support, including the testing, approval, and deployment of Windows Updates.

> **NOTE VISTA SECURITY AND PATCH SUPPORT**
>
> Mainstream support for Windows Vista Enterprise edition expired in October 2012, and Windows Vista SP2 support will expire in October 2014.

Objective 6.1: Review

1. **Correct answer:** C

   A. **Incorrect:** Windows Update isn't the most efficient method for a large number of workstations.

   B. **Incorrect:** This tool doesn't deploy updates.

   C. **Correct:** Windows Server Update Services (WSUS) enable you to manage all your updates.

   D. **Incorrect:** This tool is an older version of WSUS.

2. **Correct answer:** C

   A. **Incorrect:** This command opens the services applet only.

   B. **Incorrect:** This command stops the service.

   C. **Correct:** This command starts the desired service.

   D. **Incorrect:** This is a generic process name.

3. **Correct answers:** A and D

A. **Correct:** Security updates are part of Windows Update.

B. **Incorrect:** Viruses would be harmful to your computer.

C. **Incorrect:** Malware would be harmful to your computer.

D. **Correct:** Service Packs are part of Windows Update.

4. **Correct answer:** E

A. **Incorrect:** This might not resolve the problem.

B. **Incorrect:** You need to remove the update.

C. **Incorrect:** Resetting the PC isn't required.

D. **Incorrect:** The problem lies with the update, not the software.

E. **Correct:** Uninstalling the update should resolve the problem.

5. **Correct answer:** C

A. **Incorrect:** This is possible but isn't the preferred option.

B. **Incorrect:** This approach isn't efficient, because unwanted updates will continue to be presented.

C. **Correct:** This prevents the unwanted updates from reappearing.

D. **Incorrect:** Turning off the updates won't provide the richest app experience.

Objective 6.2: Thought experiment

Only the 470 Windows 8 Enterprise PCs could be configured to use the Storage Spaces feature. Only these machines are running Windows 8 and have two disks. One disk will be used by the system volume, which will allow the other disk to be configured in a Storage Pool.

If additional disk drives were purchased or the Windows 7 machines were upgraded to Windows 8, more machines could benefit from the Storage Space feature.

Objective 6.2: Review

1. **Correct answers:** B and C

A. **Incorrect:** FAT doesn't support large volume sizes.

B. **Correct:** NTFS supports volumes up to 256 TB in size.

C. **Correct:** exFAT supports volumes up to 256 TB in size.

D. **Incorrect:** FAT32 doesn't support large volume sizes.

2. **Correct answer:** C

A. **Incorrect: Fsinfo fsutil C:** results in an error.

B. **Incorrect: Fsinfo C:** results in an error.

C. **Correct: Fsutil fsinfo ntfsinfo C:** reports whether the drive supports the Advanced Format specification.

D. **Incorrect: Fsutil fsinfo C:** results in an error.

3. **Correct answers:** A, B, and C

A. **Correct:** Converting a MBR disk to GPT disk or GPT to MBR is possible in Disk Management.

B. **Correct:** Extending and shrinking a volume is possible in Disk Management.

C. **Correct:** Converting dynamic disk to basic disk is possible in Disk Management.

D. **Incorrect:** Hiding a disk isn't possible within Disk Management.

E. **Incorrect:** Repairing a disk isn't possible within Disk Management.

4. **Correct answer:** B

A. **Incorrect:** You shouldn't defragment SSD drives.

B. **Correct:** You should delete unwanted files by using the Disk Cleanup tool.

C. **Incorrect:** You shouldn't defragment SSD drives.

D. **Incorrect:** This will run the chkdsk tool but won't resolve the space problem.

E. **Incorrect:** You shouldn't defragment SSD drives.

5. **Correct answer:** D

A. **Incorrect:** Parity requires three drives to be available. Currently, you have three drives, but one is used as the system volume.

B. **Incorrect:** The simple type won't provide any fault tolerance.

C. **Incorrect:** A three-way mirror requires three drives to be available. Currently, you have three drives, but one is used as the system volume.

D. **Correct:** With two spare drives, a two-way mirror is possible and provides fault tolerance if one disk fails.

Objective 6.3: Thought experiment

You could manually inspect each machine to extract the information and update your checklist manually.

Some of the required items relate to performance metrics (such as available disk space), whereas others relate to items that would be captured by each computer Event Log (such as logon attempts).

To save time and automate the process, you could use an Event Collection to collect some of the specific events. Disk-related and process-related data could be collected via the Performance Monitor tool to configure a user-defined Data Collector Set, which can then be used to update the checklist.

Objective 6.3: Review

1. **Correct answers:** C and D

    A. **Incorrect:** The WEI rating doesn't affect Windows 8 performance.

    B. **Incorrect:** Disk Space doesn't affect the WEI rating.

    C. **Correct:** The amount of RAM installed affects the WEI rating.

    D. **Correct:** The processor speed affects the WEI rating.

2. **Correct answer:** B

    A. **Incorrect:** Apps isn't a correct tab displayed in Task Manager.

    B. **Correct:** Processes, Performance, App History, Start-up, Users, Details, and Services are the correct tabs displayed in Task Manager.

    C. **Incorrect:** Perfmon isn't a correct tab displayed in Task Manager.

    D. **Incorrect:** Processors isn't a correct tab displayed in Task Manager.

3. **Correct answer:** D

    A. **Incorrect:** Converting the disk won't speed up performance.

    B. **Incorrect:** The bottleneck is the disk, not the processor.

    C. **Incorrect:** The bottleneck is the disk, not the swap file.

    D. **Correct:** Replacing the disk with a fast SSD will improve disk performance.

4. **Correct answers:** A and B

    A. **Correct:** Trust This PC is a feature supported in the Action Center.

    B. **Correct:** Storage Spaces is a feature supported in the Action Center.

    C. **Incorrect:** Location Settings isn't a feature supported in the Action Center.

    D. **Incorrect:** Family Safety isn't a feature supported in the Action Center.

5. **Correct answers:** C and D

    A. **Incorrect:** Windows logs aren't found in the Windows Logs folder.

    B. **Incorrect:** The Auditing log isn't found in the Windows Logs folder.

    C. **Correct:** Forwarded Events are found in the Windows Logs folder.

    D. **Correct:** Security logs are found in the Windows Logs folder.

CHAPTER 7

Configure backup and recovery options

As the author of *Troubleshoot and Optimize Windows 8 Inside Out* from Microsoft Press, I know better than some of the importance of maintaining regular backups of your files and data and how to use the operating system's recovery options. My email inbox is often full of reader questions, and comments on Facebook, Twitter, and YouTube are always plentiful.

This objective guides you through not just the new and existing ways to back up both data and Windows 8 itself, but also through some best-practice tips that go beyond the scope for the final exam. This includes tips both for systems administrators and also topics that users can be educated about.

Objectives in this chapter:

- Objective 7.1: Configure backup
- Objective 7.2: Configure system recovery options
- Objective 7.3: Configure file recovery options

Objective 7.1: Configure backup

In the same way that Windows 8, being the most stable, reliable and robust version of Windows ever seen, comes with more recovery and repair tools than any version of the operating system before it. This robustness also means, ironically, that Windows 8 includes more file backup tools than any previous Windows version.

These tools include a full-file backup solution, now hidden away slightly in the Windows 7 File Recovery options of the Control Panel but still as fully functional as its predecessor and not just for restoring backups created in Windows 7. A SkyDrive app is built into Windows 8 and although this is suitable only for viewing files you have already stored in SkyDrive, the desktop software can be downloaded as part of the free Windows Essentials Suite and can be used for both file backup and syncing files between computers. Finally, there's the new File History feature, which acts as both backup and a file-versioning tool.

Although SkyDrive is unlikely to be covered in your exam, it's included here for completeness because it's such a useful and valuable tool that many Windows 8 users will likely want to take advantage of, especially if they have multiple Windows 8 tablets, laptops, and computers.

> **This objective covers the following topics:**
> - Use Microsoft SkyDrive
> - Use Windows 7 File Recovery

Using Microsoft SkyDrive

SkyDrive has a split personality in Windows 8. By default, the operating system comes with an app that allows users to browse their existing SkyDrive storage and open files so that they can work on them. For many users, this is a good solution and perhaps all that they need, certainly in the workplace.

The reason for this is that the new Microsoft Office 2013 suite also integrates with SkyDrive and makes it the default save location for all new files, unless you specify otherwise. The only limitation with this is that users must be logged in with a Microsoft account (formerly known as a *Live ID*) connected to a SkyDrive account. This is reasonably likely with Windows 8, because the operating system offers a Microsoft account login option for the first time.

For home users using Office 2013, SkyDrive is great because it not only means that they can access all their documents from anywhere in the world using any computer that has an Internet connection, but also that all their documents are backed up to the cloud in real time, all the time.

In the workplace, things are quite a bit different because files are commonly stored locally on file shares and often need to be accessible to many people within the workplace for sharing and collaboration. This isn't something that SkyDrive makes easy, because you still need to set file sharing manually in the web interface, and sharing settings are limited to only individual files and folders.

To get around this, Microsoft provides a desktop SkyDrive program as part of the Windows Essentials suite (formerly known as the *Live Essentials Suite*) that allows users to store all their files locally on their computer and back them up using synchronization to SkyDrive in the cloud.

When installed, SkyDrive shows up as a Favorite file location in File Explorer and can be accessed just as you would any other network drive location. What's more, you can instantly see the file synchronization status of individual files and folders via small icons overlaid on the file icons in File Explorer.

Other services also offer this functionality, but SkyDrive is now a built-in feature of all Microsoft products from Windows and Office to Windows Phone. This ubiquity makes the service genuinely useful.

In large part, SkyDrive is now useful because of the devices that users are commonly using in their daily home and business lives, such as smartphones, tablets, and ultrabooks.

These relatively new form factors for computing equipment don't come with large amounts of on-board storage, primarily because of the high cost of large-capacity storage chips. It's common to find tablets with 32 GB or 64 GB of storage, ultrabooks and professional grade tablets with no more than 128 GB of storage, and smartphones with as little as 4 GB.

Tablets and ultrabooks also need to store the Windows operating system itself as well as any programs and apps you have installed. Therefore, it's easy to see how very little space can be left for files, especially if you also have an image backup on board.

Now that Windows 8 and Windows Phone both have the built-in ability to read and open SkyDrive-stored files, and Office 2013 has a default save option, storing files locally becomes less important. Suddenly, your entire file library is available to you wherever you are. If you open and modify a file from the cloud, those modifications are synched back to your desktop computer(s) containing the master copies of those files, using the desktop SkyDrive sync.

Smartphones, tablets, and ultrabooks are highly desirable targets for thieves because they have a high resale value and are small and light enough to steal and hide easily. However, with the files not actually stored on the devices themselves, but rather in the cloud and pro-tected behind a user password, even removing the storage from a device won't necessarily allow a criminal access to the files. (The one exception would be possible local temporary file stores—but they aren't a concern unless government authorities want access to them.)

Using cloud backup with SkyDrive or other cloud services then, is one way to circumvent the limitations caused by many tablets and ultrabooks not shipping with Trusted Platform Module (TPM) chips that support hardware data encryption. Windows RT does come with a BitLocker equivalent that's secure, but Windows 8 Pro tablets don't support the same feature.

When you install SkyDrive on the computer with the Windows Essentials Suite, the app will want to synchronize your C:\Users folder; however, this causes some difficulties for more advanced users, especially in the workplace. Because it's so common to fix computer prob-lems by simply reimaging the hard disk or partition on which Windows is installed, any files that are also stored in this location are wired, or at least replaced, with earlier versions when the restore takes place.

The gist of this is that if the SkyDrive folder suddenly contains earlier versions of files or—worse—no files at all, that problem could be replicated in the cloud storage space and then synchronized with all the other computers running SkyDrive for that Microsoft account.

Setting the SkyDrive sync folder to a location other than the default C:\Users folder is always advisable.

SkyDrive comes equipped with its own recycle bin that can help if a disaster occurs. You can find a link to the SkyDrive recycle bin in the bottom left of the window when logged into the SkyDrive service from a web browser (see Figure 7-1).

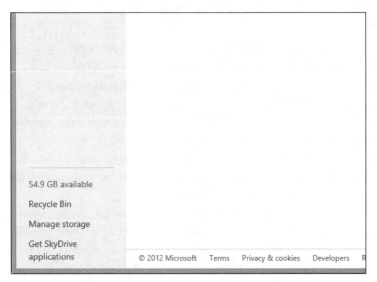

54.9 GB available

Recycle Bin

Manage storage

Get SkyDrive
applications

© 2012 Microsoft   Terms   Privacy & cookies   Developers   R

FIGURE 7-1 SkyDrive's own recycle bin

This recycle bin simplifies recovery of files that have been accidentally deleted. You simply select the check box for the file or files to be restored, right-click, and choose Restore from the options that appear.

Using Windows 7 File Recovery

Because File History isn't a full backup solution, does a full backup solution still exist in Windows 8? The good news is that it does; you can find it in the peculiarly named Windows 7 File Recovery options in the Control Panel (see Figure 7-2).

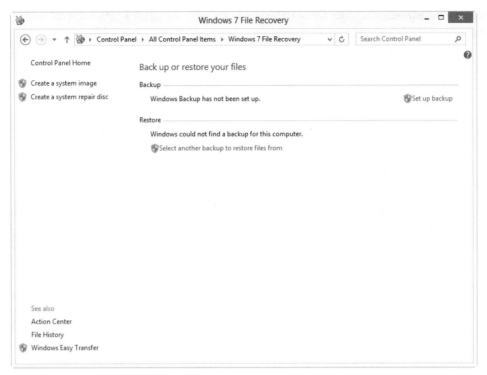

FIGURE 7-2 The Windows 7 File Recovery window

Why is it called *Windows 7 File Recovery*? File History, covered in detail in Objective 7.3, "Configure file recovery options," is a new quick and convenient way to manage backups for the files you work on and use the most. However, a great many Windows 7 and Windows Vista users have relied on the built-in file backup facility those operating systems provided to keep copies of files safe and secure.

Microsoft has left the backup facility intact to enable users of those operating systems to recover previously made backups; however, the good news is that all the backup and imaging features from Windows 7 still work in Windows 8. This includes both file backup and operating system imaging.

Using file backup

The file backup feature in Windows 8 isn't a file-by-file copy; it's not intended for easily grabbing individual files out of a backup for later restoration using File Explorer. Instead, it creates a compressed file containing the backed-up files. On the face of it, you can consider that this makes the backup more secure—and you can still open the file and drill down to see the contents.

You set up a backup by clicking the Set Up Backup link in the Windows 8 File Recovery panel. You are then be asked where you want to store the backup (see Figure 7-3). You can store the backup on an internal or USB-connected hard disk or on a network location. Windows 8 won't allow you to store this backup on CD/DVD/Blu-Ray removable media.

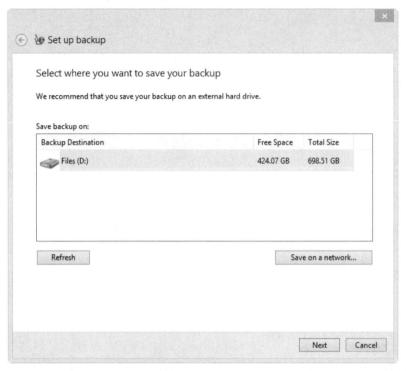

FIGURE 7-3 Setting up Windows backup

By default, the backup software also wants to keep an image copy of Windows. The next page informs you that this is one of the components it wants to include in the backup. Select the Let Me Choose option to disable this (see Figure 7-4).

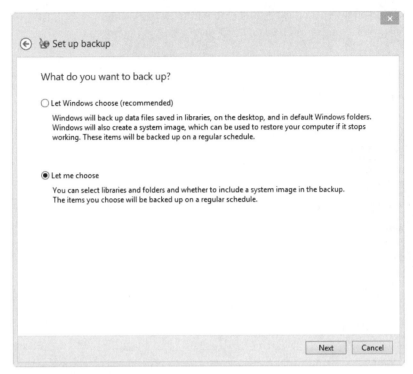

FIGURE 7-4 Choosing what you want to back up

If you choose to decide what you want backed up, notice at the bottom of the next page that Windows 8 still wants to include an image backup copy of Windows, although you can clear that option, as shown in Figure 7-5. Here you can also choose what to include and exclude in the backup. This could include additional internal hard disks or partitions, or you can choose to exclude some library locations from the backup if you have copies of those files elsewhere.

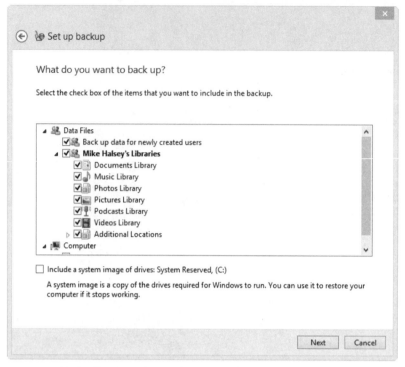

FIGURE 7-5 Having fine control over what you can back up

On the final page (see Figure 7-6), you can review the backup options you've selected and then confirm these settings. However, you can also change the schedule at which backups are performed by clicking the Change Schedule link. For example, you might want to change the time and day(s) when backups are performed to when you are likely to be using the computer, so that it's switched on, but not at a time when you're using it for processor or disk-intensive tasks.

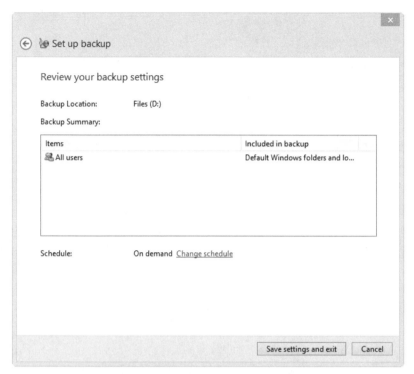

FIGURE 7-6 Modifying the schedule on which a backup takes place

Windows backup works incrementally. The first backup run creates a full backup of everything, but subsequent runs create an incremental backup that contains only the files that have changed since the original backup was made. As a result, the standard Windows backup software might be unsuitable for users who prefer a file-by-file backup. For most users, however, it remains an excellent option.

Monitoring and recovering file backups

After your first backup is completed, the Windows 7 File Recovery window changes to show the status of your file backups, including the time and date of the most recently performed backup (see Figure 7-7). Here you should see additional options, including a Restore My Files option for restoring all or part of a backup. In the main pane of the page, in addition to manually starting a backup, you can change all backup options, including changing the backup location and the schedule on which the backup takes place.

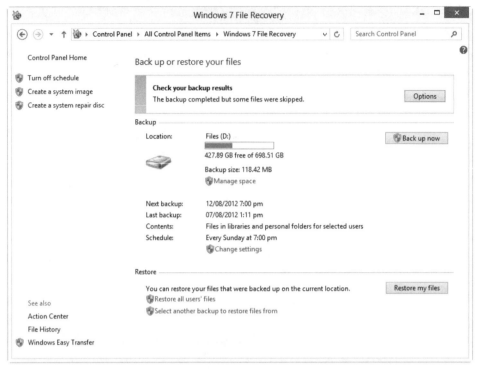

FIGURE 7-7 The status of your file backups in Windows 7 File Recovery

If a problem occurs with the backup, you are alerted at the top of the page with a color-coded alert. In Figure 7-7, the alert tells you that some files weren't backed up (which occurred because I cancelled the backup before it completed).

 Thought experiment

Designing a backup solution for a small business

In the following thought experiment, apply what you've learned about the objective. You can find answers to these questions in the "Answers" section at the end of this chapter.

You need to create a backup solution that's suitable for a small business. The company has 10 PCs, of which one also acts as a file server, the central repository for all files that everybody in the company uses.

By using the file backups tools available in Windows 8 and downloadable for the operating system from Microsoft, design a lightweight and effective file backup solution that will allow users to access Microsoft Office 2013 files on the road.

Objective summary

- Windows 8 includes two main file backup solutions: Windows 7 File Recovery and File History.
- Windows 7 File Recovery backup will include a system image backup automatically unless you tell it not to.
- The main backup solution can be saved to local, removable, and network locations.

Objective review

Answer the following questions to test your knowledge of the information in this objective. You can find the answers to these questions and explanations of why each answer choice is correct or incorrect at the end of this chapter.

1. Where can you find the file backup solution in Windows 8?

    A. File History

    B. Windows 8 File Recovery

    C. Windows 7 File Recovery

    D. Backup and Restore

2. How much free storage do you get with a personal SkyDrive account?

    A. Up to 100 GB

    B. 7 GB

    C. 25 GB

    D. None

3. What does the file backup utility allow you to save?

    A. Documents and folders

    B. Libraries, documents, and folders

    C. Libraries and the content of any internal hard disk

    D. Libraries, the content of any internal hard disk, and a system image

4. Where does the file backup utility allow you to store backups?

    A. CDR/DVD-R/BD-R

    B. CDR/DVD-R and USB-attached drives

    C. CDR/DVD-R/BD-R, USB-attached drives, and network locations

    D. USB-attached drives and network drives

Objective 7.2: Configure system recovery options

You have seven ways available to resuscitate Windows 8 in the event of a problem. These solutions range from two simple utilities that rely on Windows 8 booting to the desktop (even if that's just in safe mode) through no fewer than three different reimaging tools. In short, the most stable, robust, and reliable Windows version to date has more ways to rescue it should something go wrong than any previous version of the operating system.

I like to refer to this as the *Windows Recovery Tool index*, which means that the number of available rescue and recovery tools in Windows seems to increase at roughly the same rate at which stability problems with new versions are eliminated.

> **This objective covers the following topics:**
> - Configure system restore
> - Determine when to choose last known good configuration
> - Perform a complete restore
> - Perform a driver rollback
> - Perform a push button refresh or reset
> - Configure startup settings

Configure System Restore

The oldest and most venerable recovery tool in Windows 8 is System Restore, as shown in Figure 7-8. When Windows XP first introduced System Restore, it was often derided for being a place where malware could hide, which resulted in many people from turning this useful feature off. This all changed with the introduction of User Account Control (UAC) in Windows Vista, however, and in Windows 8 System Restore continues to be one of the easiest to use and most useful rescue and recovery tools.

You can find System Restore easily by searching for *restore* on the Start screen, and clicking Create a Restore Point in the Settings search results.

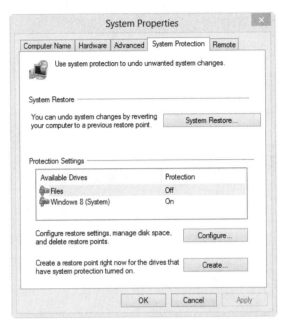

FIGURE 7-8 Controlling System Restore in Windows 8

System Restore is most useful for repairing little problems with Windows 8, such as a poorly written piece of software or hardware driver that causes the operating system to become unstable or not start properly, or a problem during startup that causes problems with the operating system. These are the types of issues that all operating systems installed file-by-file onto a hard disk can experience occasionally.

System Restore keeps a snapshot of critical Windows 8 files in a System Reserved folder on each disk (if you ever wondered what those folders are for). Windows 8 creates a restore point automatically whenever you perform a task such as installing a desktop program (but not apps), when you install or update a driver, or perform a Windows Update.

You can create a restore point in the main System Restore panel manually by clicking the Create button. You can control how much hard disk space is reserved for System Restore (15 percent by default) by clicking Configure and moving a slider. You also can turn System Restore off from here—but that's not recommended.

When you want to restore Windows using the System Restore feature, click the System Restore button to launch the System Restore wizard. On the page that appears, you can choose from either the most recent restore point or a previous custom restore point that you specify (see Figure 7-9).

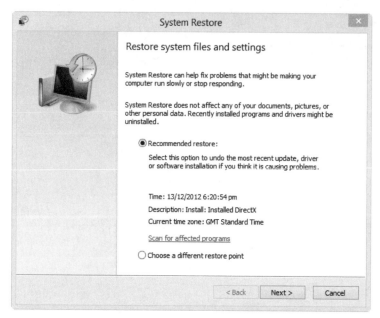

FIGURE 7-9 Restoring Windows 8 using System Restore

You can find out what programs (again, this doesn't apply to apps) are affected when you restore to the most recent restore point by clicking the Scan For Affected Programs link. A dialog box appears, telling you which programs, features, and updates are affected (see Figure 7-10).

FIGURE 7-10 System Restore, telling you which programs and updates will be affected

Should you choose a custom restore point, the page changes to display the most recent restore points, but you can select the Show More Restore Points check box to see all the restore points that Windows 8 has saved (see Figure 7-11). Notice, however, that the number of saved restore points depends on how much hard drive space is reserved for them.

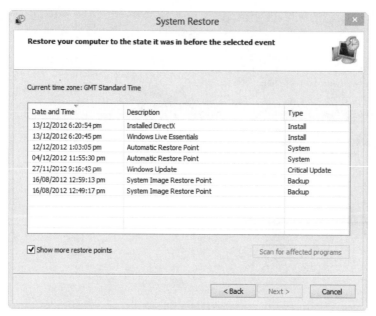

FIGURE 7-11 Choosing a custom restore point

Again, you can select a restore point and click Scan For Affected Programs to check what will be changed by rolling back this particular update and what desktop software will be affected by it.

You can also invoke System Restore from the Windows 8 boot menu (press F8 at Startup or hold down the Shift key while restarting the computer). You need to click through the first couple of screens in the startup menu. On the first screen, click the Troubleshoot option, and then click Advanced Options on the next screen. At that point, you should see an option to use System Restore to repair the computer (see Figure 7-12).

> **NOTE ACCESSING THE WINDOWS 8 BOOT MENU**
>
> You can also access the boot menu by starting the computer from a System Rescue Disc or a Recovery Drive, or by clicking the Repair Your Computer option (instead of Install) from your original Windows 8 installation DVD.

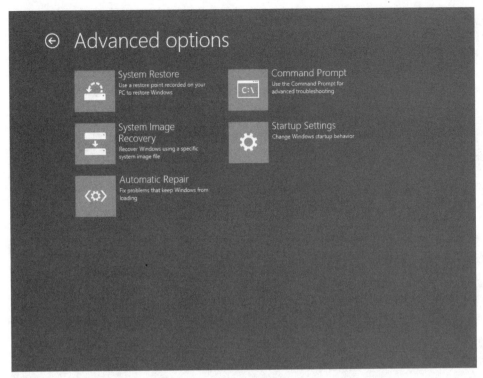

FIGURE 7-12 Invoking System Restore from the boot menu

Using Safe Mode

All this talk about System Restore leads to a discussion of Safe Mode, which is a special startup mode for Windows 8 that loads only critical drivers and services. Safe Mode can be useful when you need to run a System Restore but where whatever has changed recently on the PC is preventing you from stably starting Windows normally.

In Figure 7-12, you can see how to access System Restore from the Windows 8 boot menu. In that same menu you can click Startup Settings, which let you change the behavior of the Windows 8 boot menu, effectively restoring the older-style boot menu from earlier Windows versions.

This Startup Settings menu (see Figure 7-13) includes a few options not available in the new boot menu, including such useful features as Disable Automatic Restart On System Failure, which can enable you to read the message on a blue screen. Here, though, you should see three Safe Mode options. Standard Safe Mode is the one you want to use to be able to effectively use System Restore.

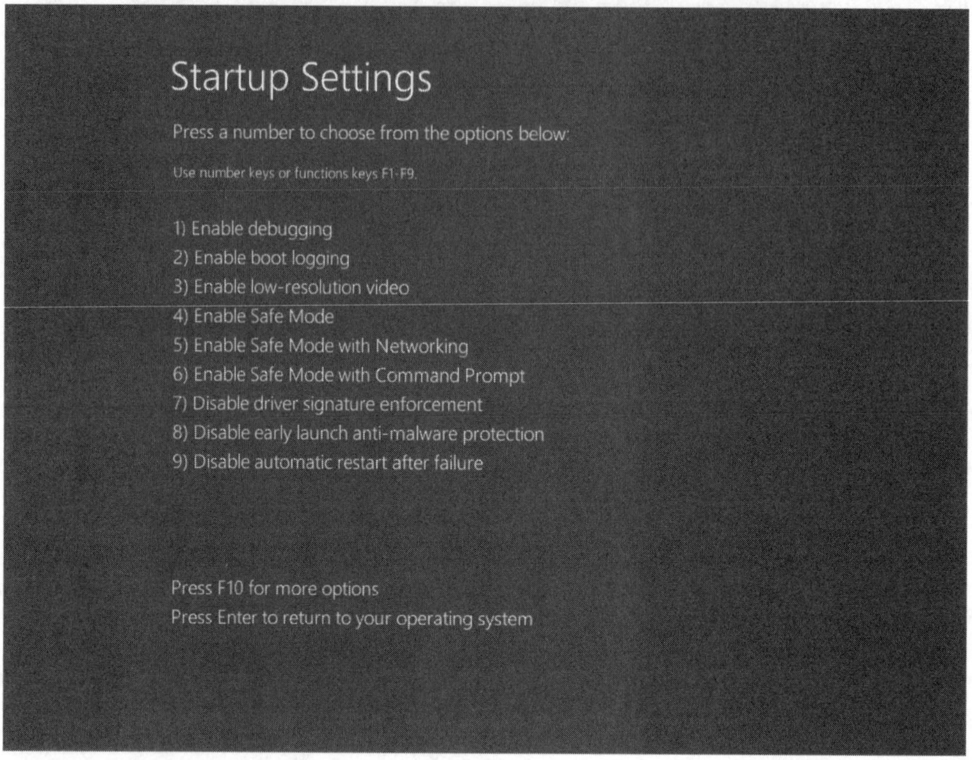

Startup Settings

Press a number to choose from the options below:

Use number keys or functions keys F1-F9.

1) Enable debugging
2) Enable boot logging
3) Enable low-resolution video
4) Enable Safe Mode
5) Enable Safe Mode with Networking
6) Enable Safe Mode with Command Prompt
7) Disable driver signature enforcement
8) Disable early launch anti-malware protection
9) Disable automatic restart after failure

Press F10 for more options
Press Enter to return to your operating system

FIGURE 7-13 The Windows Startup Settings boot menu

Invoking safe boot mode

Safe Mode isn't the only option for dealing with problematic Windows 8 installations, however. You can use the safe boot mode option, which you access from the System Configuration options in Windows 8.

To start the System Configuration utility, search for *msconfig* on the Start screen. On the first tab, notice the options for Selective Startup and Diagnostic Startup. These invoke the standard Safe Mode, but the Boot tab provides many useful options, including safe boot mode (see Figure 7-14).

Safe boot is different from Safe Mode in that it allows you to do more when the operating system is loaded. By default, Safe Mode doesn't load your graphics drivers, forcing you to work in a very low-resolution environment. Crucially, it also prevents access to many administrative features in the operating system.

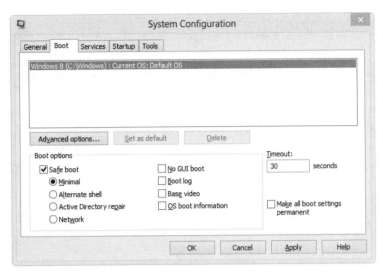

FIGURE 7-14 Invoking safe boot mode

Safe boot avoids these limitations by allowing all the useful drivers to load, such as graphics and networking, and allowing an administrator full unfettered access to the Windows administrative controls while still preventing less critical drivers and software from starting. This is an excellent diagnostic and repair mode for Windows and one that I can recommend. However, after you are finished with safe boot mode, you must switch it off in MSConfig the same way that you switch it on.

Refreshing your PC

Windows 8 is unique among operating systems in that when it is installed it keeps a backup image copy of itself handy in case you need to restore it, a very useful feature. This feature, called *Refresh,* is available through the PC Settings panel, in the General section. Although Refresh isn't quite as complete a solution as a system image backup, which is discussed shortly, it's so simple and straightforward to use that even a novice can do it, saving useful man hours for tech support staff.

Refresh isn't without its problems, however. Although it keeps all your user accounts, settings, and files, it also restores the rest of your copy of Windows 8 to the state it was at when you first installed it—meaning, it removes all the installed apps and desktop programs, which you then need to reinstall.

A way around this problem is to create a separate Refresh image. Any apps and programs you have installed at the time you create this custom Refresh image are kept within the image. However, note that any settings within your desktop software, such as email accounts in Outlook, are wiped and have to be reconfigured after the Refresh process is complete.

To create a custom Refresh image, run the command prompt as an Administrator. You can do this most easily by pressing Windows+X and clicking Command Prompt (Admin) from the options that appear.

At the command prompt, type the **recimg /createimage C:\RefreshImage** command. You can specify which folder to use, and the process will take between 10 minutes and an hour, depending on how much software you have installed. You can keep the custom refresh image on a separate hard disk or partition if you want.

You can have multiple Refresh images if you want, and switch between them using the command *recimg /setcurrent / C:\RefreshImage\Image1*. You can check which image is currently set as the default by using the command *recimg /showcurrent*.

Resetting your PC

You access Reset, like Refresh, from PC Settings under the General section. Reset varies because it doesn't use a custom image, nor does it keep any user files or accounts on the computer. Instead, this feature completely resets the computer to the state it was in when it was first shipped or when Windows 8 was first installed (whichever came later).

Using System Repair Disc and Recovery Drive

Even though the System Repair Disc and the Recovery Drive have different names, are created in different ways, and use different media, they are otherwise completely identical. These drives allow you to boot your Windows 8 computer to the boot menu, where you can perform diagnostic and repair operations. So what are the differences between these two options?

- A System Repair Disc is a bootable CD or DVD you create by opening the Windows 7 File Recovery page from Control Panel and then clicking the Create A System Repair Disc option in the left side panel. You also are prompted to create a system repair disc when you perform a complete system image backup of Windows 8.

- A Recovery Drive can be copied only to a USB flash drive (any size). You create one by using the Recovery option in Control Panel. A Recovery Drive improves on the features available with a System Repair Disc not only in the size and portability of the media, but also in that if the computer has a default system image backup—perhaps created by the computer manufacturer when the computer was sold—you also can add that image to the flash drive, as shown in Figure 7-15 (you need a USB flash drive of 32 GB or more to store this Windows image). So if Windows 8 and your backup image fail completely, perhaps because of a hard disk failure, you can still restore the original image.

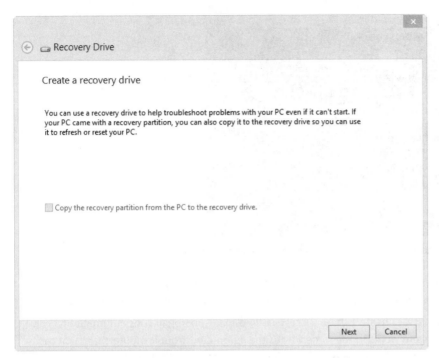

FIGURE 7-15 Creating a recovery drive

Using Startup Repair

The previous discussion of System Restore and Safe Mode mentioned the Windows 8 boot menu. You can access this menu in several different ways:

- Press F8 at Startup.

- Restart the computer while pressing the Shift key.

- Start the computer from a System Repair Disc or Recovery Drive.

- Start the computer from your original Windows 8 installation DVD or flash drive and, rather than click Install Now, click Repair Your Computer in the bottom left of the window (see Figure 7-16).

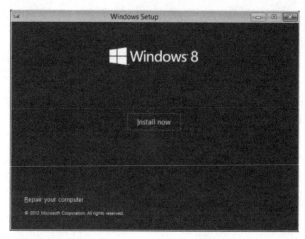

FIGURE 7-16 Accessing the boot menu from Windows 8 installation media

From here, you can manually run Startup Repair by clicking Troubleshoot on the boot menu, clicking Advanced Options, and then clicking Automatic Repair (refer to Figure 7-12).

If Windows 8 fails to start three successive times, Startup Repair runs automatically. This automated system works in the same way as the automated troubleshooters that you can access in the Action Center by resetting Windows components to their default state. This capability means that Startup Repair can fix many problems, such as corrupt startup files. It can't repair every problem, however, which is when you might need to repair the Windows 8 Startup files manually.

Manually repairing Windows 8 Startup

You can manually repair and rebuild the Windows 8 boot files by opening the command prompt from the Advanced Troubleshooting Boot options. From there, you can manually repair the Windows 8 boot files as follows:

1.   Type **BcdEdit /export C:\BCD_Backup** to save a backup copy of the Windows 8 boot files, where *BCD_Backup* is the location where you want the backup stored.

2.   Type **C:** and press Enter.

3.   Type **cd \boot** and press Enter to navigate to the Windows 8 boot folder, where the rescue commands you need are found.

4.   Type **attrib bcd –s –h –r** and press Enter, which will allow you to modify the Windows 8 boot files.

5.   Type **ren C:\Boot\bcd C:\Boot\bcd.old** and press Enter to make a backup copy of the BCD boot file.

6.   Type **Bootrec /RebuildBCD** and press Enter to force Windows 8 to rebuild its boot files.

Should these steps not work for any reason and you want to reimport the original boot files, use the *BcdEdit /import C:\BCD_Backup* command to reimport your backed-up files.

Some additional commands that you can use with the Bootrec command are as follows:

- /FixMBR creates a new Master Boot Record file for the computer.
- /FixBoot writes a new boot sector to the hard disk. This is useful if the boot sector has become corrupt, perhaps through the installation of a different operating system in a dual-boot configuration.
- /ScanOS provides a list of all the installed operating systems that the repair system can find.

Performing a system image backup

A system image backup has for decades now been the preferred backup option for system administrators and IT professionals. An option to create a full system image exists in Windows 8; you can find it in the Control Panel by clicking Windows 7 File Recovery.

In the left panel, notice a link to Create A System Image, which you can click to begin the process (see Figure 7-17).

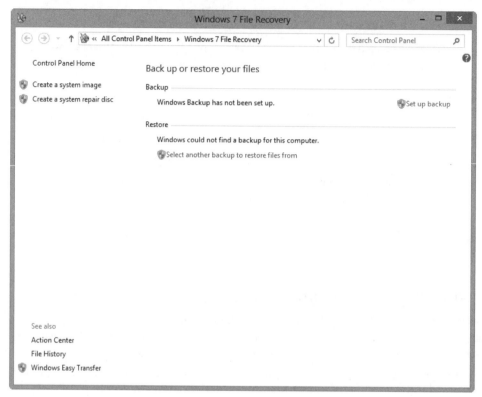

FIGURE 7-17 The Back Up Or Restore Your Files page in the Windows 7 File Recovery window

When you begin the process of creating a System Image, you are first asked where you want the backup image to be stored (see Figure 7-18). Each option here has pros and cons.

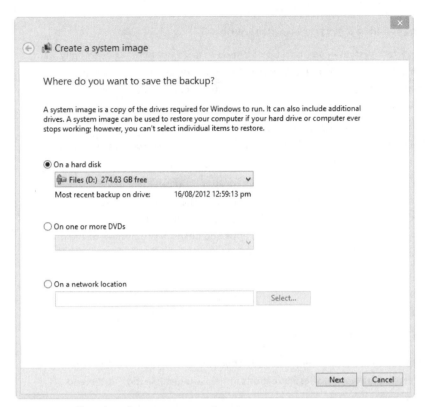

FIGURE 7-18 Choosing where to store your image

For individual computers, storing the system image on the same computer is often best, so it can be restored quickly and easily. To do this, however, you need a second physical hard disk or an already partitioned hard disk because you can't store the image on the same physical partition as your copy of Windows 8.

DVDs can sometimes be a good option, but if you have a lot of software installed, you might require many discs—and those can degrade over time, depending on the quality of the original disc.

Network locations have advantages, especially if all the computers in the office have the same physical hardware and software configuration. If that's true, you have to store just a single image for all the computers, and each can access it.

However, you shouldn't choose a network location if the computer connects to the network via Wi-Fi. Such image backups can be restored only from the Windows 8 boot menu, where no Wi-Fi drivers are loaded. You should save an image to a network location only if the computer connects to the network with a physical Ethernet cable.

After you select the location for the backup image, you can select which hard disks and partitions (if you have any extra ones) to include or exclude from the backup.

Thought experiment
The Locked-Out User

In the following thought experiment, apply what you've learned about the objective. You can find answers to these questions in the "Answers" section at the end of this chapter.

Following a system configuration change, the computer is misbehaving, locking the user out of features to which he should otherwise have access. He's using the main Administrator account on the computer and can't change the necessary options to allow him full access to the operating system's features.

You need to develop the best solution to use to troubleshoot and repair this user's problem.

Objective summary

- System Restore provides a great deal of useful information about restore points.
- You can use the Refresh Your PC option to create and store multiple backup images for a PC.
- Creating recovery media for CD/DVD and USB drives involves several options, but both offer same recovery features.

Objective review

Answer the following questions to test your knowledge of the information in this objective. You can find the answers to these questions and explanations of why each answer choice is correct or incorrect at the end of this chapter.

1. Which of these isn't a recovery tool for Windows 8?

    A. Safe Mode

    B. System Restore

    C. Refresh

    D. Startup Repair

2. How can you access Windows Startup Repair in Windows 8?

    A. Press F8 or Shift+F8 at startup

    B. F8, Shift+F8, Recovery Drive, Recovery Disc

    C. Auto start, F8, Shift+F8, Recovery Drive, System Repair Disc, Windows installation media

    D. Auto start, F8, Shift+F8, System Repair Drive, Recovery Disc, Windows installation media

3. Where can you find the option to create a system image backup?

    A. Backup and Restore

    B. Windows 8 Boot Menu

    C. Windows 7 File recovery

    D. Recovery

4. How does safe boot mode vary from Safe Mode? Choose all that apply.

    A. It's activated manually from the Windows desktop and runs each time the computer starts until deactivated.

    B. It loads more drivers and allows more control over Windows 8 than Safe Mode.

    C. It's activated from the new graphical Windows boot menu.

    D. You run it from a USB flash drive.

Objective 7.3: Configure file recovery options

Windows has provided a file-versioning tool for some years now called *Previous Versions*. This feature integrated well with Windows Server but was little used, and was a basic versioning tool unable to compete with the likes of Apple's Time Machine. Now, however, Windows 8 has a new file-versioning tool, File History, that's much more feature-complete and polished. For the first time, it's both quick and straightforward to restore earlier versions of files.

Before exploring File History in depth, you will examine why users might want to restore previous versions of files and how File History compares to file-backup solutions.

Restoring previous versions of files can be extremely useful in all kinds of situations, from users, who are so afraid of losing things that they press Ctrl+S (or Shift+F12) regularly when working on documents (occasionally saving changes we hadn't intended to), to people who work on complex files, perhaps program code, who might need to roll back a whole series of changes they've made to a document.

Using File History as only a backup solution isn't recommended. Certainly, it keeps a copy of all your files, and you can keep the copy in any location including a USB-attached hard disk or a network drive, but File History is intended to be used to restore files that have changed. It's just not set up to restore everything, all your deleted files, or files otherwise in a manner that you would expect a full file backup program to do.

Nor does it keep all the files stored in a manner whereby you can simply use File Explorer to pick out the file or files you need to restore. Windows 8 still includes a full file backup solution as detailed in Objective 7.1, "Configure backup."

This objective covers the following topics:

- Configuring file restore points
- Restoring previous versions of files and folders
- Configuring File History

Working with File History

Windows Server 2003 first introduced the concept of previous file versions to the Windows desktop. This feature allowed the operating system to reserve a certain amount of hard disk space on which it would store earlier copies of files that had changed. It did this using the Windows Shadow Copy feature that permits copying of locked (in-use) files.

In Windows 8, this feature has been further refined and should be familiar to anybody who has used the Time Machine feature on an Apple Mac. It works by using a second hard disk, partition, external hard disk, or network location to store earlier versions of files as they are saved and modified on the computer.

You can access File History (see Figure 7-19) directly from Control Panel or by searching for *file history* on the Start screen, where you will find it in the Settings results.

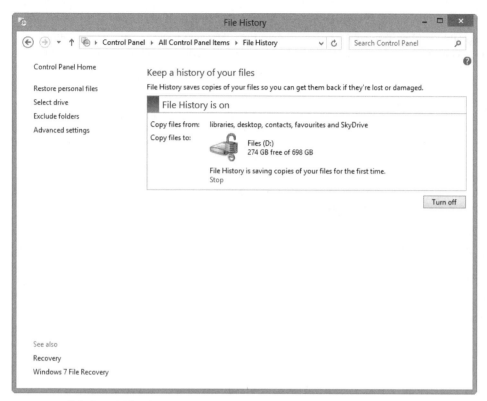

FIGURE 7-19 Windows 8 File History

> **NOTE RUNNING FILE HISTORY AND WINDOWS BACKUP**
>
> Windows 8 won't allow you to use Windows Backup and File History at the same time, and File History will insist that the Windows Backup schedule be deactivated for File History to work.

File History has been refined and expanded enormously from the old Previous Versions feature. When you first run it, File History creates a full and complete backup of all your files (except the ones you have deliberately set to exclude, as explained shortly). After this backup is complete, File History will, as scheduled, create a versioned copy of every file that has changed since the last backup was made.

Unfortunately, the total amount of available storage for files on the File History hard disk is finite. You would typically assign hard disk space for a backup equal to the total space occupied by the files and documents to be backed up, which is perfectly reasonable. But because File History keeps multiple versions of files, the total available storage space can be filled up without a copy of every file being present.

When the total available space for File History is full, the feature can still keep copies of newly changed files but will do so by deleting the oldest files it has copies of. For example, if you play music on your computer, you might find that nearly your entire File History storage space is full of copies of MP3 tracks and very little else.

Configuring File History

It's not all bad news, though, because File History is very configurable. From its main panel you can click Advanced Settings in the left pane to choose how you want the feature to operate (see Figure 7-20).

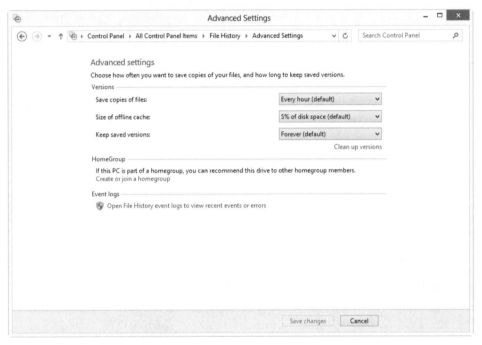

FIGURE 7-20 Configuring File History

In the Advanced Settings, you can choose how much space on the computer on which File History is used is reserved for file copies. By default, File History fills any hard drive you specify for its use. It also keeps some local copies, so that you can still restore previous versions of files if your main File History save location is unavailable, perhaps because it's a USB-attached hard disk or a network location.

You can also choose to exclude certain folder and drive locations from File History by clicking Exclude Folders on the main File History page. Doing this displays additional options for completely excluding user-selected folders from the File History feature, as shown in Figure 7-21.

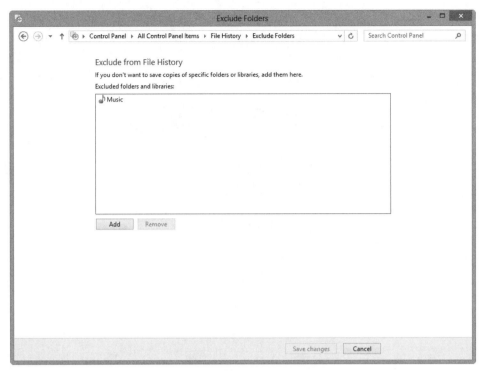

FIGURE 7-21 Excluding folders from File History

The advantage of using this feature is that you can, as in Figure 7-21, exclude the Music library or file locations such as pictures and video from the feature. This means that when you open files stored in those locations, such as playing music, the change in the last accessed date stamp doesn't result in a copy of the file being stored. If you exclude everything except your Documents library, you can rest safe in the knowledge that the feature will store only changes you make to your work documents, and nothing else.

Even if you do this, your file history can eventually become polluted with older versions of files that you'll never need. Weeding out unwanted backup files could be an impossible task were it not for a useful link in the File History Advanced Options.

Cleaning up versions

Just beneath the Keep Saved Versions option is a small Clean Up Versions link. Clicking this displays a dialog box (see Figure 7-22) where you can choose to have Windows 8 automatically clean out versions of files older than a specific time. The available options range from All But The Latest One to Older Than 2 Years.

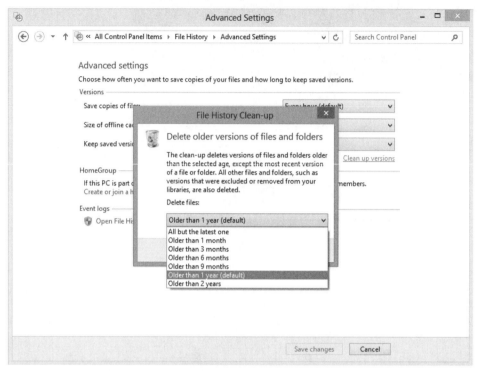

FIGURE 7-22 The File History Clean-Up dialog box

After you select which option you want and which files you want deleted, click the Clean Up button in the next dialog box (not shown in Figure 7-22) to delete those older files. Using the clean-up feature is an excellent way to maintain sufficient available hard disk space for backups, making room available for newer and more recent copies of files.

> **NOTE IF A FILE ISN'T ACCESSED, IT ISN'T COPIED**
>
> File History will make copies only of files that you open, edit, or change. It will not create a copy of files on your hard disk that you don't access.

Thought experiment

Designing a File History structure

In the following thought experiment, apply what you've learned about the objective. You can find answers to these questions in the "Answers" section at the end of this chapter.

You need to design a File History structure for the same small office as in Objective 7.1. This office has 10 computers, one of which acts as a file server for the others. You want to configure File History for the computers but need to take into account that some users might keep copies of files locally when they are initially created, but those files will be moved to the file server when they are ready to be shared with other people. The company policy for this is one month. You have a large-capacity network attached storage (NAS) drive on your network for File History backup.

What would you include in the design?

Objective summary

- The file backup solution from Windows 7 still exists and is fully featured.
- File History creates and maintains a full file backup as well as performs version control.
- You can't run File History and Windows Backup at the same time.

Objective review

Answer the following questions to test your knowledge of the information in this objective. You can find the answers to these questions and explanations of why each answer choice is correct or incorrect at the end of this chapter.

1. For what purpose would you use File History in Windows 8?

   A. File Backup and Restore

   B. File Versioning Control

   C. Creating local Storage Pools

   D. You wouldn't use File History; instead you'd use previous versions

2. What do the configuration options for File History allow you to do? Choose all that apply.

   A. Select which folder locations to include

   B. Select which folder locations to exclude

   C. Choose how much additional local hard disk storage to use

   D. Choose how often backups are deleted

3. How can you delete older copies of files that are no longer required?

   A. Open the File History recovery window and manually select all older files.

   B. Click Clean Up Versions in the Advanced File History options.

   C. Change the option for how long files are stored.

   D. Delete the File History versions and restart the backup.

Chapter summary

- SkyDrive will become more useful only as the service is refined and can be used both for backup and PC file sync.
- The File Backup feature from Windows 7 still exists and is fully featured.
- The ability to create custom refresh images can be useful for multi-purpose office PCs.
- The recovery drive option to create a USB flash drive to help fix a PC in the event of a problem is an extremely useful one.
- File History is both a complete file backup and file-versioning utility.

Answers

This section contains the solutions to the thought experiments and answers to the objective review questions in this chapter.

Objective 7.1: Thought experiment

The best backup solution would be to have the file server store a backup of every file it contains but also to have each individual laptop and (optionally) desktop PC make their own backups. In this scenario, because some files are accessed while the user is out on the road where Internet access isn't available, you need to make sure that a recoverable copy of all available files is on hand in those circumstances.

Objective 7.1: Review

4. **Correct answer:** C

   A. Incorrect: The File History feature in Windows 8 isn't a file backup solution; rather, it's a compliment to an existing file backup solution.

   B. Incorrect: Although you might expect Windows 8 File Recovery to appear in the Windows 8 Control Panel, the decision to keep the name as Windows 7 File Recovery is because the tools it contains exist with the primary intention of helping people recover files previously backed up in Windows 7.

C. Correct: You find it in the Control Panel under Windows 7 File Recovery.

D. Incorrect: The Control Panel has no Backup and Restore option.

5. **Correct answer:** B

    A. Incorrect: You can purchase up to an extra 100 GB of storage with Microsoft SkyDrive, but this amount doesn't come for free.

    B. Correct: The basic amount of storage you get for free with a personal SkyDrive account is 7 GB.

    C. Incorrect: When SkyDrive first launched, the amount of free space given by Microsoft was a very generous 25 GB. This was amended in early 2012, however, to 7 GB, which Microsoft said was ample to save the files of most ordinary Windows users.

    D. Incorrect: It's not true that you don't get any free storage with SkyDrive. Every SkyDrive user gets 7 GB of free storage for the life of the account, unless their account was created before 2012 when they will have 25 GB free for the life of the account.

6. **Correct answer:** D

    A. Incorrect: Although you can save Documents and folders, the file backup utility in Windows 8 also allows you to save libraries and a system disk image.

    B. Incorrect: Although you can save libraries, documents, and folders, the file backup utility in Windows 8 also allows you to save a the contents of any internal hard disk or partition and a system disk image.

    C. Incorrect: Although you can save libraries and the contents of any internal hard disk, the file backup utility in Windows 8 also allows you to save a system disk image.

    D. Correct: The file backup utility is very flexible and allows you to save any library, internal drive, or partition (or any part thereof) as well as a system image backup of your Windows 8 installation.

7. **Correct answer:** C

    A. Incorrect:: The file backup utility allows you to save files on USB-attached hard disks and to network locations in addition to all optical media types.

    B. Incorrect:: The file backup utility allows you to save files to network locations in addition to all optical media types and USB-attached hard disks.

    C. Correct: The file backup utility allows you to save your backups to pretty much any location, including optical media, USB-attached storage, and network storage.

    D. Incorrect: The file backup utility allows you to save files on optical media as well as USB-attached hard disks and network locations.

Objective 7.2: Thought experiment

If a user is locked out of features in the operating system that they should have access to after a system configuration change, this probably means that a Group or Security Policy change has been implemented incorrectly or that a fault with a Group or Security policy change has occurred. The best way to rectify this is to restart the computer in Safe Boot mode. This allows the user to access all the Group and Security Policy controls in the operating system, which are blocked in Safe Mode.

Objective 7.2: Review

1. **Correct answer:** A

   A. **Correct:** Safe Mode is a special Windows operating environment in which some repair and troubleshooting operations can be undertaken. It's not a recovery tool in itself.

   B. **Incorrect:** System Restore has been around since Windows XP and is a useful recovery tool for rolling back changes to Windows, such as a faulty driver update or software installation.

   C. **Incorrect:** New to Windows 8, Refresh allows even a novice user to restore a working system image of the operating system.

   D. **Incorrect:** Startup Repair can run both automatically and also manually from the boot partition, a USB or optical disc recovery medium or from Windows 8 installation media. It can reset common Windows 8 startup behaviors to their default state.

2. **Correct answer:** C

   A. **Incorrect:** Although you can access Startup Repair from the Windows boot menu, it can be accessed in many other ways, too.

   B. **Incorrect:** A recovery disc isn't a feature of Windows 8.

   C. **Correct:** You can access Startup repair in many ways, including the new and old style boot menus, a Recovery Drive (USB flash drive), System Repair Disc (CD/DVD), and the Windows 8 installation media.

   D. **Incorrect:** In Windows 8, the removable and optical storage options are called a *Recovery Drive (USB flash drive)* and a *System Repair Disc (CD/DVD)*.

3. **Correct answer:** C

   A. **Incorrect::** Backup and Restore isn't found in the Windows 8 Control Panel.

   B. **Incorrect:** You can restore a Windows 8 system image backup from the Windows 8 boot menu, but you can't create one there.

   C. **Correct:** The tool used for creating a backup image of Windows 8 is found in the Windows 7 File Recovery option of the Control Panel.

D. **Incorrect:** The Recovery panel in Control Panel doesn't contain an option for creating a system image backup of Windows, although it does allow you to restore a previously created Refresh image.

4. **Correct answers:** A and B

A. **Correct:** You activate Safe Boot Mode from the System Configuration Options (commonly known as *MSConfig*), and it remains in effect every time you start the computer until you clear it in the System Configuration dialog box.

B. **Correct:** Safe boot mode loads more drivers than Safe Mode and, crucially, it allows the user full access to Windows 8's administrative controls, many of which are blocked in Safe Mode.

C. **Incorrect:** You can access Safe Mode from the old-style DOS boot menu (available on Shift+F8), but you can activate safe boot mode only from the Windows desktop.

D. **Incorrect:** You can't run safe boot mode from a USB flash drive; it can be activated only on the Windows desktop.

Objective 7.3: Thought experiment

The main point here is that some files are kept on users' own computers and laptops until they are ready to be shared. When files are initially created in the workplace, they usually undergo many revisions, so you should ensure that File History is activated on each desktop computer and backed up to the NAS drive. Because the company policy is that files should be moved to the central file server within a month of creation, you should set the Keep Saved Versions option to one month. This ensures that these individual stores leave plenty of space on the NAS drive for a File History setup for the main file server.

Objective 7.3: Review

1. **Correct answer:** B

A. **Incorrect:** File History isn't a file backup tool in and of itself. Instead, it's a complement to a file backup tool.

B. **Correct:** The proper usage for File History is as a file-versioning tool, so you can roll files back to earlier versions or recover them easily when they have been accidentally deleted.

C. **Incorrect:** You would use the Storage Spaces function in Windows 8 to create a local storage pool. This is a very different feature to File History.

D. **Incorrect:** Previous Versions is a basic file versioning tool that has existed in earlier editions of Windows and Windows Server. It has been replaced in Windows 8 by File History, which is more fully-featured and easier to manage.

2. **Correct answers:** B and C

   A. **Incorrect:** By default, File History includes all the libraries you have set up in Windows 8. File History can't include other file and folder locations. To include these in File History, they must be added to a library.

   B. **Correct:** You can select which file and folder locations you want to exclude from File History.

   C. **Correct:** You also can specify local storage to be used by File History, in case you can't access the default storage location (which might be on a network).

   D. **Incorrect:** You can choose how long versions of files should be stored for in the File History options, but to delete files you need to click the Clean Up Versions option.

3. **Correct answer:** B

   A. **Incorrect:** The File History recovery window is designed to aid in the *recovery* of files, not their deletion. However, this would be an extremely laborious way to delete old files, and you would risk also deleting newer ones.

   B. **Correct:** You can click the Clean Up Versions link in the File History advanced options to manually delete older versions of files, freeing up valuable hard disk space for new files.

   C. **Incorrect:** Although you can choose how long versions of files are stored for, and changing this option would achieve the desired outcome, this isn't the correct way to delete older versions of files.

   D. **Incorrect:** Deleting your entire file history backup also deletes all the newer files that you want to keep. You should clean up the files in the advanced options instead.

Index

Symbols

A

B

configuring. See also setting

M

R

W

X

Z

About the authors

ANDREW BETTANY is a Microsoft Most Valuable Professional (MVP), recognized for his Windows expertise, and a member of the Microsoft Springboard Technical Expert Panel.

As leader of the IT Academy at the University of York, UK and Microsoft Certified Trainer, Andrew delivers learning and consultancy to businesses on a number of technical areas including Windows deployment and troubleshooting.

He has created and manages the "IT Masterclasses" series of short intensive technical courses, www.itmasterclasses.com, run through his own training company Deliver IT Training Ltd.

Passionate about learning and helping others, he frequently donates his time to work with Microsoft. He is a frequent speaker and proctor at TechEd conferences worldwide. In 2011 he delivered a "train the trainer" class in earthquake-hit Haiti to help the community rebuild their technology skills.

Very active on social media, Andrew can be found on LinkedIn, Facebook, and Twitter. He lives in a village just outside of the beautiful city of York in Yorkshire (UK).

MIKE HALSEY is the author of several books on Microsoft's operating system, including *Troubleshoot and Optimize Windows 8 Inside Out* (Microsoft Press, 2012), *Beginning Windows 8* (Apress, 2012), the best sellers *Troubleshooting Windows 7 Inside Out* (Microsoft Press, 2010), and *Windows 8: Out of the Box* (O'Reilly, 2012).

An English and math teacher by trade, he also holds a Microsoft Most Valuable Professional (MVP) award (2011, 2012, 2013) and is a recognized Windows expert. Mike has an open mailbag at *mike@MVPs.org* and can also be found on Facebook, Twitter, and YouTube as HalseyMike. He lives in Yorkshire (UK) with his rescue border collie, Jed.

What do you think of this book?

We want to hear from you!
To participate in a brief online survey, please visit:

microsoft.com/learning/booksurvey

Tell us how well this book meets your needs—what works effectively, and what we can do better. Your feedback will help us continually improve our books and learning resources for you.

Thank you in advance for your input!